World Yearbook of Education 2009

World Yearbook of Education Series
Series editors: Terri Seddon and Jenny Ozga

World Yearbook of Education 2009

Childhood Studies and the Impact of Globalization: Policies and Practices at Global and Local Levels

Edited by
Marilyn Fleer, Mariane Hedegaard and Jonathan Tudge

Routledge
Taylor & Francis Group

NEW YORK AND LONDON

First published 2009
by Routledge
270 Madison Ave, New York, NY 10016

Simultaneously published in the UK
by Routledge
2 Park Square, Milton Park, Abingdon, Oxon OX14 4RN

Routledge is an imprint of the Taylor & Francis Group, an informa business

© 2009 Taylor & Francis

Typeset in Galliard by
HWA Text and Data Management, London
Printed and bound in the United States of America on acid-free paper by Sheridan Books, Inc.

Library of Congress Cataloging-in-Publication Data
World yearbook of education 2009 : childhood studies and the impact of globalization : policies and practices at global and local levels / [edited by] Marilyn Fleer, Mariane Hedegaard, Jonathan Tudge.
    p. cm. – (World yearbook of education)
Includes bibliographical references and index.
1. Child development – Cross-cultural studies. 2. Education and globalization – Cross-cultural studies. I. Fleer, Marilyn. II. Hedegaard, Mariane. III. Tudge, Jonathan.
LB1117.W67 2009
370.72--dc22   2008029188

ISBN10: 0–415–99411–X (hbk)
ISBN10: 0–203–88417–5 (ebk)

ISBN13: 978–0–415–99411–8 (hbk)
ISBN13: 978–0–203–88417–1 (ebk)

Contents

Figures

Tables

Contributors

Nihal Ahioğlu is assistant professor of Educational Sciences in the Faculty of Education, University of Kastamonu, Turkey. Ahioglu received her PhD (2007) in educational psychology from the University of Ankara. Her thesis was about cognitive interactions between parents, siblings and children aged 4–5 from families of low socioeconomic status. She also studies child-rearing practices, parental participation at school, poverty and child development, history of childhood, play and toys. Her publication includes Ahioğlu, N., & Güney, N. (Eds.) (2007) *Popular culture and child*.

Jytte Bang (PhD) is associate professor at University of Copenhagen. Her work has focused on knowledge epistemology and how to overcome the dualistic split of knowledge representation. She has studied high school students' knowledge about physical maters. She is involved in a project about comprehensive school students' knowledge formation in home and school activities. She combines a cultural-historical and ecological perspective in her research approach. A recent publication is *Elevens alsidige personlige udvikling – et dialogredskab* [Students' general personal development – a tool for dialogue] (2007) with Mariane Hedegaard and Niels Egelund, Dansk Psykologisk Forlag.

Louise Bottcher finished her PhD at University of Copenhagen 2008. Her research deals with children with cerebral palsy, their learning and development. She has worked as a school psychologist for four years.

Angela Uchoa Branco works at the Institute of Psychology, University of Brasilia, and has coordinated the Laboratory of Microgenesis in Social Interactions since 1995. She has been a Visiting Scholar at Duke University and at the University of North Carolina, USA. From a systemic sociocultural constructivist approach, her research team aims at investigating the microgenesis and ontogenesis of social interactive patterns among children, as well as between children and adults, particularly the role of teacher–student interactions in teaching–learning processes and knowledge construction. The development of cooperation, competition and individualism, the co-construction of values and beliefs related to social motivation and patterns of interdependence have been a special topic of investigation. Dr. Branco edited with Dr. Jaan Valsiner the book *Communication and metacommunication in human development* (Info Age Publishing, 2004).

Seth Chaiklin (PhD) is a Reader in the Department of Education at University of Bath, UK. His research interests include cultural-historical science (i.e., analysis of practice), psychology of subject-matter teaching, strategies for the development of professional practice ("practice-developing research"), and conceptual roots of cultural-historical theory. From 2002 to 2008, he was president of the International Society for Cultural and Activity Research (ISCAR). Selected publications include "The zone of proximal development in Vygotsky's theory of learning and school instruction" (2003, in: *Vygotsky's educational theory in cultural context*), *Radical-local teaching and learning* (2005, with M. Hedegaard), *Activity theory and social practice: Cultural-historical approaches* (1999, edited with M. Hedegaard & U. J. Jensen), and *Understanding practice: Perspectives on activity and context* (1993, edited with J. Lave).

Julian Elliott is currently Professor of Education at Durham University. Originally a teacher of children with special educational needs in mainstream and special school settings, he subsequently practised as an educational (school) psychologist before entering higher education. His research interests include cross-cultural studies of educational policy and practice, the assessment of reading disorders, behaviour management, achievement motivation, and dynamic assessment. His most recent books (co-authored with various colleagues) are: *Children in difficulty: A guide to understanding and helping*, 2nd edition, Routledge (2004); *Frameworks for thinking*, Cambridge University Press (2005); *Motivation, engagement and educational performance*, Palgrave Press (2005); and *Western psychological and educational theory in diverse contexts*, Routledge (2008).

Marilyn Fleer is Research Director of the Centre for Childhood Studies at Monash University, Melbourne, Australia. She holds the foundation chair of Early Childhood Education, and is the president of the International Society for Cultural and Activity Research (ISCAR).

Lia B. L. Freitas is a professor of Psychology at the Federal University of Rio Grande do Sul, Brazil. She completed her doctorate at the University of São Paulo, in Brazil. In 2004, she worked as a Visiting Scholar in the Center for Youth, Family, and Community Partnerships at the University of North Carolina at Greensboro, in the United States. Her research deals with child development, focusing primarily on the construction of values and moral feelings. She has written two books published in Brazil: *The production of ignorance at school: A critical analysis of literacy practices in the classroom* and *The theory of morality in Jean Piaget's work: An unfinished project*.

Artin Göncü is professor of Educational Psychology and Early Childhood Education in the College of Education at the University of Illinois at Chicago, and the Chair of the Department of Educational Psychology. Göncü received his PhD (1983) in developmental psychology from the University of Houston. His publications include Göncü, A., & Gaskins, S. (Eds.) (2007) *Play and development*, LEA; Göncü, A. (Ed.) (1999) *Children's engagement in the world*, Cambridge; Göncü, A. & Klein, E. (Eds.) (2001) *Children in play, story, and school*, Guilford; and Kessel, F. & Göncü, A. (Eds.) (1984) *Analyzing children's play dialogues*, New Directions for Child Development, Jossey-Bass.

Mariane Hedegaard (D Phil) is professor in developmental psychology and head of the centre PPUK (Person, Practice, Development and Culture), University of Copenhagen. Her research focus is on child development in a cultural-historical perspective and the formation of personality (i.e. concepts, motives, identity) in school and home. Her recent publications include: Hedegaard, M. (2002) *Children's learning and development*; Hedegaard, M. & Chaiklin, S. (2005) *Radical local teaching and learning*; Hedegaard, M. & Fleer, M. with Bang, J. & Hviid, P. (2009) *Studying children: A cultural-historical approach*.

G. G. Kravtsov is a Professor within the Vygotsky Institute at the Russian State University for the Humanities with a special interest in the Arts.

Elena E. Kravtsova is the head of the Vygotsky Institute at the Russian State University for the Humanities and granddaughter of L. S. Vygotsky.

Ana Cristina Mantilla is a PhD student in the Faculty of Education at Monash University, Peninsula Campus, Melbourne, Australia.

A. Bame Nsamenang is associate professor of psychology and learning science at the University of Yaounde [ENS], Cameroon. He also directs the Human Development Resource Centre, a research and service facility. His research focus is on children and adolescents and he is committed to contributing to an Africentric developmental science, as it can enrich global psychology. He has published and/or guided influential works on early childhood development and adolescence in Africa. His theoretical foundation is interactive contextualism and biological embedding, which he considers the core determinants of human thriving, health, competence and developmental learning.

Dolphine Odero-Wanga is a Senior Lecturer in the department of Applied Community Development Studies at Egerton University, Kenya. Her area of research interest includes child and family development in social and cultural contexts. She has done research in socialization of urban Luo children in Kenya, and challenges of raising children orphaned through HIV/AIDs in Kenya. She is currently involved in research focusing on various ways in which Kenyan families address poverty through involvement in small-scale business ventures.

Bert van Oers is professor in Cultural-historical Theory of Education at the Free University in Amsterdam. His research interests concentrate on the relationship between school learning and (identity) development at primary school age. In particular he is interested in the potentials of play as a context for learning and development.

Serap Özer is an assistant professor of Psychology in Doğuş University, Istanbul, Turkey. She received her PhD in Clinical Psychology from University of South Florida (1981). Her area of research is children and mental health. Her research interests are in the area of children's psychological evaluations. Her most recent publication is on the Bender Gestalt test performance of Turkish children (*Perceptual & motor skills*, 2007).

Gloria Quiñones is a PhD student at the Centre for Childhood Studies, Faculty of Education at Monash University, Peninsula Campus, Australia. She would like to acknowledge the support received from Monash University (Monash Graduate Scholarship) and CONACTY Mexico. These two institutions have supported me in my PhD studies.

C. M. Patricia Rivalland is a PhD student in the Faculty of Education at Monash University, Peninsula campus, Melbourne, Australia.

Terri L. Shelton is Director of the University of North Carolina at Greensboro's Center for Youth, Family, and Community Partnerships and Professor in the Department of Psychology. She received her PhD in Clinical Psychology with a minor in Child and Family Studies and has 25 years of experience in clinical intervention, community-based treatment outcome research, teaching and technical assistance focused on children and youth at risk and their families. In her role as Director of the Center, she oversees over $4 million in federal, state, and local grants and contracts that build the capacity of families, service providers, researchers, teachers, and communities to ensure the health and well-being of youth by engaging partnerships that bridge research, policy, and practice. Her research interests include designing and evaluating family-centered, culturally congruent, coordinated services in community-based settings. She is co-author of the text *Assessing attention-deficit/hyperactivity disorder* and the monograph, *Family-centered care for children needing specialized developmental services.*

Tania M. Sperb is a professor of Psychology at the Federal University of Rio Grande do Sul, Brazil. She completed her MS and PhD (1989) in developmental Psychology at the University of London. Before working as a professor at the University she worked as a clinical and educational psychologist. Her research focuses on children's cognitive and language development and she has published a number of papers in this area. She is one of the editors of the book *Sociocognitive development: Brazilian studies on theory of mind*, published in Brazil.

Anna Stetsenko is a Full Professor and Program Head in the PhD Program in Developmental Psychology and faculty member in the PhD Program in Urban Education at the Graduate Center of the City University of New York. Stetsenko's central research interests focus on developing cultural-historical activity theory especially in its applications to teaching and learning. She has published widely on this topic, drawing on her knowledge of diverse sociocultural and educational contexts (gained through research and teaching experiences in the US, Germany, Switzerland and Russia) with the goal of developing a comprehensive foundation for effective schooling and instruction. She has organized international panels, symposia and workshops on this topic and serves on editorial boards of several journals in this field.

Holli A. Tonyan (PhD) is currently an assistant professor of Psychology at California State University, Northridge, but work for this publication was conducted when she was a lecturer in Early Childhood Education at Monash University in Melbourne, Australia. Her research has focused on the interpersonal dimensions of infants' ability to regulate their emotions during the context of everyday interactions, including distress, play, and stress. Her research interests include understanding the ways in which children and the important people in their lives (peers, other children and adults) understand and develop new ways of negotiating the emotional challenges and joys across contexts and throughout development in home and child care/educational settings. Her work draws from her experiences in infant care and early childhood educational settings.

Jonathan Tudge is a professor of Human Development and Family Studies at the University of North Carolina at Greensboro, United States, and has been a visiting professor at several Brazilian universities and at the University of Tartu, Estonia. He completed his undergraduate and master's degrees in England, at Lancaster and Oxford respectively, and his PhD at Cornell University in the United States. Before becoming a professor he worked as a teacher of young children in England, Russia, and the United States. His research examines cultural-ecological aspects of young children's development both within and across a number of different societies, particularly focusing on the years prior to and immediately following the entry to school. He has authored or co-authored three books, including *The everyday lives of young children: Culture, class, and child rearing in diverse societies* (2008), New York: Cambridge, and published over 60 journal articles and book chapters.

Series Editors' Introduction

This 2009 volume of the *World Yearbook of Education* focuses on the construction of childhood and the place of education in global-local policies and practices. It continues the work, since the 2005 volume, of interrogating the effects and implications of globalisation in and on education. It also breaks new ground for the series with its focus on younger children and early years education.

'Constructing childhood' is the organising theme in the 2009 *World Yearbook of Education*. Volume editors, Marilyn Fleer (Australia), Mariane Hedegaard (Denmark) and Jonathan Tudge (US), argue that global discourses about young children and their development constitute policies and practices which define 'childhood' and the way it is enacted in everyday settings and relationships between adults and children. Historic inequalities between what they term the 'poor majority and rich countries from the industrialized (minority) world' (p. 3) means that normative principles anchored in the life experience of the minority world are generalised to all communities, world wide. Yet conditions within the majority world make it difficult for children, adults, nations and education systems to meet these norms. This one-sided minority world endorsement of 'good practice' means that local meanings and practices of childhood and development are marginalised. It sets some children, adults and communities up to fail. Equally other communities are recognised and rewarded because they better fit the global (but minority) norm.

In developing this argument the editors conceptualise 'global' effects in childhood and child development within a distinctive 'wholeness approach'. They recognise that global discourses travel and disrupt prevailing practices in local spaces so 'global–local' practices are in dynamic interplay and have unpredictable outcomes. They then plunge down into particular places and spaces to examine the way this 'global–local' interplay constitutes relationality that is enacted as particular located and ordered identities, practices and cultures. The editors draw on cultural historical and social ecological theories in this methodology. This framing highlights the way every local site or 'place' exists as a particular play, and politics, within hierarchical, horizontal and differently scaled (i.e., local, national, regional, transnation) relations of power. This 'wholeness approach' contributes in important ways to our knowledge about the 'global politics shaping local childhoods'.

The 2009 volume carries forward our commitments as series editors for the *Routledge World Yearbook of Education*. Our aim is to make this *World Yearbook of Education* a source for truly global analysis of contemporary transformations in education and societies. We make serious research available as a resource in uncertain times and as a contribution to shaping future education policy and practice towards building a better world. To this end we:

- Invite scholars to edit each volume because they are recognised experts in their fields who approach their fields with global research horizons;
- Recruit volume editors, and encourage them to recruit chapter authors, from all parts of the world. Our goal is to open up a global dialogue about education and research. This democratic impulse recognises the historic structuring of research in which the Global north has predominated over the global South (Connell, 2007). It takes the idea of a *World* Yearbook seriously and attempts to open a space where the voices of education researchers from both metropoles and peripheries can be heard in conversation; and
- Encourage volume editors to think globally with an eye to the future in developing their volume of the *World Yearbook of Education*. Specifically, we invite them to be ambitious by using the volume to initiate and profile a global research dialogue and to define a cutting edge agenda for future education research in their field. This is an invitation to chart new possibilities for education research informed by global horizons and diverse research voices, from centres and peripheries.

The 2009 volume of the *World Yearbook of Education* clearly carries this agenda for global education research forward through its investigations of education and childhood. We are delighted that scholars of the calibre of Fleer, Hedegaard and Tudge have taken up these challenges in preparing the 2009 *World Yearbook of Education*. Their work brings us perspectives on childhood, children's development and child rearing which challenge established traditions of early childhood education research. Their insights into children, and being a child today, contribute to a global politics that does not just form children but constructs our collective global future.

Terri Seddon and Jenny Ozga
Melbourne and Edinburgh, 2008

References

Connell, R. (2007) *Southern theory: The global dynamics of knowledge in social science.* Sydney: Allen and Unwin.

Series Editors' Details

The World Yearbook of Education series has been edited by Jenny Ozga and Terri Seddon since 2006.

Jenny Ozga is Professor of Educational Research and Director of the Centre for Educational Sociology at the University of Edinburgh (www.ces.ed.ac. uk). Before joining CES in 2000 she was Professor of Education Policy and Dean of Social Sciences at Keele University. Her research is in education policy, broadly defined, which includes research on policy-making as well as on specific areas of policy. The ways in which policy elites regroup and maintain their positions is one of her core areas of enquiry, along with comparative policy studies, policy networks; the 'Europeanisation' of education policy, the changing governance of education; the relationship between knowledge and policy, and policy for the teaching profession.

Terri Seddon is Professor of Education at Monash University, Melbourne. Her research is on the social organization of education as a social institution. This work is cross-sectoral in orientation, looking at schools, vocational and higher education, and workplace and community learning contexts in order to understand learning, work practices and organisational and decision-making processes in diverse learning spaces. She explores the social organisation of learning and the way it is organised, regulated and practiced within different settings which are each subject, in different ways, to economic reform and the increased individualisation of social life. She has particular research interests in partnership work and the challenges in constructing knowledge-sharing networks and collective agency across boundaries.

From 2009, the series editors' team will be extended to include Professor Gita Steiner-Khamsi, Teachers College, Columbia, and Professor Agnès van Zanten, Centre National de la Recherche Scientifique (CNRS), Paris.

1 Constructing Childhood

Global–Local Policies and Practices

Marilyn Fleer, Mariane Hedegaard and Jonathan Tudge

At the global level there has been an increasing discontent with how children have been named, reified, and measured. Prevailing Eurocentric and North-American notions of "childhood" and "development" hold sway in how "childhood" is constructed and how "development" is theorized. Benchmarks about progression are viewed as universal, and little has been done to disrupt the colonization of families who have children who do not fit the Eurocentric milestones and who are asked to change their family practices in order to be "ready for learning." In this book, we explicitly provide a series of windows on the construction of childhood around the world, as a means for conceptualizing and more sharply defining the emerging field of "global–local childhood studies." Providing research evidence of the nature and range of childhood contexts across countries provides a conceptual platform in which to draw comparisons and to build new understandings of the concept of childhood.

The agenda that is developed throughout this book is concerned with the specific dimensions of contemporary construction of "childhood," specifically the way globalized discourses constitute instruments (e.g. practices of policy and marketization) which disrupt, re-shape or contest family practices that educate and care for children. In this way, the book seeks to actively explore childhood studies from a range of perspectives, including those derived from education, sociology, and psychology. We begin this critique by drawing upon cultural-historical and ecological theory in order to build a dialectical relationship between global and local contexts to provide a conceptually rich discussion of "childhood" and children's development. This perspective lies in contrast to the globalized practices of policy and marketization that we criticize. In providing a perspective of "global–local" that is dialectically framed, we move beyond the binary concepts of "individual" and "universal" or "general" and "particular." Through this, we seek to give insights into how different countries address contemporary *global politics shaping local childhoods*.

Initially, it might be helpful to consider two of the ways in which the word "global" has been conceptualized. At times it has been used to mean "universal," in the sense that development is sometimes viewed as occurring in much the same way in any part of the world. From this point of view, understanding how development takes place in any one group of human beings adequately explains how development does, or should, occur in any part of the world. In this perspective, a single measuring stick is adequate to determine who has developed optimally and who is deficient in one or more ways.

But the term "global" has also been used in the sense of globalization, or the spread of ideas from one part of the world (typically conceived as the United States or western Europe) to the rest of the world, in an apparent process of economic, ideological, or educational colonization (see Nsamenang, this volume). These two senses of the word are linked, to the extent that if development is thought of as universal and a certain way of thinking, or behaving, or believing is viewed as the best among one group of people in one part of the world, it makes perfect sense to export conditions likely to allow more people in other parts of the world to attain the same ways of thinking, behaving, and believing.

In our view, and that of the authors of the following chapters, these two related senses of the term "global" are dangerous. Culture is so heavily implicated in developmental processes that one has to consider local considerations about what should be viewed as optimal in children's development. In other words, many measuring sticks have to be employed, rather than just one, to assess development in different cultural groups. If this is the case, one clearly must be cautious about the spread of ideas, or economic or educational institutions, from one society to others (or from a dominant group within a society to others that have been marginalized), whether in a form of active processes of colonization or by creating the conditions under which local or marginalized groups come to value aspects of the "modern" world.

What Does Global–Local Mean Across Communities?

It is important to note, however, that we are not advocating a local versus global approach to study children's development. The global–local distinction can lead to a dichotomization of the understanding of what is meant by "global–local studies of childhood and children's development." In psychology, education, and sociology dichotomies (such as mind–body, nature–nurture, society–subject, etc.) have flowered. In ecological and cultural-historical approaches these dichotomies are transcended and turned into dialectical and complementary relationships. As Branco (this volume) argues, to understand children's development one must consider "the intertwined nature of both general (species specific) and local (socioculturally specific) aspects of human development." Problems arise when "global" is only conceptualized as:

- universal, transcending specific times and places
- general laws, transcending unique cases and events
- theoretically abstract practices

and local as:

- specific places and times
- unique cases and events
- concrete practices.

The aim is to understand how a global approach to childhood and children's development always has to include reference to specific times and places, and at the same time how general laws of children's development have to encompass unique cases and events, and theoretical conceptions of children's development have to relate to concrete practices. The particular events in a child's development cannot be understood in themselves without using theoretical concepts, and theoretical conceptions of childhood and children's development are worthless if they cannot be related to concrete practices in all their complexities.

In this book we present research that draws upon a theoretical wholeness approach in researching "global–local policies and practices"

- that provide insights into and critiques policy imperatives, pedagogical processes, and cultural contexts
- that provide insights into how different countries address contemporary global–local tensions
- that foreground the educational context, through research in institutions such as family, school, child care and preschool.

The chapters in this book examine research from birth to twelve years, across institutional contexts (families, schools, child care, informal learning centers, community spaces), and within both poor majority and rich countries from the industrialized (minority) world. Contributors to this book provide many different windows into the global–local study of childhood and children's development from birth to 12, and through these presentations of research, provide new insights into how studies of children's development can be framed. However, the periodization of childhood is not uncontested, and in drawing upon sociological theories, the next section seeks to explore the tensions found in the naming of "childhood."

Are Globalized Views of "Childhood," "Children's Development," and "Learning" Being Constructed or Politicized?

Traditional critiques have foregrounded the problems with uniformity and coherence in relation to the concept of childhood. Henricks (1997) argued that in the 1800s childhood had not been conceptualized as universal. It was the early 1900s that saw middle-class communities determine an identity for children constructing a "modern view of childhood." "Childhood" became constructed and reconstructed into age periods and took on a public identity. However, constructions of "childhood" evolved over time from Rousseauian Naturalism, Romanticism, and Evangelicalism. Similarly, wage-earning labour was transformed into a period of "childhood," the term "juvenile delinquent" was created, a "child study" movement was founded, "children of the nation" was conceived as a public phrase, "psycho-medicine" emerged, and finally "children of the welfare state" was invented (see Henricks, 1997, pp. 35–36). Henricks determined that modern childhood was "legally, legislatively, socially, medically, psychologically, educationally and politically institutionalized" (p. 35). Kincheloe (2002) argued that along with the institutionalization of childhood came a way for describing children in universal terms. For example, young children were referred to as "non-social" or "pre-social," and later came the notion of "normal" and "abnormal" phases of children's development, which were taken up into the public psyche in relation to children's growth and development in many Western countries. Kincheloe (2002) wrote:

> By undermining an appreciation of the diversity and complexity of childhood, such viewpoints have often equated difference with deficiency and sociocultural construction with the natural. The complicated nature of childhood, child study, child psychology, social work for children, and childhood education demands rigorous forms of analysis. (p. 76)

Each of these disciplines has now embarked upon a serious critique of how children and therefore "childhood" has been positioned within their field.

We are now seeing an overwhelming number of critiques that have been undertaken within and across early childhood education, developmental psychology, history, and cultural studies that suggest that "childhood" is a cultural construction (Cannella & Kincheloe, 2002; Prout & James, 1997). Much of this literature states that the "child" as a construct is "reified as the 'other' and is seen as innocent (i.e., simple, ignorant, not yet adult), dependent (i.e., needy, unable to speak for themselves, vulnerable, victims), cute (i.e., objects, play-things, to be watched and discussed)" (Cannella, 2002, p. 3). In line with more recent, postmodern studies of childhood (Cannella & Kincheloe, 2002), this book takes an interdisciplinary, critical, and international view of "childhood." Indeed, because of interdisciplinary research, how children are viewed has changed and, we argue, will continue to change, over time. In this book, children have been positioned as central agents within the studies reported in the chapters that follow. For example, in Section I, Fleer and Quiñones discuss the concept of "children as researchers" from both a sociological and cultural-historical perspective.

Some authors in international cultural studies have suggested that as researchers we must remember that any discourse can be dangerous and that it should continually require historical and political examination. Cultural-studies scholars suggest that the discourses can be used to "generate a childhood studies that critiques itself, attempts to decolonize, and struggles to construct partnerships with those who are younger in the generation of human possibility" (Cannella, 2002, p. 8). Others (see Kasturi, 2002, p. 41) have argued that critical cultural studies seek to emphasise the "political dimensions of culture and society" and to examine the relations among culture, knowledge, and power in relation to children.

Postmodern critiques of "childhood," in putting forward the notion of "postmodern childhood studies," emphasize the need for the "disruption of the adult/child dualisms that predetermine people and generate power for one group over the other" (Cannella, 2002, p. 11). This line of critique moves beyond simply rejecting dualisms, but constructs the child as a political agent. In challenging universalism, postmodern childhood studies attempt to generate new possibilities for children. For instance, researchers have critiqued "children" and "childhood" in relation to policy development (Newburn, 1996; Oppenheim & Lister, 1996; Parton, 1996; Pilcher, 1996; Winter & Connolly, 1996), the children's rights movement (Franklin & Franklin, 1996), representations in art and popular print such as cards, magazines etc (Higonnet, 1998), education, entertainment and advertising (Kenway & Bullen, 2001).

As scholars have critiqued and debated the cultural construction of "children" and "childhood," the corporate world has actively used the construct of "childhood" to "create, sustain, and legitimate a type of consumer ethic that has come to dominate the landscape of childhood imagination" (Kincheloe, 2002, p. 42). Steinberg and Kincheloe (1997) and Kincheloe (2002) have argued that few scholars have noticed what they call the "corporate construction of childhood." In recognition of the immediacy and depth of information made available to children through new technologies, and through the broadening worldview of children as a result of easy exposure to information, corporations have actively targeted and redefined "childhood." Kincheloe (2002) stated:

> Corporate producers, marketers, and advertisers, recognizing the dynamics before other social agents, have reduced prior market segmentations based on chronological age to only: (a) very young children and (b) all other youth. Abandoning divisions suggested by developmental psychology, such business operatives realize how blurred age categorization has become. (p. 79)

The corporate world has redefined childhood in relation to marketing criteria. Market research by the corporate world has shown that in Western (Jipson & Paley, 2002; Kasturi, 2002; Scott, 2002) and also some Asian communities (Shon, 2002; Viruru, 2002) children are enjoying a "kidworld" (Cannella & Kincheloe, 2002) or "Kinder-culture" (Steinberg & Kincheloe, 1998) that runs covertly in parallel with the "adult world" (Kasturi, 2002; Pollock & Van Reken, 1999; Scott, 2002). Kincheloe (2002, p. 103) argued that when children are "[d]rawing on this technology-enhanced isolation, children turn it into a form of power. They know things that mom and dad don't. How may parents understand the relationship between Mayor

McCheese and the French Fry Guys in McDonaldland?" Children are enjoying the power of generating their own discourse (Scott, 2002), worldly input, and technological knowledge expertise (as a result of being able to operate technologies more easily than adults) (Provenzo, 1998), and through this children have problematized the traditional beliefs of "childhood" as "innocent," "cute," and in "need of protection" (Cannella, 2002; Henricks, 1997; Higonnet, 1998). Kincheloe (2002, p. 83) stated that "traditional notions of childhood as a time of innocence and adult-dependency have been challenged by children's access to corporate-produced popular culture."

Alongside arguments that center on children's agency has been a growing number of studies that also have shown the impact of the corporatization of childhood. For example, Petterson (2005), in researching consumption and identity in Arabic cultures through an analysis of Arabic children's magazines, noted that Egyptian communities are concerned for how their children can simultaneously be modern and Egyptian. He argued that a form of hybridity of cultures prevails—that is, rather than dualities of "*galabiyya* vs. jeans and button down shirts," "veil vs. the salon hair style," and "sermon vs. TV" what is observed is "the sheikh with a cell phone, the televised sermon, the veil, selected for color and pattern, as style accessory" (p. 196). For some groups in the corporate world, the hybridization has become a form of colonization. For instance, "Disney's geographies appropriate and commodifies space, while the histories restructure time for corporate convenience. Disney is viewed as constructing and presenting specific, ideologically loaded stories and lessons for consumers to learn" (Kasturi, 2002, p. 44). Through this process, cultural groups become invisible or stereotyped. Kasturi (2002) suggested that "the unproblematized representations of race, class, and gender in Disney 'stories' (e.g., movies, comics, parks)" and on their websites (p. 45) scale up the U.S. set of highly questionable values to a global form of colonization. She argued that "Disney's power lies in this subconscious form of colonization" (p. 43). However, the tensions between local and global forms of colonization are well known to the corporate world, as argued by Kincheloe (2002):

> So concerned is McDonald's about implanting this perception of localization/personalization in the mind of the public that the company actually employs a vice-president for individuality. The stated function of this office is to make "the company feel small" despite the reality of globalization. In Beijing, McDonald's markets itself to the Chinese people not as an American but as a Chinese company. (p. 87)

Similarly, in the course of researching popular children's culture, through an analysis of the Beanie Babies, Scott (2002) argued that along with many other artefacts are products "that have lubricated the wheels of materialist globalization, a complex site of both agency and control. Beanies join with many other Euro-American artefacts in the construction of a global capitalist hegemony..." (p. 72).

The authors of various chapters in this volume make similar points about the impact of these colonizing tendencies. Citing their previously published work (Artar, Onur & Çelen, 2002; Göncü et al., 1999), Göncü, Özer and Ahioğlu (this volume) state that:

> children's games are influenced by their economic and cultural context, and that decreasing frequency of games and children's reliance on ready-made toys revealed that the local meaning of childhood is being replaced by that which is introduced to Turkey through the free market economy and globalization.

Nsamenang (this volume) also mentions these problems in relation to the global impact of poor country worldviews of childhood, particularly "child development," suggesting that there needs to be a recognition of the cultural conceptualizations of "childhood," "child development theory," and the practices that flow from these views. He states:

> Are rights activities and the development community really aware that many Majority World children "hide" their true identity because contemporary ECCE [early childhood care and education] services instil shame in them for being different from the normative Western child?

Nsamenang (this volume) suggests that what should be foregrounded is a view that global childhood should be characterized by diversity. He sates that the image of the "global child" is Western-derived and "that pathologizes all 'other' images of childhood." He notes that what is actively being promoted by the "development community in [the] Majority World is a product of European and North American culture, which represents only a minority of the world's early childhoods in a multicultural universe." Further, he claims that those who do go beyond the industrialized world only locate themselves in the majority world cities, thus missing 70 percent of the world's population who live in rural communities. The dynamics between the global and the local are taken up in quite different ways in the literature, and quite different critiques of "children" and "childhood" are offered by scholars working within particular theoretical perspectives, particularly those adopting a postmodern perspective.

Writing from related perspectives, Elliott, Tudge and Odero-Wanga, Freitas, Shelton, and Sperb, and Branco (all in this volume) draw attention to the ways in which views of "appropriate" ways of thinking about and dealing with children and adolescents have been spread by North American and West European scholars to other parts of the world. Elliott, for example, shows how Western educators have attempted to export their ideas to the Russian context, despite the fact that there was a great deal to admire in the Soviet educational system and much that is lacking in its North American equivalent. Similarly, Freitas and her colleagues (Freitas et al., this volume; Freitas, Shelton, & Tudge, 2008) note the ways in which North American approaches to early childhood education have been applied in Brazil, including a two-tiered system (education of the "whole child" for the children of the rich, "care" or a deficit-inspired model to "improve" the children of the poor). Branco's chapter, written from a cultural-historical perspective, raises the additional issue of the impact on Brazilian early childhood education of competition among children, which she sees as having been influenced by market forces to the detriment of more collaborative and interdependent ways of being. One additional issue, however, is the fact that Western and North American ideas do not always have to be imposed on parts of the majority poor world, but are sometimes accepted along with McDonald's and Starbucks as emblematic of becoming "modern."

Childhood labor is another contested area, as many scholars from Western cultural contexts have actively sought to question such practices. However, other scholars have suggested that views of "childhood" and therefore "childhood labor" are framed from within communities, and that Eurocentric or middle-class views of what constitutes work should be culturally located and not globalized. These scholars suggest that locally relevant models should be constructed and named, and globalized definitions should be questioned (see Stephens, 1995). Assumptions about how "childhood" is being conceptualized in these discussion about "childhood labor" should be critiqued. Göncü, Özer and Ahioğlu (this volume) suggest that "the economic interdependence common in low-income households influences values about family, and children's and women's places in specific terms." Further, Tudge and Odero-Wanga (this volume) demonstrate nicely how the views expressed in the 1980s in relation to Kenyan communities must now be understood as a particular period in time, as most Kenyans lived in rural communities. With the rapid movement of families into cities, Kenyan children, particularly those from middle-class backgrounds, spend much less time involved in labor. Although the urban working-class children from Kenya in their comparative study worked more, Tudge and Odero-Wanga (this volume) show that Kenyan middle-class children spent no more time at work than did children in many cities from the industrialized world. These findings draw our attention not only to the need to move beyond literature published some time ago, but also the significance of how views of some groups of children become treated as reflecting universal aspects of development, and reified, despite the diversity of circumstances and chances that occur across and within particular communities either in a specific country or across the world.

In this section we have examined the literature that has critiqued "childhood" and "children" with a view to better understanding the "global construction of childhood" and to introduce some of the key ideas inherent in the chapters within this book. In the next section we examine a new view of "children" and "childhood studies."

A Wholeness Approach to Researching "Childhood" and "Child Development"

In noting the tensions inherent in discussing "childhood studies" this book seeks to move beyond the problematization of terms and concepts and offer new insights. In this book "childhood and children's development" is framed from a wholeness perspective. A wholeness approach includes a global–local dialectic in which childhood and children are seen in interdependent relation to their activities, institutional practices, and societal conditions. This approach can both be used to conceptualize childhood in general and to follow single children in their different everyday institutional settings. It could also be used in relation to specific problems such as researching children's use of "other persons as role models in educational practices." Wholeness is not one thing but is a relational concept beginning with the aims held by people. For us, it is important to understand children's development as anchored in local practices, such as the aim of teachers to have children "being compliant in the classroom" (see Elliott, this volume) or exhibiting cooperative behavior (see Branco, this volume), and this practice needs to be seen as related to theoretical concepts about children's development. For example, in some societies interdependence is a highly valued developmental outcome, as observed in the former Soviet Union (as reported by Elliott, this volume). However, the wholeness approach also includes the influences on development that shape and change local practices which come from other groups. For example Elliott (this volume) speaks of how education was so highly valued by youth in schools, but in recent times social conditions have generated disillusionment and diminished respect for education due to its inability to improve the economic situation of people within Russia. A wholeness approach to understanding "global–local childhoods" is only possible when all of these cultural-historical conditions are brought together.

Children develop through participating in everyday practices in societal institutions, but neither society nor its institutions (i.e. families, kindergarten, school, youth clubs, etc.) are static but change over time in a dynamic interaction between person's activities, institutional traditions and practices, societal discourse, and material conditions. Several types of institutional practices in children's social situations influence children's life and development. At the same time, children themselves influence the institutions in which they are situated: they change their families by their arrival, their particular temperamental qualities, the ways in which they interact with their parents and siblings, and so on; they change their kindergartens and schools by arriving there with unique past experiences, different motivations and interests, the relationships they establish with their peers and their teachers, and so on. Children's development can be seen as diverse possibilities for socio-cultural tracks through different institutions. The chapters in this book provide a range of rich examples of diverse possibilities. Stetsenko (this volume) shows how these socio-cultural tracks have in the past been informed by an incremental view of development, where the universal perspective prevailed.

Her theoretical work shows an expansive view of development "where people come to know themselves and their world... [and] ultimately come to be human *in and through* (not in addition to) the processes of collaboratively transforming their world in view of their goals and purposes." Similarly, Tudge and Odero-Wanga (this volume) draw on cultural-ecological theory (see Tudge, 2008), to show the ways in which young urban Kenyan children, from both middle-class and working-class backgrounds, develop in the course of initiating and engaging in their everyday activities.

In developmental psychology much research has focused on children's cognitive and emotional development without considering the traditions in the settings of children's everyday life. So for us the question is: How can studies of children's activities in everyday institutional settings (such as family and school) across different nation states contribute to an understanding of children's development that transcends these setting? And how can a wholeness approach be formulated that both can be used to understand children in their everyday activities in local communities and as sharing global aspects of childhood? To approach these questions one has to focus upon what is understood as a wholeness approach, and also to formulate a research approach that conceptualizes children in their everyday activities across nation states, institutional borders and local settings. We conceptualize institutional practices as part of an elaborated account of a wholeness approach where the different instances/aspects create conditions for each other. That is, when we think about children we look at the children within the institution of their family, their local community practices within institutions such as clubs, sporting groups, and the formal learning institutions that they attend, such as school or child care. This is foregrounded by van Oers (this volume) when he discusses the pedagogy of developmental teaching. In his research he notes the importance of organizing learning to reflect the wholeness of community within the classroom through the generation of everyday home and community practices within the children's learning environment. Van Oers states "The aim of Developmental Education can also be described as the enhancement of persons' abilities to participate independently and critically in sociocultural practices of their community."

Given that this book focuses on researching childhood and children's development, the concept of institutional practice has to be seen in connection with the upbringing and education of children, and how children's active participation in their everyday practices influences the practices themselves and thereby becomes part of their learning and development conditions. That is, we consider both the child-rearing practices and experiences of children in families at the same time as we note the way these children participate in the practices of schooling. When children step into an institution, such as a school, they bring with them their everyday life from home as part of "who they are." We believe that the child's everyday life at home, as embedded within the child, has to be included in the institutional practice of the school, and through this influences the conceptualization of his or her learning and development.

Theoretical approaches that have focused on the same problem to develop a wholeness approach can be found in both *the cultural-historical activity* research with Lev Vygotsky (1998) and A. N. Leontiev (1978), which has evolved into a Scandinavian research tradition (Hedegaard, 2002, 2008; Hundeide, 2003), and *the ecological approach* best represented by Urie Bronfenbrenner (2005) and Bronfenbrenner and Morris (2006), and adapted by Tudge (2008). Both cultural-historical and ecological theories share the position that understanding development requires taking simultaneous consideration of activities and interactions, characteristics of the individuals involved in those activities and interactions, and the cultural setting, as developed over historical time, that gives meaning to those activities and interactions. Trying to understand development by focusing only on the level of the individual and his or her activity or only on practice or context are seen as insufficient in both theories; instead, they require a wholeness approach.

Critiques have also arisen from other approaches such as the "deconstruction of psychology" formulated by Erica Burman or the "interpretive reproduction" approach as formulated by William Corsaro (2005). All these approaches see diversity in societal practices and traditions as central as well as point to the importance of values in research about children's development and childhood. They all oppose the prevailing Eurocentric and North-American notions of "childhood" and development as presented above.

An educational approach needs to formulate what is conceptualized as good development; such conceptions have to be anchored in the relation between societal practices and the values that connect with these so that development cannot be viewed as universal progression. Scholars who have not considered a group's values about what constitutes good development or a good childhood have judged these things as though they can be measured on a single Eurocentric or North American scale. Families whose children do not "measure up" on this scale are viewed as having deficits whose practices need to change to ensure "good" development. Globalizing pressures that try to ensure that all children around the world are raised in similar ways clearly stem from the idea that local practices are counter-productive if they do not fit well with a supposedly universal set of markers for good development.

By contrast, this book explicitly seeks to provide a series of windows on the construction of childhood in relation to different societal demands and value systems around the world, as a means of conceptualizing and more sharply defining the emerging field of global–local childhood studies. For instance, Nsamenang (this volume) has shown the relations between global views of what constitutes "good early childhood education and care practice," and local constructions of "childhood" and "childhood development." In his analysis he has problematized the disjunction between minority (usually Western) views of early learning and care and majority worldviews, showing how the dynamics between majority and minority worldviews are resulting in a form of colonization. Bottcher (this volume), in undertaking a case study of two children with cerebral palsy in a primary school context, has shown the dialectical interactions between the social and biological, accentuated through the physical constraints imposed. Her work nicely illustrates the relations between neurobiological constraints, child motives, and child thinking and acting. She shows how children "with lesions to their brains change and develop actively in and with changing demands and possibilities in the social settings similar to the way normal children do, even though their conditions for doing so are different." Her work provides another window into how "childhood" and "childhood development" can be conceptualized, and also illustrates that no single measuring stick is sufficient to assess development, even within a single society. Göncü, Özer & Ahioğlu (this volume) show in their analysis of the Turkish context that "children's activities are determined by the economical and value contexts of their communities." That is, when family time and energy are devoted to the collective enterprise of income generation and collective domestic chores, then how children play and how they spend their time is significantly influenced. These local and within-community variations in children's activities are not always well understood or considered. They provide valuable insights, not only in terms of the data generated, but also through their locally framed methodologies. In this section we have examined the global–local tensions inherent in contemporary thinking about childhood studies with a view to realizing a new perspective on the global–local study of childhood—a wholeness approach. In the next section we seek to explicate this approach specifically in relation to education.

Foregrounding the Educational Context Through Research in Institutions Such as Family, School, Child-Care and Preschool Contexts

Education in the context of this book on childhood studies can be found as a critical interface between theoretical concepts of children's development and local family practices—that is, seeing "education" in broad terms as the instruments and practices of learning which are located both within and outside families.

In this connection, it is important not to use the time and space distinctions for family studies naively so they become physical concepts but instead to use them to specify the relations of institutions within a societal frame. A society gives conditions for its institutions, and institutions reflect generational changes that both are dependent on and influence societal change (James, Jenks & Prout, 1998). Hedegaard and Fleer (this volume) provide insights into how the family institution creates possibilities for development in relation to societal conditions. It is through the everyday practices of the family that family-specific values, motives, and beliefs are encountered and transformed by the participants. The transitions between everyday activities, the demands and conflicts within the activities, as well as the modelling by siblings and parents are detailed for two children—one in Australia and one in Denmark. At this everyday level it is possible to see how constraints and demands at the societal level, as well as the general conception of family life impact upon the day-to-day activities of children in their family. For example, living in Australia where community resources are geographically distant means families need a car. Being poor in Australia means that you don't have a car and this sets up different opportunities for development.

In Bang's chapter environmental affordance perspective is introduced and presented as an important factor in the study of development. She argues that "environment should be studied from an integrated historical/cultural *and* a functional perspective" environment is not a neutral term; instead "the environment of a child becomes that which the child perceives as available to action". This availability is related to social others and the self experience. Bang demonstrates her understanding in interpretation of a student's learning in a mathematics class where both artefacts, teachers, students, and the child's self experience have affordance in learning activity, and space dimensions.

The relational concept of "time and space" can also be considered from the perspective of how a society depicts differences in childhood across nation states, where regional diversity and changes in practice are evident. Elliott (this volume) provides a good example of this when discussing the changes emerging both within Russian society and within the former Soviet schooling system as a result of both economic change and an opening up of values from outside the country. Similarly, Tudge and Odero-Wanga (this volume) call attention both to the passage of historical time in Kenya and to the different impact historical changes have had on middle-class and working-class Kenyan families. A practice perspective in relation to "time and space" provides the possibility to transcend the rational conceptions of this dimension and opens up space for tradition and values as part of change. Fleer, Tonyan, Mantilla and Rivalland (this volume) in their analyses of how Western play theory is used in local play practices, draw attention to how both local and societal tensions in relation to values are shaped and constituted through "time."

At another level, how institutions shape or are shaped by different views of "children" and "childhood" (both institutional and societal) become evident in the studies reported in this book. Bottcher (this volume), drawing upon cultural-historical theory, has foregrounded the dialectical relations between the social context (school), and the activities of two children with cerebral palsy that she was studying. Rather than viewing "childhood" in isolation from the institutional context in which children participate, Bottcher (this volume) focuses on the dialectical relations between them, and through this shows how "normal children" and "children with cerebral palsy" can be reconceptualized. Her work reframes thinking in education. It repositions "biological constraints," in this case cerebral palsy, like all other biological constraints, such as being small or being large, so that the focus of attention is in relation to the activity and how this generates (or not) motives for learning for the participants in her study.

Freitas, Shelton and Sperb (this volume) in foregrounding the historical component of Vygotsky's cultural-historical theory, have undertaken an analysis of Brazilian views and policies of early childhood care and education in relation to the views and policies espoused in the United States. Their work shows local institutional agency, despite global domination. In examining the dominant minority (Western) worldview, often positioned as universal, on what matters for early childhood care and education, they note that the "general principles about the care and education of young children take on local nuances." Policies and practices are enacted or imagined with local understandings. They suggest that

> in order to understand the global–local tension involved in implementing early childhood care and education policies in any society it is essential to know the history of that society, given that the changes that take place are always a transformation of what had been and not a simple substitution of the old by the new.

Their work points to the institutional agency found within early childhood education and care in Brazil, and provides a platform for thinking about the global–local construct in relation to institutions within and across countries. Institutional agency has also been noted in a study by Fleer, Tonyan, Mantill, and Rivalland (this volume) on the theories of play that were being drawn upon to inform early childhood professionals' practice in a child-care center in Australia. The staff (particularly the unqualified staff) used the language of Western theories of play, but constructed their own labels in order to explain their observations of children at play. As has been argued by Göncü, Özer and Ahioğlu (this volume), "none of schooling, play, or labor takes place as uniformly as was expected by Western theorists and policy makers." Whilst the theories of play had colonized their professional practice, they were identifying problems and were working towards new understandings in relation to theorizing their practices. As with Freitas, Shelton and Sperb (this volume), the global or universal terms used in early childhood, in this case the theories of play, are also being nuanced at the local level. In contrast, Göncü, Özer and Ahioğlu, in their study of Turkish children, families and education system, argue that most Turkish scholars publish in Turkish, and as such, the theories and practices of child development and education are unavailable to the rest of the world. They state that in relation to Turkish preschool play "we do not know of studies that examine the middle-class caregivers' values about or participation in the play of children." Through locally relevant research, scholars in Turkey have not needed to draw upon research or theories from outside of their own society for framing up locally relevant practices.

The traditional practice in society by many countries is to separate care and education (see Freitas et al., this volume), and this has also been mirrored in the separation of family and schooling. In contrast, Kravtsov and Kravtsova (this volume) have brought together the institution of the "family" with the institution of the "school" through the creation of the Golden Key Schools in Russia. They argue that "life is organized on the principle of the family, where all adults, without exception, participate in the upbringing of the children... and [the schools are] a continuation and extension of the child's own family."

The multi-age settings, combined with an easy flow of practice between the school and the home, generate a learning context where separation between institutions is less evident. With an orientation towards space in the first year, followed by the foregrounding of time in the second year (e.g. time periods through history as well as "minutes," "seconds," and "hours"), and finally in the third year the focus is on materials (e.g. folk art and other cultures), learning is generated through teamwork across settings. The Golden Key Schools support both horizontal and vertical learning across contexts and over time.

Another aspect of education that has been noted in this book is the tension between education and development. Chaiklin and Hedegaard (this volume) suggest that "education is a societal practice, children's development is a consequence of their participation in societal practices, and therefore education has a significant role in children's development." In their chapter their analyses have occurred in relation to education and development on a general analytical level, on a general practice level, and on a concrete societal level. Here they introduce the concept of radical–local teaching and learning. The concept radical–local combines the cultural-historical theory of education with local practice. "The designation 'radical–local' is meant to emphasise the integration of general intellectual concepts ('radical' in the sense of 'root') with the local content and conditions for children's lives."

Van Oers (this volume) also makes reference to the dialectical relations between education and development through detailing how developmental teaching has been theorized and enacted in practice in the Netherlands. He suggests that 10 percent of schools have adopted this approach to their teaching because of a dissatisfaction with the prevailing reductionist view of pedagogy and learning and a growing interest in cultural-historical activity theory. He states

> From our Developmental Education perspective we believe that meaningful learning that can stimulate critical identity development can only blossom in activities that have adopted a format that is based on clear rules, that stimulates involvement in the actors, and that allows (at least) some degrees of freedom. This format is characteristic for play activities (see van Oers, 2005), but we extrapolated the format to all meaningful activities in the Developmental Education curriculum. That is why we characterise the whole Developmental Education curriculum as a *play-based curriculum*. This includes both playful learning activities in the primary grades, and the inquiry-based learning activities in the upper grades of primary school. This format of the activities in school creates the basic conditions for emancipation, identity formation and meaningful learning.

Developmental teaching positions children as not just consumers of society, learning the required curriculum, but rather as critical participants who are not only shaped by their learning community but who also contribute towards and shape curriculum possibilities.

In this section we have foregrounded some of the arguments put forward by authors of chapters in this book. We have noted the relations between society at large and the institutions found within that society, we have also considered more broadly how Western minority worldviews pass into institutional practices and are resisted or taken up, and we have considered within-nation institutions and the borders (or not) between the institution of the family and the institution of schooling. Finally, we have examined how education and development are dialectically related, and how a local–radical view can be transformative of traditional educational practices. We now move towards examining the framing of research for studying global–local childhoods.

Researching and Critiquing Policy Imperatives, Pedagogical Processes and Cultural Context

One of the main themes in this book is that research with children should not be detached from children's everyday practices. Psychological and educational research activity has generally been shown to run parallel with educational and everyday practice (see Chaiklin & Hedegaard, this volume). This points to the alternative of researching children in practice, where researchers entering this practice can be conceptualized as part of the research practice. But to do this we also have to conceptualize research as located within children's social situations. For example, Fleer and Quiñones (this volume) discuss how traditional approaches to childhood studies have positioned the child center stage, and have marginalized the researcher. In listening to the voice of the child, the researchers have been made invisible. Yet a wholeness perspective acknowledges that the researcher is a part of the research context, not simply seen as a static being influencing the research (as it is often reported), but rather someone who engages with the children, offering possibilities for interaction and discussion. The researcher is not a play partner, but has a specific "research role," and his or her role must be taken into account when examining the data that are generated. Similarly, children are not researched as though they were on their own. Fleer and Quiñones argue that a "children's consultation culture… is premised upon an ideology that simply listening to children equates with generating robust research data." They argue that foregrounding the child is not enough. The researcher in their interactions with the child, and how they enter the field, how they are positioned or position themselves (what role they take), must be made visible and understood. This is understood as a "relational ontology of human development and learning that places *relations* between individuals and their world at the core of this development" (Stetsenko, this volume). The psychological, educational and sociological sciences researchers have to see themselves as part of the practice, paying tribute to societal demands.

When we see childhood research as practices that are related to societal demands, the researcher's own value base unfolds.

Traditional Western psychological, educational, and sociological research, like other institutional practices, have been located within modern societies that have the "universal" goal of progress. We do not free ourselves from these societal values when we undertake research within other countries, unless we see the research context as related to "studying localized societal demands reflected in concrete practices" (Kravtsova & Kravtsov, this volume). For instance, these authors illustrate four easily observable values in the daily life of any person of any age as concrete practices:

> The ability to act in the space surrounding the child. The skill to organise one's personal space according to the goals of the activity; Orientation to time, the skill to develop, construct a sequence of actions and to plan them; The ability to work with various materials, to use their properties and peculiarities in one's own activity; The development of the ability to analyse one's own actions, to reflect, to understand oneself as the subject of these activities.

Here progress as value statements for the institution are assumed, and research within this institutional context seeks to determine these developments.

When going into a young nation state to look for a new kind of research into children's development, we must ourselves question or acknowledge the extent to which our research assumes some type of universal goal in relation to the demands and societal practices which children have to meet. Otherwise we risk finding or framing research based on Eurocentric and North-American notions of childhood and children's development. We do not conquer new knowledge by going to young nation states unless the focus of the research is related to societal demands when researching childhood practices. What we seek to avoid is reproducing the dominating science traditions.

Göncü, Özer & Ahioğlu (this volume) actively positioned themselves as researchers of global–local childhood, transcending the dominating traditions in research. They were interested in how children played in rural communities in Turkey. To do this, they designed a study which not only captured the occurrence and frequency of play, but also examined the meaning of play within the particular cultural communities. They argue: "This meant that both the examination and the interpretation of children's play need to take place according to the cultural priorities of children's communities." To achieve this, Göncü and his colleagues observed in naturalistic settings, and they interviewed the adults who were in the environment at the time (e.g., grandparents). Interviews and observations were videotaped.

We need to conceptualize the diversity of family values as seen from different institutional and societal perspectives in our research in order to better understand the diversity of views on what constitutes "childhood" and "childhood development." Generating a diversity of research in order to capture broader and better understandings of children and childhood is essential for increasing scholarly knowledge in global–local childhood studies. Through this, we begin to better understand the interdependence between worldviews, methodologies and methods. For example, Bang (this volume) draws our attention to the child–environment reciprocity in an activity setting, seeking out small and great novelty. Here novelty refers to the "presence of things and people in specific context, but also to the presence of an absence (temporality/historicity) of societal processes" as the child interacts with the environment. In the study of global–local childhoods, Bang (this volume) argues that in studying "potentials for small and great novelty within an activity setting means studying what kind of activities are going on in which particular environment, how does a child participate in ongoing activities, and how does he or she experience/feel about this." The dialectical relations between the local research context and the worldview and methodology of the researchers come into play.

Conclusion

In this chapter we have explored how a wholeness approach to the global–local study of children can provide new insights into how we think about childhood studies and how we may go about researching child development and learning within and across institutions and countries. Throughout this book we have positioned the global–local study of children, childhood, and development through a wholeness lens. The chapters that follow further problematize the cultural construction of childhood (Section I), elaborate more on the theoretical ideas introduced in this chapter (Section II) and finally, they expand on the educational implications of contemporary global–local thinking (Section III).

References

Artar, M., Onur, B., Çelen, N. (2002). Çocuk Oyunlarında Üç Kuşakta Görülen Değişimler [Changes in Children's Games Through Three Generations]. *Çocuk Forumu* 5(1), 35–39.

Bronfenbrenner, U. (Ed.) (2005). *Making human beings human: Bioecological perspectives on human development* (pp. 3–15). Thousand Oaks, CA: Sage.

Bronfenbrenner, U., & Morris, P. A. (2006). The bioecological model of human development. In W. Damon (Series Ed.) & R. M. Lerner (Vol. Ed.), *Handbook of child psychology: Vol. 1. Theoretical models of human development* (6th edn, pp. 793–828). New York: John Wiley.

Brooks, S. (2002). Making poverty pay: Children and the 1996 Welfare Law. In G. S. Cannella & J. L. Kincheloe (Eds.), *Kidworld childhood studies, global perspectives, and education* (pp. 21–38). New York: Peter Lang Publishing.

Cannella, G. S. (2002). Global perspectives, cultural studies, and the construction of a postmodern childhood studies. In G. S. Cannella & J. L. Kincheloe (Eds.), *Kidworld childhood studies, global perspectives, and education* (pp. 3–18). New York: Peter Lang Publishing.

Cannella, G. S., & Kincheloe, J. L. (Eds.), (2002). *Kidworld childhood studies, global perspectives, and education.* New York: Peter Lang Publishing.

Cannella, G. S., & Viruru, R. (2002). (Euro-American constructions of) education of children (and adults) around the world: A postcolonial critique. In G. S. Cannella & J. L. Kincheloe (Eds.), *Kidworld childhood studies, global perspectives, and education* (pp. 197–214). New York: Peter Lang Publishing.

Corsaro, W. A. (2005). *The sociology of childhood,* 2nd edn. Thousand Oaks, CA: Pine Forge Press.

Diaz Soto, L., & Inces, R. Q. (2002). Children's linguistic/cultural human rights. In G. S. Cannella & J. L. Kincheloe (Eds.), *Kidworld childhood studies, global perspectives, and education* (pp. 181–196). New York: Peter Lang Publishing.

Franklin, A., & Franklin, B. (1996). Growing pains: The developing Children's Rights Movement in the UK. In J. Pilcher, & S. Wagg, (Eds.) *Thatcher's children? Politics, childhood and society in the 1980s and 1990s.* (pp. 94–113). London & Bristol: Falmer Press.

Göncü, A., Tuermer, U., Jain, J., & Johnson, D. (1999). Children's play as cultural activity. In A. Göncü (Ed.), *Children's engagement in the world: Sociocultural perspectives,* (pp. 148–170). Cambridge, UK: Cambridge University Press.

Grieshaber, S. (2002). A national system of childcare accrditation: Quality assurance or a technique of normalization? In G. S. Cannella & J. L. Kincheloe (Eds.), *Kidworld childhood studies, global oerspectives, and education* (pp. 161–180). New York: Peter Lang Publishing.

Hedegaard, M. (2002). *Learning and child development: A cultural-historical study.* Aarhus, Denmark: Aarhus University Press.

Hedegaard, M. (2008 in press). Child development from a cultural-historical approach: children's activity in everyday local settings as foundation for their development. *Mind Culture and Activity.*

Henricks, H. (1997). Constructions and reconstructions of British childhood: An interpretative survey, 1800 to the present. In A. James, A. & A. Prout (Eds.), *Constructing and reconstructing childhood* (pp. 34–62). London & Philadelphia: Falmer Press.

Higonnet, A. (1998). *Pictures of innocence: The history of crisis of ideal childhood.* London: Thames and Hudson.

Hundeide, K. (2003). *Børns livsverden og sociokulturelle rammer* [Children's life word and sociocultural frames]. Copenhagen: Akademisk forlag.

James, A., & Prout, A. (1997). *Constructing and reconstructing childhood.* London & Philadelphia: Falmer Press.

James, A., Jenks, C., and Prout, A. (1998). *Theorising childhood.* Cambridge, UK: Polity Press.

Jipson, J. A., & Paley, N. (2002). A toy story: The object(s) of American childhood. In G. S. Cannella & J. L. Kincheloe (Eds.), *Kidworld childhood studies, global perspectives, and education* (pp. 123–136). New York: Peter Lang Publishing.

Kasturi, S. (2002). Constructing childhood in a corporate world: Cultural studies, childhood, and Disney. In G. S. Cannella & J. L. Kincheloe (Eds.), *Kidworld childhood studies, global perspectives, and education* (pp. 39–58). New York: Peter Lang Publishing.

Kenway, J. & Bullen, E. (2001). *Consuming children: Education-entertainment-advertising.* Buckingham & Philadelphia: Open University Press.

Kincheloe, J. L. (2002). The complex politics of McDonald's and the new childhood: Colonizing Kidzworld. In G. S. Cannella & J. L. Kincheloe (Eds.), *Kidworld childhood studies, global perspectives, and education* (pp. 75–122). New York: Peter Lang Publishing.

Leontiev, A. N. (1978). *Activity, consciousness, and personality* (M. J. Hall, Trans.). Englewood Cliffs, NJ: Prentice-Hall. (Original work published 1975)

Newburn, T. (1996). Back to the future? Youth crime, youth justice and the rediscovery of "authoritarian populism". In J. Pilcher, & S. Wagg (Eds.), *Thatcher's children? Politics, childhood and society in the 1980s and 1990s* (pp. 61–76). London & Bristol: Falmer Press.

Oers, B. van (2005). Carnaval in de kennisfabriek [Carnaval in the knowledge factory]. Inaugural address. Amsterdam: VUpress.

Oppenheim, C., & Lister, R. (1996). The politics of child poverty 1979–1995. In J. Pilcher, & S. Wagg (Eds.), *Thatcher's children? Politics, childhood and society in the 1980s and 1990s* (pp. 114–33). London & Bristol: Falmer Press.

Parton, N. (1996). The new politics of child protection. In J. Pilcher, & S. Wagg (Eds.), *Thatcher's children? Politics, childhood and society in the 1980s and 1990s* (pp. 43–60). London & Bristol: Falmer Press.

Peterson, M. A. (2005). The JINN and the computer: Consumption and identity in Arabic children's magazines. *Childhood: A Global Journal of Child Research, 12*(2), 177–200. London, Thousand Oaks and New Delhi: Safe Publications.

Pilcher, J., & Wagg, S. (1996). *Thatcher's children? Politics, childhood and society in the 1980s and 1990s.* London & Bristol: Falmer Press.

Pollock, D. C., & Van Reken, R. E. (1999). *Third culture kids: The experience of growing up among worlds.* Maine, USA & London: Intercultural Press.

Prout, A., & James, A. (1997). A new paradigm for the sociology of childhood? Provenance, promise and problems. In A. James & A. Prout (Eds.), *Constructing and reconstructing childhood* (pp. 7–33). London & Philadelphia: Falmer Press.

Provenzo, E. R. Jr. (1998). Video games and the emergence of interactive media for children. In S. R. Steinberg & J. L. Kincheloe (Eds.), *Kinder-culture* (pp. 103–114) Colorado: Westview Press.

Scott, D. (2002). What are beanie babies teaching our children? In G. S. Cannella & J. L. Kincheloe (Eds.), *Kidworld childhood studies, global perspectives, and education* (pp. 59–74). New York: Peter Lang Publishing.

Shon, M.-R. (2002). Korean early childhood education: Colonization and resistance. In G. S. Cannella & J. L. Kincheloe (Eds.), *Kidworld childhood studies, global perspectives, and education* (pp. 137–150). New York: Peter Lang Publishing.

Steinberg, S. R., & Kincheloe, J. L. (1998). *Kinder-culture.* Colorado: Westview Press.

Stephens, S. (Ed.) (1995). *Children and the politics of culture.* Princeton, NJ: Princeton University Press.

Tudge, J. R. H. (2008). *The everyday lives of young children: Culture, class, and child rearing in diverse societies.* New York: Cambridge University Press.

Viruru, R., (2002). Postcolonial ethnography: An Indian perspective on voice and young children. In G. S. Cannella & J. L. Kincheloe (Eds.), *Kidworld childhood studies, global perspectives, and education* (pp. 151–160). New York: Peter Lang Publishing.

Vygotsky, L. (1998). *The collected works of S. L. Vygotsky: Volume 5:* New York: Plenum Press.

Winter, K., & Connolly, P. (1996). "Keeping it in the family": Thatcherism and the Children Act 1989. In J. Pilcher & S. Wagg (Eds.), *Thatcher's children? Politics, childhood and society in the 1980s and 1990s* (pp. 29–42). London & Bristol: Falmer Press.

Part I

The Constructions of Childhood Development and Learning

2 Cultures in Early Childhood Care and Education*

A. Bame Nsamenang

"Cultures in early childhood care and education" (ECCE) partly refers to the obvious differences in the cultural values and practices that define childhood and inform and guide cultural curricula and services for the nurturing of children into competent citizenship in the huge variety of children's circumstances worldwide (Nsamenang, 2008a). The notion of cultures in early childhood is ingrained in the fact that cultural communities the world over impose their cultural curricula onto the biology of human development. In fact, "various cultures ... recognize, define and assign different developmental tasks to the same biological agenda" (Nsamenang, 1992, p. 144). Therefore, culture should be central to any discourse or policy statement on early childhood development and ECCE services. Whiting and Whiting (1975) proffered culture as a *provider of settings* for childcare and development. Culture contours and sharpens the nature of many features of the developmental context. "Culture, as in social heritage and cultural tools, is a determinative complement of genotype that shapes human psychosocial differentiation in the direction of a given people's cultural meaning systems" (Nsamenang, 2008a, p. 73).

The goal of this chapter is to expose, through archival research, the diversity that characterizes the global state of early childhood care and education (ECCE). From a focus on a select literature available to the author, it glimpses into the different facets by which some cultures raise competent children, pondering why the field gives less attention to the vibrant variety of the ECCE services of the Majority World (Kagitçibasi, 1996) while highlighting those of Anglo-American cultures. While evidence acknowledges diversity, current understandings have yet to translate into the theory, research, intervention, and pedagogy of international psychology (Stevens & Gielen, 2007) in terms that mirror the immense variation in global developmental trajectories and the cultural curricula that generate them. Are rights activists and the development community really aware that many Majority World children "hide" their true identity because contemporary ECCE services instill shame in them for being different from the normative Western child (Vandenbroeck, 1999)? Therefore, the chapter does not judge as rogue scholarship the questioning of why the development community is advocating the reinforcement of institutional services that generally subvert the ECCE systems of Majority World peoples and enclaves of inner city children in the Western world, thereby denying rights, dignity, even humanity, to the vast majority of the world's children and families.

Human development and being are transactional processes. The child, for example, is impacted by, and in turn influences the nature of the caregiving and social environment (Grieve, 1992). Most developmental theories admit the primal role of genotype, but I place an accent on the salience of the changeable contexts and conditions in which children live and individuation occurs (Ngaujah, 2003; Nsamenang, 2006). "When that is accepted and understood, the need is to recognize the importance of cultural conceptualizations of childhood, and of the child development theories and practices that follow on from these in a given culture" (Smale, 1998, p. 3).

The Social Construction of Childhood

Worldwide, ECCE services for children of 0–8 years are an actively negotiated set of social relationships (Prout and James, 1990). They have evolved from women's familial duty to professional service in need of more status and funding that accrues from institutional universalism (Nsamenang, 2008b). The "work" stands to lose the status and control that powerful interest groups feel is their right, although it is at the expense of those who the groups are expected to serve (Callaghan, 1998). How can early childhood development science, "a 'fuzzy-bounded' discipline coping with its own history, contribute to building a universal science across cultural boundaries" (Super & Harkness, 2008, p. 107)?

The contribution would be more meaningful if "childhood is to be understood as a social construct …" (Jenks, 1982, p. 12). "Comparative and cross-cultural analysis reveals a variety of childhoods rather than a single and universal phenomenon" (Prout & James, 1990, p. 8). Childhood as constructed in the West has been understood as "a protected realm" (Golden, 2005, p. 1), a point elaborated by Stephens (1995, p. 4): "modern children are supposed to be segregated from harsh realities of the adult world and to inhabit a safe, protected world of play, fantasy, and innocence". But to what extent is the school, like the ECCE centre, still the protected area it was designed to be in the face of recent evidence of violence and rights abuses by adults, who should care for and protect children?

The idea of the social construction of childhood carries immediate relevance to and utility for acknowledging and upholding the huge variety of childhoods found throughout the world, yet it is a viewpoint that is seldom cited nor articulated in policy statements and service programs by advocates, researchers, policy planners, practitioners and other actors in the ECCE field. Instead, the mainstays of the ECCE mindset and landscape remain mainstream psychology and child development perspectives that continue to focus on an image of the "global child" that is Western-derived (Pence & Hix-Small, 2007) and that pathologizes all "other" images of childhood. Thus, the ECCE that is actively being promoted by the development community in the

Majority World is a product of European and North American culture, which represents only a minority of the world's early childhoods in a multicultural universe in need of discovery (Nsamenang, 1999). This implies that the ECCE that is highlighted in the first EFA goal is Anglo-American, which interprets with difficulty into non-western cultures, a policy scenario that undermines the rights of Majority World children to a cultural identity as enshrined in the UNCRC. A Western storyline per se is not problematic but it becomes tricky when its universalistic claims to absolute truth deprive the Majority World of the right to its own meaningful knowledge systems and practices (Moss, 2005). Imagine that "at least 86 percent of all children and adolescents" (Gielen & Chumachenko, 2004, p. 82) live in Majority World countries, but the norms for their "appropriate development" originate in Western nations that in reality are the Minority World, which houses only a quarter of the world's child and adolescent population. In addition, institutional ECCE stops on the edges of most Majority World cities, thereby bypassing the community-based ECCE services of 70 percent of the world's rural peoples. ECCE programs appropriately should draw strength from rich Majority World cultures and the wisdom of their timeless traditions (see Callaghan, 1998), but they generally do not.

Given the raging outcry by the Western media about adolescent "irresponsibility", is there really any clear evidence (Vogelaar, 2005) that ECCE is "an instrumental, frontline strategy for achieving poverty reduction goals" (Arnold, 2004, p. 2)? The purported indicators for the promissory value of ECCE are derived from the developmental norms of Western middle-class child development, as those of the Majority World are just beginning to emerge (Britto, Engle, & Alderman, 2007). What is not so obvious in analyses of early childhoods is the fact that the professed benefits from ECCE have been so emphasized as to render trite any imagination of obstacles or the injury children may suffer when their ecological and cultural realities diverge from those that inspire ECCE's emancipatory goals. For instance, "Under what circumstances do ideas and research tools now traditional in the profession prove useful for advancing human development in Africa, and when do they become misleading or, worse, exploitative" (Super & Harkness, 2008, p. 107)? It is equally not clear why advocacy or policy for investment in such goals focuses more on a universalism motive than on moving forward functional services that reach children in the cultural contexts in which their communities could fully participate (Lanyasunya & Lesolayia, 2001). It is perhaps in recognition of the necessity for contextual relevance that Hoskyn, Moore, Neufeld, LeMare, and Stooke (2007, p. ii) reminded the field to "always contextualize our study findings, our policies, our programs in the sociohistorical and cultural contexts from which they arise." This is an essential requirement for appropriate ECCE services and research given that "human development always occurs in a specific cultural context" (Dasen & Jahoda, 1986, p. 413).

Every culture invests in children, not as an endstate but in recognition that today's adults are a product of their childhoods. Accordingly, all societies make provisions for children's basic needs and initial learning from the earliest age to support survival and the development of their intelligence and personalities, as well as their integration into society (Evans, 2002). Despite the diversity that marks ECCE systems globally, their common attribute is ideological or philosophical positioning regarding the meaning and purpose of human life, which may be explicit or implicit. We are referring here to worldview, which interprets as a theory of the universe, by which "a theorist's view of development," for example, "is closely tied to his or her view of human nature, a view intimately tied to his or her conception of how the universe works" (Nsamenang, 1992, p. 210). Such theories further introduce diversity into visions and forms of ECCE by positioning every cultural community to prefer aspects of nature and child states to cherish.

There are of course, universal and universalizing "standards", but they tend to be actualized differentially across cultures. In general, humanity's universal needs for survival, wellbeing and self-fulfillment are not satisfied in a universal manner. Often, one culture's most satisfying style turns out as another's most loathsome mode. Thus, an essential but rarely examined feature of ECCE is how the world's diverse peoples care for, educate and guide children into mature and responsible competence. But we cannot assume that all practices, in principle, are positive merely because they conform to specific cultural values and norms. Some of them can be as destructive as they are misleading. In every culture there are practices that may disrupt human thriving and wellbeing, such as female genital mutilation, inequity, and the paternalism of "civilizing" benevolence to backward peoples. A rights-based position envisions ECCE as a "liberal" project of empowerment and guidance of societies to improve their ways of ensuring the survival, development, and wellbeing of their young and not the adoption of imported models. Although it is worthwhile investing in human capital to speed up per capita income growth, we consider such a strategy a partial solution to the healthy development of children. Wholesome child development begins with the satisfaction of basic needs and involves much more than capital investment and intellectual enrichment (Nimnicht, Arango, & Hearn, 1987).

Facets of Parenting Programs and Perspectives in Cross-Cultural Practices

Across the globe, human beings survive and thrive in varied ecological and cultural circumstances. Similarly, cultures vary in the values they place on the child and the extent to which they organize the contexts in which children develop and how they learn. We consider the world's systems of how societies organize developmental learning in two basic forms: a didactic or instructional perspective and a participatory mode (Nsamenang & Lamb, 1995). Western and to an extent Islamic systems of ECCE basically are didactic, wherein children learn in contrived contexts remote from livelihood activities. By contrast, learning within the ECCE of Majority World family traditions requires children from an early age (Nsamenang, 2008b) to engage in ongoing cultural and economic activities as valued *participants in cultural communities* (Rogoff, 2003, p. 3).

The context, content and methods of ECCE differ from one country and community to another as well as within the same country. In practical terms, "individuals and families have a complex array of different identities that derive from ethnicity, religion, profession and region. More of these can and should be accentuated" in ECCE work (Bram, 1998, p. 23). Differences equally emerge from such structural factors as political regime, economic policies, and social security systems. These and other factors reveal the contextual nature of parenting, the goals and services for child development and the cherished developmental outcomes in their considerable cross-cultural variation.

As ecology and culture, the developmental context constitutes a key factor that structures ECCE in every society. In fact, ECCE is context-bound. An important facet of early childhood context is *parental belief systems* (Sigel, McGillicuddy-DeLisi, & Goodnow, 1992). These are cultural beliefs, scripts, and values (Super & Harkness, 1986) that confer on parents and other cultural agents the knowledge, affective disposition, and attentive orientation to raise culturally competent children, often without regard to whatever advocacy or purportedly "civilized" intervention is in place. Given the difficulty, if not impossibility, of imagining parenting independent of culture (Krappmann, 2001), Super and Harkness (1986) offered the developmental niche as a theoretic heuristic to bridge the three core fields of early childhood development, namely, anthropology, parenthood, and psychology.

Parenting Within the Developmental Niche Framework

How children live, develop and learn are shaped by the ideological, historical, ecological, and sociocultural imperatives of their early years. Every culture offers parental ethnotheories or "a framework for understanding the ways that parents think about their children, their families and themselves, and the mostly implicit choices that parents make about how to rear the next generation" (Harkness et al., 2001, p. 12). The multiple forces that shape childhood arrangements, parenting and the educational ideas on which children develop can be subsumed under the developmental niche paradigm.

The developmental niche model addresses the interrelated facets of the settings in which children live and grow and how parents and others perceive the role and task of socializing and educating offspring. The framework consists of three components, namely, the physical and social settings of early childhood, the customs and practices of child rearing and the psychology of caretakers [including teachers and peer mentors]. This incorporates their beliefs, values and attitudes to children and their development as well as the political and social systems that organize parenting and education. In arranging these sub-systems in their own terms, cultural communities the world over prioritize and stress different values, practices and child outcomes. As such, the developmental niche is a holistic heuristic that permits structuring and integration of the different strands of any "niche" in which children develop. Thus, it permits the weaving together of the diverse ways every cultural community arranges to handle the micro-niches and daily routines of early childhood as they link the child with different levels of the macro-system like the school, participatory processes of informal sectors, and social or religious institutions.

A crucial but often ignored facet of early childhood realities is how humanity's universal needs of thriving, health, nutrition, education, intelligent behavior, responsible attitudes, social integration, and self-fulfillment, are guided and socialized or educated across the world's diverse cultures. Actually, the same need is often fulfilled in different ways by different cultures. Accordingly, we can presume that appropriate research on or monitoring how the developmental niche shapes ECCE services would reveal different parenting profiles, divergent ECCE arrangements, and dynamic developmental pathways.

Variety of Parenting Programs and Childcare Arrangements

The primary focus of ECCE is on basic early childcare arrangements involving the division of time, energy and responsibility among childcare, provisioning, and other activities relevant to child survival (Lancaster, Altman, Rossi, and Sherrod, 1987). It is also about initial learning, ECCE actors and settings. While the satisfaction of basic needs is assumed, ECCE content, physical arrangements and human resources are problematic in every country. Although international advocacy prefers institutional ECCE, it is not yet universal, even in some industrial countries. For example, "at least 25% of children in the United States are cared for by family, friends, or neighbors" and U.S. "State regulatory standards for informal care vary quite a bit" (Susman-Stillman, 2005, p. 241). In industrializing nations like Nigeria, women combine mothering and paid work relatively successfully because housemaids, nannies, daycare centers, nursery schools and the kindergarten are available (Ogbimi & Alao, 1998). Even with the "one-child policy" in "the world's largest geopolitical community" – China (Ho, Peng & Lai, 2001, p. 7) – early childcare arrangements not only vary from family to family, but also change during the year to contain parental employment circumstances (Yajun, Li & Champagne, 1999).

Underlying parenting programs or ECCE arrangements in both industrial and industrializing countries are parenting motives and values, which vary across ecologies and cultures, illumining the global variety of cultural conditions that are created for early childhood. In point of fact, children's behavior and activities tend to foreshadow parental beliefs and values (Acuna & Rodrigo, 1994; Nsamenang & Lamb, 1995). These "play a directive role in shaping the developmental niche and consequently the development" of children (Super et al., 1996, p. 3). Cross-cultural variation of parental motives and parenting programs inform an approach to ECCE that requires understanding the diversity of childhood context in historical perspective. For instance, Uribe, LeVine and LeVine (1994, p. 41) describe contexts in which Mexican children are reared wherein the "central point is that the Mexican communities generating immigrants to the United States have been changing as environments for child development, particularly in their conditions of health, fertility, parental education, and media exposure, as well as their family attitudes, childrearing practices, and differentiation by socioeconomic status (SES)."

A report of cross-cultural gender role differences by Munroe and Munroe (1975) and "the varieties of social behavior of children brought up in different parts of the world" (Whiting & Whiting, 1975, p. vii), like the mere acknowledgement of the diversity in early childhood conditions and childcare arrangements around the world, carry obvious significance for the status of ECCE in general and the *EFA Global Monitoring Report 2007* in particular. The field would benefit from objective exploration of ECCE motives, that is, whose interests ECCE services and who the child outcomes they produce serve. In addition, what child outcomes do varied parenting values and practices produce? It is in this light that the lack of homogeneity even in Western European and Anglo-American countries reported by Harkness and colleagues (2001): "differences that seem to be maintained in spite of geographical proximity or linguistic relatedness" (Grusec & Rudy, 2001, p. 16), add force to inclusivity thinking in ECCE. In other terms, it is essential to realize and act on the fact that ethnocultural models foster ECCE under a variety of circumstances of child life and parenting, ranging from contexts in which parenting and sibling caregiving are normative (see Krappmann, 2001; Weisner, 1987), though condemned by international advocacy, to settings in which deliberate childlessness and sneers against welfare services for parents and their children are growing. Imagine that in Britain, for example, a pension scheme that proposed to offer working mothers some time off work to care for children was challenged as "unfair," in the face of a declining population (Winnett, 2005). A more extreme experience in ECCE history is the "one-child policy" in China (Ho et al., 2001).

It seems obvious from the foregoing discussion that even a cursory appraisal of the cross-cultural evidence and state of the ECCE field would expose multiple ways of raising culturally healthy and competent children. It would further reveal children's resilience in amazingly divergent circumstances.

Parenting Practices and Child Outcomes: Children's Resilience in Adversity

Parental values organize daily parenting programs and routines for child and family life (Harkness & Super, 1996). Parents' cultural belief systems channel elements of the larger culture to children. Zeitlin (1996) for one justifies how the feeding habits of Nigerians that non-Africans regard as counterproductive are useful. On their part, Weisner, Matheson, and Bernheimer (1996) thought that American parental beliefs on the importance of early "stimulation" for optimal child development could lead to an unnecessary concern about the earliest possible interventions for children with developmental delays (Harkness & Super, 1996). Thus, the huge variety in parenting practices results in differentiation in desirable cultural child outcomes.

Whereas Miller and Chen (2001) reviewed research on culture and parenting whose diversity Goodnow (2001) claimed to be daunting, Sagi and Aviezer (2001) reported examples of what, in principle, looked like unfavorable childrearing conditions that output positive child outcomes. One plausible explanation for this possibility is that rarely have theorists and interveners focused on understanding the "surrounding support network" (Sagi & Aviezer, 2001) of the adversity, which provides a secure base for the healthy development of children in adverse conditions. Thus, across the posited adversity of Majority World ECCE, children are more resilient than has hitherto been conceptualized. The regrettable reality is that current ECCE interventions tend to theorize and design into informality or extinction ideologies and practices that are quite functional and useful to many children, whose routine conditions are judged as adverse (Nsamenang, 2007).

But "what the dominant group calls deviant or dysfunctional might be quite functional from the point of view of the people involved. If this were the case, then street boys might be the more resilient children among the urban poor, while the less resilient children are unable to leave home, and are forced to live in conditions that are unsuitable to child rearing practices (deviant!)" (Aptekar, 1994, p. 2). Thus, exclusivity is pervasive in the field because what fails to conform to Anglo-American developmental appropriateness or has never been "imagined in developmental theories" (LeVine, 2004, p. 163) is simply tagged as adversity. It is therefore decisive to ponder whether Majority World peoples "neglect the needs of their infants and toddlers for stimulation, interaction, and affection, or these needs have been exaggerated by child development specialists [and advocates] who mistake Anglo-American ideologies of the second half of the twentieth century as the universal requirements of human infants" (LeVine, 2004, p. 158).

Prospects for Majority World Contribution to Early Childhood Care and Education

Culture defines competent parenting and desirable child outcomes and "colours all the activities connected with a particular group" (Bram, 1998, p. 23). This fact of culture obliges contextualization of approaches to initiating children into lifelong learning. That "in all societies, throughout human history, people have educated their children" (Reagan, 1996, p. ix) reinforces this obligation. Although every culture introduces children to learning its cultural curriculum, Eurocentric ECCE services for the majority of the world's children, as with Mayan-Ixil children in Guatemala, have been offered within a deficit model of "none of these children receive initial education" (Tzay, 1998, p. 18). As such, ECCE interventions, as exemplified by that of San preschool children in Botswana, are best interpreted as "against a background of people forced to adopt a new lifestyle" (Cohen, 2001, p. 5). This is an affront on the children's right to own identity, as it undermines their background and represents intolerance of human diversity (Vandenbroeck, 1999). Most of the recommendations promoted by ECCE "experts" for developmentally appropriate and science-based parenting and childrearing practices tend to denigrate the alternative parenting values and practices of the non-Western world.

For most Majority World children and those in minority enclaves of Western societies, the advocated ECCE services are restrictive and inappropriate; they ignore and circumvent the worldviews and values of the beneficiary communities. Thus, in common with similar cultural groups worldwide, the Mayan-Ixil people experience institutional ECCE as "rigid and mechanical, and it does not allow laughter and play" (Tzay, 1998, p. 19), the preoccupation of children. By contrast, in the free spirit of the activity settings of Majority World peer cultures, children are not prodded into learning by intervention; they mostly undertake self-generated activities, therein engaging in generous play and self-motivation (Nsamenang, 2005a). "Play, which is the essence of childhood, should be a quintessential feature of a child care program, particularly as the child may spend the majority of his/her waking hours in the child-care setting" (Jacobs, 1994, p. 1). Cognitively more stimulating is the fact that the unavailability of commercial toys disposes most non-Western children, at least in Africa, into imitative construction of objects available in their environments or "creating" their own playthings from local materials. Such "creations" express ingenuity and recognizing them as "products" enhances children's self-worth. There is therefore need to recognize and learn from an open community-based ECCE curriculum, which, more than a didactic institutional one, rouses and reinforces children's abstract and spatial thinking and cognitive and creative abilities (Segall, Dasen, Berry, & Poortinga, 1999) that exist already in the culture, which needs them (Ogbu, 1994).

Through the assumption that all children learn a universal culture, the dominant ECCE narrative introduces an insidiously destructive factor of naïve acquiescence to the institutionalization of ECCE (Dahlberg, Moss, & Pence, 1999; Moss, 2005) as a "right" of all children and their families regardless of their circumstances. This approach not only marginalizes other forms of ECCE but also fails to recognize a child's right to own cultural identity. It is contrary to the "new commitment" to the "discovery" that "All cultures can contribute scientific knowledge of universal value" (UNESCO, 2003, p. 1). Culturally oriented approaches to support development during the early years require understanding difference in all its complexity and subtlety which, for example, immigrant or acculturating groups encounter as they attempt to integrate into the dominant cultures. A major program of settlement of Jewish immigrants from Russia and central Asia into Israeli society exemplifies this point. A culturally appropriate approach to EECE should build on the strengths that exist already in the community; therein permitting informed community participation and more effective reaching out to children in their own cultural contexts. As Bram (1998) perceptively highlights, accurate knowledge of the cultural group is an essential and salient element in developing and applying culturally sensitive services, particularly against the dominant values of " *Western* societies that tend to lump all cultural groups from developing countries into one category" (Bram, 1998, p. 24).

Generalized perceptions like the above constitute blinders that prevent advocates, policy planners and researchers as well as practitioners and field staff from distinguishing subtle differences between cultural communities. In the Israeli settlement program, "the sociological distinction went hand in hand with negative labeling attitudes that ranged from a sense of superiority to contempt" (Bram, 1998, p. 24). In fact, "Many child development programmes around the world fail to recognize and respect families' and communities' achievements and resourcefulness in raising their children, often against extraordinary odds" (Arnold, 2004, p. 25). "Those who have worked in international development are keenly aware that research based on a predominantly Western paradigm is part of the story, but not the full story needed to move forward effectively in local development" (ECDVU, 2004, p. 46). Yet, culturally oriented ECCE approaches and genuine sensitivity to context-relevant services remain an illusion in the field.

The field has yet to realize that the "differentness" of Majority World "cultures provide opportunities for learning and development which simply do not exist in the West and therefore are not considered by the predominant theories" (Curran, 1984, p. 2), rights instruments and the so-called best practices. Two examples of Majority World contribution are Kagitçibasi's (1996) image of family and human development "from the other side" and Nsamenang's (1992) interpretation of human ontogenesis as a cumulative process of social integration into the cultural community that "differs in theoretical focus from the more individualistic accounts proposed by Freud, Erikson, and Piaget" (Serpell, 1994, p. 8). The field can gain from early care and socialization research in Africa (e.g., Nsamenang, 1992; Serpell, 1996), Japan (Chen, 1996), and Navajo (Chisholm, 1996), which depicts child development in garden metaphors (Cole, 1988; Erny, 1968) as alternative to the organismic and mechanistic models dominant in Western perspectives. Garden metaphors connote not only vitality but also a gradual unfolding of human abilities and sequential attainment of levels of maturity and responsibility throughout ontogeny. However, Japanese metaphors have undergone greater adjustment to Western "modernity" than those of other parts of the Majority World.

The Changing Patterns of Early Childhood Care and Education: Different Levels and Scales

Most children around the world survive and thrive not only in the adversity and poverty that is their daily routines but must equally cope with waves of societal change and technological transformations, often with considerable resourcefulness and resilience that expertise seldom perceives. ECCE "experts", who are in short supply or non-existent in most parts of the world, appear to have been "educated" not to see and value the niches in which children develop. There is "a blindness and inability", for example, "to see and value Africans in the African context" (Callaghan, 1998, p. 31). Therefore, it is advisable to make endeavor to understand ECCE in the light of the cultural background of children's lives and communities – *which also change* (Rogoff, 2003, p. 4).

ECCE expertise seems to encounter difficulty to conceptualize ECCE services as for children growing within a nested system of relationships affected by multiple levels of the structural systems and surrounding environments which influence the child directly and indirectly (Bronfenbrenner, 1979; Chauhan & Kshetrapal, 2004). This blindness forcefully contributes to the apparent lack of scale, impact, and replication of most ECCE programs that so far reach only a tiny minority of the populations "experts" should serve. Although the idealized centre-based ECCE facility is useful to working parents who have access to no other means of "arrangement" for their children, this model only serves a minority of the world's families, given the availability of family-based services in the Majority World. Accordingly, in most communities the mainstreaming and idealization of centre-based ECCE only undermines people's strengths and their more functional community-based ECCE efforts. In fact, Western concepts of educationalization "have devalued indigenous cultures and traditions so much that they are [now] seen as being anti-progressive and somewhat outdated" (Callaghan, 1998, p. 30).

In reality, due to its high cost and the differing resource bases, the replicability and sustainability of institutional ECCE still remains questionable for the majority of the world's peoples (Callaghan, 1998). It is for this reason that ECCE programs that *support* rather than *replace* parents and families in their role as children's first educators (Bernard van leer Foundation, 1994) and cognitive stimulators (Nsamenang, 2004) are needed and deserve advocacy. This insight convinced Callaghan (1998, p. 33) that "the future of the African child lies deep within the African family and the rich, strong, living, growing, sustaining African culture which is reflected" in Africans, but which ECCE experts and interventionists insidiously condemn by sidelining or out-phasing from service programs, school curricula and development planning (Nsamenang, 2005c). Community-oriented programs are common in Latin America. They offer useful extension opportunities, which assist families and communities to increase income by generating resources within the community as productive services for children (Bernard van Leer Foundation, 1986).

All Majority World cultures have been exposed to external, especially Western, influences, the effects of which should not be underplayed. But despite tumultuous changes, nowhere in the Majority World has this led to the total collapse of local institutions and indigenous knowledge systems, though they are in difficulty. Instead, indigenous and imported psychologies now live together in the same individuals and communities (Nsamenang & Dawes, 1998), and are both useful, although they sometimes collide or transgress one another. The intermingling or rivalry varies greatly within and between continents, regions, nations, communities, social classes and ethnicities, even within the same family and across developmental stages. Thus, Majority World children are receiving ECCE in a disorganizing hybridism that does not seem to be given the programmatic attention required in redressing inherent tensions and conflicts. Indeed, current childhood realities and parenting values in the colonized world are a hybrid cultural character, a product of indigenous and modern factors. As a result, in most Majority World societies, as in middle-class Argentine society, "there are no clear rules about how to behave as a parent" (Bornstein et al., 2004, p. 183). Similarly, Kenyan parents "have been caught up in the web of cultural transition where there are no longer clearly defined values and moral codes of behavior that should be instilled in children and young people" (Cohen, 2001, p. 6).

In actuality, across the globe ECCE has undergone "a dramatic trans-formation from a service for women who 'unfortunately' had to be employed out of the home, to a service enabling independence and liberation for women from full-time mothering" (May, 2000, p. 56). In consequence, the total responsibility for children, which was accepted by most parents and local communities in previous generations, has been altered radically as a result of "modernization", as institutions and social structures have become larger and less identified with specific communities. In New Zealand, as in most hybridized societies, ECCE ideologies vary from beliefs in children being "better off in their own homes no matter how miserable their conditions may be" to being cared for in advocated full-time, sponsored institutional day care (Meade & Podmore, 2002, p. 7). The most blinding and upsetting error with the transformations in Majority World contexts, however, is the attractive temptation to approximate the adoption of Western models to a desire to "civilize" to be like Europe and North America. The adoption is best interpreted as a reactive response to inescapable but tolerable irritants that are perceived as unfair and ephemeral. The field could gain from the resilience of indigenous traditions because, in spite of the suffering in the Majority World against the promises of scientific positivism and the allure of modernizing developmentalism (Nsamenang, 2005c), most non-Western communities and Mayan-Ixil peoples "have jealously preserved their culture and its values" (Tzay, 1998, p. 18).

The dualism of contemporary childhood environments come alive in *Images of Childhood* (Hwang, Lamb & Sigel, 1996) and *Following Footsteps* in "countries as widely spread as Jamaica and Kenya, Ireland, the USA, Botswana, Colombia, Trinidad and Honduras" (Cohen, 2001, p. 7). The evidence from these and other sources abridges into the point that most ECCE programs are narrowly focused on distinct aspects of early childhood, failing to attend to the wider contexts of wholesome development that program delivery fails to capture. This is because the emphasis in the overwhelming majority of cases is on social marketing and program delivery (Callaghan, 1998) instead of on meeting the needs of real children and their families in the contexts of their daily lives. It is not difficult to discern the hesitation, which stands against the evidence, to voice the failure of the "capturing" narrative to understand diversity and differences in order to address the ECCE needs of Majority World children. The confusion and tension this engenders remains largely unattended, as the ECCE field instead jilts and estranges most children from the meaningfulness of their cultural life into aspiring for an elusive "modernity" in Euro-western-type ECCE services.

To summarize, the field has failed to contemplate and theorize the complexity of contemporary childhood conditions in Majority World interventions. This implies that the stark realities of the ECCE field in most parts of the globe are only peripherally and "belligerently" being tackled. We continue to trivialize and marginalize the dynamic dualism of the ECCE realities of Majority World contexts instead of exploring their hybrid diversity for edifying scholarship, creative theorizing, and innovative and empowering methodologies.

Issues With Early Childhood Care and Education Policy Instruments and Quality of Services

In historical perspective, the ECCE story stretches into recounting every culture's inclusive fitness considerations to prepare its next generation. A narrower viewpoint begins with Western Infant Schools in the 1820s and accentuates internationally with the UN adoption of the Convention of the Rights of the Child on November 20, 1989 (Pence, 2004). The narrower version has become the dominant narrative, which now pathologizes the wisdom of centuries of the rich traditions with which all societies throughout history have cared for and educated their children (Reagan, 1996). Such a lopsided history is as constricted as it engenders exclusion and carries far-reaching policy implications. First, core ECCE issues remain largely unspoken. Discourse on ECCE quality, for instance, typically posits Anglo-American values and developmental benchmarks as a frame of reference to which all other cultural groups should aspire, instead of perceiving quality in its multicultural dimensions of children and their learning of competencies in the familiar cultural contexts with which they identify and within which they make sense of the universe.

Second, ECCE discourse generally portrays interventions as "neutral", implicitly depicting Majority World livelihoods as developmentally inappropriate. In fact, the list of "inappropriate" practices resembles "practices that are culturally preferred among various peoples outside the United States, whereas the 'appropriate' list describes the practices preferred by contemporary upper-middle-class Americans" (LeVine, 2004, p. 152). Euro-American truth claims thus dominate international rights instruments and policy positions, therein localizing or excluding locally embedded ECCE services. Many strategies even fail to acknowledge the natural settings and humanity of Majority World children. Third, the advocated ECCE is not articulated from childhood realities but mostly contrived from the perceptions and theorizations of astute gatekeepers in agencies that essentially are allergic, if not hostile, to

Majority World mentalities, lifestyles and forms of ECCE. One point of view holds that the CRC was "developed far from the lived experience of children, their families and communities" (Reid, 2006, p. 18). In addition, it is not quite obvious if the family is still "the best promoter, provider and protector of children's rights" (Claiborne & One, 2007). Reid (2006) contends that a growing body of powerful interest groups and professionals led by advocates has "captured" children's rights from parents and families.

Fourth, there are no universal child-outcomes to which all cultural communities aspire or would agree; there is great diversity in desirable child states and endpoints of development. LeVine (2004) believes Majority World peoples have as much a right as Minority World populations to have culturally preferred practices regarding the care and destiny of offspring. That forms of ECCE the world over are franked in cultural agendas for desirable child states somehow limits the possibility of an ECCE approach that is universally appropriate for all cultures. Although the Treaty on the Rights of the Child internationalizes ECCE issues, it resolutely bestows "a legal status on the right of one's own identity; on respect for the background of every child" (Vandenbroeck, 1999, p. 13). In so doing, it tacitly inserts the accommodation of human diversity into ECCE policy positioning and program development. Fifth, although the guidelines donors and experts offer are "roadmaps" or "toolkits" for visualization of policy (e.g., Vargas-Barón, 2005), such guiding principles, regrettably, are virtual "prescriptions" in much of the Majority World. This is because the scourges of colonization and the unforeseen effect of Western schooling now constitute unexamined roadblocks that incapacitate Majority World policy planners from stepping out of Eurocentric policy boxes to creatively imagine lucid and coherent policies and program strategies that appropriately address their stark realities. Most of the ongoing capacity building initiatives in Africa train technical experts rather than visionaries who will be able to deal successfully with the global geopolitical and technological challenges of the coming decades. They are not specifically focused on developing transformational leaders, at least for Africa (Saasa, 2007).

Sixth, ECCE policy and program development demands evidence-based policies, but it is unclear why donors and international experts formulate policy and design programs on childhood realities that grossly diverge from those they experience in the field. The emphasis is on indicators devised by experts aligned to the United Nations system, the World Bank and the international donor community but not on the needs of children in their daily routines. It is not rogue to ask whether the guidelines and toolkits of these advocates and policy makers contain any content on the ECCE realities of the majority of the world's children. In addition, we must be concerned with why the development community hesitates to address the apprehensions and conflicts inherent in ECCE work but instead adopts the global child image (Pence & Hix-Small, 2007). Imagine the rights issues, the disrespect and disempowerment inherent in current strategies that formulate into irrelevance or extinction of Majority World people's parenting approaches and childcare arrangements. Such efforts persist in the face of evidence that "there is far more to child development than preschool, and that if the school system is not congruent with home circumstances, the children will have to make immense efforts to achieve any form of success" (Cohen, 2001, p. 7).

In the seventh instance, ECCE has evolved into a professional field that requires advocates and experts, who are notable by their scarcity and cultural irrelevance in the Majority World. However, this state of the field rouses apprehension whether expertise is a procedural issue, a matter of universal knowledge and know-how or that of applying context-relevant knowledge and skills (Nsamenang, 2005c). Scott (1998) contends that experts lack the knowledge that can come only from practical experience. Given the lack of consensus amongst experts and the shifting realities that diversity and pluralism stir, to what extent can an expert, native-born or expatriate, objectively and sensitively ground best practices on the daily routines and expectations of children and their families in recipient communities? This casts in sharp relief not only the apparently ambiguous role of the expert policy planner but equally provokes a call to critical discourse of what ECCE expertise portends for and the shape and direction it has given to the field. Recognizing that everything is not bad, but that everything is potentially dangerous (Foucault, 1980), the critique of ECCE policy and program development should expand to include even the best intentions of researchers and the development community, including the UN system.

Eighth, an ultimate policy matter pertains to "rights". Although a rights-based approach, in principle, recognizes the legitimate right of children to beliefs and practices that accurately reflect their cultural heritage, no ECCE policy should condone the destructive aspects of any culture, such as female genital mutilation, child marriages, marginalization of the girl child, domination by another culture, etc. While the focus ought to be on "guided" empowerment to reinforce positive and constructive aspects of every ECCE system, keen attention must focus on eliminating the destructive elements of any culture's ECCE. A rights-based ECCE policy is inclusive of all patterns of ECCE and should policy into instant extinction Eurocentric strategies that marginalize or exclude Majority World forms of ECCE from the field.

Finally, an urgent policy matter, albeit an important gap in ECCE work, concerns the little attention given to fathers and men as caregivers and resource-holders. Research-based evidence indicates that fathers are significant to children's development, even when absent (Nsamenang, 2000). Although the paternal role is one-half of parenting, in the Third Millennium it largely still is a "forgotten" contribution (e.g., Lamb, 1975) in ECCE work. The big picture of *Supporting Fathers* (Bernard van Leer Foundation, 2003) to engage in ECCE services should reverse this state of the field, as a matter of urgent priority.

Conclusion

An evidential truth claim from our study is the staggering variety that characterizes the global landscape of ECCE services, broadly defined. The other truth claim is about whose interest truly is in focus in policy instruments and program orientations (Nsamenang, 2008b). As they stand today, policy instruments and program values are not in favor of the recipients of donor largess and their communities; they insidiously albeit forcefully serve and promote the visions and interests of the international community, Western donors and their advocates.

In fact, powerful interest groups, advocates and gatekeepers of the field give little to no systematic attention to diversity, as that variety is sidelined and dominated by policy instruments that force Anglo-American visions of ECCE on Majority World early childhoods that are generated and sustained by starkly different developmental theories and cultural realities. Developmentally appropriate practices, for instance, "present an appearance of science-based knowledge in a formula based heavily on [Anglo-American] cultural ideology" (LeVine, 2004, p. 151). In the face of scarce human resources in general and early childhood capacity in particular in many countries of the Majority World, the so-called development cooperation, donor charities in support of ECCE work and the research ethos only perpetuate the continuing supremacy of Euro-Western models.

In principle, the UN and scientific rhetoric are right to have posited culturally sensitive planning and implementation of programs for children and their families, say in Africa. However, in the field there seems to be a grave disconnection between universal principles and the degree to which they are acknowledged and actualized in the livelihoods of early development. "Is this due to the subtle intrusion of Western beliefs and values, perhaps derived in turn from the Western-oriented education of local functionaries? Such an interpretation cannot be dismissed, but we suggest that it is also important to recognize the universal organizational imperatives of bureaucracies" and their assumed emancipatory value (Super & Harkness, 2008, p. 109). While "many aspects of human development and functioning are no doubt universal, such universality cannot be postulated on the basis of research in a single cultural group; it must be demonstrated empirically across a variety of human populations" (Dasen & Jahoda, 1986, p. 413). Thus, revision of current narratives and efforts is the more obliging given the elasticity with which human offspring adapt and thrive in harshly dissimilar ecologies and cultures worldwide. Furthermore, we ought to become keenly sensitive to a realism of the field, that compulsive proselytization of Anglo-American ECCE realities and values may upset and indeed stunt Majority World children by denying them a right to their UNCRC-enshrined cultural identity and heritage.

Which rights instrument permits anyone to move children and families forward by intervening their culturally embedded daily routines into informality or extinction? Can the development community give a healthier and respectful attention to the ECCE services of Majority World children through culturally sensitive enhancement approaches instead of persisting with heavy investment to replace them or to normalize them to elusive Western-derived standards, as if diversity were wrong about the nature of children? Should ECCE research inform or interrogate policy (Urban, 2006)? How does research use the evidence that in many Majority World settings significant learnings occur in child-to-child processes and peer interstimulation than any theory or policy had envisaged so as to discontinue the efforts and the tremendous resources spent on intervention research that forces costly Western models that depend on adult prodding of children's developmental learning in cultures in which children are accredited agents of their own socialization and learning (Pence & Nsamenang, 2008).

The Eurocentrism of the EFA first goal evokes ECCE services that initiate Majority World children into an educationalization process and economization mindset through which, at varying stages of development, they systematically gain in unfamiliar knowledge and skills sets, which increasingly alienate them from their cultural roots and livelihoods. It stealthily transforms, say Africans, into "ignorant experts" who are inept about their own undesirable circumstances (Nsamenang, 2005c, p. 179). As such, it instead inhibits much of the Majority World from achieving the MDGs in culturally meaningful ways. If children are *Africa's challenge* (Garcia, Pence & Evans, 2008), it is due to the unexamined failure of longstanding but continuing investment to replace Africa's timeless traditions of family-based ECCE practices with Western institutional patterns. The expectation, given the accentuating efforts "to expand and improve comprehensively early childhood care and development" in sub-Saharan Africa (Ansu, 2008, p. xix) in the face of a deepening crisis with children, is to shape shift to gain from and enhance Africa's "successful" practices of "childrearing within the framework of an African culture for centuries" (Callaghan, 1998, p. 31). Nevertheless, we see unwarranted doggedness to set up Western-type institutional centers in Africa.

"If survival depended on the triumph of the strong, then the species would perish. So the real reason for survival, the principle factor in the 'struggle for existence,' is the love of adults for their young" (Maria Montessori, cited in Vargas-Barón, 2005). Love for offspring, like ECCE services within which such love is revealed, "is packaged in a wide variety of cultural and emotional expressions, such that no way of loving children might translate as a universal fact of humanity" (Nsamenang, 2007, p. 10). Adult–child bonding as attachment research espouses constitutes only one form of expressing affectionate care to children; other ways deserve attentive charting through culture-sensitive research. The success of such research, like ECCE programming in Africa, as apparent in the first MDG and highlighted in EFA *Global Monitoring Report 2007*, will depend on a delicate act of balancing and enhancing "the benefits imagined in institutionalizing and educationalizing childhood," as anchored on the wisdom of indigenous African practices but as extended by insights from imported ECCE, while attentively addressing the vocal but silent and mixed motives of stakeholders and the apprehensions they engender (Nsamenang, 2008b, p. 145).

Note

* This paper was commissioned by the Education For All Global Monitoring Report as background information to assist in drafting the 2007 report. On request, permission was granted to the author to revise it for publication as a book chapter.

References

Acuna, M. & Rodrigo, M. J. (1994). *Parental beliefs, every day family activities, and environmental quality.* Paper presented at the 13th Biennial Meetings of the ISSBD, Amsterdam, the Netherlands.

Ansu, Y. (2008). Foreword. In Garcia, M., Pence, A., & Evans, J. L. (2008), *Africa's future, Africa's challenge: Early childhood care and development in sub-Saharan Africa* (pp. xix–xx). Washington, DC: The World Bank.

Arnold, C. (2004). Positioning ECCD in the 21st century. *Coordinators' Notebook*, 28, 1–36.

Bernard van Leer Foundation (1984). *Multi-cultural societies: Early childhood education and care, summary report and conclusions.* The Hague: BvLF.

Bernard van Leer Foundation (1986). *The parent as prime educator: Changing patterns of parenthood.* The Hague: BvLF.

Bernard van Leer Foundation (1988). *Children and community: progressing through partnership.* The Hague: BvLF.

Bernard van Leer Foundation (1994). *Building on people's strengths: Early childhood in Africa.* The Hague: BvLF.

Bernard van Leer Foundation (2003). *Supporting Fathers.* Contributions from the International Fatherhood Summit 2003. BvLF. The Hague, The Netherlands.

Bornstein, M. H. (2001). Some questions for a science of 'Culture and parenting' (… but certainly not all). *ISSBD Newsletter*, 1 (38), 1–4.

Bornstein, M. H., Haynes, O. M., Pascual, L., & Painter, K. M. (2004). Competence and satisfaction in parenting young children: An ecological, multivariate comparison of expressions and sources of self-evaluation in the United States and Argentina. In U. P. Gielen & J. Roopnarine (Eds.), *Childhood and adolescence: Cross-cultural perspectives and applications* (pp. 166–195). Westport, CT: Praeger.

Bram, C. (1998). A culturally oriented approach for early childhood development. *Early Childhood Matters*, 89, 23–29.

Britto, P. R., Engle, P., & Alderman, H. (2007). *Early intervention and caregiving: Evidence from the Uganda Nutrition and Early Child Development Program.* Unpublished manuscript.

Bronfenbrenner, U. (1979). *The ecology of human development.* Cambridge, MA: Cambridge University Press.

Callaghan, L. (1998). Building on an African worldview. *Early Childhood Matters*, 89, 30–33.

Chauhan, G. S. & Kshetrapal, N. (2004). Community Program in Laxminagar 1 and 2. Baroda, India: Baladji Education and Medical Charity Trust.

Chen, S.-J. (1996). Positive childlessness: Images of childhood in Japan. In C.-P. Hwang, M. E. Lamb & I. E. Sigel (Eds.), *Images of childhood* (pp. 113–118 Mahwah, NJ: Erlbaum.

Chisholm, J. S. (1996). Learning 'respect for everything': Navajo images of development. In C.-P. Hwang, M. E. Lamb and I. E. Sigel (Eds.), *Images of childhood* (pp. 167–183). Mahwah, NJ: Erlbaum.

Claiborne, L. B. & One, S. T. (2007). Book review: *From innocents to agents: Children and children's rights in New Zealand* by Michael Reid. Maxim Institute, Auckland. 2006. *New Zealand Journal of Social Sciences Online* http://www.rsnz. org/publish/kotuitui/2007/05.php (Site visited 19/02/08).

Cohen, R. N. (2001). Foreword. In A. Njenga & M. Kabiru, *In the web of cultural transition: A tracer study of children in Embu District of Kenya.* The Hague: Bernard van Leer Foundation.

Cole, M. (1988). Cross-cultural research in the sociohistorical tradition. *Human Development,* 31, 137–157.

Curran, H. V. (1984). Introduction. In H. V. Curran (Ed.), *Nigerian children: Developmental perspectives* (pp. 1–20). London: Routledge and Kegan Paul.

Dahlberg, G., Moss, P. & Pence, A. (1999). *Beyond quality in early childhood services.* London: Falmer Press.

Dasen, P. R. & Jahoda, G. (1986). Preface to special issue on the impact of psychology Third World development. *International Journal of Behavioral Development,* 9 (4), 413–416.

ECDVU. (2004). Case studies: Positioning ECCD: The Early Childhood Development Virtual University. *Coordinators' Notebook,* 28, 46–47.

Erny, P. (1968). *L'Enfant dans la pensee traditionnelle d'Afrique Noire* [*The child in traditional African social thought*]. Paris: Le Livre Africain.

Evans, J. L. (2002). Beginning on the seventh floor. *ADEA Newsletter,* 14 (2), 3–6.

Foucault, M. (1980). *Power/knowledge: Selected interviews and other writings.* Brighton: Harvester.

Garcia, M., Pence, A., & Evans, J. (Eds.), *Africa's future—Africa's challenge: Early childhood care and development in sub-Saharan Africa.* Washington DC: The World Bank.

Gauvain, M. (1995). Thinking in niches: Sociocultural influences on cognitive development. *Human Development,* 38, 25–45.

Gielen, U. P. & Chaumachenko, O. (2004). All the world's children: The impact of global demographic trends on economic disparities. In U. P. Gielen & J. Roopnarine (Eds.), *Childhood and adolescence: Cross-cultural perspectives and applications* (pp. 81–109). Westport, CT: Praeger.

Golden, D. (2005) Childhood as protected space? Vulnerable bodies in an Israeli kindergarten. *Ethnos,* 70 (1), 79–100.

Goodnow, J. (2001). Commentary: Culture and parenting: Cross-cultural issues. *ISSBD Newsletter,* 1 (38), 13–14.

Grieve, K. W. (1992). Play based assessment of the cognitive abilities of young children (pp. 5.6–5.21). Unpublished doctoral thesis, Unisa, Pretoria.

Grusec, J. E. & Rudy, D. (2001). Commentary. Culture and parenting: Expanded horizons. *ISSBD Newsletter,* 1 (38), 16.

Harkness, S. & Super, C. M. (Eds.) (1995). *Parents cultural beliefs systems: Their origins, expressions and consequences.* New York: Guilford Press.

Harkness, S., Super, C. M., Axia, V., Eliasz, A., Palacios, J., & Welles-Nystrom, B. (2001). Cultural pathways to successful parenting. *ISSBD Newsletter,* 1 (38), 9–13.

Ho, D. Y. F., Peng, S.-Q., & Lai, A. C. (2001). Parenting in mainland China: Culture, ideology, and policy. *ISSBD Newsletter,* 1 (38), 7–8.

Hoskyn, M., Moore, D., Neufeld, P., LeMare, L., & Stooke, R. (2007). Letters from the editors. *Child Development, Health & Education,* 1 (1), pp. i–iii.

Jacobs, E. V. (1994). Introduction. In Goelman, H. & Jacobs, E. V. (Eds.), *Children's play in childcare settings* (pp. 1–19). Albany, NY: State University of New York.

Jenks, C. (Ed.) (1982). *The Sociology of childhood: Essential readings*. London: Batsford.

Kagitçibasi, C. (1996). *Family and human development across cultures: A view from the other side*. Mahwah, NJ: Lawrence Erlbaum.

Krappmann, L. (2001). Commentary: No parenting independent of culture. *ISSBD Newsletter*, 1 (38), 15–16.

Lamb, M. E. (1975). Fathers: Forgotten contributors to child development. *Human Development*, 18, 245–266.

Lancaster, J. B., Altman, J., Rossi, A. S., & L. R. Sherrod (Eds.) (1987). *Parenting across the lifespan: Biosocial dimensions*. Hawthorne, NY: Aldine de Gruyter.

Lanyasunya, A. R. & Lesolayia, M. S. (2001). *El-barta Child and Family Project: Working papers in early childhood development, No. 28*. The Hague: Bernard van Leer Foundation.

Laosebikan, S. (1982). *A constituency for clinical psychology in Nigeria: Implications for training*. Paper read at the 2nd Annual Convention of the Nigerian Association of Clinical Psychologists, Benin City, Nigeria.

Larson, J. (1998). *Perspectives on indigenous knowledge systems in Southern Africa: Discussion paper no. 3*. Washington, DC: World Bank.

Le Roux, W. (2002). *The challenges of change: A tracer study of San preschool children in Botswana*. The Hague: Bernard van Leer Foundation.

LeVine, R. A. (1974). Parental goals: A cross-cultural view. *Teachers College Record*, 76, 226–239.

LeVine, R. A. (2004). Challenging expert knowledge: Findings from an African study of infant care and development. In U. P. Gielen & J. Roopnarine (Eds.), *Childhood and adolescence: Cross-cultural perspectives and applications* (pp. 149–165). Westport, CT: Praeger.

May, H. (2000). The 'playground' of early childhood policy: Social and political change versus social and political order. In NZEI Te Rui Roa (Eds.), *Policy, practice and politics: Early childhood millennium conference, July proceedings*. Wellington: NZEI Te Rui Roa.

Meade, A. & Podmore, V. N. (2002). *Early childhood education policy and coordination under the auspices of the Department/Ministry of Education: A case study of New Zealand*. Early Childhood and Family Policy Series No. I-2002. Paris: UNESCO.

Miller, J. G. & Chen, X. (2001). Introduction to the longitudinal research on human development: Approaches, issues, and new directions. *ISSBD Newsletter*, 1 (38), 1.

Moss, P. (2005). *From children's services to children's spaces: Re-thinking early childhood*. Abingdon: RoutledgeFalmer.

Munroe, R. L. & Munroe, R. H. (1975). *Cross-cultural human development*. Prospects Heights, IL: Waveland Press.

Munroe, R. L., Munroe, R. H., & Whiting, B. B. (1981). *Handbook of cross-cultural human development*. New York: Garland.

Ngaujah, D. E. (2003). *An eco-cultural and social paradigm for understanding human development: A (West African) context*. Graduate Seminar Paper (supervised by Dr. Dennis H. Dirks), Biola University, CA.

Nimnicht, G., Atrango, M. M. & Hearn, L. (1987). *Meeting the needs of young children: Policy alternatives*. Occasional Papers No, 2. The Hague: BvLF.

Nsamenang, A. B. (1992). *Human development in cultural context: A Third World perspective.* Newbury Park, CA: Sage.

Nsamenang, A. B. (1999). Eurocentric image of childhood in the context of the world's cultures: Essay review of images of childhood, edited by P. Hwang, M. E. Lamb, & I. E. Sigel. *Human Development*, 28, 159–168.

Nsamenang, A. B. (2003). Conceptualizing human development and education in sub-Saharan Africa at the interface of indigenous and exogenous influences. In T. S. Saraswathi (Ed.), *Cross-cultural perspectives in human development: Theory, research, and applications* (pp. 213–235). New Delhi: Sage.

Nsamenang, A. B. (2004). *Cultures of human development and education: Challenge to growing up in Africa.* New York: Nova.

Nsamenang, A. B. (2005a). The intersection of traditional African education with school learning. In L. Swartz, C. de la Rey, & N. Duncan (Eds.), *Psychology: An introduction* (pp. 327–337). Cape Town: Oxford University Press.

Nsamenang, A. B. (2005b). African family traditions: Education. In C. Fisher, & R. Lerner (Eds.), *Encyclopedia of applied developmental science* (pp. 61–62). Thousand Oaks, CA: Sage.

Nsamenang, A. B. (2005c). Educational development and knowledge flow: Local and global forces in human development in Africa. *Higher Education Policy*, 18, 275–288.

Nsamenang, A. B. (2006). Human ontogenesis: An indigenous African view on development and intelligence. *International Journal of Psychology*, 41, 293–297.

Nsamenang, A. B. (2007). A critical peek at early childhood care and education in Africa. *Child Health and Education*, 1 (1), 14–26.

Nsamenang, A. B. (2008a). Culture and human development. *International Journal of Psychology*, 43 (2), 73–77.

Nsamenang, A. B. (2008b). (Mis)understanding ECD Africa: The force of local and global motives. In M. Garcia, A. Pence, & J. Evans (Eds.), *Africa's future, Africa's challenge* (pp. 135–149). Washington, DC: The World Bank.

Nsamenang, A. B. & Dawes, A. (1998). Developmental psychology as political psychology in sub-Saharan Africa: The challenge of Africanisation. *Applied Psychology: An International Review*, 47 (1), 73–87.

Nsamenang, A. B. & M. E. Lamb (1994). Socialization of Nso children in the Bamenda Grassfields of northwest Cameroon. In P. M. Greenmailed & R. R. Cocking (Eds.), *Cross-cultural roots of minority child development* (pp. 133–146). Hillsdale, NJ: Erlbaum.

Nsamenang, A. B. & M. E. Lamb (1995). The force of beliefs: How the parental values of the Nso of Northwest Cameroon shape children's progress towards adult models. *Journal of Applied Developmental Psychology*, 16 (4), 613–627.

Ogbimi, G. E. & Alao, J. A. (1998). Developing sustainable day care services in rural communities of Nigeria. *Early Child Development and Care*, 145, 47–58.

Ogbu, J. U. (1994). From cultural differences to differences in cultural frames of reference. In P. M. Greenfield & R. R. Cocking (Eds.), *Cross-cultural minority child development* (pp. 365–391). Hillsdale, NJ: Erlbaum.

Pence, A. (2004). *ECD policy development and implementation in Africa.* Early Childhood and Family Policy Series No. 9-2004. Paris: UNESCO.

Pence, A. R. & Hix-Small, H. (2007). Global children in the shadow of the global child, *International Journal of Educational Policy, Research, and Practice*, 8 (1), 83–100.

Pence, A. & Marfo, K. (2004). Capacity building for ECD in Africa: Introduction to Special Issue. *International Journal of Educational Policy, Research & Practice*, 5 (3), 5–12.

Pence, A. & Nsamenang, A. B. (2008). Respecting Diversity in an Age of Globalization: A Case for Early Childhood Development in Sub-Saharan Africa, Bernard van Leer Foundation Working Paper, No. 51, The Hague: Bernard van Leer Foundation.

Prout, A. & James, A. (1990). A new paradigm for the sociology of childhood? Provenance, promise and problem. In A. James & A. Prout (Eds.), *Constructing and reconstructing childhood: Contemporary issues in the sociological study of childhood* (pp. 7–34). London: The Falmer Press.

Reagan, T. (1996). *Non-Western educational traditions: Alternative approaches to educational thought and practice*, 2nd edn. Mahwah, NJ: Erlbaum.

Reid, M. (2006). *From innocents to agents: Children and children's rights in New Zealand*. Auckland: Maxim Institute.

Rogoff, B. (2003). *The cultural nature of human development*. Oxford: Oxford University Press.

Rose, N. (1999). *Powers of freedom: Reframing political thought*. Cambridge: Cambridge University Press.

Saasa, O. S. (2007). *Enhancing institutional and human resource capacity for improved performance*, 7th Africa Governance Forum: Building the Capable State in Africa. New York: UNDP

Sagi, A. & Aviezer, O. (2001). The rise and fall of children's communal sleeping in Israeli Kibbutzim: An experiment in nature and implications for parenting. *ISSBD Newsletter*, 1 (38), 4–6.

Saraswathi, T. S. (1998). Many deities, one God: Towards convergence in cultural psychology. *Culture and Psychology*, 4 (2), 147–160.

Scott, J. C. (1998). *Seeing like the state: How certain schemes to improve the human condition have failed*. New Haven, CT: Yale University Press.

Segall, M. H., Dasen, P. R., Berry, J. W. & Poortinga, Y. H. (1999). *Human Behavior in Global Perspective*. Boston: Allyn & Bacon.

Serpell, R. (1993). *The significance of schooling: Life-journeys into an African society*. Cambridge: Cambridge University Press.

Serpell, R. (1994). An African social ontogeny: Review of A. Bame Nsamenang (1992): Human development in cultural context. *Cross-Cultural Psychology Bulletin*, 28 (1), 17–21.

Serpell, R. (1996). Cultural models of childhood in indigenous socialization and formal schooling in Zambia. In C.-P. Hwang, M. E. Lamb & I. E. Sigel (Eds.), *Images of childhood* (pp. 129–142). Mahwah, NJ: Erlbaum.

Sigel, I. E., McGillicuddy-DeLisi, A. V., & Goodnow, J. J. (Eds.) (1992). *Parental beliefs systems: The psychological consequences for children*. Hillsdale, NJ: Erlbaum.

Smale, J. (1998). Culturally appropriate approaches in ECD. *Early Childhood Matters*, 89, 3–5.

Stephens, S. (1995). Introduction: Children and politics of culture in "Late Capitalism". In S. Stephens (Ed.), *Children and the politics of culture* (pp. 3–48). Prentice, NJ: Prentice University Press.

Stevens, M. J. & Gielen, U. P. (2007). *Toward a global psychology: Theory, research, intervention, and pedagogy*. Mahwah, NJ: Lawrence Erlbaum Associates.

Super, C. M. & Harkness, S. (1986). The developmental niche: A conceptualization at the interface of child and culture. *International Journal of Behavioral Development*, 9, 545–569.

Super, C. M. & Harkness, S. (2008). Globalization and its discontents: Challenges to developmental theory and practice in Africa. *International Journal of Psychology*, 43 (2), 107–113.

Susman-Stillman, A. (2005). Child care: Infant and toddler. In C. B. Fisher & R. M. Lerner, *Encyclopedia of applied developmental science*, Vol. 1 (pp. 240–242). Thousand Oaks, CA: Sage.

Tobin, J. J., Wu, D. Y. H., & Davidson, D. L. H. (1989). *Preschool in three cultures: Japan, China and the United States*. New Haven, CT: Yale University Press.

Tzay, C. (1998). Guatemala: Working with the Mayan-Ixil people. *Early Childhood Matters*, 89, 18–22.

UNESCO (2003). *Declaration on science and the use of scientific knowledge*. http://unesco.org/genera (Site visited: 4/24/2003).

Urban, M. (2006). *Strategies for change: Reflections from a systematic, comparative research project*. Paper presented to the Early Childhood Care and Education Policy seminar on "A Decade of Reflection from the Introduction of the Childcare Regulations 1996 through to today", Dublin, Ireland.

Uribe, F. M. T., LeVine, R. A., & LeVine S. E. (1994). Maternal behavior in a Mexican community: The changing environments of children. In P. M. Greenmailed & R. R. Cocking (Eds.), *Cross-cultural roots of minority child development* (pp. 41–54). Hillsdale, NJ: Erlbaum.

Vandenbroeck, M. (1999). *The view of the Yet: Bringing up children in the spirit of self-awareness and knowledge*. The Hague: BvLF.

Vargas-Barón, E. (2005). *Planning policies for early childhood development: Guidelines for Action*. Paris, UNESCO.

Vogelaar, J. (2005). Foreword. In E. Vargas-Barón.,*Planning policies for early childhood development: Guidelines for Action* (pp. iii–iv). Paris: UNESCO.

Weisner, T. S. (1987). Socialization for parenthood in sibling caretaking societies. In J. B. Lancaster, J. Altman, A. S. Rossi, & L. R. Sherrod (Eds.), *Parenting across the lifespan: Biosocial dimensions* (pp. 237–270). Hawthorne, NY: Aldine de Gruyter.

Weisner, T. S., Matheson, C. C., & Bernheimer, L. P. (1996). American cultural models of early influence and parent recognition of developmental delays: Is earlier always better than later? In S. Harkness & C. M. Supper (Eds.), *Parents' cultural beliefs systems: Their origins, expressions and consequences* (pp. 496–531). New York: The Guilford Press.

Whiting, B. B. & Whiting, J. W. M. (1975). *Children of six cultures: A psycho-cultural analysis*. Cambridge, MA: Harvard University Press.

Winnett, R. (2005). Blair's pension offer to mothers: 3 billion pound election pledge. *The Sunday Times*, No. 8,417, 1 & 16.

Yajun, Z., Yi, L. & Champagne, S. (1999). *Childrearing in Hubai village, China*. Working Papers in Early Childhood Development No. 25. Bernard van Leer Foundation: The Hague, The Netherlands.

Zeitlin, M. (1996). My child is my crown: Yoruba parental theories and practices in early childhood. In S. Harkness & C. M. Supper (Eds.), *Parents cultural beliefs systems: Their origins, expressions and consequences* (pp. 407–427). New York: The Guilford Press.

Zeitlin, M. F., Megawangi, R., Kramer, E. M., Colletta, N. D., Babatunde, E. D., & Garman, D. (1995). *Strengthening the family: Implications for international development*. Tokyo: United Nations University Press.

3 Cultural Practices, Social Values and Childhood Education

The Impact of Globalization

Angela Uchoa Branco

Human development occurs along a complex process of systemic change that takes place over ontogenetic time within particular historical and sociocultural contexts (Bruner, 1997; Ford & Lerner, 1992; Valsiner, 2007). The sociocultural genesis and the constructive role of individuals concerning their own development have been well established by contemporary developmental theorists (e.g. Bruner, Rogoff, Valsiner, Wertsch). However, many theorists and practitioners still face many challenges. First, there is the development of creative methodologies to approach the multiplicity of interdependent factors playing a central role in developmental processes, taking into account the intertwined nature of both general (species specific) and local (socioculturally specific) aspects of human development. Second, there is the challenge of the ethical and necessary translation of scientific knowledge about human development into corresponding social practices and activities to foster child development within the various cultural contexts within which children are embedded since the moment they are born.

In this chapter I will address the subject of similarities/convergences, and dissimilarities/divergences in human developmental processes, the major role played by globalization on most societies' values, practices, and childhood education, and the need to investigate such impact at the microlevel of everyday social interactions. My intention is to overcome dichotomies opposing universal *versus* local, culturally oriented, scientific knowledge construction in psychology, but still keeping the polarity of opposites for analytical purposes (see the concept of *inclusive separation*, Valsiner & Cairns, 1992). Another important goal of the chapter is to underline the centrality of communication, metacommunication and motivation in meaning-construction processes occurring within school contexts, which contribute in significant ways to promote or inhibit child learning and development.

To begin with, it is very important to stress what I mean by "universal" aspects of human development. Aware of the need to include general biological features and genetic dispositions of human beings, here I also employ the concept of "universal" to designate the non-controversial assumption—among socioculturalists—that *culture* is the central and most distinctive species-specific characteristic of human beings. In other words, culture consists of our universal and ingrained quality, the one that allows us to actually become human. Therefore, no developmental theory is possible without simultaneously considering universal *and* local aspects of human characteristics, and much of the reasoning pervading this chapter takes a dialogical, systemic, and complex perspective considering the range of possible generalizations of the processes under study.

According to the proposal of this book, it is necessary to analyze the interface between local and global contexts, namely, the local–global dynamics that contribute to the emergence of the broad range of definitions of childhood, schooling, and other cultural practices. Such practices provide the contexts within which children socialize and develop according to dynamics that promote either similar, or diverse, directions to their development. Trajectory diversity encompasses development, at its plural and intermingled dimensions, as affectivity, cognition, language, social and self characteristics, plus dynamics. Thus, while considering the impact of globalization, I will *focus on the analysis of both general and local intertwined processes* which understanding can contribute to advance solid scientific knowledge, namely, robust theoretical accounts of human development. Moreover, such comprehension will bring forth some important local information linked to culturally structured contexts not always under scrutiny by developed countries' scientific production on the subject of child development.

Cultural Practices, Human Values and the Impact of Globalization

From a systemic view, contemporary psychology needs to elaborate its theoretical models on the assumption of a mutual constitution between cultural practices and human values. The dialogically constructive nature of activities, and the semiotic world within which the person participates, engages in specific actions, creates and negotiates meanings, both consist of the setting—or cultural context—within which human development takes place.

According to this approach, both activity and symbolic levels of human experience play a fundamental part in developmental processes that entail change and relative stability, basic principles of a systemic theoretical framework to explain human development. Goal-oriented actions and meaning co-construction constitute the major processes through which the developmental flow finds its way throughout the cultural landscape that supports human beings along their life experiences, i.e., ontogenesis.

The conceptualization of the mutual constitution of practices and values allows for a better understanding of the tremendous impact of globalization on even remote cultures like Amazonian tribes, and small rural villages located in the poorest regions of the world. The evidence of the economic, political and social power of capitalism is vast and overwhelming. Considered by some as a collectivist culture (Triandis, 1995), Brazil has definitely become an extremely competitive and individualistic country. Clearly, we cannot think of Brazil as a homogeneous entity, since historically, economically, ethnically, and culturally, Brazilian diversity is huge (as huge as in the United States, for example) (see Freitas, Sperb, & Shelton, this volume). The contrasts are incredible, especially concerning the enormous gap between the rich and the very poor portion of its population. Notwithstanding, Brazil had some tradition of solidarity among the poor, and peaceful conflict resolution among most of its people (Milani & Branco, 2004). Military confrontations have been avoided in different ways throughout its 500 official years of existence, and the struggle to find peaceful alternatives to solve problems has frequently been mentioned by historians. Even in the worst years during the dictatorship, struggles were made to avoid massive, out-of-control military confrontations. The continuous intimacy with violence (mainly structural, socio-economic violence) throughout the country, and during all of Brazil's history, did not prevent Brazilian people from showing a certain degree of cooperation and clear efforts to maintain a certain level of acceptance and tolerance in relation to each other (Milani & Branco, 2004). Unfortunately, however, this scenario has changed in recent decades.

Due to generations of structural and socio-economic violence, and to the overflow of competitive, individualist and consumerist cultural messages from a bulky capitalist ideology, the people of Brazil are increasingly observing not just the violent encounters broadcast to the world, but particularly a progressive wave of daily events proving the individualistic, paranoid, and dog-eat-dog dispositions among people. Such social and subjective perceptions and action dispositions ultimately created resistance and fear of interacting with other people, social isolation, and a decrease in spontaneous help and cooperation among all social classes, particularly in Brazil's ever-growing cities (Branco et al., 2004a, 2004b). Even in rural areas the same trend towards isolation, violent conflict management, and low self-esteem can be observed. And why is that so? Apart from the global economy and its reflections at all different levels of community interchanges and living conditions in the so-called "developing" countries, what is easily verified is the impregnation, internalization, or appropriation of individualistic and competitive practices and values in various social contexts. They are easily observed in everyday practices, particularly within children's most prominent contemporary developmental contexts: the family and the school. The internalization and proliferation of values and practices conducive to an intense individualistic/competitive flow, which emanate from media to educational activities, urgently demand better explanations of how such internalization processes take place, thus participating in the ontogenesis of values and the emergence and consolidation of certain social practices. Despite the general relevance of the analysis that will follow, I would like to particularly stress the sort of cultural canalization structures, processes and mechanisms that educational settings are, almost without exception, offering to our children during their school years.

A word of caution, however, is necessary: globalization does not only, and exclusively, bring unfortunate social and developmental negative consequences. It may, and frequently does, broaden perspectives in narrow-minded mentalities, and it allows for planetary, international access to information, which certainly contributes, in a general sense, to the wonders and welcome accomplishments of freedom and democracy. In terms of social relationships, happiness, and socio-affective quality of life, however, the tough face of globalization may represent a dangerous route towards less tolerance and willingness to cooperate in the construction of a peaceful and better world for everyone. To some extent this may seem like a paradox, but that is exactly what is happening. Thus, if we expect a positive change in such negative aspects—the "dark side"—of globalization, rigorous research associated with theoretical and methodological elaborations needs to be pursued by social and human scientists, particularly in the domains of psychology.

The need for healthier social interactions among people demands a deep understanding of how the potential of globalization perspectives can be positively interconnected with cultural, political, ethnic and other sorts of diversity. Above all, the acknowledgment of democracy prevails as the best means to fulfill the challenge of conciliating the inevitable global planning of politics with the deep and consequential respect for diversity. It also implies the deconstruction of prejudice at all levels of human and social relationships, which ultimately will result in mechanisms of inclusion and collaborative development among individual and nations.

Culture, Socialization and Meaning Construction

From a theoretical perspective, the cultural-historical approach, proposed by Vygotsky in the late 1920s, elaborates on the fundamental assumption of the sociogenesis of human development proposed by Baldwin at the end of the 19th century. Sociogenetic mechanisms, though, still need to be unveiled by psychological research at the microgenetic level. Some authors designate such micro processes as "internalization" (e.g. Lawrence & Valsiner, 1993; Valsiner, 1987, 2001), others as "appropriation" (e.g. Cole, 1998; Matusov, 1998; Wertsch, 1998), or participation (e.g. Rogoff, 1990, 2003), but the major conceptual goal consists of shedding some light on the ways in which social, environmental messages are transformed and incorporated by individuals living in specifically structured contexts, through their social interactions. Also, the relationships between sociogenesis, microgenesis, and ontogenesis need to be further investigated in their dynamics and complexities.

While studying such micro processes, however, the socio-historical and economic macro level must be taken into account as a figure–background systemic framework for understanding human phenomena (Damon & Lerner, 1998). Depending on the research question or issue under study, the target changes (background aspects come to the foreground, and vice versa). But the simple mention of the sociogenesis of human development can just be empty talk if researchers do not dare to analyze data, raise interesting hypotheses, and theorize on consistencies and regularities, as well as on contradictions and the emergence of novelties (Branco & Valsiner, 2004; Valsiner, 2005, 2007).

Socialization

Socialization traditionally meant "learning how to live together with others". From the cultural-historical, or sociocultural, perspective, though, it never received the same scientific attention that was directed towards the study of cognitive and language processes. Therefore, most that has been studied and theorized about socialization, motivation and moral development comes from the contributions of classical authors from social learning, behavioristic, or Piagetian constructivist theoretical backgrounds (e.g. Cole & Cole, 2004; DeVries, Zan, Hildebrandt, Edmiaston & Sales, 2004; Damon & Eisenberg, 1998). From my perspective, though, the analysis of sociogenetic processes that allows for the emergence of human superior functions brings theory very close to the study of socialization processes. It is nonsensical to separate or establish barriers and frontiers between those fundamental dimensions of human development, namely, socio-affective and moral development, on the one hand, and cognitive and language development, on the other.

What we mostly detect while analyzing the literature is a lot of discourse about the unity of affect and cognition, but when it comes to investigative goals, very rarely is studied the social motivation that inspires moral actions and beliefs or different kinds of social interdependence—such as cooperation, competition, and individualism. There are few who directly address such issues (e.g. Ratner, 2002; Rogoff, 2003; Shweder & Much, 1987; Tappan, 1992; Valsiner, 2007). To adopt a sociocultural approach, though, is to take a systemic (e.g. Ford & Lerner, 1992; Thelen & Smith, 1998), and transdisciplinary perspective over developmental processes, with a special emphasis on meaning-construction processes (e.g. Bruner, 1997; Shweder, 1991; Valsiner, 2007).

Meaning-Construction Processes

Meaning-construction processes should be at the center of psychological scientific investigation. The complex nature of such processes (e.g. Morin, 1999; Rey, 2003), however, cannot be overestimated. Motivation, affect, values and beliefs play a very significant role in processes like memory, logic operations, language, and so many other processes located at the domains of intellect and emotions. Likewise, the study of personality and self development cannot discard the active part played by those phenomena which are difficult to categorize or analyze, namely, those "hot", affect-laden processes.

Meaning-construction processes occurs as different individuals (e.g. Fogel, 1993; Chaiklin, 2001), or different I-positions of the same individual (e.g. Hermans, 2001; Salgado & Hermans, 2005), confront each other in dialogue (Bakhtin). Such processes are fluid, dynamic, but yet available for analysis, particularly of the hermeneutic kind (Ratner, 2002; Shweder & Much, 1987). They take place in specific cultural-historical contexts, within the social practices of specific groups, and also vary as participants and participant's relationships are taken into account. In other words, meaning co-construction processes are, indeed, communication and metacommunication processes, where information is exchanged and novelties are constantly being created (Fogel, 1993; Fogel & Branco, 1997).

At each social encounter, individuals' goal orientations are negotiated according to different levels of intensity. Convergent goal orientations usually characterize the interactions as affiliative, positive, productive, and even cooperative, when the goal is shared and can be reached by all the participants. In some other situations, divergent goal orientations prevail, and then two possibilities emerge: active negotiation leading to conflict resolution, or disruption. In some situations, the quality of the interaction "frame" (a concept to be explained later) is ambiguous or ambivalent, and the consequences can also entail further negotiations or plain disruption. When the dialogue occurs between one individual's different I-positions, similar (or at least equivalent) processes may occur. However, in such cases, as the relative stability of the self system must be preserved, a greater effort is made to keep the system (the person) going with a relative sense of integration, coordination and stability. Psychopathologies are, thus, the results of failed attempts in those directions.

Meaning is here conceptualized as dynamic and fluid (Brockmeier & Harré, 2001; Bruner, 1990), and it is exactly this openness property that allows for negotiation, creativity, and human development. The semiotic dimension, understood as the field where meaning-making processes take place, should be considered to be of very special interest for knowledge construction about human development and related phenomena, like education. It is also positioned at the central stage where communication and metacommunication weave together power relations and relationships among people.

Power Relations and the Power of Relationships and Social Interactions: Communication and Metacommunication

Now I want to address the issues more directly concerning the discipline of psychology. Despite the necessity of keeping in mind the existence of multiple colonizing mechanisms at the macro level, there is a whole level of investigations of microprocesses that remain unknown (Foucault, 1996). Much has been said about oppression, unfair hierarchies, and the dominance of inequality among people and societies. However, together and beyond repressive power mechanisms we already know that power relations impregnate human relationships and interactions, generating plural negative and unwelcome consequences at both social and subjective levels. Overall, the notion of symbolic power, and its ubiquity to the point of self-sacrifice and the like, need further analysis and deeper scrutiny. The new paradigms inspiring contemporary thinking in philosophy, in social and human sciences, and developmental theory have definitely broadened the scope of our understanding concerning the pivotal role of language, and the several levels of semiotic functioning for the constitution of individuals and groups participating in both collective and particular practices within the contexts of societies.

Psychology, I think, has a lot to contribute exactly at the less analyzed level of microgenesis of human psychological processes in interaction with sociocultural processes and activities. Psychology can assume the task of unveiling the mechanisms through which power relations—constituted at a macro level (see Foucault's contributions to social sciences)—actually transform, or actively *take* form and exert their power at the micro level of human interactions and relationships (Hinde, 1996). The power of microgenetic theoretical and methodological approaches to promote change and development is still to be fully explored and demonstrated (Lavelli, Pantoja, Hsu, Messinger & Fogel, 2005; Siegler & Crowler, 1992; Valsiner, 2007). The positive thing is that researchers are increasingly aware of the potential and productive investigative path provided by the study of communication, metacommunication and meaning-construction processes at microgenetic time (Branco & Valsiner, 2004; Fogel & Branco, 1997). Therefore, conceptualizing and elaborating on such issues will certainly help psychologists to find better explanations for the existence and probability of specific life trajectories, and their consequences to the development of individuals and societies.

Communication can be conceptualized as the process that conveys co-construction of meanings through the dynamic interplay of signs expressed by a multitude of communicative channels. It is a complex and broad phenomenon of endless co-construction and co-creation of meanings by the participants of social interactions. From a sociocultural perspective, it plays a crucial part in the dynamics of internalization/externalization processes (Valsiner, 2007) that give rise to self and culture. Internalizations and externalizations are both oriented by the dominant influence of affective semiotic processes and social suggestions existing within culturally organized contexts, what has been designated by Valsiner (1987, 2007) as "cultural canalization processes."

Metacommunication, conceived as part of communication, refers to "communication about communication." The concept was first used by Watzlavick, Beavin and Jackson (1967) and later by Bateson, Goffman, and many other investigators (e.g. Branco & Valsiner, 2004; Stambak & Sinclair, 1993). The initial emphasis on nonverbal communication, however, expanded to the analysis of verbal and nonverbal action domains. Metacommunication indicates the quality of the interactive frame (Goffman, 1974) co-constructed by individuals in interaction (Branco, 1998, 2003; Fogel, 1993; Fogel & Branco, 1997). The affective quality of such frames— or contexts for meanings interpretation—is continuously negotiated between the participants, as each person interprets and gives specific meanings to each other's actions. Such negotiation processes, however, do not necessarily entail a permanent awareness on the part of the individuals in interaction. This means that interpretations very often are influenced by non-acknowledged emotional and motivational states actually experienced by the participants, but which are not within the individuals' field of awareness. This may generate completely different interpretations—or meaning-making processes—depending on which kind of frame is being configured among individuals. Often enough, each participant's interpretations do not necessarily coincide, which leads to misunderstandings and ambivalences. In short, the metacommunicative dimension of communication engenders the joint creation of metacommunication frames. As individuals proceed in their interactions, such frames are permanently negotiated at both verbal and nonverbal levels, and negotiation processes lead to the emergence of a dynamic meanings co-construction.

Metacommunication

People communicate with each other about relational and non-relational issues. Relational meanings are constantly created during the interaction, whereas non-relational contents tend mostly to emerge as verbal episodes. Although mostly nonverbal, sometimes metacommunication occurs at a verbal level, and it is designated as verbal metacommunication. Verbal metacommunication, though, only emerges episodically, when participants verbally refer to relational aspects of their communication.

The way people coordinate their gestures, postures, facial expressions, paralinguistic cues and so on, permanently creates a unique quality to every single frame of their interaction. The complex interpretation of all sorts of signs that are being used by the participants leads to the co-creation of meanings, and this process can be considered as a sophisticated artwork. Children are very good at interpreting the quality of an interactive frame, and very sensitive to affectively positive (friendly) versus negative (rejecting) metacommunicative frames.

Sometimes metacommunication indicators are in contradiction with each other, giving rise to embarrassing or uncomfortable ambiguities (Bateson, 1972; Watzlavick et al., 1967). When a teacher tells a student "Good job!" but her eyes, facial expression, and body posture suggest no enthusiasm, or even a negative evaluation, the child feels bad about the work, and may suppose s/he is not good enough to accomplish the task according to the teacher's expectations. In the worse scenario, the child will feel bad about him/herself, which contributes to the emergence of negative self conceptions such as self-esteem (Tacca & Branco, 2003).

We can ask: but how are we to study such processes? The development of adequate methodologies to investigate complex phenomena from a dynamic and co-constructive approach has always represented a challenge for developmental psychology. As we tried different approaches, we came to the conclusion that variations of microgenetic methods definitely were the most productive way to identify the dynamics of social interaction processes. Considering, now, the centrality of communication and metacommunication processes to child development and education, I will next present some data and ideas concerning their occurrence in a very important context: the school.

Communication and Metacommunication Within Significant Life Contexts: The Special Case of Schools

The singularity of school contexts concerning the easier access for professional guidance and cultural canalization efforts to promote positive social values and significant education aiming at excellence in terms of professional qualification and citizenship is fabulous. Even though critical discourses about the conservative, unfair role of schools abound (*à la* Bourdieu), their potential to promote change and development remains less translated into actual knowledge about *how* to effectively promote the desirable changes, meaning knowledge that translates into anything beyond politically correct discourses. Those changes concern critical thinking and positioning, socio-historical awareness of inequalities, intolerance and prejudice, and concrete efforts to develop practices conducive to democratic values and positive, moral development. Therefore, investigations of how educational contexts participate in the ontogenesis of values, social practices among students, and subjective characteristics of individuals, are long-awaited and extremely welcome among theorists and practitioners. Schools, indeed, may open possibilities to promote proactive engagement in activities leading to positive social practices and values that may result in the continuous constructive processes weaving a progressive, daily culture of peace. This is particularly true in poor contexts, and poor countries.

Educational contexts provide the unique possibility to foster and cultivate alternative experiences towards cooperation and actual inclusion. It is important to clarify that here the term inclusion means the opposite of prejudice and discrimination of any sort. No doubt the collaboration of family, media and other social agents are very important to help creating effective cultural canalization towards inclusion and cooperation, but, at school, some initial steps can be put forward by specific smart and laborious teams: teachers and professionals dedicated to sponsor and encourage child development.

Taking into account the above-mentioned unit of analysis constituted by affect-cognition, childhood education necessarily needs to give the same relevance to social objectives as it usually attributes to intellectual, cognitive and linguistic goals. Unfortunately, most of the studies conducted in Brazil— and also in other countries, to my knowledge—show the prevalence if not the dominance of intellectual goals over social, moral or emotional development (Branco & Mettel, 1995). One of the worst consequences of such distortion is the lack of planning and orientation concerning the major, fundamental role played by *motivation* for all teaching–learning and self-development processes that take place within educational contexts.

The perspectives for children's development according to a sociocultural constructivist approach are optimistically promising, even for those challenged by any type of special needs, including poverty conditions (Patto, 1999). Scientific knowledge and creativity must be put in motion to provide the best conditions for education and development. This happens not only because providing better material conditions may unexpectedly promote actual development for those in need of adequate teaching and/or access to educational tools and methodologies; it happens, as well, because the major resource of educational institutions are *people* genuinely willing (motivated) and properly prepared (knowing how) to contribute to the education of a vast range of children with their singularities and personal characteristics.

Also, I think it is particularly important to keep in mind that the child is active, and the part played by affect and motivation can never be overestimated. To speak the child's language means to develop a significant trust relationship between the interacting partners, establishing a positive, affiliative frame. This accomplishment is, definitely, a must within educational contexts (Branco, 2003; McDermott, 1977). It is very interesting to notice how well-known processes do work in different contexts: an excellent example is the Pygmalion effect, or the "self-fulfillment prophecy" (Rosenthal & Jacobson, 1983). In research developed in Brasilia, Tacca and Branco (2003) confirmed the power of positive—and negative—expectations by second-grade teachers, and how children, in their narratives, appropriated their teachers' voices when describing their own abilities, problems, and personality characteristics (like the *"I'm too slow and not very smart"* kind of self-evaluation). This effect is generated by communicative and metacomunicative processes, as analyzed in the previous section.

There are many studies confirming the power of motivation, and how motivations arise from affective, good-quality relationships between teachers and students and among peers (DeVries et al., 2004; Tacca & Branco, in press). Culture, emotions and subjective experiences all contribute to the quality of successful or unsuccessful teaching–learning processes, as well as to healthy or unhealthy trajectories of self-development.

Martins de Oliveira (1994) provides a very good example about how self-conceptions and self-evaluations are profoundly related to the quality of social interactions within the classroom. The object of her investigation was self-esteem evaluations among 3rd grade students attending a public school in the city of Campinas, in the state of Sao Paulo, Brazil. The particular issue under investigation was how black students (the terminology "Afro-descendents" is too rarely used in Brazil) co-constructed their identity, and how they positioned themselves as subjects, or individuals. Did their phenotypical characteristics play any role concerning ethnic identity (or a sense of belonging to an ethnic group)? Were they impregnated by the persistent racist ideology of "whitenization" of the Brazilian population, proposed by late 19th and early 20th century intellectuals (Carone & Bento, 2002) as a way to "improve the quality" (sic) of the Brazilian people? From a historical-cultural perspective, Martins de Oliveira used many interesting procedures, and was cleverly able to access children's written productions about themselves. In her book, she highlights the cases of two black girls, who used different Portuguese words to refer to themselves: "preta" (black), and "morena" (no corresponding word in English). The word "morena" acquired a very singular and interesting meaning among Brazilian people: on the one hand, traditionally (historically) it was, and still is, used to designate "brunettes," or white girls with black eyes and hair; on the other, many people started using the word in the 20th century to designate a "colored" person who was probably descendent of black with white ethnic groups, or any other sort of ethnic combination that resulted in different shades of dark skin.

In her work, Martins de Oliveira (1994) demonstrates the impact of powerful characteristics such as race, socioeconomic status and gender in establishing dominance relations among peers inside the classroom. As a substantial number of students had different shades of dark skin, different socioeconomic backgrounds, and presented various kinds of socially expected behaviors as a student, her analysis of how all those categories intermingled to yield diverse self-conceptions was very thoughtful. Of particular interest is the way she analyzed the major role of language use within the class and other contexts, and its impact over children. The girls she selected to present in her book showed particularly strong negative self-evaluations. The crucial point I want to make, though, is how it is possible—and necessary—to analyze, as she did, the materials produced by the girls without losing track of the sociocultural and historical contexts that allowed for the emergence of such negative self-evaluations.

From my point of view, here lies a great contribution of sociocultural studies. Traditional, classical studies in psychology very easily attributed those negative evaluations (or low self-esteem "problems") to the person herself, and consequently suggested procedures and strategies to raise students' self-esteem. In Martins de Oliviera's (1994) study about race and self-conceptions, though, she stresses the fundamental role of the ominous ideology ("whitenization" of the population) that still pervades our society and contaminates people's interactions, although the degree of prejudice and discrimination depends on specifically where in Brazil you do your research. Unfortunately, this sort of racist ideology is not constrained to Brazil.

The study of the mutual constitution of practices and values demonstrates that a cultural perspective provides a fresh field for innovation. The co-construction of inclusive and affiliative relationship contexts can, thus, help in canalizing positive subjective experience, considering that, simultaneously, the individual is active and constructive of her/his self-development. That means that many factors and aspects should be taken into account as self-development progresses along ontogeny. Bidirectionality and feedback–feedforward mechanisms, typical of open-systems theory (Ford & Lerner, 1992; Thelen & Smith, 1998; Valsiner, 2005), hence, have to be seriously considered in order to facilitate human development, which is also characterized by its future-orientation, or pre-adaptation processes that ultimately contribute to the emergence of welcome novelties (Valsiner, 2007).

Social Motivation and Culturally Structured Activities

The recognition of the importance of motivation for human development and education should not lead to the misconception that children should be allowed to do whatever they want. Children need goals and constraints, as we all do. However, children need to feel respected in their individuality as they follow rules that they should understand, and as they are guided throughout school tasks and activities. The display of respect, though, needs to be honest and heartfelt, otherwise children can easily perceive and disclose hidden agendas. Norms and constraints are only internalized when trust relationships provide the legitimacy for their existence.

In our research projects carried out at the University of Brasilia, in the Laboratory of Microgenesis in Social Interactions (LABMIS), our team has identified and analyzed many examples concerning the complex relationships between communication, metacommunication, motivation, values and goal orientations, and social interactive actions (e.g. Branco & Valsiner, 2004). In one such project, the aim was to identify and analyze conceptualizations and beliefs related to the major types of social motivation, or social interdependence, namely, cooperation, competition and individualism. Within the contexts of public and private schools, we investigated the narratives of 24 children and 24 adolescents of both sexes concerning this topic. The research took place in the city of Brasilia, and the qualitative methodology used included individual interviews and focal groups. Interviews were audiotaped, and focal groups were videotaped (Branco, Pinto, Pinheiro & Bernardes, 2004a, 2004b).

Results showed that both age groups had huge difficulty, for instance, in defining the concept of 'cooperation', as well as of remembering any instance of participating in, or witnessing, cooperative activities or situations. The predominance of individualistic and competitive dispositions was quite impressive. Definition and memory of competitive activities were precise and various. It was easy to bring forth examples of such activities drawn from family or school daily experiences. When the participants tried to explicate the meaning of cooperation, they almost all mentioned "help"; in other words, the idea that in cooperation all will gain something from the joint experience was absolutely alien to them. Yet, as Deutsch proposed (1949), that is exactly how cooperation is, and should be, defined (Branco, 2003; Johnson & Johnson, 1989). Collaboration was an unknown concept, always connected with "helping" the peer or the teacher to do something for their own sake. Eventually, the term came to be associated with team work, but their conceptualization of team work mostly referred to the act of putting together individual contributions to benefit the group. In short, their lack of experience or even "discourse" about cooperation was definitely amazing.

They valued competition for "real" life, but when asked about which world could be considered ideal for them, inevitably they referred to a world of solidarity and justice, characterized by non-violent forms of social interaction. All participants seemed at ease providing the interviewer with socially and politically correct answers, meaning they were ready to offer narratives compatible with social representations (Juberg, 2000; Moscovici, 2007) of what people expect others to say about a certain topic (particularly topics referring to moral domains). However, as the interview went on, and they were asked to come up with actual examples and experiences of their own, they made clear their propensity to believe that competition is the only option within contemporary society for those who want to succeed. Both children and adolescents never mentioned the possibility of subtle forms of violence ingrained in competition. Moreover, a noteworthy result was that both boys and girls provided similar narratives.

The following excerpt gives a general picture of what we found. Adam (fictitious name), 15 years old, attending a private middle-class school talks with the interviewer:

INTERVIEWER: So, and what about in life, generally speaking? Who is more successful, the person who cooperates or the person who competes?
ADAM: Nowadays, the person who competes.
INTERVIEWER: Why?
ADAM: Uh, because the market is too competitive. No, I guess that is because we ... no one are caring for anyone else. You either do your own stuff or else ... No one wants to help the other, anyway. If you do not study, for instance, you won't pass [he refers to the "vestibular", a series of examinations required for university entrance]. You will be a nobody. We can't help other people, otherwise you will end up lagging behind!
INTERVIEWER: Do you think that helping people will make you worse than the others?
ADAM: It doesn't make me worse than any others, but ... it slows me down, kind of, it makes me waste my time, time I could be studying instead of helping people ... But I wish things were not like that.
INTERVIEWER: How would you wish it to be?
ADAM: Well, to have time to help others while helping oneself, you see? Then things could work out. You help people and you also succeed. But things are not like that, I don't think that is a possibility ...

According to Adam, today's market is very competitive, and the fact that no one cares for anyone else is an explanation for why helping others belongs to a kind of outdated utopia. In real life, it just makes the person waste his/her time, and "lag behind". Individualism and competition are presented by Adam—and almost the whole group of participants, boys and girls—as an inevitable "fact of life." The interesting thing, though, is that when further questioned about the subject, he tries to compromise with the criterion of "response desirability," and suggests that it would be nice if he could help and be successful at the same time. However, he does not believe it is a realistic thing to do. The problem here, as described before, is that it seems to him—and to most of the participants—that cooperation is not an option at all. The way I see it, this happens because they too rarely experience, either at school or at home, cooperative activities or practices. And when they do, that kind of social interdependence among people is never stressed, or categorized as being "cooperative." It seems that in our society, at least in Brazil, as many research studies have confirmed (Palmieri & Branco, 2007), cooperation is not even a concept to classify certain sorts of activities.

The similarities between Adam's and Claudia's narrative is striking. Claudia is an 11-year-old girl attending a public school. According to her,

> I think people today are too selfish, and also envious. They are always competing, everyone wants to be successful and they don't care for each other. I'm not talking about everybody, but most people are too competitive …

In short, arguments like Adam's and Claudia's could be detected in practically all participants' discourses. Such results did not come as a surprise, but the intensity of values and beliefs concerning competition came, indeed, with an unexpected rate of recurrence.

More illustrations about the same issue, meaning lack of experience with participation, or reference to cooperative practices, come from different projects developed by our team in Brazil. Another study aimed at investigating, at a microgenetic level, how teachers conceived, evaluated, and promoted or inhibited cooperation among young children at preschools in the southern state of Parana (Branco & Palmieri, 2003; Palmieri & Branco, 2008). Results showed that both teachers investigated, from different private preschools, had no idea what the concept meant, and even worse, they had no idea about how to organize and develop an activity to promote cooperative interactions among their 5- to 6-year-old children.

In the study, we proposed to each teacher that, after an adaptation preliminary phase, she thought about and structured an activity that she believed could intentionally facilitate cooperative interactions. The structured session organized by each teacher was videorecorded for microanalysis. Then came a remarkable surprise: Teacher A conducted a typically competitive activity, and Teacher B organized a group activity that ended up with each child taking turns to perform their part to complete the group task.

Teacher A divided her class in groups of three children each. She said the group to first finish the activity would be the winner. The activity consisted of bursting balloons tied to each child's ankles. She talked and insisted so much about the importance of winning that when she timidly suggested that each child could "help" the partner within the group, children felt insulted with the idea. How come she could think they were not good enough to perform the task just by themselves? The following is an extract of the recorded interactions:

TEACHER A: When I give you the signal ... when I give you the signal the group, hand in hand, don't let go of your hands, will blow the balloons using your feet. A peer [the word "friend" was not used] may help the other to blow the balloon, within the same group, OK?

LUCA screams at her: I don't need help!

THE TEACHER looks surprised at him, and with a curious tone in her voice says: Don't you need help? Why?

ALL CHILDREN start screaming like crazy yelling they do not need help at all: Neither do I! Neither do I!, they say.

[The noise and confusion is now out of control. Children hop around, climb the tables, scream at each other.]

TEACHER A mutters, with disappointment in her voice: But ... but you ... you'll be in groups!

LUCA aggressively stomps on the floor as though he was bursting a balloon, while angrily saying: Because I take a balloon and do like this!

[Andre and Paulo then do the same with their feet, as though they were strongly bursting imaginary balloons.]

It is interesting to see how Teacher A demonstrates authentic surprise (or frustration) when she suggested that the children "help" each other inside their groups. However, from the very beginning of the activity she insisted on the competitive nature of the activity, verbally and nonverbally encouraging children with expressions such as "This time is for real!", or "...otherwise you will not win!", and so on. When she suggested the possibility of "helping one another, " she did that just once, in a very timid way, after several acts of encouragement to compete. Therefore, it seems that children interpreted her suggestion as a sign of weakness and incompetence, as though what she really meant was "If you're not good enough, you may ask for help...". That would explain the anger and frustration of children's response to her suggestion.

Teacher B, in her turn, proposed an activity that could have promoted some cooperative interactions. She divided the class in two, each group sitting at a big table. Each group had to draw a big poster, to be put on the wall as an ad for the coming school book fair. Each group received different color pencils, and she suggested they could exchange pencils. However, as the activity developed, children transformed it into separate individual tasks, taking turns to draw, and not exchanging anything. That happened with a little help from the teacher, for once in a while she herself inhibited pencil exchanges during regular classroom activities. Therefore, it was as though the children interpreted the activity according to their typical classroom practices.

Further evidence came from the interviews with the teachers (Palmieri & Branco, 2008). None, according to their own narrative, knew what to do, or how to organize an activity aiming at promoting cooperation. Teacher A asked for her mother's help, who advised her to promote the above-described balloon activity. Teacher B asked the principal, who literally told her to develop "any group activity, for all such activities promote cooperation."

During the interviews with the teachers, many questions were posed to explore their discourse concerning conceptions, values and beliefs relative to socialization and social interdependence. Both defined cooperation as "help," exactly in the same way as the children and adolescents who participated in the other study. Teachers also mentioned "help the teacher" as a good example of cooperation. Child–child cooperation was apparently something alien to them. In short, in our projects we have confirmed the *mutual* dialectical constitutive relationship between social practices, on the one hand, and values and beliefs, on the other. Such results corroborate other evidence and thinking in cultural psychology (e.g. Rogoff, 1990, 2003; Shweder, 1991; Valsiner, 2001, 2005, 2007).

The Meaning of Cultural Canalization Efforts and Constructive Conflicts: Towards Democracy, Justice, Inclusion and Peace

Dumon (1985), Velho (1987), Jares (2002), Curry and Goodheart (1991), Maturana and Varela (1995), Morin and Prigogine (2000), Sloan (2005) and many others insist on the urgent need to investigate the socio-historical-cultural origins of individualism and competition that flourish all over the world, spread not only by the power of capitalism, but also by the associated symbolic power of values and beliefs. The alternatives to globalized capitalism are timid and too local at the present time. Therefore, we still have to learn how to deal with poverty, social exclusion, intolerance, prejudice and, sometimes, face the demands to avoid or change the trajectory of military and violent confrontations between people, groups and nations. The state of the arts in politics, economy, and the sociocultural dimensions of the civilized world claim for creativity, but mostly, claim for *cooperation*. This is true at both global and face-to-face interactional levels. We need to co-construct alternative ways to deal with diversity and divergences. As said before, conflicts can be constructive (Valsiner & Cairns, 1992), but hostile aggression and destruction will never be the answer. By collaborating with each other, all nations and people can construct mutual acceptance, respect, and a fundamental sense of planetary solidarity. Knowledge of such level and broad scope can only be created by diverse minds interested in creating solidarity with the efforts of different cognitive, affective, cultural approaches we can find in contemporary nations and societies.

Many may doubt the value of arguing for a utopia of a cooperative, peaceful world. However, peace and democracy, as other major human values and virtues, must not stand as a promise of a final state of affairs, but must prevail as a compass to orient individual and collective actions, practices, and activities. If today's poverty, unemployment, and social exclusion go hand in hand with prejudice, intolerance, competition and individualism, it is high time to implement proactive policies and courses of action to promote change and development.

Such endeavors include researchers and all sorts of professionals and workers. Hence, research in the general field of education, encompassing family, schools, community, media, religious contexts and the like is required throughout the world. All can profit from the investment of all, rich or poor, from east to west, from north to south. Today it is already possible to present to the world community important indicators of sociocultural canalization processes that generate and fortify some human values over others. If we think that competition and individualism are not a good bet for the present or the future of humanity, it is certainly necessary to start working hard in the opposite direction. A critical and detailed analysis at both macro and micro levels is, thus, absolutely indispensable to provide the goals and tools to attain our objectives. We already know some things that could be done (the literature is vast, see Jares, 2002; Rogoff, 2003; Staub, 1991, and many others), but much more needs to be accomplished in terms of research to provide further knowledge, and particularly in terms of actual political determination, at general and local levels.

When we analyze and discuss issues like justice, human rights, democracy, freedom and social responsibility, we are talking about the viability of peaceful co-existence, dignity, and happiness. All such values are nothing if they are not translated into the routine of daily, everyday-life interactions and relationships between real people, in real contexts. And nothing is more difficult than to translate a set of good intentions and bright discourses into actual living experiences, where divergent encounters can lead to constructive conflict and negotiation.

Why are we living through a time of depression, anxiety and low self-esteem? How can scientific psychology contribute to the development of a culture of peace and happiness? It is time for a qualitative leap from moral and political discourses to the achievement of new social practices, in accordance with new life paradigms. I would say it is time to stop blaming the sociopolitical system, and better observe our own relationships and interactions. By doing so, we can actually open the venue for true alternative, longed-for transformations at both the micro and macro levels that will have a significant impact on life on this planet.

References

Branco, A. U. (2003). Social development in social contexts: cooperative and competitive interaction patterns in peer interactions. In J. Valsiner & K. Connolly (Eds.), *Handbook of developmental psychology* (pp. 238–256). London: Sage.

Branco, A. U. & Mettel, T. P. L. (1995). O processo de canalização cultural das interações criança-criança na pré-escola. *Psicologia: Teoria e Pesquisa*, 11 (1), 13–22.

Branco, A. U. & Palmieri, M. W. (2003). *Shall we cooperate or compete? The ambiguities of meaning construction in the context of preschool activities.* Paper presented at the IX European Conference of Child Development, Milan, Italy, August.

Branco, A. U., Pinto, R., Pinheiro, M., & Bernardes, P. (2004a). *Cooperation, competition and individualism: 11-year-old children's belief orientations and moral implications*. Paper presented at the 34th Meeting of Jean Piaget Society, Toronto, June.

Branco, A. U., Pinto, R., Pinheiro, M., & Bernardes, P. (2004b). *Motivação social na perspectiva de adolescentes do 1º ano do ensino médio* [Social motivation in junior High School adolescents]. Paper presented at the XXXIV Reunião da SBP, Ribeirão Preto, São Paulo, October.

Branco, A. U. & Rocha, R. (1998). A questão da metodologia na investigação científica do desenvolvimento humano [The issue of methodology in the scientific investigation of human development]. *Psicologia Teoria e Pesquisa*, 14 (3), 251–258.

Branco, A. U. & Salomão, S. (2001). Cooperação, competição e individualismo: pesquisa e contemporaneidade [Cooperation, competition and individualism: Research and contemporaneity]. *Temas em Psicologia da SBP*, 9 (1), 11–18.

Branco, A. U. & Valsiner, J. (1997). Changing methodologies: A co-constructivist study of goal orientations in social interactions. *Psychology and Developing Societies*, 9 (1), 35–64.

Branco, A. U. & Valsiner, J. (2004). *Communication and metacommunication in human development*. Greenwich, CT: Information Age Publishing.

Brockmeier, J. & Harré, R. (2001). Narratives: problems and promises of an alternative paradigm. In J. Brockmeier & D. Carbaugh (Eds.), *Narrative and identity: Studies in autobiography, self, and culture* (pp. 39–58). Amsterdam & Philadelphia: John Benjamins.

Bruner, J. (1997). *Atos de significação* [Acts of meaning]. Porto Alegre: ArtMed Editora.

Carone, I. & Bento, M. A. (2002). Psicologia social do racismo: estudos sobre branquitude e branqueamento no Brasil [Social psychology of racism: Studies on whiteness and whitening processes in Brazil]. Petrópolis, Rio de Janeiro: Vozes.

Chaiklin, S. (2001). *The theory and practice of cultural-historical psychology*. Aarhus: University of Aarhus.

Cole, M. (1998). *Cultural psychology: A once and future discipline*. Cambridge, MA: Harvard University Press.

Cole, M. & Cole, S. (2004). *O desenvolvimento da criança e do adolescente* [Development of children and adolescents]. Porto Alegre: ArtMed Editora.

Curry, R. O. & Goodheart, L. B. (1991). *American chameleon: Individualism in trans-national context*. London: Kent State University Press.

Damon, W. & Eisenberg, N. (1998). *Handbook of child psychology*, 5th edn: Vol. 3, *Social, emotional, and personality development*. New York: Wiley.

Damon, W. & Lerner, R. A. (1998). *Handbook of child psychology*, 5th edn: Vol. 1, *Theoretical models of human development*. New York: Wiley.

Deutsch, M. (1949). A theory of cooperation and competition. *Human Relations*, 2, 129–152.

DeVries, R., Zan, B., Hildebrandt, C., Edmiaston, R., & Sales, C. (2004). *O currículo construtivista na educação infantil: práticas e atividades* [Constructivist curriculum in early child education: Practices and activities]. Porto Alegre: ArtMed.

Dumont, L. (1985). *O individualismo: uma perspectiva antropológica da ideologia moderna* [Individualism: An anthropological perspective of modern ideology]. Rio de Janeiro: Rocco.

Fogel, A. (1993). *Developing through relationships. Origins of communication, self and culture*. Chicago: University of Chicago Press.

Fogel, A., & Branco, A. U. (1997). Metacommunication as a source of indeterminism in relationship development. In A. Fogel, M. Lyra, & J. Valsiner (Eds.), *Dynamics and indeterminism in developmental and social processes* (pp. 65–92). Hillsdale, NJ: Erlbaum.

Ford, D. H. & Lerner, R. M. (1992). *Developmental systems theory: An integrative approach.* London: Sage.

Foucault, M. (1996). *Microfísica do poder* [Microphysics of power]. Rio de Janeiro: Graal.

Goffman, E. (1974). *Frame analysis: An essay on the organization of experience.* Cambridge, MA: Harvard University Press.

Hermans, H. J. (2001). The dialogical self: Towards a theory of personal and cultural positioning. *Culture & Psychology*, 7 (3), 243–282.

Hinde, R. A. (1996). Describing relationships. In A. E. Auhagen & M. Salisch (Eds.), *The diversity of human relationships* (pp. 7–35). New York: Cambridge University Press.

Jares, X. R. (2002). *Educação para a paz: sua teoria e prática* [Peace education: Theory and practice]. Porto Alegre: ArtMed.

Johnson, D. W. & Johnson, R. T. (1989). *Cooperation and competition: Theory and research.* Minnesota: Interaction Book Company.

Jurberg, M. B. (2000). Individualismo e coletivismo na psicologia social [Individualism and collectivism in social psychology]. In *Paradigmas em psicologia social: a perspectiva latino-americana* [Paradigms in social psychology: A Latin American perspective]. Petrópolis: RJ: Vozes.

Lavelli, M., Pantoja, A. P. F., Hsu, H., Messinger, D., & Fogel, A. (2005). Using microgenetic designs to study change processes. In D. M. Teti (Ed.), *Handbook of research methods in developmental science* (pp. 40–65). Baltimore, MD: Blackwell.

Lawrence, J. A. & Valsiner, J. (1993). Conceptual roots of internalization: From transmission to transformation. *Human Development*, 36, 150–167.

Madureira, A. F. A., & Branco, A. U. (2005). Construindo com o outro: uma perspectiva sociocultural construtivista do desenvolvimento humano [Constructing with the other: A sociocultural constructivist perspective on human development]. In M. A. Dessen & A. L. Costa Jr. (Eds.), *A ciência do desenvolvimento humano: tendências atuais e perspectivas futuras* [The science of human development: Contemporary trends and future perspectives] (pp. 90–112). Porto Alegre: ArtMed.

Martins de Oliveira, I. (1994). *Preconceito e auto-conceito: identidade e interação em sala de aula* [Prejudice and self-esteem: Identity and interaction in the classroom]. Campinas, São Paulo: Papirus.

Maturana, H. & Varela, F. (1995). *A árvore do conhecimento* [The tree of knowledge]. Campinas: Workshopsy.

Matusov, E. (1998). When solo activity is not privileged: Participation and internalization models of development. *Human Development*, 41, 326–349.

McDermott, R. (1977). Social relations as contexts for learning in schools. *Harvard Educational Review*, 47 (2), 198–213.

Milani, F., & Branco, A. U. (2004). Assessing Brazil's culture of peace. *Peace and Conflict—APA (American Psychological Association)*, 10, 161–174.

Morin, E. (1999). Por uma reforma do pensamento [For a reform in thinking]. In A. Pena-Vega & E. P. Nascimento (Eds.), *O pensar complexo: Edgar Morin e a crise da modernidade* [Complex thinking: Edgar Morin and the crisis of modernity] (pp. 7–34). Rio de Janeiro: Garamond.

Morin, E. & Prigogine, I. (2000). *A sociedade em busca de valores* [Society in search for values]. Lisbon: Instituto Piaget.

Moscovici, S. (2007). *Psychoanalysis.* Cambridge: Polity Press.

Palmieri, M. W. (2003). *Cooperação,competição e individualismo na pré-escola: análise de contextos de desenvolvimento* [Cooperation, competition, and individualism in preschool: Analysis of developmental contexts]. Doctoral dissertation, University of Brasília.

Palmieri, M. & Branco, A. U. (2007). Educação infantil, cooperação e competição: análise microgenética sob uma perspectiva sociocultural [Early children education, cooperation, and competition: Microgenetic analysis from a sociocultural perspective]. *Psicologia Escolar e Educacional,* 11, 1–10.

Patto, M. H. S. (1999). *A produção do fracasso escolar: histórias de submissão e rebeldia* [The production of school failure: Histories of submission and rebellion]. São Paulo: Casa do Psicólogo.

Ratner, C. (2002). *Cultural psychology: Theory and method.* New York: Plenum.

Rey, F. G. (2003). *Sujeito e subjetividade:uma aproximação histórico cultural* [Subject and subjectivity: A historical-cultural approach]. São Paulo: Thompson.

Rogoff, B. (1990). *Apprenticeship in thinking: Cognitive development in social context.* Cambridge: Oxford University Press.

Rogoff, B. (2003). *The cultural nature of human development.* New York: Oxford University Press.

Rosenthal, R. & Jacobson, L. (1968). *Pygmalion in the classroom: Teacher expectation and pupils' intellectual development.* New York: Rinehart and Winston.

Salgado, J. & Hermans, H. (2005). The return of subjectivity: From a multiplicity of selves to the dialogical self. *E-Journal of Applied Psychology: Clinical Session,* 1 (1), 3–13.

Shweder, R. (1991). *Thinking through cultures: Expeditions in cultural psychology.* Cambridge, MA: Harvard University Press.

Shweder, R. A. & Much, N. C. (1987). Determinations of meaning: Discourse and moral socialization. In W. M. Kurtines & J. L. Gewirtz (Eds.), *Moral development through social interaction* (pp. 197–244). New York: Wiley.

Siegler, R. S. & Crowler (1991). The microgenetic method: A direct means for studying cognitive development. *American Psychology,* 46 (6), 606–620.

Sloan, T. (2005). Globalization, poverty, and social justice. In G. Nelson & I. Prilleltensky (Eds.), *Community psychology: In pursuit of liberation and well-being.* New York: Palgrave Macmillan.

Stambak, M. & Sinclair, H. (1993). *Pretend play among 3-year-olds.* Hillsdale, NJ: Erlbaum.

Staub, E. (1991). A conception of the determinants and development of altruism and aggression: Motives, the self, and the environment. In C. Zahan-Waxler, E. M. Cummings, & R. Iannotti (Eds.), *Altruism and aggression: Biological and social origins* (pp. 135–164). Cambridge: Cambridge University Press.

Tacca, M. C., & Branco, A. U. (2000). *Teach and learn: Co-creation of meanings in teacher–students interactions within structured contexts.* Paper presented at the III Conference for Sociocultural Research, July, Campinas, Brazil.

Tacca, M. C., & Branco, A. U. (in press). Processos de significação na relação professor-alunos: uma perspectiva sociocultural construtivista [Meaning processes in teacher–students' relationship: Sociocultural constructivist perspective]. *Psicologia em Estudo, UFRN.*

Tappan, M. B. (1992). Texts and contexts: Language, culture, and the development of moral functioning. In L. T. Winegar & J. Valsiner (Eds.), *Children's development within social context* (vol. 1, pp. 93–117). Hillsdale, NJ: Lawrence Earlbaum Associates.

Thelen, E., & Smith, L. (1998). Dynamic systems theory. In W. Damon & R. Lerner (Eds.), *Handbook of child psychology*, 5th edn: Vol. 1, *Theoretical models of human development* (pp. 563–634). New York: Wiley.

Triandis, H. C. (1995). *Individualism and collectivism.* San Francisco: Westview.

Valsiner, J. (1987). *Culture and the development of children's action.* Chichester: Wiley.

Valsiner, J. (1994). Culture and human development: A co-constructionist perspective. In P. van Geert & L. Mos (Eds.), *Annals of theoretical psychology*, vol. 10. New York: Plenum.

Valsiner, J. (2001). *Comparative study of human cultural development.* Madrid: Fundación Infancia y Aprendizaje.

Valsiner, J. (2005). Soziale und emotionale Entwicklungsaufgaben im kulturellen Kontext. In J. Asendorpf & H. Rauh (Eds.), *Enzyklopädie der psychologie*, Vol. 3, *Soziale, emotionale und Persönlichkeitsentwicklung.* Göttingen: Hogrefe.

Valsiner, J. (2007). *Culture in minds and societies.* New Delhi: Sage.

Valsiner, J., Branco, A. U., & Dantas, C. (1997). Socialization as Co-construction: Parental belief orientations and heterogeneity of reflection. In J. E. Grusec & L. Kuczynski (Eds.), *Parenting and children's internalization of values* (pp. 283–306). New York: Wiley.

Valsiner, J. & Cairns, R. (1992). Theoretical perspectives on conflict and development. In C. V. Shantz & W. W. Hartup (Eds.), *Conflict in child and adolescent development* (pp. 15–35). New York: Cambridge University Press.

Velho, G. (1987). *Individualismo e cultura.* Rio de Janeiro: Zahar.

Vygotsky, L. S. (1978). *Mind in society.* Cambridge, MA: Harvard University Press.

Vygotsky, L. S. (1986). *Thought and language*, 2nd edn. Cambridge MA: MIT Press.

Watzlavick, P., Beavin, J. H., & Jackson, D. (1967). *Pragmatics of human communication: A study of interactional patterns, pathologies and paradoxes.* New York: W. W. Norton.

Wertsch, J. W. (1998). *Mind as action.* New York: Oxford University Press.

Wertsch, J, del Rio, P., & Alvarez, A. (1998). *Sociocultural studies of the mind.* Cambridge: Cambridge University Press.

4 Childhood in Turkey

Social Class and Gender Differences in Schooling, Labor, and Play

Artin Göncü, Serap Özer and Nihal Ahioğlu

The sociocultural approaches to the study of child development have aptly illustrated that dominant Western theories do not take into account variations in childhood and thus lead to ethnocentric characterizations of children of the non-Western world. This is due to the fact that patterns proposed for Western children's development are seen as universal standards, and deviations from such patterns are interpreted as deficits or idiosyncrasies of the children of comparison in question. Examples of this stance can be seen easily in many different lines of research. For instance, previous cross-cultural research on children's pretend play interpreted some non-Western children's relative lack of involvement in this activity as an indication of children's deficit rather than a result of the conditions of context within which children grow up (Göncü & Gaskins, 2007).

A glance at the sociocultural research of the last decade quickly reveals that a number of factors such as the economical structure of children's communities, adult values, and children's gender, among many others, play a significant role in the activities available for children's participation and the appropriation of skills from them (e.g., Göncü, 1999; Rogoff, 2003; Tudge, 2008). That is, the presence of an activity or children's engagement in it is determined not only by children's abilities but also by whether or not such activity can be afforded by children's communities or is seen as appropriate for children's participation. For example, research on children's play indicates that middle-income Western and non-Western caregivers engage in play with their young children whereas rural caregivers do not participate in play due to lack of time and the value that play is children's business. Indeed, some of the variations are vividly present even in the same nation and at the same socioeconomic level. For example, research shows that while middle-class Irish-American caregivers see children's play as a developmentally appropriate teaching tool and participate in pretend play activities with their youngsters (Haight, 1999), Korean-American caregivers see play as a fun activity in which children engage when they do not have school work to do (Farver, 1999).

The present chapter aims to contribute to the evolving sociocultural stance that children's development can be best understood when it is examined in relation to the contexts in which it occurs. In order to make this case, we present different portrayals of childhood in Turkey. Our choice is motivated by several important factors. First, because of its geographical position, political history, and cultural lives, Turkey has always remained between the East and West, and this stance has led to internal tensions in Turkey. Currently, there are many conflicting voices regarding whether Turkey is a Western or a Middle Eastern nation as identification with one or the other has implications for a number of social policies. For example, from its promulgation of a constitution in 1923, Turkey emerged as a Western nation declaring that it is a secular nation and that men and women have equal rights. Despite this background, however, today's Turkey includes voices that call for integration of Islam into children's schooling, and qualifying individuals' freedom according to their gender and sexual orientation.

Second, Turkey is a country that is in the process of transformation from agricultural to industrial, from rural to urban, and from traditional to modern. These transformations are influenced by and reflect changes that occur at a global level. For example, Turkey aims to become a member of the European Union; it is struggling to improve its economical wealth, rate of literacy, and conditions of living, as it tries very hard to prepare its young population for its anticipated future. Different communities' responses to these kinds of external pressures combined with internal tensions result in contexts of childhood that can vary in Turkey from one neighborhood to another within a radius of a few miles. It is possible to observe an urban 7th grader who is going to school 35 hours a week, learning a foreign language, is going to special prep courses 14 hours a week, and getting special tutoring for selection exams for high school education during the remaining hours. It is also possible to see his/her rural counterpart who is spending all the hours that remain from school in "household chores" such as minding animals or working in the fields. Therefore, the exploration of childhood in Turkey provides evidence for our thesis that although different communities of children in Turkey share certain cultural features throughout the country, they live "next to" one another with their unique cultural traditions. Each community of children can be best understood only when they are examined in relation to their own contexts.

Our third reason for focusing on portrayals of childhood in Turkey relates to the fact that all three authors are originally from Turkey and received our undergraduate degrees there. This shared background enables us to use a common language in constructing this chapter. However, our ethnic and schooling differences situate us in a uniquely advantageous position of being able to compare different views within Turkey and to present their similarities to and differences from Western characterizations. Göncü is a Turk of Armenian ancestry, first-generation urban, and was educated in Turkish in public schools. He is a developmental psychologist who has been living in the United States for over 30 years and working as a professor of educational psychology and early childhood education. Özer is of Turkish ancestry from Greece and Albania, urban, and was educated in English in a private school. She has been working as a professor of clinical psychology in Turkey although she got her degree in the United States. Ahioğlu is also of

Turkish ancestry from Greece and Turkey, first generation urban, attended public schools, got her degree in Turkey, and has been working as a professor of education there.

The fourth reason why we decided to focus on Turkey is that although there is some work in the area of child development and education in Turkish, much of it is not available to non-Turkish speakers. With notable exceptions (e.g., Kağıtçıbaşı, 1996), Turkish scholars publish only in Turkish. Most of the published work in English focuses only on specific areas of child development such as play in early childhood (Göncü, 1993; Göncü, Jain, & Tuermer, 2007). Thus, it is our goal to make available for the international community knowledge about childhood in Turkey. In keeping with the focus of this book, we cover childhood from the preschool years up to eighth grade, 14 years of age. However, when necessary we make reference to adolescence as the boundaries between childhood and adolescence can shift depending on cultural expectations.

Our chapter is based on the theory of Vygotsky and activity theory (Leont'ev, 1981; Göncü, Tuermer, Jain & Johnson, 1999) stating that children's development can be best described as a process of their participation in and appropriation from cultural activity. Therefore, to understand what children learn, and how they do so, we need to identify the activities that are available to children. In addition, in following our thesis that the economic structure of children's communities, the adult values, the communication of adult values to children, and the cultural traditions influence children's activities, we seek to examine how such features of Turkish culture affect the types of activities afforded for children, and the kinds of skills children appropriate from those activities (Göncü et al., 1999, 2007).

This framework fits squarely with the types of pragmatic problems with which we are struggling in describing childhood in Turkey. As we discuss below, the three activities that vary along class and gender lines are schooling, income-producing labor and chores, and, to some extent, play. In addition, these three activities are those with which the international community of scholars and policy makers are also struggling. That is, none of schooling, play, or labor takes place as uniformly as was expected by Western theorists and policy makers (Rogoff, 2003; Tudge, 2008; Whiting & Edwards, 1988). Since participation in these activities raises important problems for Turkish caregivers and educators as they also raise problems at the global level, we focus on these three activities. In what follows, we first describe children's schooling and labor along with the legal context that set the stage for these activities. In discussing schooling we provide a general description of the structure of schools and classrooms, the nature of instruction, the curriculum, and offer some insights about teacher–student interactions. In the ensuing section, we describe the work life of children, the kinds of jobs children have, the apprenticeship system, and the power relations in work life as well as children's income. Finally, we provide a description of children's play activities, focusing on whether or how children's play in different institutions such as home and school receives support. We also discuss the kinds of play and games played by children in different communities. Our chapter ends with conclusions about how to advance the conditions of childhood in Turkey.

Schooling in Turkey

The Familial and Class Background of Schooling

It is helpful to begin with a general introduction to social class and gender differences in child-rearing at home and offer some population statistics, as this background facilitates understanding issues surrounding children's schooling, labor, and play. After this, we describe preschool and primary school education.[1]

According to the 2007 census, the population of Turkey is 71 million, with an average family size of 4.5, although this number can reach 7.5 in some eastern and low-income provinces. This is due to the fact that most families are extended. The primary reason for this appears to be economic. According to some Turkish scholars (e.g., İmamoğlu & İmamoğlu, 1992; İmamoğlu & Karakitapoğlu-Aygun, 2007; Kağıtçıbaşı, 1981, 1996), a collectivist stance towards life deriving from economic and emotional interdependence results in a large family size including children, parents, grandparents, and sometimes other relatives.

The economic interdependence common in low-income households influences values about family, and children's and women's places in specific terms (Ayyıldız, 2005; Kağıtçıbaşı, 1996; Miral, 1982; Özyurek, 2004). Women's primary roles are seen as contributing to family development and within-home labor (Hortaçsu, 1995; Kağıtçıbaşı, 1996). This has a direct influence on the availability of schooling for girls and women. Only 11 million women are graduates of primary school and there are 6 million women who are illiterate, with the majority of them living in rural eastern provinces. Of the adult female population, only 24 percent hold paid employment (TUIK [Turkish Statistical Institute], 2008a). Consistent with this pattern, low-income families value boys more than girls due to boys' potential contribution to the economic well-being of the family, although families at all income levels value boys due to the belief that generational continuity is maintained through the male line (Kağıtçıbaşı, 1981; TUIK, 2008b).

Historically, mothers are responsible for taking care of children regarding their health, nutrition, and social form of conduct while fathers and grandparents are responsible for decisions about children's education and schooling (Onur, 2007). Child-rearing at home emphasizes children's socialization into society with desires for children to have professions with high income, acquire appropriate conduct and traditions, and respect the elders (Ahioğlu, 2008). In general, parents follow a traditional reward-and-punishment pattern in teaching children both social and cognitive skills (Buldukoğlu & Kukulu, 2008; Gözütok, Er, & Karacaoğlu, 2006; Hortaçsu, Kalaycıoğlu, & Rittersberger-Tılıç, 2003; Kırcaali-İftar, 2005; Onur, 2007). Physical punishment is common at all SES levels. Approximately, 33 percent of families use physical punishment as a socialization device (TUIK, 2008b). This is so despite the fact that laws about children's rights strictly prohibit corporal punishment and state that control of children as such is punishable by law.

There are social class differences in families' provision of support for different areas of children's development. For example, low-income households that constitute 18 percent of the population provide less support for cognitive development than do middle-income families (Kağıtçıbaşı, 1981) although both low- and middle-income households provide support for language acquisition (Ahioğlu, 2007; Rogoff, Mistry, Göncü, & Moiser, 1993). Families in the mid- to high-income range value schooling and hold high educational aspirations for their children (Rogoff et al., 1993), provide activities and toys that support cognitive and physical development in the form of computers, educational books and toys, and private courses in music and sports (TUIK, 2008b). Low-income families tend to send their children to Quranic schools for them to receive religious education during their free time. However, sending children to Quranic schools is seen with increasing frequency in the middle-income range as well. In an effort to enhance education at home in low-income households, the ministries, universities, and civic organizations provide support programs such as the mother–child education project (Bekman & Gürlesel, 2005).

Preschool Education

The goals and substance of education in Turkey are determined by the Turkish Constitution and the Ministry of Education (MEB [Ministry of Education], 2008a).[2] In Turkey, preschool education is voluntary, and takes place in a number of different institutions including private schools, in preschools embedded in primary schools, and in those that are housed in social service agencies. Including the preschools established by the minorities and foreign organizations, there are 20,675 preschools, 33,213 classrooms, and 24,775 preschool teachers. The teachers are either college graduates with a degree in education or graduates of two-year vocational schools. The latter work only on contract bases and they are not included in the official statistics. That is why the statistics do not reflect the actual number of teachers serving in preschools. The educational program, as determined in 2005 by the Ministry of Education, is developmentally appropriate, emphasizing developmental and individual differences and is based on children's play and daily experiences rather than decontextualized academic learning. However, due to family pressures, in some preschools it is possible to find children being taught how to read and write, although this is not a priority of the proclaimed preschool education (Ayhan, Oğuz & Oktay, 2004). Family involvement is encouraged (Gürkan, 2003).

Although there are 7 million children between 3 and 5 years of age, of these only 640,849 children attend preschool (MEB, 2008b). The majority of the children who receive preschool education are between 5 and 6 years old. According to UNESCO, although the percentage of 3- to 5-year-old children who attend preschool in 203 nations averages 37 percent, this number is 8 percent in Turkey (UNESCO, 2006). However, according to the reports of MEB and TUIK, this rate is even lower and specified as 4.5 percent (Ural & Ramazan, 2007).

There are cultural and legal explanations for this low rate. Legally, preschool education is voluntary and therefore is not seen as necessary. This, combined with the high rate of poverty of 18 percent and the high tuition fees for preschool education, limits low-income children's attendance at preschool. However, initiatives by government and civic organizations for low-income families are leading to increases in low-income children's preschool attendance. All of this indicates that there is a gross inequality against the poor regarding preschool education.

Primary Education

In Turkey, primary education is for typically and non-typically developing children, it is required, and is free of charge. In the 2006–07 school year, there were 34,656 primary schools, 387,351 classrooms, 402,829 teachers, and 11 million children in primary schools.

Unfortunately, as these statistics indicate, there is a shortage of classrooms and teachers. In the 2006–07 academic year, 217,290 students had education in classrooms with 60 students, 660,177 students were in classrooms with 50–59 students, and 1,918,573 students received education with 40–49 other students. In other words, 28 percent of all students received education in classrooms with 40 or more students (Karip, 2007). The Ministry of Education is struggling to address the shortage of teachers and other limitations by providing transport, integrated classrooms, pilot programs, and boarding schools. Such programs are especially beneficial to children in eastern and rural Turkey.

The governmental policy for elementary education is described as "reaching, using, and reproducing knowledge." The program is defined as child-centered, encouraging critical thinking, creativity, problem-solving, communication, inquiry, decision-making, and improving interpersonal skills. In addition, the program encourages learning by doing in a cooperative manner. Thus, elementary education aims to support both academic and social growth in a child-centered manner.

However, elementary education as practiced is different from how it is proclaimed, a struggle that appears to be common in developing countries. (Also see Freitas, Shelton, & Sperb, this volume.) There are problems in elementary education in Turkey. These can be summarized as children who are excluded from elementary education, sex discrimination, physical punishment, and the examination for access to high school education. Regarding the former, although there has been an increase in the numbers of children who attend elementary schools, the schooling rate is lower in Turkey than it is in some other developing countries. There are 13 million children of elementary school age but according to 2006–07 statistics only 90 percent of children attend elementary school. In ten cities this rate is as low as 75 percent (TUIK, 2008c). Rural children and girls constitute the majority of children who have reduced access to elementary education.

Girls constitute 61 percent of children who are excluded from elementary education. The reasons for this include the differential valuation of girls and boys, the schooling of the parents, and income level. Traditional and religious values result in the expectation that girls should be good wives and mothers and, as a result, their schooling is not valued. Especially in low-income households, girls are expected to support their family income and assist in taking care of household chores; therefore, they are not allowed to attend school. Since primary education has become compulsory, girls' attendance in primary schools has increased, but the exclusion of girls from schooling and their dropout rate is still higher than that of boys. This difference is more noticeable between 6–7 and 12–13 years, i.e., between 1–2 and 6–7 grades (Kavak & Ergen, 2004).

Traditional values influence the ways in which children are "disciplined" in Turkish schools. As Onur (2005) states, physical punishment is a common way of controlling children in primary schools in Turkey, in a tradition that extends from the Ottoman era to the modern Turkish Republic. It is justified as a form of child education and rearing. Physical punishment is approved by parents who often say to the teachers "While you get his flesh, let me keep his bones only." In the case of girls, this belief becomes all the more textured in the Turkish equivalent of the saying "Save the rod, spoil the child" that is used only for girls. Gözütok, Er and Karacaoğlu (2006) stated that from 1992 to 2006, teachers used physical punishment with increasing frequency and increasing intensity.

Finally, the third problem that elementary education struggles with is the high school entrance examination. This examination determines which high school children will attend.[3] To prepare for this examination, children enroll in special courses, either private courses or courses offered by their schools. This puts their regular education on the back burner and results in stress and depression for the children.[4] In recent years, this system has been changed to include children's level of educational knowledge and skills, grade point average, and social skills, and such evaluations have begun to take place at grade 6 (MEB, 2008c). It is believed that focusing on the process of children's educational development instead of performance only on one test will prove to be a better assessment device and less stressful for children.

In summary, primary education is limited and limiting in Turkey. It privileges the urban as opposed to rural, high-income as opposed to low-income children, boys as opposed to girls. The recent efforts to promote education for low-income children and girls aim to promote their attendance and success in elementary education but their consequences remain to be seen. Also, the highly punitive educational system as observed in the increasing rate of corporal punishment does not allow the child-centered educational system espoused for elementary schools.

Child Labor in Turkey: Facts and Figures

Child Labor and Social Class

We start out by stating that the expectation of labor or any other economic contribution by children is almost nonexistent in urban, middle- and upper-income families in Turkey. Unlike in Western societies such as the U.S., in urban middle-income neighborhoods, it would be almost impossible to find a child who will wash cars, or baby-sit for a fee. Acceptance of a fee for such a job by a young person would be considered an insult to the family honor. Middle-class youngsters are not encouraged to get summer jobs and an attempt to do so is frowned upon. Children are told primarily that "their job is to get an education." If poverty is not an issue, parents are economically supportive of their children for quite a long time. Even college students are not expected to earn any money. They are only expected to fulfill their educational requirements, i.e., attend school.

Historically, children's participation in labor and household chores has been common in Turkey in low-income households or if children choose not to pursue high school education. Although there has been a decrease in children's participation in income-producing activity during the last decade, two recent recessions and migrations from rural to urban areas have contributed to demands on all members of the family to contribute economically (Bakırcı, 2002). As a result, children continue to participate in income-producing labor activity in rural areas, in low-income households, or if they do not pursue their schooling.

According to current Turkish laws, following the guidelines of the International Program for Elimination of Child Labor (IPEC) of the International Labor Organization (ILO), children under 15 years of age are not permitted to have gainful employment. Children who are 14 years old and have completed the primary level of education may engage in "light employment" that will not deter them from continuing their schooling or harm their health, mental, and moral development (Bakırcı, 2004). However, given the fact that 26 percent of Turkey's population is under age 14, and many of these children come from low-income households (TUIK, 2007), it is plausible to expect that many children may be involved in economic activities.

The existing statistics show a significant decrease in child labor in Turkey from 1994 to 2006. Child labor surveys conducted in 1994 indicated that 8.5 percent of children between 6–14 years were economically active and 24 percent were engaged in domestic chores. These figures showed significant improvement on the survey in 2006 (TUIK, 2006); the percentage of economically active children in this age group dropped to 2 percent. In addition, in 2006, 39 percent of children listed some household chores as their responsibilities.

Two points are worth noting about these statistics. First, a primary reason responsible for the drop in child employment that was observed in the figures from 1994 to 2006 is the legislative change that took place in 1997, which increased compulsory education years from five to eight (Dayıoğlu, 2006a). That is, children are now required to stay in school longer, therefore reducing the potential for work. Second, although it is difficult to determine whether "household chores" should be considered as child labor or family work, we feel that these activities should be considered as labor since they entail participating in income-producing labor such as working in the family fields, minding animals, and picking fruit from the trees. Although no direct pay is involved in these activities, families' livelihoods depend on them.

When we look at who does what kind of work at present, we see that girls comprise the majority of the children who participated in households chores (59 percent). Of the 6–14 year olds who were employed, the majority of them worked in agriculture (57 percent), and the majority of the children who were engaged in economic activity were from rural areas (73 percent) (TUIK, 2006). Most (38.4 percent) children state that they work to contribute to the family income, while others (20 percent) work to aid in the economic activity of the family in other ways (CSGB [Ministry of Work and Social Security], 2005). In households with a working child (under 18), the child's income was 13 percent of the total family income.

Many children live in low-income homes where parents have little schooling and a large number of children (Dayıoğlu, 2006b). In such families, schooling and employment are not seen as compatible. In the 6–17 age group, 68.5 percent of children who are employed are not in school. In contrast, of the 6–14 year olds who are in school, only 2 percent are economically active, and 39 percent are responsible for household chores (TUIK, 2006).

While these figures may provide some insight into child labor in Turkey, they may not fully reflect its reality and should be treated with caution for a number of reasons. For example, many who work on the street and in small shops in urban areas are invisible to the system. Also, children of rural families who do not own their land participate in labor along with their elders on the land of others and these children also do not figure in the statistics (CSGB, 2005). Finally, nomadic groups such as the Romany with working children do not appear in "household surveys" or "labor surveys" although it was found that in these families children's participation in work is not a choice but a way of life (Akkan, Karatay, Erel, & Gümüş, 2007). This is best illustrated in an interview with a father who stated: "How should I send that child to school, let's say I do, he gets off at noon, or afternoon, how am I supposed to put bread on the table? Who supports me? Of course I want a future for my child, but ... "[5] (Akkan et al., 2007, p. 77).

Child Labor and Gender

Although traditional values about gender roles are changing, they continue to influence how extensively girls are involved in activities outside of the home. Traditional values encourage girls to stay at home, act only as is deemed to be appropriate, and not be engaged in activity with unfamiliar people of the opposite sex. For example, Köksal and Lordoğlu (1993) reported that only very few adolescent girls worked as apprentices and those who did explained their working conditions as "selected by my father, owner is a friend of my father, looks after me." Also, there was a difference in the type of jobs held by girls and boys; girls worked in textiles while boys were in production-oriented activities (e.g., carpentry, upholstery, and auto maintenance). Also, Karatay (2000) reported that more than 90 percent of the children who worked on the streets in such jobs as vendors were boys. In contrast, in rural areas girls are represented more in household chores (64 percent of 6–14 year olds), consistent with the traditional female role in society and the socialization process for girls (Bolak, 2002). The negative relationship between poverty and school attendance is especially apparent for girls; that is, there is a tendency to keep boys in school, and this is in turn reflected in girls becoming "house workers" early on (Dayıoğlu, 2006b). It is very telling that 23.1 percent of the 12–14 age group were categorized as "housewives" in the 1994 Household Labor survey (Bakırcı, 2002).

Trade-Off Between Schooling and Labor: The Case of Apprenticeship

Historically, one of the pathways leading to adulthood has been the learning of a trade through apprenticeship. Children or young adults were placed into the hands of a "master craftsman" who did not "employ" these children in the true sense of the word, but "educated or guided" them in his craft such as shoe or jewelry making. In this system, children participate in the activity that Lave and Wenger (1991) called "peripheral participants," observing the master and engaging in the "fetch and carry" part of the trade. Gradually, they assume more central roles assisting the master, and eventually move on to the position of journeymanship where they are allowed to perform the trade under the approval of the master. They became master only when they can perform the trade independently.

Today it is still possible to see many Turkish children join the work force as apprentices between the ages of 13 and 18. They are expected to continue the theoretical part of their education at least one day a week in school. By law, they have to be paid 30 percent of minimum wage, and have social security benefits covered by the State. However, many of the children working as apprentices are outside of this formal system since many employer-masters wish to stay outside of registered, tax-paying formats (Ünlühisarcıklı, 2001). Usually, apprentices are children who did not wish to continue school or were unsuccessful in school. Existing data indicate that 63 percent of apprentices left school as a result of the conviction that the educational system would not provide them with the necessary chances for advancement (Köksal & Lordoğlu, 1993). Many of the children who work within this context indicate that they are not working for economic reasons. However, this claim needs to be taken with caution because research indicates that while 70 percent of these children claim that their income is not important for the family, more than 70 percent give part or all of their wages to their mothers (Köksal & Lordoğlu, 1993).

There are some gender differences in apprenticeship. Most of the male apprentices have selected this pathway to learn a trade and expect to build a future on it. In contrast, girls indicate that they are mostly working to save money for marriage or out of boredom. It seems that for girls apprenticeship is usually seen as an object of socialization, passing the time and earning money while waiting to get married; for boys it is an alternative to education in terms of building a future (Köksal & Lordoğlu, 1993).

Apprentices view their experiences as positive and report that they are learning a trade. However, at first glance they appear to spend their time in the fetch and carry part of the job that does not provide them with much training (Fidan, 2004). Existing preliminary work corroborates the self reports of apprentices indicating that 15- to 21-year-old apprentices show fewer clinical symptoms than their counterparts in school. It is possible that having a job contributes to their sense of identity, responsibility, and individuation (Bildik, Tamar, Vesek, Bukusoğlu & Aydın, 2005; Hocaoğlu, Kandil & Bilici, 2001). This preliminary finding should be interpreted with caution since depending on the area of industry, conditions may be detrimental to the psychological or even physical health of children (Akış, Irgil, Pala & Aytekin, 2004).

Although there have been some changes in the apprenticeship system, the basic form of skill acquisition remains the same. Learning by watching and imitating is still the main mode of traditional apprenticeship training. Feedback about apprentices' performance is a significant part of training. Feedback takes the form of didactic instruction and demonstration. In order for the apprentice to advance, the approval of the master is very important (Ünlühisarcıklı, 2001). Apprentice–master relations are typically authoritarian and power-imbalanced, entitling the master with the power to reward and punish the apprentice both in and out of trade. As a result of this, many apprentices indicate that they frequently feel fear of the verbal abuse they may face when they make a mistake (Fidan, 2004).

In summary, the patterns regarding child labor are consistent with patterns of schooling. Low-income children engage in income-producing labor in order to support their families while middle-income children attend school. As indicated earlier in the quote from the Romany father, even very low-income families desire their children to get schooling. Children leave school only if all the other options are closed to the family. Children may choose apprenticeship if the path to formal schooling is not open to them, and if they need income. Even in low-income households, girls' employment for income is not encouraged and they are expected to stay at home, working there, rather than go to school.

Children's Play

Children's play and games are studied less extensively than their schooling and labor. Parallel to the work in the Western world, the existing research focuses on the relation between play and other areas of development such as cognition and affect. There is a paucity of research on expression of play forms and their frequencies. This may be due to a number of factors. For example, play is often seen as a spontaneously occurring activity of childhood that does not need intervention. Also, the urgency with which children are encouraged to succeed in school or bring bread to the family table may gain greater research priority than play whose returns may not be so immediate. As we discuss below, this may be especially true for older children at all income levels.

Existing work indicates that urban middle-income families value young children's play and participate in it with enthusiasm. As revealed in their interviews, the caregivers' emphasis on play was motivated by mothers' schooling and knowledge that play contributes to children's development (Göncü, Mistry, & Mosier, 2000; Rogoff et al., 1993). We found that Turkish caregivers provided play opportunities and toys for their one- to two-year-old sons and daughters just like their Western counterparts. They became children's peers in play as they participated in this activity. Caregivers' support of play took many forms including pretend play (e.g., enacting social roles such as mother–baby role play), physical play (e.g., rolling on the floor), language play (e.g., making up words), object play (e.g., exploration and manipulation of objects), and games with rules (e.g., peek-a-boo). Moreover, they used play as an educational device in giving language lessons to their children. For example, a mother used the pictures on a pencil box in creating a language play experience for her child and giving a vocabulary lesson.

Regarding the play of Turkish preschool children, we do not know of studies that examine middle-class caregivers' values about or participation in the play of children. However, informal observations in high-income communities by all three authors indicate that a similar pattern of parental involvement continues during the preschool years. Families' involvement in play is ever-present both at home and also in the kind of preschools children attend. In the preschools that follow developmentally appropriate practice, free play is supported and instruction is provided through play. It is plausible to expect that peer interaction is encouraged more than adult involvement during this period.

It is interesting to note that children's play is valued and encouraged in low-income rural communities as well. Our work that described the play of children between 4 and 6 years in a village in Western Turkey illustrates this (Göncü, Tuermer, Jain, & Johnson, 1999; Göncü, Jain, & Tuermer, 2007). We designed the study to show that the occurrence and frequency of children's play as well as its meaning emerge as an extension of children's cultural heritage. This meant that both the examination and the interpretation of children's play need to take place according to the cultural priorities of children's communities. We observed children and their families with minimal interference after having become familiar with them. We also interviewed children's parents and relatives such as grandmothers when/if they were around and interested. We videotaped and then transcribed all the interviews and observations.

With regard to the caregivers' values about play, our analyses indicated that, in general, low-income caregivers value play for both boys and girls since, as they stated, play contributes to different areas of children's development. However, the low-income rural caregivers differed from their middle-income counterparts in that they did not think it was their business to participate in preschool children's play, stating that children play on their own with their siblings and friends, and that adults do not have time for play due to their work load. Finally, although they valued play they did not think about it in relation to children's schooling since preschool did not exist in this village.

Children engaged in a wide variety of play. Some of these kinds of play were like those found in Western theory and in the activities of Western children such as pretend play that occurred both with and without objects. When children used objects, these were often discarded materials such as chewing gum wrappings or materials that existed naturally such as mud and tree branches. Children had very few toys. Also, consistent with the Western children's activities, the Turkish village children engaged in physical play, and games with rules such as hide and seek.

In addition, and in keeping with our thesis, we found that children exhibited play forms that illustrated different features of their culture. We expected that play as a cultural activity would take place with the tools of cultural expression common in children's communities. In support of this, we found that children used features of oral traditions common in their community. The play forms that expressed this were language play, teasing, and sound and rhythm play. While language play has been observed in the play of Western children, the latter two were not mentioned previously or were not encouraged. For example, teasing is often interpreted as an insulting behavior and children are discouraged from teasing one another in middle-income Western schools. However, both sound and rhythm play and teasing appeared as legitimate cultural play forms in this Turkish community. Teasing often occurred as mock insult while sound and rhythm play involved improvising the intonation pattern of language or simply playing with music.

Based on these findings we concluded that play is valued by low-income Turkish villagers and is encouraged as a peer activity. Moreover, play is influenced by children's culture and may have both universal and local manifestations. This finding corroborated a historical study indicating that children's war games have reflected cultural traditions since Ottoman times (Onur, 2007). Finally, our findings suggest that play is seen as a legitimate activity for both boys and girls during infancy and the preschool years.

Unfortunately, there is only very limited research addressing the play of Turkish children during the elementary school years. In one notable study, Artar, Onur and Çelen (2002) interviewed 10-year-old village children, their parents, and grandparents with the purpose of examining generational changes in the occurrence and frequency of games with rules. The authors reported that both the kinds of games and the frequency of occurrence decreased from the first to the third generation (i.e., the children). The first generation learned the games mostly through observation or participation while the third generation learned through instruction. Gender differences were apparent in where children played the games, what materials they used, and in game preferences. The first two generations did not know about store-bought toys whereas the third generation almost always used ready-made toys. All three generations reported that parents did not play games with them. Nor did they intervene in children's games. Parents worked and they expected children of this age to do work such as minding the animals, working in the fields, and cooking. Consistent with Göncü et al. (1999), the authors concluded that children's games are influenced by their economic and cultural context, and that the decreasing frequency of games and children's reliance on ready-made toys revealed that the local meaning of childhood is being replaced by that which is introduced to Turkey through the free market economy and globalization.

We found only one study that examined the play of Turkish urban children during the elementary school years. In a naturalistic observational study, Çok, Artar, Şener, and Bagli (2004) examined children's games in school yards and on the streets in low-, middle-, and high-income communities in Ankara. The study was conducted to examine socioeconomic status (SES) and gender differences in the kinds and frequency of games played by the 6- to 12-year-old children of the capital of Turkey. The findings revealed both social class and gender differences. Children in the low SES neighborhood played on the streets more than did children in the upper SES. The authors interpreted this difference as indicating that the upper-income children had other resources than the streets to rely on while the low SES children needed the community for their play. There were also differences in the themes expressed in the games; the low SES children expressed traditional themes more than the upper SES children did, although children at all SES levels included themes from popular culture in their games. The authors found that games were gender segregated at all SES levels: girls played with other girls while boys preferred to play with other boys.

What remains as a mystery is what happens to the play of children after 12 years of age. While we do not have data to support the following claim we have poignant observations to state that for different reasons in both middle- and low-income communities play decreases as children get older. In urban middle-income households, the pressure put on children to perform successfully in high school entrance examinations leads to lessening of play involving peers. In these families, children appear to use the internet as an outlet in their solo worlds. In low-income families the pressure is even harder; we suspect children are expected to do well both in school and in their income-producing labor although they end up in labor. It may well be that the absence of research on the play of older urban children is an indication of the sad expectation that play in these communities is in danger of extinction.

In conclusion, as we stated in the beginning, our analyses show that children's activities are determined by the economic and value contexts of their communities. As such, depending on the income level of children and adult values about children and their gender, the activities afforded to children vary. Turkey is a rapidly changing, dynamic young country reflecting a transition from a traditional, extended, rural, and interdependent family system to a Western, urban, nuclear family system where independence and individuation are valued (Kağıtçıbaşı, 1996). It is frequently assumed that a shift from one to the other will take place with modernization and socioeconomic development. However research from collectivistic cultures such as Turkey indicates that other syntheses are possible, extending and nuancing the continuum. For example, in one such synthesis there emerges an "emotional interdependence" in middle-income communities where material interdependence and the value of the child as an economic asset cease but psychological value and emotional dependence and needs for closeness continue. Looking at children's schooling, labor, and play from this perspective, we can conclude that in the sections of society where poverty is effective, where there are difficulties meeting basic needs, being a collectivist culture requires children to do their part, i.e., contribute to the economical advancement of family at the expense of school and play. In such collectivistic low-income communities, childhood is not accorded a special, distinctive, and protected place. In contrast, in other layers of the society where the education level and earning power of the parents increase, children are expected to do their part in terms of getting the best education possible that not only will help their future but will also elevate the social status and prestige of the family. In these family structures there is warmth, emotional expression and a decrease in authoritarian control (Sunar, 2002). The result of these values and child-rearing practices would be the "autonomous-relational self" as defined by Kağıtçıbaşı (1996) where the child has an agency as she or he maintains affective ties with the family. As such, the urban Turkish middle-class family seems to have made a synthesis of some of the positive aspects of collectivist and individualistic societies (Sunar, 2002).

That said, we also feel that Turkey has the following important challenges ahead: 1) Traditional gender roles and increasing religious emphasis disadvantage girls affording them lesser opportunities and power in society than boys (e.g., Bolak, 2002). If Turkey wants to remain loyal to its constitution that men and women have equal rights, this gender inequality should be overcome. 2) If Turkish caregivers and teachers want to honor children's rights and treat children as human beings with dignity, they should abandon physical punishment. 3) In a similar vein, children's participation in labor should be conducted only according to laws without abusing them.

Notes

1 The terms primary and elementary school will be used interchangeably.
2 As such, formal education in Turkey consists of preschool education (3–5 years), primary education (6–14 years), high school education (15–18 years) and higher education.
3 There are three types of high schools in Turkey: private with an emphasis in a foreign language with high tuition and fees; government high schools with an emphasis in a foreign language that are free of charge; and government high schools with education in Turkish. The first and the second require passing a highly competitive entrance examination; the second is desired by the largest segment of society since it is free.
4 One assistant principal alluded to the damage caused by this exam by stating that "children have become race horses" as a result of this competition.
5 The father means that if the child goes to school, he will not have time to work.

References

Ahioğlu, E. N. (2007). Alt Sosyoekonomik Düzeydeki Ailelerde Anne, Baba ve Kardeşler ile 4–5 Yaşlarındaki Çocuklar Arasındaki Bilişsel Etkileşimler [Cognitive interactions between parents, siblings and children of 4–5 years at low socioeconomic level]. Unpublished Doctoral Thesis, Ankara Universitesi, Egitim Bilimleri Enstitüsü, Egitim Bilimleri Anabilimdalı, Ankara.

Akış, N., Irgil, E., Pala, K., & Aytekin, H. (2004). Gemlik çiraklik eğitimi merkezinde çalişan çocuklarin çalişma koşulları ve sorunları [Work conditions and problems of children working in the Gemlik apprenticeship center], *Türkt Tabipleri Birliği Mesleki Sağlık ve Güvenlik Dergisi* 15–20.

Akkan, B. E., Karatay, A., Erel, B., & Gümüş, G. (2007). *Romanlar ve sosyal politika* [Romanys and social politics]. Istanbul: Cem Ofset.

Artar, M., Onur, B., & Çelen, N. (2002). Çocuk Oyunlarında Üç Kuşakta Görülen Değişimler [Changes in children's games through three generations]. *Çocuk Forumu*, 5 (1), 35–39.

Ayhan, H., Oğuz A. & Oktay, A. (2004). *21. Yüzyılda Eğitim ve Türk Eğitim Sistemi* [Education in the 21st century and the Turkish Educational System]. Istanbul: Dem Yayınları.

Ayyıldız, T. (2005). Zonguldak il merkezinde 0–6 yas çocugu olan annelerin çocuk yetiştirme tutumları [Child-raising attitudes of the mothers of 0–6 year old children in the centrum of Zonguldak]. Unpublished Master's thesis, Zonguldak Karaelmas Universitesi, Saglık Bilimleri Enstitüsü, Çocuk Saglığı ve Hastalıkları Hemsireligi Anabilim Dalı, Zonguldak.

Bakırcı, K. (2002). Child labour and legislation in Turkey. *International Journal of Children's Rights*, 10: 55–72.

Bakırcı, K. (2004). Türkiye'de çocuk ve genç İşçiliği [Child and youth labor in Turkey]. *Görüş*, 3, 52–56.

Bekman, S. & Gürlesel, C. F. (2005). *Doğru Başlangıç: Türkiye'de Okul Öncesi Eğitim* [Right beginning: Preschool education in Turkey]. Istanbul: TÜSİAD.

Bildik, T., Tamar, M., Vesek, S. Bukusoğlu, N. & Aydın, C. (2005). The mental health of young workers: A pilot study. *Social Behavior and Personality*, 33, 295–306.

Bolak, H. (2002). Family work in working class households in Turkey. In R. Liljeström, & E. Özdalga (Eds.), *Autonomy and dependence in the family. Turkey and Sweden in critical perspective* (pp. 239–263). Istanbul: Swedish Resarch Institute in Istanbul.

Buldukoğlu, K. & Kukulu, K. (2008). Maternal punishment practices in a rural area of Turkey. *Child: Care, Health and Development,* 34 (2) 180–184.

Çok, F., Artar, M., Şener, T. & Bagli, M. (2004). Kentlerdeki Açik Alanlarda Çocuk Oyunlari: Ankara Örneği[Children's outdoor games in the cities]. In B. Onur & N. Güney (Eds.), *Türkiye'de Çocuk Oyunları: Araştırmalar* [Children's play in Turkey: Studies] (pp. 73–82). Ankara: A.U. Cocuk Kültürü Araştırma ve Uygulama Merkezi Yayınları.

CSGB (2005). *Türkiye'de çocuk işçiliği : Sorun bizim* [Child labor in Turkey: The problem is ours]. Istanbul: Work and Social Security Ministry publications.

Dayıoğlu, M. (2006a). Patterns of change in child labour and schooling in Turkey: The impact of compulsory schooling. *Oxford Development Studies,* 33, 195–211.

Dayıoğlu, M. (2006b). The impact of household income on child labor in urban Turkey. *Journal of Developmental Studies,* 42, 939–956.

Farver, J. A. M. (1999). Activity setting analysis: A model for examining the role of culture in development. In A. Goncu (Ed.), *Children's engagement in the world: Sociocultural perspectives* (pp. 99–127). New York: Cambridge University Press.

Fidan, F. (2004). Psychological and social aspects of the child labor question. *Trakya Universitesi Sosyal Bilimler Dergisi,* 4, 30–49.

Göncü, A. (1993). Guided participation in Kecioren. In B. Rogoff, J. Mistry, A. Göncü, & C. Mosier, *Guided participation in cultural activity by toddlers and caregivers.* Monographs of the Society for Research in Child Development, 58, (7, Serial No. 236, pp. 126–147).

Göncü, A. (Ed.) (1999). *Children's engagement in the world: Sociocultural perspectives.* New York: Cambridge University Press.

Göncü, A. & Gaskins, S. (Eds.) (2007). *Play and development: Evolutionary, sociocultural, and functional perspectives.* Mahwah, NJ: LEA.

Göncü, A., Jain, J., & Tuermer, U. (2007). Children's play as cultural interpretation. In A. Göncü, and S. Gaskins (Eds.), *Play and development: Evolutionary, sociocultural, and functional perspectives* (pp. 155–178). Mahwah, NJ: LEA.

Göncü, A., Mistry, J., & Mosier, C. (2000). Cultural variations in the play of toddlers. *International Journal of Behavioral Development,* 24, 321–329.

Göncü, A., Tuermer, U., Jain, J., & Johnson, D. (1999). Children's play as cultural activity. In A. Göncü, (Ed.), *Children's engagement in the world: Sociocultural perspectives* (pp. 148–170). Cambridge University Press.

Gözütok, F. D., Er, K. O., & Karacaoğlu, C. (2006). *Okulda Dayak (1992 ve 2006 Yılları Karşılaştırması* [Physical punishment in school: 1992 and 2006 comparison] *Bilim ve Aklın Aydınlığında Eğitim,* No. 75.

Gürkan, T. (2003). *Okul Öncesi Eğitim Programının Temel Özellikleri. Ne Yapıyorum? Neden Yapıyorum? Nasıl Yapmalıyım?* [The foundations of preschool education; What am I doing? Why? How should I do it?]. Istanbul: YA-PA Yayınları, 78–97.

Haight, L. W. (1999). The pragmatics of caregiver–child pretending at home: Understanding culturally specific socialization practices. In A. Göncü (Ed.), *Children's engagement in the world: Sociocultural perspectives* (pp. 128–147). New York: Cambridge University Press.

Hocaoğlu, Ç., Kandil, S. T., & Bilici, M. (2001). Çiraklik eğitim merkezi öğrencileri ile orta öğrenim öğrencilerinin ruhsal durumlari üzerine karşilaştirmali bir çalişma [A comparative study looking at the psychological situations of apprentice students and secondary level students], *Ibni Sina Tıp Dergisi,* 6, 161–169.

Hortaçsu, N. (1995). Parents' education level, parents' beliefs and child outcomes. *Journal of Genetic Psychology*, 156 (3), 373–383.

Hortaçsu, N., Kalaycıoğlu, S., & Rittersberger-Tılıç, H. (2003). Intrafamily aggression in Turkey: Frequency, instigation, and acceptance. *Journal of Social Psychology*, 10, 145–161.

ILO IPEC Reports (2008). http://www.ilo.org/public/turkish/region/eurpro/ankara/programme/ipec.htm.

İmamoğlu, E. O. & İmamoğlu, V. (1992). Life situations and attitudes of the Turkish elderly toward institutional living within a cross-cultural perspective. *Journal of Gerontology: Psychological Sciences*, 47, 102–108.

İmamoğlu, E. O. & Karakitapoğlu-Aygun, Z. (2007). Relatedness of identities and emotional closeness with parents across and within cultures. *Asian Journal of Psychology*, 143, 2, 163–184.

Kağıtçıbaşı, C. (1981). Çocuğun değeri: Türkiye'de değerler ve doğurganlık [The value of children in Turkey]. Istanbul: Bogazici University Press.

Kağıtçıbaşı, Ç. (1996). *Family and human development across cultures: A view from the other side*. Mahwah: NJ: Lawrence Erlbaum Associates.

Karatay, A. (2000). İstanbul'un sokakları ve çalışan çocuklar (The streets of Istanbul and working children). *1. İstanbul Çocuk Kurultayı Araştırmalar* Kitabı [1. Istanbul Child Symposium Research Book]. Istanbul: Istanbul Çocukları Vakfı.

Karip, E. (2007). İlköğretimde Kalite: Avrupa Birliği Kalite Göstergeleri Çerçevesinde Kalitenin Değerlendirilmesi. TED Egitimde Yeni Ufuklar III Sempozyumu: "Okul Öncesi Egitim ve Ilköğretimin Sorunlari: Gelecege Bakis." 12–13 Nisan, Ankara.

Kavak, Y. & Ergen, H. (2004). *Türkiye'de ilköğretime katilim ve okula gidemeyen cocuklar.* [Participation in primary education in Turkey and children who cannot go to school], TED Egitimde Yeni Ufuklar II: Egitim Hakki ve Okula Gidemeyen Çocuklar Sempozyumu, 3–4 Aralık, Türk Egitim Dernegi, Ankara.

Kırcaali-İftar, G. (2005). How do Turkish mothers discipline children? An analysis from a behavioural perspective. *Child: Care, Health and Development*, 31, 2, 193–201.

Köksal, S. E. & Lordoğlu, K. (1993). *Geleneksel çıraklıktan çocuk emeğine: Bir alan Araştırması* [From traditional apprenticeship to child labor: A field study]. Istanbul: FES.

Lave, J. & Wenger, E. (1991). *Situated learning: Legitimate peripheral participation.* New York: Cambridge University Press.

Leont'ev, A. N. (1981). *Activity, consciousness, and personality.* Englewood Cliffs, NJ: Prentice-Hall.

MEB (2008a). Türk Milli Eğitim Sistemi. http://www.meb.gov.tr/duyurular/duyurular2006/takvim/egitim_sistemi.html, accessed 01.28.2008.

MEB (2008b). Milli Eğitim İstatistikleri.http://sgb.meb.gov.tr/istatistik/meb_istatistikleri_orgun_egitim_2006_2007.pdf, accessed 01.28.2008

MEB (2008c). 64 Soruda İlköğretime Geçiş Sistemi ve Seviye Belirleme Sınavı Örnek Sorular. http://oges.meb.gov.tr/ (accessed 05.05.2008).

Miral, S. (1982). Üç değişik sosyo-kültürel kesimde çocuk yetiştirme tutumlarının araştırılması. [Exploration of child rearing attitudes in three different socioeconomic groups]. Unpublished Medical Proficiency Thesis. Ege Üniversitesi Tıp Fakültesi, İzmir.

Onur, B. (2005). *Türkiye'de çocukluğun tarihi* [History of childhood in Turkey]. Ankara: Imge Yayınevi.

Onur, B. (2007). *Çocuk, tarih ve toplum* [Child, history and society]. Ankara: Imge Yayınevi.

Özyurek, A. (2004). Kırsal bölge ve şehir merkezinde yaşayan 5–6 yaş grubu çocuğa sahip anne-babaların çocuk yetiştirme tutumlarının incelenmesi [Researching the child-rearing attitudes of rural and urban parents with 5–6 year old children]. Unpublished Master's Thesis. Gazi Üniversitesi, Eğitim Bilimleri Enstitüsü, Ankara.

Rogoff, B. (2003). *The cultural nature of human development.* New York: Oxford University Press.

Rogoff, B., Mistry, J., Göncü, A., & C. Mosier. (1993). Guided participation in cultural activity by toddlers and caregivers. *Monographs of the Society for Research in Child Development*, 58 (7, Serial No. 236).

Sunar, D. (2002). Change and continuity in the Turkish middle class family. In R. Liljeström & E. Özdalga (Eds.) *Autonomy and dependence in the family. Turkey and Sweden in critical perspective.* Istanbul: Swedish Resarch Institute in Istanbul.

Tudge, J. (2008). *The everyday lives of young children: Culture, class, and child rearing in diverse societies.* New York: Cambridge University Press.

TUIK, (2006). *State Institute Statistics News Bulletin*, 61.

TUIK, (2007) State Institute of Statistics. Yaş grubu ve cinsiyete gore Türkiye nüfusu [Turkish population based on age and sex], accessed 01.02.2008, http://tuikapp. tuik.gov.tr/adnksdagitimapp/adnks.zul.

TUIK (2008a). State Institute of Statistics. Population, Housing and Demography. http://www.turkstat.gov.tr/Start.do;jsessionid=RgjkLgQWnFBPYZfLWqJbJnx Q9Jw1sMhyxR0brzR23BNn8Vxn1vQz!-2099033630, accessed 01.02.2008.

TUIK (2008b). State Institute of Statistics. Population, Housing and Demography: Family Structure. http://www.turkstat.gov.tr/VeriBilgi.do?tb_id=64&ust_id=11, accessed 01.01.2008.

TUIK (2008c). State Institute of Statistics. Education, Culture and Sport Statistics. http://www.turkstat.gov.tr/Start.do;jsessionid=RgjkLgQWnFBPYZfLWqJbJnx Q9Jw1sMhyxR0brzR23BNn8Vxn1vQz!-2099033630, accessed 01.02.2008.

UNESCO (2006). Strong Foundations: Early Childhood Education, EFA Global Monitoring Report. http://www.unesco.org/education/GMR/2007/Full_ report.pdf, accessed 28.01.2008.

Ünlühisarcıklı, O. (2001). Training on the job in Istanbul: A study of skills acquisition in carpentry and car-repair workshops, *International Review of Education*, 47, 5 (pp. 443–458).

Ural, O. & Ramazan, O. (2007). Türkiye'de Okul Öncesi Eğitiminin Dünü ve Bugünü. [The yesterday and today of early education in Turkey], TED Egitimde Yeni Ufuklar III Sempozyumu: "Okul Öncesi Egitim ve Ilkögretimin Sorunlari: Gelecege Bakis." 12–13 Nisan, Ankara.

Whiting, B. B. & Edwards, C. P. (1988). *Children of different worlds: The formation of social behavior.* Cambridge, MA: Harvard University Press.

5 A Cultural-Historical Reading of "Children as Researchers"

Marilyn Fleer and Gloria Quiñones

> To what extent are children recognized as citizens and as active members of the community who can be included within, rather than excluded from, the communitarian agenda of the recent government? (James & James, 2001, p. 214)

Many governments around the world are seeking to gather children's perspectives and through this gain insights into how to organise, manage and design community resources (see Gallagher, 2004). For example, in Ireland two major studies were undertaken to document and pay attention to the perspective of young children and youth in policy, planning and reform. A follow-up study was also undertaken by the National Children's Office, the Children's Rights Alliance and the National Youth Council of Ireland (2005) to gain insights into how to create, plan and invite children's participation in the development of policy participation and consultation. In one of the projects children were invited to be members of a Development Committee which sought to design the use of space in a family support building in order to create a child-friendly environment.

Research that focuses on "children's voices" in the development of policy in the UK has been enshrined in the UK Children Act (1989) (James & James, 2001). The Act acknowledges "children's voice and agency" but in their analysis of how the Act is operationalised, James and James (2001) argue that although 'children (are) having more, rather than less rights of participation' (p. 212), and according to Komulainen (2007) their voices are 'still not taken into account in decision-making processes that directly affect children's lives' (p. 11). In contrast to Komulainen (2007), Oberg and Ellis (2006) suggest there is a new paradigm for doing research that respects children's perspectives and gives a voice to children through a range of opportunities and choices for expressing their views.

In this chapter, we present a discussion of the methodology and methods for a study which was commissioned by the City of Melville (pseudonym) to find out children's leisure, sport and recreational needs so that resourcing and policy changes could be made to make the City of Melville a more "child-friendly city". Through this case example we discuss the concept of "children as researchers" in order to illustrate and critique this trend in minority rich countries. We seek to actively move away from what Diaz Soto and Swander (2005) have called "imperial eyes":

> Research "through imperial eyes" describes an approach that Western ideas about the most fundamental things are the only ideas possible to hold, certainly the only rational ideas, and the only ideas that can make sense of the world, reality, of social life, and of human beings. (p. 2)

Children as Researchers: Approaches and Assumptions

Several researchers have investigated a range of methods for hearing "children's voices" (e.g. Clark, 2004; Hatzinikolaou & Mitakidou, 2005; Martinez-Roldan, 2005; Sun, 2005; Swander, 2005). One of the techniques frequently used for designing research with children involves photographs. Cook (2007) aimed to construct a fun methodology with cameras as the main data collection tool. This research acknowledges children's perspectives and focuses on shifting into a more "child-centric research focus". Photographs were used as a "way of hearing children's voices". Cook (2007) suggests that photographs can represent children's thoughts and understandings.

Punch (2002) argues that the way in which researchers perceive childhood and view children, influences how they position children in the research, and therefore how the children are ultimately understood. Researchers that view children as social actors think about research methods which are child-friendly. Punch (2002) argues that child-friendly research tools include drawings, photographs, PRA (participatory rural appraisal) techniques, spider diagrams and activity tables, diaries, worksheets, and combining visual and written techniques with traditional methods.

Another perspective for listening to young children, known as the "Mosaic Approach", has been proposed by Clark (2004, 2005). The Mosaic Approach uses integrated techniques to combine the visual and the verbal (Clark, 2004, 2005). Triangulated documentation includes observations, child conferencing, cameras (photographs), tours, map making, and interviews. It is argued that all these techniques lead the researcher towards better understanding children's priorities.

Jones (2004) suggests that research methods that position the child as central involve locating the child in an educational journey which features inquiry and exploration. Jones (2004) argues that researchers must pay attention to how an institution initiates children's involvement in research. Jones (2004) believes that little thought is given to the positioning of children within a study design. In contrast, Kellett (2005) argues that some researchers strongly position children as researchers and support children with using their own natural "inquisitive methods" to become actors of research. For instance, Kellett (2005) fostered in children the idea of children (10–14 years old) thinking of themselves as researchers, and through this supported them to benefit from being researchers engaging with improving their own learning context.

Barker and Willis (2003) describe from a geographical perspective how "children as researchers" can examine space. In drawing upon a multi-method approach, they argue that it is more likely that children from different ages, background and abilities will be engaged, and through this the diversity of experiences of children will be reflected in the data generated.

Researchers are actively seeking ways in which to engage children in the research process. Those discussed above illustrate a diversity of approaches for involving children in research. Their motives for this engagement vary, from providing research methods which "work with children" through to discussing the philosophical and ethical dimension of either involving or excluding children from the research process.

There are basic assumptions that we believe underpin the movement towards "children as researchers" which have not been adequately questioned. Through exploring these assumptions, we can better understand and limit how the concept of "children as researchers" may be positioned in our own work. First, the trend to "hear children's voices" has proliferated in many European and European heritage communities. It is likely that countries which use childrearing practices which separate children out from their communities (see Rogoff, 2003) must find ways of "re-introducing children" back into their communities when undertaking research. As such, the concept of "hearing children's voices" must be understood within its own cultural communities, where children have traditionally not had responsibilities (e.g. shared in home and community work and events) or have been isolated from their communities through sleeping arrangements (e.g. separate bedrooms), and specialised care and learning institutions (e.g. childcare). Jipson and Jipson (2005) have also noted that differences between rural and city life are important factors in research, where working on the farm means everyone pitching in, which is very different to growing up in cities where much of the paid work takes place away from children's lives. They argue that how children and therefore childhood is conceptualised is based on researchers' own personal experiences of childhood or is "socially transmitted within academic disciplines as part of the cultural capital of their fields" (p. 37). Komulainen (2007) argues that the 'notion of the child's "voice" is, despite being a powerful rhetorical device, socially constructed' (p. 11).

Further, the children's consultation culture that has emerged is premised upon an ideology that simply listening to children equates with generating robust research data. James (2007) in drawing upon the critiques and developments in anthropology, has argued most convincingly that "giving voice to children" 'masks a number of important conceptual and epistemological problems' (p. 261). She argues that there is a real problem of translation, interpretation and mediation of children's voices. How do researchers deal with the diversity of children's comments, experiences and lives – are they clumped together under the singular category of children's voices? Gutierrez-Gomez (2005) illustrates how Spanish-speaking children respond, rather than remain silent, when their own language is used. Do researchers organise their research tools in ways which engage culturally diverse children, and allow culturally diverse responses to be given and categorised beyond a single "children's voice"? Malewski (2005) claims that 'uncritical approaches to knowledge production' often 'equate equal treatment across social groups with equality', leaving diversity unnoticed (p. 217).

James (2007) thoughtfully asks the question 'does such research carried out by children necessarily represent a more accurate or authentic account of children's issues that can better inform policy' simply because they are children (pp. 262–263)? James (2007) in referring to Geertz (1988) discusses the concept of "ethnographic ventriloquism" where 'the claim to speak not just about another form of life but to speak from within it' (Geertz, 1988, cited in James, 2007, p. 145) is prevalent and can be problematic, and she notes that without careful methodological considerations, "children as researchers" could become a form of ventriloquism.

A Cultural-Historical Approach to Studying Children: the Dialectical Relations Between Children, Their Families and Their Communities

Much of the contemporary literature in early childhood research has drawn upon the sociology of childhood and has focused our attention on how children have been traditionally positioned within the research process – as subjects rather than active agents (see Diaz Soto, 2005). The discussions have found traditional research wanting, and in working beyond a postmodern perspective, the published works have offered new insights into undertaking research with young children (James & Prout, 1997). This literature strongly advocates that young children be given a voice in the research process, and that this voice holds a privileged position within the outcomes of the research – with some suggesting that a child's perspective is the central and only voice to be considered. We have been inspired by these discussions, because we also think that the child's perspective has not been sufficiently discussed in research (Punch, 2002). However, we are also mindful that the child-centered perspective has tended to only give one view among a range of potential perspectives (see Komulainen, 2007), including the family perspective, the teacher's perspective and the researcher's perspective (see Hedegaard, 2005a). By singling out "the child" and only focusing the research lens on "the child", we believe that a form of individualism is foregrounded, silencing important interactions and contexts which shape and are shaped by the child's engagement in the world. These engagements give meaning to the child's perspective, and therefore cannot be excluded from research. As such, we have drawn upon cultural-historical theory because it offers other possibilities for positioning children in the research, without compromising the "voice of the child". We believe this will allow us to recast the lens to the "many voices of the culturally diverse children" that participate in research.

A cultural-historical approach to studying children in everyday settings allows researchers to move beyond just studying the child's perspective on the particular societal conditions they are located in – as is common in contemporary sociologically inspired research projects on the "child as researcher". Cultural-historical theory allows researchers to not just study children's everyday life from the child's perspective, but it focuses on transcending these settings by generating concepts from the research. In particular, cultural-historical research seeks to map the motives, goals, and values of all the participants. In drawing upon Hedegaard's (2005a) seminal theorisation of cultural-historical research, we come to better understand how investigations are dialectically framed to capture the perspective of teachers, the families, the institutions the child attends, and the community. The latter are framed around the cultural practices which shape what communities invite their children to pay attention to in learning the goals, values and motives within that society.

Cultural-historical research positions the child in the study in ways which allow for the child's voice or perspective to be heard. However, at the same time cultural-historical research also captures the other perspectives of the participants so that it is possible to illuminate the institutional and cultural conditions that create the social situation that the child is in. It is only possible to understand the child's perspective when the other conditions which give meaning to the child's voice or which are illustrations of what the child has voiced, are also gathered. It is necessary to gather other perspectives, in order to study how the child participates in the social settings and how others contribute to the child's interactions. In this way it is possible to investigate the social situation of the child, and to therefore be able to interpret the child's perspective – so that *the voice of the child is not just heard, but understood.*

The central tenet of cultural-historical research is acknowledging the individual child in the study design, and at the same time acknowledging that the child is an active participant in a collective community. That is, the child develops her or his own unique perspective, giving voice to her/his views and at the same time the child also becomes a member of a community, embracing institutional and cultural values, beliefs and motives.

Hedegaard (2005a) has shown how the child's perspective can be framed within a study design in ways which also allow data to be gathered on the contexts which give meaning to the child's voice. The child is not viewed as an "individual voice" disembedded from the different contexts she/he can be found. Hedegaard (2005a) suggests that at the societal level, there are cultural traditions that are located in and valued by particular communities. There are institutions that a child engages in, such as "the family", "the school" and "preschool or childcare". At the individual level, the child's perspective is documented in ways which show the relations between the societal and institutional perspectives. That is, a child's voice is about their social and cultural contexts, and for very young children these can best be gained in situ. These constructs provided us with a framework for positioning the child as central in the research, and at the same time allowed us to consider the institutions in which the child was an active agent.

Study Design

Research Question

The study sought to gain an understanding of the sport, recreation and leisure needs of children and their families within the City of Melville, Australia. In particular, the study sought to gain insights into the perspectives of children, as embedded in their family practices, and the City of Melville environment (community and school).

Background to the Study: Building Child-Friendly Cities

As has been argued earlier, we can gain a tremendous amount of understanding about the world we live in by involving children in our research. Not only can children inform us about the sport, recreation and leisure needs for themselves and their families, but they can also provide a worldview that is both insightful and targeted. A "child's perspective" framed from within cultural-historical theory was adopted as the main methodology for researching the children's and their families' recreational, sports and leisure needs. The approach of the research was to mirror the objectives of the City of Melville's *Recreation and Leisure Strategy*, through:

- Partnerships: a methodology that values and respects the contribution of children to the project
- Promotion: effective consultation with children, Council officers, and other stakeholders
- Planning: focused recommendations regarding the sport, recreation, and leisure needs of children and their families in the City of Melville
- Provision: timely reporting and accurate representation of infrastructure, demographic, Local Government Authority, and policy trends
- Participation: an effective relationship with the research contractor, the City of Melville.

The Recreational and Leisure Strategy forms part of a general international trend for local governments to adopt policy and implementation strategies which are child-friendly. For instance, UNICEF's Innocenti Research Centre promotes building a *Child Friendly City* (see UNICEF, 2004). This document provides a framework for developing a Child Friendly City. This framework promotes local systems of governance that commit to 'fulfilling children's right' (p. 1).

A Child Friendly City is committed to the implementation of the Convention on the Rights of the Child for every young citizen. Some of these rights include: influencing decisions about their city, expressing their opinion on the city they want, walking safely in the streets on their own, having green spaces for plants and animals, and living in an unpolluted environment (see UNICEF, 2004).

Some of the foundations for building a Child Friendly City and that are important for our research relate to the aims of these projects: *best interests* (article 3) and *listening to children and respecting their views* (p. 7). In the *best interests* (article 3) a Child Friendly City ensures that the best interests of the child are foregrounded and the government takes actions on issues that affect children directly or indirectly in ways which ensure that all are aware of the impact new policies will have on children. In *listening to children and respecting their views* (article 12) in a Child Friendly City 'children are seen and heard … their views are taken seriously in their neighbourhoods and schools and in their families' (p. 7). These principles were taken into account when researching children's needs in relation to leisure, recreation and sport in the City of Melville.

In their progress report, the City of Melville stated that it aimed to gain accreditation as a Child Friendly City from UNICEF. Some of the areas the City of Melville are building on to be accredited as a Child Friendly City include:

- identification of services, facilities and programs and events;
- a policy called A Great Start that aims to advocate and coordinate the development of child and family centred services in the municipality;
- a children's submit which involved children under twelve and their families and aimed to elicit ideas and feedback about what will make Melville a better place to live.

A cultural-historical study design ensured that the City of Melville's perspective in relation to children and children's voices could be foregrounded in the data generation process and therefore in the analysis.

Sample: Five schools were selected for involvement in the study. The particular schools were selected because they were inner city schools with significant cultural diversity (e.g. families from Vietnam, China, Somalia, India, and some from European heritage communities) and four of the five schools serviced low socioeconomic communities. A total of 305 children were involved in the research.

Research approach

In order to gain an understanding of the different perspectives, protocols were established which featured three steps:

- environmental walks and in-class Children's Think Tank
- environmental walks in the community and interviews with children
- community-based Children's Think Tank.

These steps are discussed in detail below. Details of the participating schools, students and data collected are given in Table 5.1.

Table 5.1 Data gathered in school and year level of students

Schools	Year levels participating	Sample size (total number of children involved in environmental walk)	Total number of environmental photos taken	Total number of work samples (drawings and written material)	Number of families participating (cameras and Think Tank)	Total number of family-community photos	Total number of diary entries
St. Joseph Primary School	Year One Year 3 & 4 Year 6	76	416	76	3	297	17
South Clara Primary School	Year One Year 3 & 4 Year 6	114	255	19	9	411	18
Caria Primary School	Prep Year One Year 3 & 4 Year 6	49	286	30	7	386	19
Holy Family Primary School	Prep Year One Year 3 & 4 Year 6	19	374	11	3	216	12
Melin Primary School	Prep Year One Year 3 & 4 Year 6	47	452	50	2	252	6

Environmental walks: Researchers arrived at the school and an environmental walk was planned with children. At first, the researchers stimulated active engagement in the research by introducing the children to digital cameras and digital video cameras. The aim of the project was to learn about children's sport, leisure and recreational needs, and this was explained to children in different ways. For the very young children, a puppet set the scene (tell the "bear" or "Chip" about their environment) and wishing stones allowed the children to wish for the things they would like to see in their environment (Figures 5.1a, 5.1b and 5.1c). For the middle years, children acted as spies, undertaking an important assignment to document what was in their environment and to discuss what they would like to have to support their recreational, sport and leisure needs (Figures 5.2a and 5.2b). The older children were given digital video cameras and asked to join a news team, producing a report on their environment that could be screened on TV (Figure 5.3). These narratives supported the children in learning how to use the technology. After this introductory practice session, the children were given information on the City of Melville's request to find out their sport, recreational and leisure needs.

Interviews: The children were interviewed whilst on their environmental walk, and also at the conclusion of their walk. Children's photographs (taken whilst on the walk) were screened immediately following their walk,

(a)

(b)

(c)

Figure 5.1   Photographing the environment (including using wishing stones to wish for what they want in the environment)

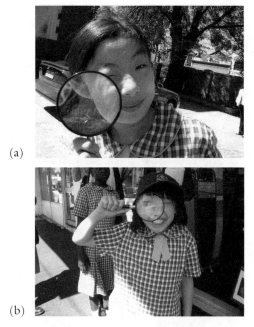

(a)

(b)

Figure 5.2 Being spies, investigating the environment (photographing the evidence)

Figure 5.3 Children dressed as spies – on a mission

and children discussed their priorities. In addition, all participating children recorded (as individuals or in groups) their ideas immediately after their environmental walk. The drawings or writing provided a further vehicle for children to express their needs regarding sport, recreation and leisure.

Disposable cameras and interviews: From each school, twenty children and their families were selected (with help from the teacher) to undertake an environmental walk over the weekend. Disposable cameras were given out immediately following the data gathering environmental walks (including drawings/writing and group interview sessions) (Figures 5.4a and 5,4b). The selected children were asked to repeat what they had experienced with their families over the weekend or after school. Children kept a diary of their activities. Disposable cameras were developed within ten days of the initial interviews, and participating children were interviewed on a one-to-one basis. Children viewed their photos on computer, and interviewers asked

(a)   (b)

Figure 5.4   Creating a news report (using video cameras to film their documentary/
news report)

the children to comment on what they had photographed and why. Specific
questions were asked about their sport, recreational and leisure needs at the
time of the interviews.

Children's Think Tanks

Class Think Tank: The children took photographs on their environmental
walks, and these photos were projected onto the wall. The children discussed
the photographs, commenting on the play activities and other activities
that occurred in the sites photographed. All comments were video or
audio taped.

School and Community Think Tank: From the disposable camera
photographs and child interviews, approximately three photos and comments
were chosen for each child, and these were screened at the Children's Think
Tank (Figure 5.5). The choice of photos was based on representation, as well
as differences across the groups. All comments were video or audio taped. The
Children's Think Tank, which was held after school hours, allowed families
to discuss the children's ideas in the context of their daily living conditions
in the City of Melville.

Analysis

The analysis sought to show the motives and intent of the *children* within the
context of the family's goals and values, and societal conditions, as discussed
by Hedegaard (2005a). In examining the norms and values of the society
alongside of the goals and values of the institution, it is possible to understand
the child's project. The unit of analysis was not the individual child, but
rather the evolving and dynamic interactions of the children within their
environment as they photographed/video-taped their specific local context.

The dynamic research context included how children (from a child's
perspective) view their living conditions, that is, how they lived in their
society and engaged with their surrounding "societal conditions" in relation

Figure 5.5   Children's Think Tank

to sport, leisure and recreation. The children's social situation was analysed in relation to how they played in their communities.

The children's perspective could only be understood in relation to the "families' project" and the City of Melville's project. It was important to not just listen to the child's perspective, but to understand it more thoroughly through gaining insights into what the families noted about their everyday life and living conditions. Family interviews allowed for a broader and deeper understanding of the children's perspectives to emerge.

Hedegaard (2005b) describes children's motives as:

> Motives are longer-lasting dynamics giving directedness to a person's life and characterizing his or her own personality across different situations. A person's motives are related to each other, so the most meaningful motives are related to each other, so the person is that which dominated but in the same situation several motives can be functioning. In actual situations a motive can be realized through different intended activities. (pp. 192–193)

We analysed the data in relation to:

- What were the children's motives for playing in their environment?
- How the child's goals were met or could be met through finding out what were the children's leisure and recreational "needs" (from a societal or City of Melville perspective).

- What were the goals and motives within the society and institutions in which the children were located and what was valued in relation to sport, leisure and recreation by the children?

The findings

Children as researchers: "child's eye" perspective

Through the children documenting their community environments, during school time, individually at home, and with their families, it was possible to gain a "child's eye perspective" on what their communities were like to live and play in. The research approach foregrounded the children's critique of their environments as they discussed what they liked, what was missing, and what was problematic. The direct connections between the children and their social and physical worlds meant that the digital mapping visually positioned what mattered to the children and made it easier for them to talk about their needs. For example, the children took photos of spaces that they used on weekends and after school which either demonstrated a concern for safety, or which focused on the need to repair existing resources. Some examples are shown in Figure 5.6.

> That's the stairs – it looks freaky; we need safer stairs. Sometimes you see dirty things lying around, and no bins, and lots of people's litter in there. (Jack)

Figure 5.6   Concern for safety

That's the security guard, to check if good people come and visit, not strangers who steal stuff. So much safer for us to live. If people are visiting they have to sign and call that person with the flat's phone. (Jack)

Safe equipment in the parks because some of the playgrounds have plastic which is burnt and not safe for little children and metal that is bent. (6-year-old girl)

The children made many valuable suggestions for how their environments could be improved. For example, in the study the children suggested that their environment should be regularly maintained. Broken equipment and recreational and leisure facilities, such as seating in parks, should be repaired. They suggested that bins be provided so that litter could be disposed of properly. In addition, they wanted the City of Melville to deal with the syringes that are left regularly around the parks and school-community grounds. Similarly, the children wanted the City of Melville to deal with the dog droppings, as they were a health hazard, and a most unwelcome addition to their environment. Cook (2007) suggests that 'The child's perspective, being a fragile notion, can then easily be crushed by adults who cannot move from their own version of an experience or, in the urgency of their research, find it difficult to see the alternative interpretation' (p. 44). The study design, through its iterative nature of using photography, provided many opportunities for the children to express their views, and through this make many important and valuable suggestions over an extended period of time. For example, many children suggested that flower gardens be designed for the areas around the flats and school, since this was where the children spent most of their time. In addition, the children wanted more grass and trees and some form of security set up to help them feel safe when playing. As Cook (2007) contends, 'A child's vision may be sharper than an adult's, yet the adult may miss what is being demonstrated because it does not fit their version of reality' (p. 44). Some examples of children's reality and their suggestions for improvement follow:

GIRL ONE: There are so many druggies and they fight and swear.
GIRL TWO: ... and people get scared and go.
GIRL ONE: Sometimes I see from the window some druggies are fighting in the night.
GIRL THREE: ... and there is this dog and the owner doesn't care if he bites someone ... and he chased this little girl and bit her!

That is where I live in (level 11). There is a park the tree was blocking so I couldn't take a picture. There is a school on the other side call Richmond West. I play in 106 park (they call it, the people). I played there when I get home here. There is an exercise park opposite there; on the side there is a cow. Adults talk around the cow. We can play tiggy around there. For little kids it's dangerous. Around our age is pretty good to play around. (Roseanne)

I went to the park, but I need to come back to go the toilet and were going back to the park, but then my mum said it was getting late and I already played in the park. There aren't any toilets in the park. I live in a flat and there is a park down in the building. I can take care of myself but I am not allowed. I wish there are some nice adults, maybe in my dreams. (Milka)

Children went beyond giving critiques of the environment and how to improve the general safety and look of their play spaces, they also provided valuable design ideas for play spaces. First, they suggested creating more spaces specifically for children to play. The children spoke about the lack of play facilities close to the flats, and stated that the school grounds were an important space for them. They gave many suggestions for modifying playgrounds:

We should get some bird feeders so that more birds will come and people will think it is a good place to have a picnic. (Reuben)

We need bigger fences for stopping druggies to come to our garden and ruining our gardens. (Liang)

I think the environment needs more chairs and more paper bark trees. We liked the fresh air and the big trees. We also think there should be more paths and more rubbish bins. There should be a big clump of rocks and a river running though it called The Running River!!!! I wish there was a swimming pool! (Kathy and Beliz)

The children initially discussed the placement of an existing basketball ring, suggesting that because it was oriented towards the sun during their play periods, the children would look into the sun when trying to shoot a basketball. They also discussed the placement of the square ball markings on the pavement, stating that the courts were mostly in the main thoroughfare, resulting in conflict when passing children bumped their precision patting of the ball within the court. The children recommended swapping the square ball courts with the basketball court.

One of the significant features of the study design was the opportunity for the repetition of data gathering with children so that the purpose and opportunity for expressing views could be maximised. This strength has been noted by Cook (2007) who suggests that 'A vital element of the photographs was the opportunities they offered to revisit situations with the children, to listen intently to their talk and to be able to change our views' (p. 44). In our study, children went on a number of environmental walks – at school and at home. This meant that the children could revisit their ideas across contexts, and within small and large groups. The viewing of their data both individually and collectively through projecting photographs, supported the repetition of the research process and provided further opportunities for discussion. For example, the children spoke continually about their wishes for more greenery in their environment.

> Slowly the natural environment is fading away. If we don't do anything about it soon we may just end up with a world of only concrete. (Melinda)

The children focused their responses around the grey environment that greets them each day as they walk to school or to play in their neighbourhood. Of particular concern were the visual pollution (graffiti, broken facilities) and the air pollution. Consequently, the children's comments reflected the need for a brighter and cleaner environment in which to spend their recreational time (Figures 5.7a and 5.7b). The depth of this need became more apparent over the duration of the data gathering period across four of the five schools. The fifth school was located in an upper to middle class environment surrounded by trees and parks. The children's suggestions there focused generally on having 'more of the same' – that is, more trees and more shade.

Another important design feature of this study was the opportunity for the children to be able to practise being researchers alongside experienced researchers. The environmental walks helped the children to ask questions of each other, to document what they were observing or had noticed before, and to collectively discuss their findings. This experience, in turn, gave them skills and confidence in undertaking the same task at home with their families. Practising using the equipment, viewing their images, and writing, drawing and talking about their experiences, were all done in relation to informing the City of Melville about their needs. They took these research skills to their family context and expanded the data about the needs of children and families within their community. As has been noted by Habashi (2005) in her research, children can take an active 'role in understanding the research questions and provide[d] insights in the analysis process' (p. 31). She suggests that traditionally researchers have not critically reflected upon the role adults take in research and noted how their activities may restrict children's voices

(a)   (b)

Figure 5.7   Concerns for the physical environments

'especially when their views challenge our status quo' (p. 34). Assuming children cannot engage in the research process means that children will not be given this opportunity. Wyngaard (2005) has warned 'how can this research be a transformative act, versus an oppressor-oppressed, researcher-researched relationship, *if* I've already formulated the questions?' (p. 78). Yet, the research question was posed not by the researchers, but rather by the City of Melville, who had a genuine interest in finding out what were the children's sport, recreational and leisure needs. As such, the children were not engaging in an act or role playing being researchers, but rather their role was important and authentic. The public display of their data through the Children's Think Tanks was further evidence to the children of the importance of their work for changing the City of Melville environment.

Families: Helping to Understand Children's Perspectives

In this study, the data generation process, the viewing of the data, and collective analysis of the data at the Children's Think Tanks, were a dynamic rather than a static process. The children not only shared their individual family environmental walks during their interviews with the researchers, but also representative and divergent images and interviews were shared at the Children's Think Tanks with the families. The children's comments provided a discussion context which the families could engage in. Importantly, the family comments gave deeper understanding of the children's comments. As Cook (2007) has suggested 'what we glean from children is more of an indicator of meaning, rather than an absolute' (p. 44). For example, the children discussed safety. However, this could be better understood when the families outlined their particular environmental context in more detail:

> As the families viewed the photographs at the Think Tank one mother commented that she lived in a high rise flat, with her school aged child and a baby. She was a single mother and found it very difficult to allow her school aged child to go down into the park below. She said the children (at the Think Tank) were right, they couldn't go down unsupervised, it was simply unsafe. She felt frustrated when her child wanted to go to the park below, because she couldn't supervise him when she had cooking to do or when her baby was sleeping. (field notes, St Joseph's School)

Jipson and Jipson (2005) through their methodological critique of issues of power and voice in children's research have asked, 'How can we capture another's reality when it is continually changing and when the other is a child?' (p. 42). In our study, involving the families was important because it provided confirmation of what mattered to the children. For example, the families also discussed the difficulties of using the "green space available" which put into context why the children only used the open spaces immediately available to them around their homes and school:

PARENT ONE: There is lots of green spots in this map, but there are not actually parks. The park we went to is actually not shown, the one we went to called Spider Park.
(Shows where she lives) There is absolutely nothing close to where we live.
PARENT TWO: What's nice is there is kids' play equipment here. (Showing on map Princess Park) to get there we have to drive, to get to Royal Park, so kids can bike ride, we have to drive, so you have to drive. Safely is just a nightmare, there is parking. Royal Park is nice for adults and dogs, but there is nothing for toddlers or grade one and two, there's no skate park.
PARENT ONE: There is no playground.
PARENT TWO: There is no tennis courts, there is a dog fountain there (Showing on map South Royal Park). That is the only one in the whole Royal Park. There are no toilets.

I noticed there is one [fountain] on Royal Park [that] is quite lovely. There is only one in the whole park. (Parent comment)

There is no fenced playground; the playground here is near roads, [you need] to watch them every second, because it is an open area. You have to watch them and chase them every second ... (Parent comment)

Understanding the children's comments in relation to "greener" not "greyer" environments could be understood very clearly from the environmental walks. However, the noise pollution and air pollution could not be easily seen in the photographs. Cook (2007) has suggested that the 'repeated engagement with the children slowed down the adult journey to deciding upon meanings' (p. 42). In walking with the children from their home/school grounds to open parks within 100 metres of where they lived, it was possible to see why these beautiful spaces were not being used. The four-lane highway between their homes and the park was like the Great Wall of China. In addition, the busy roads around their communities, and the heavily used street parking meant that bike riding and general playing in their communities was almost impossible for the children. Without adult supervision for all ages of children living in the community, safety would be a real issue. As Cook (2007) has noted 'It needs to be recognized that photographs are not an absolute representation of a given state, but a tool to help understandings develop' (p. 43).

Through examining the children's perspective, through their role as researchers interviewing their families, and through the Children's Think Tanks, it was possible to build a deeper and richer understanding of the children's perspective. That is, not only were their voices heard, but they were more likely to be understood through this dynamic and iterative research design.

Conclusion

Some of the methodological insights gained when undertaking a cultural-historical reading of "children as researchers" included better understanding the data generated from the children's documented play experiences when families also interrogated the data; repetition of data gathering with children so that the purpose and opportunity for expressing views could be maximised; children practising to be researchers with support before they worked independently at home and in the community gathering data; and viewing data generation and analysis as a dynamic rather than a static process.

The researchers – both children and adults – had an authentic research challenge. They wanted to find out what the children's needs were in the City of Melville for sport, leisure and recreation. The study design allowed this research question to be studied, and for the children to take a central role in this process. Although, the study design foregrounded the children's perspective, their perspective could be better understood when the cultural-historical context of the children's interactions and play spaces were studied alongside the children's photographs, interviews and Think Tank discussions.

Only when the child's voice is viewed as a dialectical relation to their social and physical context, can the methodological discussions move forward. The methodological assumption inherent in the design reported in this chapter suggests that there is no child's voice if there is no way of capturing their views so that someone can hear them, and there is no research with children if there are no children. One assumes the other, and our theoretical assumptions and research methods must account for this dialectical relationship. A child's voice cannot be disembedded from the living world, it must be framed as part of the world; and theoretical insights into research can only be gained when this dialectical position is taken. This new view of "children as researchers" moves the debate closer to answering the sticky question posed by Woodhead and Boyden (1997, quoted in James & Prout, 1997, p. xi) so long ago when they complained of the 'practical problems of universalistic concepts of childhood' and the 'cultural specificity of particular childhoods' as needing to be recognised. When children act as researchers they do so in their own cultural contexts, and how they interact as researchers will be determined by the communities that seek to engage them in this process. What is generated through this culturally specific research process, with its culturally specific research questions, will be used, validated and valued from within its cultural community. As with longstanding debates on etic and emic validity, the question of data generated through children acting as researchers, will also be open to scrutiny when the specific methods are imported without consideration of the specific cultural community from which they were generated.

The culturally diverse research projects outlined in the edited volume by Diaz Soto and Swander (2005) begin to redress the "imperial eyes" problem introduced in the introduction to this chapter. "Children as researchers" as a methodological construct must be understood as a Western construction, and must be re-theorised each time it moves into other cultural contexts. The study reported in this chapter generated its own methods and methodological assumptions which were relevant for the children living in the City of Melville. The concept of "children as researchers" could not be imported and used from its European heritage roots, without carefully considering the Australian context – as a culturally diverse community with specific cultural practices and environmental features. The study reported in this chapter provides a dialectical framework for building culturally specific methods within specific cultural communities, which take into account cultural environments and cultural practices when positioning children as researchers. Whilst "children as researchers" has been positioned as a global construct, how it is realised locally must be re-theorised and reconstructed each time it enters a new cultural community.

Acknowledgments

This chapter draws upon research undertaken by a very large group of people who supported the overall study by acting as research assistants, as team leaders for gathering data in particular schools or by providing technical assistance: Dr. Joce Nuttal, Dr. Beverley Jane, Dr. Trent Brown, Ms. John Gipps, Dr. Amy Cutter-Mackenzie, Dennise Rado-Lynch, Carlene Whitten, Jacinta Bartlette, and Corine Rivalland. Without their contributions, the overall project could not have been undertaken. We would like to thank the children and practitioners who have made this research possible. Without your voice, participation and enthusiasm this research could not have been done. All methodological and research methods reported here and any limitations noted by the reader are the sole responsibility of the first author.

References

Baker, J. & Willis, S. (2003). "Is it fun?" Developing children centred research methods. *International Journal of Sociology and Social Policy*, 23 (1/2), 33–58.

Clark, A. (2004). The Mosaic approach and research with young people. In V. Lewis, M. Kellett, C. Robinson, S. Fraser, & S. Ding (Eds.), *The reality of research with children and young people* (pp. 142–156). London: Sage Publications.

Clark, A. (2005). Ways of seeing: using the Mosaic approach to listen to young children's perspectives. In A. Clark, A. Kjorholt, & P. Moss (Eds.), *Beyond listening. Children's perspectives on early childhood services* (pp. 29–49). Bristol: Policy Press.

Committee Report Progress Report (2007). Investigation into UNICEF Accreditation as a Child Friendly City. Retrieved March 13, 2007 from http://www.melville. gov.au/pdf.

Cook, T. (2007). What the camera sees and from whose perspective. Fun methodologies for engaging children in enlightening adults. *Childhood*, 14 (1), 29–45.

Diaz Soto, L. & Swander, B. (2005). *Power and voice in research*. New York: Peter Lang Publishing.

Gallagher, C. B. (2004). "Our town": Children as advocates for change in the city. *Childhood*, 11 (2), 251–262.

Grover, S. (2004). Why won't they listen to us? On giving power and voice to children participating in social research. *Childhood*, 11 (1), 81–93.

Gutierrez-Gomez, C. (2005). Children's retelling. In L. Diaz Soto & B. Swander (Eds.), *Power and voice in research* (pp. 191–204). New York: Peter Lang Publishing.

Habashi, J. (2005). Freedom speaks, In L. Diaz Soto & B. Swander (Eds.), *Power and voice in research* (21–34). New York: Peter Lang Publishing.

Hatzinikolaou, A. & Mitakidou, S. (2005). Roma children: Building "bridges". In L. Diaz Soto & B. Swander (Eds.), *Power and voice in research* (pp. 125–135). New York: Peter Lang Publishing.

Hedegaard, M. (2005a). *Child development from a cultural-historical approach: Children's activity in everyday local settings as foundation for their development.* Unpublished manuscript, International Society for Culture and Activity Research, Seville.

Hedegaard, M. (2005b). Strategies for dealing with conflicts in value positions between home and school: Influences on ethnic minority students' development of motives and identity. *Culture & Psychology*, 11 (2), 187–205.

Hendrick, H. (2000). Child as a social actor in historical sources. In P. Christensen & A. James (Eds.), *Research with children: perspectives and practices* (pp. 36–61). London: Routledge.

James, A. (2007). Giving a voice to children's voice: practices and problems, pitfalls and potentials. *American Anthropologist*, 109 (2), 261–272.

James, A. & James, A. (2001). Tightening the net: Children, community, and control. *British Journal of Sociology*, 52 (2), 211–228.

James, A., & Prout, A. (1997). *Constructing and reconstructing childhood. Contemporary issues in the sociological study of childhood*, 2nd edition. London: Falmer Press.

James, A., Jenks, C., & Prout, A. (1998). *Theorizing childhood*. Cambridge: Polity Press.

Jipson, J. & Jipson, J. (2005). Confidence intervals: Doing research with young children. In L. Diaz Soto & B. Swander (Eds.), *Power and voice in research*. (pp. 35–43). New York: Peter Lang Publishing.

Jones, A. (2004). Involving children and young people as researchers. In V. Lewis, M. Kellett, C. Robinson, S. Fraser, & S. Ding (Eds.), *The reality of research with children and young people* (pp. 113–130). London: Sage Publications.

Kellett, M. (2005). *How to develop children as researchers. A step-by-step guide to teaching the research process*. London: Paul Chapman.

Komulainen, S. (2007). The ambiguity of the child's voice in social research. *Childhood*, 14 (1), 11–28.

Malewski, E. (2005). Epilogue. When children and youth talk back: Precocious research practices and the cleverest voices. In L. Diaz Soto & B. Swander (Eds.), *Power and voice in research* (pp. 215–222). New York: Peter Lang Publishing.

Martinez-Roldan, C. (2005). Bilingual children in literature discussions. In L. Diaz Soto & B. Swander (Eds.), *Power and voice in research* (pp. 177–190). New York: Peter Lang Publishing.

National Children's Office, the Children's rights Alliance and the National Youth Council of Ireland (2005). *Young Voices. Guidelines on how to involve children and young people in your work*. Dublin: Stationery Office.

Oberg, D. & Ellis, J. (2006). Theme: Researching with children and youth. *Alberta Journal of Educational Research*, 52, (3), 107–110.

Punch, S. (2002). Research with children: The same or different from research with adults? *Childhood*, 9 (3), 321–341.

Riggio, E. (2002a). Child friendly cities: Good governance in the best interests of the child. *Journal of Environment and Urbanization*, 14 (2), 45–58.

Riggio, E. & Kilbane, T. (2000). The international secretariat for child-friendly cities: A global network for urban children. *Journal of Environment and Urbanization*, 12 (2), 201–205.

Rogoff, B. (2003). *The cultural nature of human development.* New York: Oxford University Press.

Sun, Y. (2005). Listening to the voices of Chinese immigrant girls. In L. Diaz Soto & B. Swander (Eds.), *Power and voice in research* (pp. 89–104). New York: Peter Lang Publishing.

Swander, B. (2005). Kenyan street children speak through art. In L. Diaz Soto & B. Swander (Eds.), *Power and voice in research* (pp. 137–149). New York: Peter Lang Publishing.

UNICEF, Innocenti Research Centre (2004). *Building Child Friendly Cities, A Framework for Action.* Retrieved March 13, 2007 from http://www.childfriendlycities.org/resources/index_conceptual_framework.html.

Wyngaard, M. V. (2005). Culturally relevant pedagogy: 4Rs – BEIN' REAL, In L. Diaz Soto & B. Swander (Eds.), *Power and voice in research* (77–88). New York: Peter Lang Publishing.

6   The Power of Motives

The Dialectic Relations Between Neurobiological Constraints and Activity in Child Development

Louise Bottcher

During the development of typical children, the culturally and historically formed requirements are usually in accordance with the biological maturation of the child. Organic development of the brain, of the body and of the speech apparatus supports the social and cognitive development. One example of this is that a child usually begins school at a time when it is cognitively and motivationally ready for the challenges offered by the school. At the same time, the requirements at school are fitted to the particular age of the children; shorter days and easier tasks at younger ages, longer school days and more difficult tasks later on. In the normal child one only sees one line of development, because the two lines of development – biological and social – coincide and merge one into the other (Vygotsky, 1993). But this might not be the case for the child with a neurobiologically based developmental disorder, because the physical world and the social institutions are first and foremost intended for children with normal neurobiological constitutions. What is seen is an incongruence between biologically based abilities and the structure of the social institutions, an incongruence which completely reorganises the development of the child (Vygotsky, 1993). Still, the presence of a congenital brain lesion does not need to be regarded as an invariant determinant of the child's activities and actions, even though this conception is often found in the literature on children with brain lesions. Through the concept of *neurobiological constraints*, I will unfold an understanding of how children with lesions to their brains change and develop actively in and with the changing demands and possibilities in the social settings similar to the way normal children do, even though their conditions for doing so are different. The aim of this chapter is to present an understanding of how the childhood of a particular child, typical or atypical, is constructed from the dialectic relations between neurobiological constraints and local cultural-historical institutional practices. As such it is an integration of theories of neurobiological development in a cultural-historical framework of understanding children and child development.

Neurobiological Constraints

Without doubt, the activity of all children is biologically constrained because the different cognitive functions, all of which are necessary for activity, are dependent on a neural basis. An understanding of the neurobiological constraints is necessary, although not sufficient, to understand how the particular life course of a child is shaped. The child cannot develop specific competencies before the neural tissue supporting them is sufficiently matured. Simultaneously, the activity of the child impacts on the neurobiological constraints through experience-dependent changes in the neural system (Greenough et al., 1987). To understand how the maturation and development of the brain is a necessary condition for child development, I use the concept *neurobiological constraint*. In my use of the concept of constraint, I rely on the definition by Valsiner (1997):

> A constraint is a regulator of the move from the present to the immediate future state of the developing organism–environment system, which delimits the full set of possible ways of that move, thus enabling the developing organism to construct the actual move under a reduced set of possibilities. (p. 180)

Valsiner (1997) uses the concept in order to analyse relations between the child and the socio-cultural system with an emphasis on how actions are constrained by socio-cultural regulations in the form of access to objects, ways of acting and semiotic constructions. The concept is not employed to denote biological factors, although it is possible to trace diffuse references to neurobiological development in sentences such as "… if parents try to teach the child a new skill which, given the child's present state of development, is beyond his or her *immediate learning possibilities*, then the effort will fail" (Valsiner, 1997, p. 200, italics added). By diffuse I mean that the role of neurobiological development in relation to the development of children's actions is not explicated. Still, the use of the concept of constraints as "a primarily dynamic, and secondary (potentially) relative stable, organizational device" is compatible with neurobiological theories of neural development. The neural system too functions as a dynamic system, in which stable, yet changeable systems of interconnections between neurons and groups of neurons arise throughout the development of the child. This dynamic system supports the different cognitive and emotional functions (Stiles, 2000); psychological functions that enable us to organise and interpret our experiences and act in different social settings.

The neural system is a necessary condition for action, but how does the neural system as a biological constraint affect the development of a child? And just as important, how does the activity of the child modify the neural system? To answer these questions, Valsiner's concept of constraint will be elaborated with concepts from both developmental neuropsychology and cultural-historical activity theory. Two case studies of boys with cerebral palsy and their use of a personal computer in school will be used to illustrate the dialectic relation between neurobiological constraints, child motives and child thinking and acting.

Cerebral palsy (CP) is a group of developmental disorders, which are due to an early non-progressive lesion of the central nervous system. The main symptoms of CP are disorders of movement and posture, but other symptoms are often seen simultaneously; disturbances of sensation (vision or hearing) and perception (understood as the capacity to incorporate and interpret sensory information), global or specific cognitive difficulties (such as distractibility), communication disorders, and seizures (Bax et al., 2005). The consequences of a congenital or early acquired brain lesion are often wide ranging, because the much more interconnected functioning of the immature brain is associated with impairments in distributed functions such as attention or memory, which are crucial to the child who is in the middle of the process of acquiring knowledge and abilities.

The trajectory of a child with CP is by no means any more predictable than the trajectory of a child without CP. Still, some problems and developmental challenges appear more often in the life courses of children with CP than in the life course of typical children. In empirical studies, CP has been associated with restrictions in participation in day-to-day activities in childhood (Ostensjo et al., 2003), a higher prevalence of psychiatric disorders (Goodman & Graham, 1996), learning disorders (Frampton et al., 1998) and problems in peer relations (Yude et al., 1998; Nadeau & Tessier, 2006). Often, explanations have been sought in the brain lesion and cognitive functioning of the children. From the perspective of the cultural-historical school, this approach is too limited. Thinking is shaped by socio-cultural available forms in addition to the neurobiological constraints on human cognition (Scribner, 1997; Hedegaard, 2002). Cognition is not only taking place in social settings, it is social by nature. From the perspective of developmental neuropsychology, the biological constitution of a child with CP is seen as constraints on the development of cognitive functions and on the activity of the child. To approach a dialectical understanding of the relation between cognitive functions and the activity of the child, it is necessary to consider which institutional practices children with CP live their lives in.

In Denmark, children with CP go to normal schools, special classes in normal schools or special schools. The choice of school is made according to the motor impairment of the child, the type of schools within geographical reach and the preference of the child's parents, among other things. Interventions are primarily directed at the motor and sensory impairments through medical treatment and adjusted remedies, while the cognitive difficulties only to a lesser extent are taken in consideration in the life of the child with CP, especially for the children who go to normal schools. In the special schools, the teachers are more often aware of the additional cognitive difficulties, but often complain about a lack of sufficient knowledge, suitable teaching materials or both.

The activities in the particular schools present the children with CP with different developmental challenges and different possibilities of creating their own developmental challenges. A question related to the aim of this chapter of getting a more integrated understanding of the dialectic between neurobiological constraints and local cultural-historical practices is: How do the thinking and acting of the children in school modify and develop their neurobiological constraints?

Neurobiological Constraints are Shaped in and Through Activity

Researchers in the field generally agree that the cognitive functions and their neural support are never stable (Karmiloff-Smith, 1998, 2007; Bishop, 1997; Stiles et al., 2003). In order to understand the concept of neurobiological constraints, it is necessary to consider changes in the brain, which are conducted by experiences. One central mechanism is neural plasticity. Plasticity is the fundamental property of the neural system to change, generally in an adaptive way, in response to external demands experienced by the child (Stiles, 2000). The changes are seen in both the structure and the functioning of the brain. During normal neural development, an abundance of neurons and connections are lost due to competition for resources. Some cells and connections are lost due to endogenous processes, but a major part of the elimination process in the system happens in response to external activity, thereby sculpturing the cerebral system. This means that cognitive development and learning are active processes based on interaction between activity at different levels. Changes are seen in the activity in neurochemical systems, in the activity in cell assemblies, in cognitive abilities and in the activity of the child in the social setting. It is the child's thinking and acting, which in the end determines which neural potentials that are turned into actual, lasting though changeable, neural pathways.

Taken together, a neurobiological constraint is at the same time a biological reality and a regulator of actions in social settings. The active participation of the child in social settings is a precondition for development of neural connections and cognitive functions. At the same time, neural and cognitive development is a precondition for the development of the activity of the child. The growing cognitive abilities of the child enable it to participate in new ways and in new and different settings, thereby propelling both cognitive and social development. This dialectical dynamic between cognitive development and social interaction is part of the cultural-historical activity theory (Scribner, 1997). The present challenge is the integration of neurobiological development in this dialectic theory.

Social Institutional Practices and Child Motives

The neurobiological constraints and the activity of the child are socially and culturally mediated through ideas and understandings of what children are, what they need to learn and why they do as they do (Hundeide, 2003). Cognitive functioning as calculating and forming concepts are social activities, which apply and transform cultural-historical practices such as computers and calculators, language and mathematical rules. The social institutions of children are aimed at furthering child development towards goals considered desirable, among these teaching children the cultural-historical practices considered necessary in order to participate in our society. This applies to children with CP as well. The thinking and acting of children with CP takes place in socio-cultural practices just like the thinking and acting of other children do, and the neurobiological constraints of a child with CP are mediated in and through the cultural-historical practices. Taken together, the neurobiological constraints can be seen as acting at several levels, see Figure 6.1.

At the level of neural structures, the neurobiological constraints exist as a biological reality. In and through the activity of the child with CP in social settings, the neurobiological constraints are socially and culturally mediated and come to existence at the psychological level and the social level. During development, the neural structures place constraints on the development of cognitive functions, and through this, on the activity of the child in social settings. At the same time, the activity of the child feeds into both the cognitive and the neural development of the child through learning and plasticity. The relations between the levels are dialectical and the developmental trajectories of children with CP are formed by the dialectic relations between neurobiological constraints and child activity. Different cultural-historical practices for thinking and acting appear within or out of reach to the child along developmental time; sometimes the neurobiological constraints restrict the child in some kinds of activity, while at other times a particular activity of the child in the social setting enables the child to move his or her neurobiological constraints, at first at the level of psychological functions, but sometimes even at the level of neural structures.

In school a child participates in one of the most important cultural-historical practices for learning activities for thinking and acting, both of which stimulate

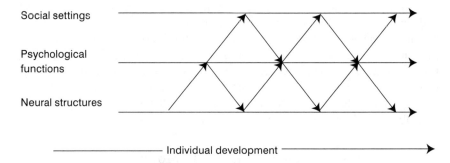

Figure 6.1 A multilevel approach to understand child activity (Adapted from Gottlieb et al., 1998)

development and fuel organisation and reorganisation at the level of neural structures. In addition, learning is not only a cognitive enterprise, but can be understood as intrinsic bound together with emotional qualities like motives. Motives are the goals which characterise the actions of children in different activities over an extended period of time (Hedegaard, 2002). Cultural values of what constitutes a good life and appropriate development are reflected in institutional practices and as child development takes place through the participation of the child in the social institutions, the cultural values become conditions for the development of motives. The dominant motives of a child originate from central and important activities (Leontiev, 1977). During childhood in our western societies, several successive dominating motives can be identified; the motive of the infant is contact with caregivers; the toddler's dominating motive is exploration of the surroundings; the dominating motive of the preschool child is play; during the first years at school the child has a learning motive which by and by is replaced by the motive to be accepted by friends and to become someone of consequence (Hedegaard, 2002). Activities are multi-motivated. Each child develops a motive hierarchy, in which one or more of the mentioned dominating motives figures along with other motives. The specific motives of a particular child are the result of former experiences in specific practices, development in interests and ideas about what it would like to do in the near future. Motives develop and change as the cognitive and emotional abilities of the child grow, leading the child to new forms of acting and participation in new institutional settings; thereby providing the child with new cognitive and emotional challenges. As such, motives are an integrated part of development.

Conflicts and Development

Conflicts might arise between the child's cognitive abilities, constrained by the developing neural system, its motives and activity. Within the cultural-historical understanding of development (Vygotsky, 1993), and in the dialectical psychology (Riegel, 1975), conflicts are generally thought of as a common and necessary condition for development. Conflicts arise whenever synchrony between different aspects of development breaks down:

> Most crises represent constructive confrontations in which the discordance and contradiction generated provide the source of every new change both within the individual and within society. (Riegel, 1975, p. 51)

As such, developmental crises or conflicts are seen as the fuel of development. In line with this, Vygotsky conceptualised interaction between the maturation of biological capacities and changes in institutional demands as the foundation of development in the social situation of the child (Hedegaard, in press). As mentioned earlier, the development of children with disabilities is often characterised by incongruence between the biological maturation and the structure of the social institutions because the social institutions and the physical world in general are suited for typical children. Seen at the level of the psychological functioning of the child, a conflict might arise if a child with cognitive impairments is placed in a school/class with normal demands and no help. Because the motives of the child arise from both personal experiences and the social institutions the child is living in (Hedegaard, 2002), the child can develop motives for activities, which might be difficult for the child to carry out due to its neurobiological constraints: for example the child with a walker, who wants to play soccer like the rest of the boys in his class.

To reach a solution, a new synchrony, the discrepancy between the present state and the required state must be within reach on the ground of neural possibilities, personal motives or social opportunities in the social institutions the child is living in. The developmental point is that once the move has begun in one area, for example in activity, development is fuelled in the remaining ones, for example motives, thinking and eventually at the level of neural activity. If the child with CP who wants to play soccer is able to accept his imperfect activity in the beginning, the soccer activity might push the neurobiological constraints and gradually improve in quality. At the same time, the child with CP must be granted the opportunity to play despite his poorer performance, not just once, but on a regular basis. The developmental conflict can only be constructive in so far as changes are possible in order to reach a new synchrony.

Empirical Study

In order to investigate the dialectic relations between neurobiological constraints, motives and activity, the author undertook a study using a case study approach combining neuropsychological testing and interview/observation.

Two boys from a large, quantitative study of cognitive impairments associated with CP were chosen to participate in the case study. Each of them was tested with a neuropsychological test battery. In addition, the primary teacher completed a questionnaire about executive functions (Behaviour Rating Inventory of Executive Function, BRIEF). Interviews were done with the teacher of each child. Participant observation was seen as the preferred method to gain knowledge about the child's everyday life at school (Hedegaard & Fleer, in press), but in one of the cases this method was considered too intrusive for the child to be willing to participate and an interview with the boy and a friend was done instead. In each case, the following research questions were used as a guide:

- How are the neurobiological constraints expressed in the activity of the child?
- How are the neurobiological constraints mediated in school activity?
- What motives does the child have?
- Which conflicts can be seen between the child's motives and activity?

During the observation, the research questions were used as guidelines for the identification of relevant situations. For the interviews, two sets of interview questions were generated from the research questions: one set for the interview with the teacher and another one for the interview with the two boys.

Case 1: Marcus

Marcus is a boy of 10 with cerebral palsy. All his four limbs are affected and to move around he must either crawl, or use his walker or his electric wheelchair. In addition to his substantial motor impairment, he has a severe visual impairment caused by his brain lesion.

Marcus is part of a resourceful upper middle class family, which receives a lot of social support. The parents have managed to get Marcus placed in a particular public school with expertise in the education of children with motor disabilities and learning disabilities, even though the school is placed in a different municipality. The school is 33 kilometres from their home and Marcus is picked up and driven home by bus each day. The school has both normal classes and special classes. The school start of Marcus was delayed by one year, and from the beginning he was placed in a special class. In the second half of first grade, he began having some of his lessons in a normal first grade class. This dual class arrangement continued in second grade, but with increasing problems, and from the beginning of third grade, Marcus' participation in the normal class was discontinued. At the time of the interview he is in the special third grade full-time. Marcus does not have a helper but the low number of children in Marcus' class makes it possible for him to receive one-to-one teaching when necessary. In school, Marcus has a personal computer because of his visual problems, which make it difficult for him to read letters and numbers in ordinary printing size.

Case 2: Angus

Angus is a boy of 12 with cerebral palsy affecting all four limbs. He is able to walk without any remedies, but uses his mini crosser for longer distances, for example from home to school (one kilometre). Angus' motor impairment includes dysarthria characterised by a weak, high-pitched voice.

Like Marcus, Angus is part of a resourceful upper middle class family. He goes to a small private school for normal children. The school has a tradition for inclusion of children with disabilities or behavioural problems in their normal classes. Angus was evaluated in kindergarten and the school did express some concern as to whether he was too disabled to be included. At that time, Angus could not walk on his own and spoke with an almost undetectable voice.

At the time of the observation, Angus goes to sixth grade. He participates in the lessons at much the same conditions as his peers, the only exception being that Angus has his personal laptop and, in some classes, a person who helps him with practicalities such as taking notes from the blackboard. Angus has the computer because it is strenuous for him to write with a pencil. He writes slowly on the computer too, but it is easier for him to make corrections.

Neurobiological Constraints Regulating the Development of Activity of Marcus and Angus

The activity of both boys is most of the time constrained by their impairments in fine and gross motor function. Although both of them struggle, neither is able to write, walk, run and so forth like other children.

The neuropsychological assessment of the two boys shows a clear difference between their cognitive functioning. The grey area in the tables denotes the area of normal functioning.

Both Marcus and Angus have a general level of cognitive functioning, measured by the WISC-III (Wechsler Intelligence Scale for Children, third version) verbal comprehension index, around the mean of normal children (Figure 6.2). Compared with each other, Angus has more scores in the high end of the normal area. Comprehension was among the last tests Marcus did and the low score probably reflects how his performance deteriorates substantially when he is tired.

As expected, Marcus showed severe problems with visual perceptual analysis such as discriminating between similar shapes or detecting differences in spatial directions (Figure 6.3). No subtest performance was in the normal area. In contrast, Angus functions in the high end of the normal area in most of the tests of visual perceptual skills.

In contrast to the preceding measures, BRIEF scores above the normal areas denote problematic behaviour, not superiority (Figure 6.4). Marcus' scores indicate problems in several areas of executive functions such as mental flexibility and ability to shift, emotional control, initiation and working memory. In contrast, Angus functions in the normal area in all measures of executive functioning, which was confirmed by the observations.

Each of Marcus' cognitive impairments, attentional (not shown), visuo-perceptual and executive, are mentioned by his teacher as something she has to take into consideration when she teaches him. But Marcus has cognitive strengths too. He has good verbal skills and although he performs below his level of verbal competence in a test of word list learning (not shown), the story is quite different in school. Marcus' teacher relates how he is able to learn a text by heart from one or two readings and "read" it from the book the following day, possibly with some support from visual cues. Also, Marcus remembers literally many shorter and longer dialogues from his favourite TV series.

Generally, Angus seems to be a boy with a level of functioning in the high end of the normal area in most of the measured cognitive areas. His dysarthria can be considered a neurobiological constraint. It is difficult for him to speak loud enough to be heard, especially when there is background noise. During observations, Angus had difficulties getting in contact with a

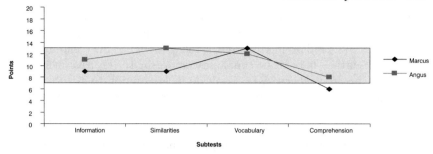

Figure 6.2   Verbal comprehension measured by subtests from WISC-III

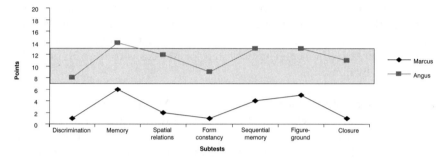

Figure 6.3   Test of visual perceptual skills measured by TVPS-R

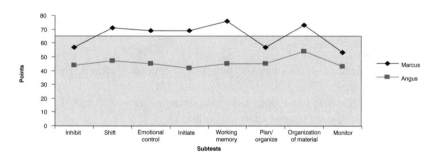

Figure 6.4   Executive function measured by the BRIEF questionnaire

teacher because she didn't hear him. Also, difficulties were observed during recess when Angus wanted to say something to one of his peers, who had trouble hearing him because the other children in the class were talking at the same time.

The Use of a Personal Computer

The reasons for giving the boys personal computers are similar, namely to remove their neurobiological constraints on learning through the incorporation of the computer. The ways in which the two boys use their computers in their thinking and activity are quite different from each other.

MARCUS' TEACHER: He has had a personal computer from the start. And in the beginning he didn't like to work at the computer. But he likes it now. He likes to sit and do math exercises, calculations, on the computer. But, of course, they have to be simple, those on the screen have to be very simple, because otherwise he won't do it. He cannot do it with a lot of different things on the screen, because then he cannot take the picture in.

Marcus' neurodevelopmental constraints make it difficult continually to find adequate material for him. His neurobiological constraints, cerebral visual impairments, executive dysfunctions, and problems with sustained attention, present obstacles to his learning and development, but in and through the use of compensating remedies such as the computer and the placement of Marcus in a class in which one-to-one teaching is a possibility, the constraints are moved. The next step for Marcus is to learn to push the constraints by himself.

TEACHER: One of the things we work on with Marcus is that he must learn to say when he needs a remedy. I would say it is one of the things we focus on with him right now. Because that is what he cannot do. He has strategies for reading, he has strategies for math, there are many things he knows how to do, but he cannot find out on his own which remedies he needs in a particular situation.

At the time of the interview, Marcus has come to recognise the computer as a learning aid.

MARCUS: Because I ... I get the pages of the book scanned, then you can get it up.
INTERVIEWER: But what does the computer do? Why is it easier to get the pages on the computer than in the book?
MARCUS: Because then it becomes bigger.

But sometimes the use of a computer during learning is in conflict with Marcus' dominating motive, which is to be part of a friendship group. While in the normal class Marcus felt different from his normal class mates. He did not make any friends in the normal class and experienced social exclusion. Marcus' dominating motive of being part of a friendship group is therefore interwoven with a motive of avoiding being different. Being the only one using a computer in class made him stand out and this might be part of the explanation for Marcus' earlier unwillingness to accept the computer as an aid. In contrast, all of the children in the special class use a computer from time to time and this might be part of the explanation of Marcus' growing acceptance of his computer.

In contrast, even though Angus is the only one in his class who depends on a computer, he does not experience the use of computer as socially excluding.

His capability on the computer seems to contribute to the building of positive peer relations:

> Angus is doing something on his computer. Samuel comes up. "Why are you doing that?" he asks. "Because it is fun", Angus answers. Angus and Samuel discuss levels in the online computer game World of Warcraft. Angus is sitting in his chair, Samuel standing behind him. "Do you want to make a motorcycle?" [on the computer], the girl sitting next to Angus asks him. But Angus gets up and follows Samuel outside, where both of them join a wild game of throwing leaves. (observation, day 1, during recess)

Angus and Samuel both play the game *World of Warcraft*, either virtually together or at Angus' home, which has two computers. Their common interest in the game is the base of a real friendship between Angus and Samuel, and when the class is about to begin a longer project work, the two boys choose each other as work partners. During the project work, Angus' computer becomes an asset because the group as a whole can use it, for example when they have to write a joint theme description for their project. Angus is very competent on the computer, even though he writes slowly and with many typos, which annoys Samuel, who would like to be in charge of the writing. But Angus is familiar with the programs on the computer and stays in charge, even though his motor disability is exposed during the activity:

> Angus shows Samuel how to do a particular operation on the computer. But Samuel gets up and leaves, and Angus shows it to Michael [a third boy in the group] instead.
>   The teacher goes to the group, Samuel returns. She comments on the theme description: it lacks a clear focus. Angus deletes some of it. The teacher leaves. Samuel makes a suggestion for a new theme description, but Angus does not write it down. "Hallo, do you remember what I just said?" Samuel says. Angus and Samuel discuss the new theme description; Angus wants something about the squires, Samuel points out that the main theme is children and adolescents. Finally, Angus comes up with a question which contains both squires and children. "That's exactly what I said before", Samuel exclaims. Angus writes the question on the computer. (Observation, day 4, project work)

The computer enables Angus to stay in charge of the theme description, because he can write and make corrections. In contrast to Marcus, Angus has incorporated the computer as an aid, which makes it possible for him to push his neurobiological constraints and function on equal terms with his peers most of the time.

It is possible that Marcus will also integrate the computer as a remedy, which makes it easier to function in learning situations. To do this, he must be able to detach himself from the problem as it presents itself and consider it at a metacognitive level: a mental operation considered to belong to the area of executive functions. The executive dysfunctions of Marcus (described by the BRIEF) make it difficult for him to reflect on the way he approaches problems, including which remedies could ease the process. Marcus' growing acceptance of the computer might present an opening. His many positive experiences of the computer as an aid might provide an alternative way for Marcus to reach an understanding of his need of different aids at a more general level, as Angus already has incorporated in his thinking and activity.

Conclusion

In order to understand how each of the two boys use their computers, the dialectic relations between their cognitive abilities, their motives and the social situation need to be taken into consideration.

The two cases illustrate how children with lesions to their brains change and develop as an active response to the changing demands and possibilities in the settings like normal children do. Still, the presence of cognitive problems, impairments in the executive functions in particular, is a wide-ranging constraint as it affects learning and development at two levels; both the learning of concrete material and the learning of how to learn best. The two levels of learning apply to children with normally functioning brains as well. But children with brain lesions are facing a double challenge; they are constrained by their cerebral condition and often their social situation is less optimal.

Angus has prospered on being met with nearly normal requirements in school, where his need of remedies and special considerations have been built into the social situation of his class over time. The present social situation provides him with plenty of opportunities to learn both curriculum and social skills at much the same pace as his peers. Angus owns both the skills and the motive to use his computer as an aid in relation to both, thereby modifying and developing his neurobiological constraints.

In contrast, the developmental trajectory of Marcus has been different and more riddled with conflicts between his neurobiological constraints and the practices for learning at school. Marcus' brain lesion makes it more difficult for him to see material and to organise it. Still, the difficulties Marcus faced in class could not be understood without appreciation of his particular motives and their conflict with the social situation of his presence in the normal class. His learning was held back by his reluctance to stand out and use necessary remedies such as his computer. Only when the conflict between the motive of social inclusion and the social situation began its resolution, could room be found to work on Marcus' learning of learning and his further development in and through the use of appropriate remedies. The institutional changes and Marcus' sprouting reflection on the usefulness of remedies might be the beginning of a major development of his neurobiological constraints.

The neurobiological constraints of typical children do not stand out in the way that neurobiological constraints of children with CP often do. Still, the differences between children with CP and typical children are continual rather than categorical. Children with brains functioning within normal expectations can be more or less intelligent as measured by intelligence tests, they might have a talent for music or experience problems with learning to read. In a group of typical children, many different learning styles and different motives for learning can be found and as they enter school, their childhood too is constructed from the dialectical relations between their particular neurobiological endowments and the local cultural-historical institutional practices for learning that they meet in school. To understand the progress or problem of a particular child's learning in school, this dialectic must be taken into consideration.

References

Bax, M., Goldstein, M., Rosenbaum, P., Leviton, A., & Paneth, N. (2005). Proposed definition and classification of cerebral palsy, April 2005—Introduction. *Developmental Medicine and Child Neurology*, 47, 571–576.

Bishop, D. V. M. (1997). Cognitive neuropsychology and developmental disorders: Uncomfortable bedfellows. *Quarterly Journal of Experimental Psychology Section A: Human Experimental Psychology*, 50, 899–923.

Frampton, I., Yude, C., & Goodman, R. (1998). The prevalence and correlates of specific learning difficulties in a representative sample of children with hemiplegia. *British Journal of Educational Psychology*, 68, 39–51.

Goodman, R. & Graham, P. (1996). Psychiatric problems in children with hemiplegia: Cross sectional epidemiological survey. *British Medical Journal*, 312, 1065–1069.

Gottlieb, G., Wahlsten, D., & Lickliter, R. (1998). The significance of biology for human development: A developmental psychobiological systems view. In W. Damon (Ed.), *Handbook of child psychology*, 5th edn (pp. 233–273). New York: Wiley.

Greenough, W. T., Black, J. E., & Wallace, C. S. (1987). Experience and brain-development. *Child Development*, 58, 539–559.

Hedegaard, M. (2002). *Learning and child development*. Aarhus: Aarhus University Press.

Hedegaard, M. (in press). Children's development from a cultural-historical approach: Children's activity in everyday local settings as a foundation for their development. *Mind, Culture and Activity*.

Hedegaard, M. & Fleer, M. (in press). A wholeness approach to child development and an argumentation for a theoretical interactive methodology to the study of children in their everyday life. Buckingham: Open University Press.

Hundeide, K. (2003). *Børns livsverden og sociokulturelle rammer* [Children's life-world and socio-cultural structures]. Copenhagen: Akademisk Forlag.

Karmiloff-Smith, A. (1998). Development itself is the key to understanding developmental disorders. *Trends in Cognitive Sciences*, 2, 389–398.

Karmiloff-Smith, A. (2007). Atypical epigenesis. *Developmental Science*, 10, 84–88.

Leontiev, A. N. (1977). *Problemer i det psykiskes udvikling. I–III* [Problems in the development of the psychic. Volumes I–III]. Copenhagen: Rhodos.

Nadeau, L. & Tessier, R. (2006). Social adjustment of children with cerebral palsy in mainstream classes: Peer perception. *Developmental Medicine and Child Neurology*, 48, 331–336.

Ostensjo, S., Carlberg, E. B., & Vollestad, N. K. (2003). Everyday functioning in young children with cerebral palsy: Functional skills, caregiver assistance, and modifications of the environment. *Developmental Medicine and Child Neurology*, 45, 603–612.

Riegel, K. F. (1975). Toward a dialectical theory of development. *Human Development*, 18, 50–64.

Scribner, S. (1997). *Mind and social practice. Selected writings of Sylvia Scribner.* Cambridge: Cambridge University Press.

Stiles, J. (2000). Neural plasticity and cognitive development. *Developmental Neuropsychology*, 18, 237–272.

Stiles, J., Moses, P., Passarotti, A., Dick, F. K., & Buxton, R. (2003). Exploring developmental change in the neural bases of higher cognitive functions: The promise of functional magnetic resonance imaging. *Developmental Neuropsychology*, 24, 641–668.

Valsiner, J. (1997). *Culture and the development of children's action. A theory of human development*, 2nd edn. New York: John Wiley.

Vygotsky, L. S. (1993). *The collected works of L. S. Vygotsky* (Vol. 2 The fundamentals of defectology (Abnormal psychology and learning disabilities)). New York: Plenum Press.

Yude, C., Goodman, R., & McConachie, H. (1998). Peer problems of children with hemiplegia in mainstream primary schools. *Journal of Child Psychology and Psychiatry and Allied Disciplines*, 39, 533–541.

Part II

Global–Local Childhood Studies

7 Vygotsky and the Conceptual Revolution in Developmental Sciences

Towards a Unified (Non-Additive) Account of Human Development

Anna Stetsenko

In this chapter, I address the core (worldview level) foundations of the Cultural-Historical Activity Theory (CHAT, taken here to refer to the Vygotsky–Leontive–Luria school)—a theoretical perspective grounded in Vygotsky's writings and further extended by several generations of this scholar's collaborators and followers both in Russia and, more recently, by a broad community of researchers on an international scene. Collaboratively developed in the early 20th century by Vygotsky and a group of enthusiastic scholars united around him (especially Leontiev and Luria), all passionately involved in the social transformations that at the time were taking place in Russia, this perspective offered—well ahead of its time—a new vision on the most profound questions pertaining to human development and human 'nature.' At the same time, it suggested a new mission for psychology as a practical-theoretical endeavor deeply imbued with the ideology of social justice and empowerment and aimed at the betterment and transformation of society (see Stetsenko & Arievitch, 2004). In my view, this theoretical perspective represents a revolutionary way to conceptualize human development that—if revealed and ascertained more coherently and directly than it has been done till now—can be seen as a precursor for the most recent breakthroughs in developmental sciences that still bears much potential for finding solutions for today's issues in these sciences both theoretically and practically.

The revolutionary import of CHAT, however, cannot be directly and easily deduced or seen from the writings of its founders. These writings, extending through several decades and comprising a vastly diversified set of ideas and methodologies, present an often contradictory and incomplete picture of human development with many gaps and internal inconsistencies. The task of bringing these ideas together in a coherent and comprehensive system that would be capable of addressing major issues related to human development and learning has not yet been accomplished. This is evident in the splitting of contemporary approaches based on Vygotsky, Leontiev, and Luria's ideas, the inconsistencies in interpreting commonalities and differences among these ideas, the disagreements in what constitutes the very basis of Vygotsky's project, and in the lack of clarity on the very question as to whether their works comprise one system of thought. What is required today, in my view, is that the very foundational premises (and their implications) implicit in the works of Vygotsky and his collaborators are revealed as one comprehensive system of ideas grounded in a novel understanding of the very phenomenon of human nature and development.

The solution I will explore in this chapter is that the revolutionary import of Vygotsky's project, including the studies of childhood, has to do with its broadly dialectical and non-reductionist, yet consistently non-dualist (non-additive) vision of human nature and development. According to this vision, human development is rooted in, derivative of, instrumental in, and constituted by the material collaborative social practices of people (i.e., human goal-directed, purposeful, collaborative activities) aimed at transforming their world. These practices, on the one hand, produce and engender social interactions and human subjectivity (mind, consciousness, and the self), and on the other hand (at mature stages of development in history and in ontogeny) are themselves reciprocally produced by these social interactions and subjectivity. Among other implications, taking the material collaborative social practices to be the irreducible core of development signifies a resolute break with the two-factorial (or hybrid type) approaches in which influences of different order (e.g., cultural and biological ones) are thought to shape, in some combination, the very course of human development.

This distinctive feature of Vygotsky's project unifies diverse works conducted within this framework (at least at initial stages in its history, cf. Sawchuk & Stetsenko, in press) and represents a well grounded (both in natural sciences such as biology and in critical-humanistic perspectives) alternative to approaches that till today remain largely stalled between the two extreme poles of (a) biological reductionism that views all development as having to do with the narrowly conceived genetic programming and operation of brain circuits and (b) narrow versions of social constructionism that reduce development to forms of discourse and other forces of supra-individual level. In offering this alternative, CHAT builds on the relational ontology of human development and learning that places *relations* between individuals and their world at the core of this development—a theme that has recently gained in popularity in developmental sciences. However, CHAT also goes beyond this recently emerging, and increasingly popular, relational view and overcomes its hidden pitfalls associated with assumptions of passivity and contemplative nature of development by positing instead an *active transformative practice as the source as well as the ultimate 'fabric' (the very matter) of psychological development*. As such, the ideas developed in CHAT (though often only in an implicit form) are still in the zone of proximal development (to use Vygotsky's expression) for contemporary views and theoretical frameworks.

This contribution entails three fundamental ideas central to understanding child development. The first idea has to do with the non-mechanistic, relational ontology that posits relations rather than separate entities (influencing each other in extraneous ways only) as a supreme reality in which and out of which human beings develop and grow, including development of psychological functions. The second idea is that relations that define human life and lie at its core are active, transformative, and collaborative—processes best captured by the notion of activity afforded by the employment of collectively created and manufactured cultural tools. The third idea is that the development of psychological processes is but part and parcel of the transformative collaborative activities—not a separate (and quite ephemeral) mental realm. In their entirety, these propositions constitute a cutting-edge approach that can truly be seen as an important precursor, and a de facto zone of proximal development, for what many now view as a conceptual revolution in developmental sciences.

Situating Vygotsky's Project in Today's Landscape: Nature-Culture Hybridity Versus Unified, Non-Additive Accounts of Development

Vygotsky's approach is broadly associated today with the notion that culture and context represent important factors shaping human development and learning. In this rendering of Vygotsky's theory, his ideas are regarded as an addition to those approaches (e.g., stemming from Piaget's works) that are perceived to focus on internal structures of the mind as being an independent reality existing in its own right and developing according to its own internal regularities and mechanisms. To take just one example from a few years ago, in a recent book on development of social cognition, Homer and Tamis-LeMonda (2005) distinguish between two approaches in developmental psychology and argue that one of them, founded on work by Piaget "has emphasized the role of cognitive processes that occur within the child," whereas the other, building on the work of *Vygotsky*, "has emphasized the role of *external, social* factors, such as dyadic engagements and the acquisition of cultural tools." The authors also state that "[r]ecent work in the field of developmental psychology has brought together these two theoretical traditions by assigning equal importance to the individual child and to the *social* environment in which the child is embedded." This is by no means a single or rare interpretation; quite on the contrary, in many contemporary works that employ Vygotsky's works, his theory is accorded with a revolutionary understanding of cultural *influences* on development.

In this and multiple other examples, human development is essentially seen as driven by various distinctive factors that act, in various combinations, to influence development through some additive process in which the influences of these factors are brought together and summed up.

This common view persists in spite of important advances of the last 15–20 years by a number of prominent Western scholars (e.g., Bruner, Cole, John-Steiner, Rogoff, Scribner, Wertsch). This is not surprising given how complex the issue of culture (e.g., in juxtaposition to nature) and its role in the dynamics of human development are and how multilayered (and often ambiguous) Vygotsky's take on this issue is. Further exploration into various layers in Vygotskian conception and its contemporary (and often rival) interpretations remains to be an important task. In particular, Michael Cole has championed integration of Vygotsky's (and other Russian scholars') writings into contemporary approaches to development and can be credited as one of the pioneers and enthusiasts of CHAT in the Western world. Through unique and substantial contributions made in his own research (e.g., Cole, 1988, 1996; Cole, Gay, Glick, & Sharp, 1971), this scholar has drawn attention to studying the impact of culture on human development and to the need to move beyond the narrow understanding of culture as a 'black box' variable. Among other contributions, Cole's research has helped to highlight the fact that Vygotsky's approach attributes an essential role to culture in human psychological processes, expounding and expanding on Vygotsky's message about the inextricable link between artifacts, mediation, and culture. While focusing on the notion of culture, Cole has suggested, in line with Vygotsky's project, that culture should be seen as the artifact-saturated environment (medium) of human life—or a pool of artifacts. According to this approach, each person can be thought of as "as acquiring their own personal culture, or personal tool kit, made up of that part of the common pool that they have come in contact with and appropriated" (Cole & Gajdamaschko, 2007, p. 208). As Cole states in another publication (1996, p. 114), "… culture undergoes both quantitative change in terms of the number and variety of artifacts, and qualitative change in terms of the mediational potentials that they embody. And as a consequence, both culture and human thinking develop."

In addition, Cole pays much attention to the interlacing and intertwining of natural and biological processes. His final conclusion is based on a dual, hybrid view of cultural and phylogenetic influences as two distinct (though interdependent) sets of factors. In Cole's (2002, pp. 316–317) words:

> In so far as it is dominated by phylogenetic influences, development is a Darwinian process of natural selection operating on the random variation of genetic combinations created at conception. But cultural change operates according to a different set of principles: cultural variations are not randomly generated, they are, rather, descended from the successful adaptations of prior generations passed down exosomatically. While natural selection has the final say, in so far as human behavior is mediated through culture it is 'distorted' by a Lamarckian principle of evolution. In acquiring culture …, culture becomes a 'second nature' which makes development a goal-directed process in a way in which phylogenetic change is not. … Human beings are hybrids.

There are many direct implications, of a principled nature, from such an approach to human development, including how the early roots of child psychological functioning are conceptualized. On this point, Cole suggests that natural forms of cognition are not replaced by cultural ones. Instead, "humans everywhere *are born possessing at least skeletal, innate mechanisms* for parsing the world in ways that enable them to make correct inferences about a variety of physical and biological phenomena" (Cole & Gajdamaschko, 2007, p. 209; emphasis added). These skeletal principles, as Cole (2002, p. 315) states are present "as early at birth as it can be tested for," providing *constraints* upon which later understanding can be built. Cole sides with Gelman's (1990) position according to which "[i]t is necessary to grant infants and/or young children domain-specific organizing structures." The conclusion drawn is that there is "a growing consensus on the model of development that combines the idea of innate skeletal constraints with the idea of cultural mediation in cultural organized, scripted activities" (Cole, 2002, p. 315). The main question then becomes, according to Cole, "under what conditions will the primitive abilities of the young infant be *realized* in appropriate behaviors that are part of its everyday life?" (Cole, 2002, p. 313).

In general, Michael Cole's push to ascertain the role of culture as a medium of development (rather than merely a factor among others), in which biological and socio-cultural factors act together to shape this process, represents an important advance over approaches that reduce development to being an outcome, exclusively, of either external (as in behaviorism) or internal (as in extreme forms of nativism) factors. Cole's perspective also provides a number of important specifications on the major composition and constituents of culture and its artifacts. There are ways, however, to build on, and expand Vygotsky's nascent understanding of development in a way that more resolutely breaks away from the multi-factorial, additive model and instead advances a unified account of development as a process with its own logic not reducible to additive effects of various forces acting on it.

As I intend to show in the following sections, Vygotsky's position on human development is more complicated (though sometimes only in subtle ways and not without its own contradictions and gaps) than the hybrid-type interpretation would grant it. This is evident, for example, in that Vygotsky (1987, p. 99) struggled to move beyond the 'principle of convergence' of external and internal influences on development when he critiqued Stern's position according to which development proceeds through a constant interaction of internal dispositions and external conditions—an example of a two-factorial model of development. Instead, Vygotsky insisted that

> It is not by the presence or absence of some specific external conditions but by the *internal logic of the process of development itself* that the necessity of critical, break-through periods [and therefore, of development itself] in a child's life is called upon. (1998, p. 192)

It might sound paradoxical that Vygotsky is talking about the 'internal logic of the development' itself, as if referring to something inside the organism ('under the skin') to describe development. This is not the case, however. A closer look at Vygotsky's logic (especially in the context of the whole corpus of his writings) suggests an alternative—and more dialectical—interpretation. For one, given Vygotsky's staunch insistence on the importance of culture/

environment in development throughout his works (including in his famous 'general genetic law' according to which psychological processes emerge from social interactions), his reference to 'internal logic of the process of development' should be viewed as having to do *not* with the processes internal to the organism per se but as hinging on a radically different notion of development altogether. In fact, Vygotsky is struggling to formulate a radically novel understanding of human development as a process sui generis—a *unitary*, that is, non-additive rather than hybrid, process with its own logic that inheres in its own dynamics and contradictions. Unlike the alternative hybrid-view of development according to which various influences are added and brought together, or interlaced and interwoven, but not merged *into one realm* of a singular process, Vygotsky is moving in the direction of overcoming this dual view of development. Granted, Vygotsky often de facto equivocates between this radically new position and the more traditional, hybrid-type approach, sometimes falling back into asserting that it is the two processes (the natural and the cultural ones) that constitute development. However, his main thesis is expressed in no uncertain terms when he states that

> All originality, all difficulty of the problem of the development of higher mental functions of the child consists in that both lines (biological and cultural) are merged in ontogenesis and actually form a *single*, although complex process. (1997, p. 15; emphasis added).

> ... the system of activity of the child is determined at each given moment by both the degree of his organic development and the degree of his mastery of tools. The two different systems develop jointly, forming, in essence, *a third system, a new system of a unique type.* (1997, p. 21; emphasis added).

Vygotsky is also very clear in his rejection of taking outside influences as the prime determinants of development.

> One of the major impediments to the theoretical and practical study of child development is the incorrect solution of the problem of the environment and its role in the dynamics of age when the environment is considered as something outside with respect to the child, as a circumstance of development, as an aggregate of objective conditions existing without reference to the child and affecting him by the very fact of their existence (1998, p. 198).

Michael Cole has also commented on this particular quote—noting Vygotsky's interest in understanding context as not just a mere outside influence on development. However, Cole's interpretation again goes in line with a 'dual' (or hybrid, additive) understanding. In particular, Cole (2003) states that

For Vygotsky, the social situation of development is a relational construct in which characteristics of the child *combine* with the structure of social interactions to create the starting point for a new cycle of developmental changes which will result in a new, and higher, level of development (and a new, relevant, social situation of development). (emphasis added)

Another possible understanding is that environment is not something outside of the child that can be added to the child's own 'internal' characteristics; rather, the child is included, right from the start, in the *ongoing process of relationships with one's environment* and it is these relationships (the give-and-take between the organism and the world) that constitute the form of life (the mode of existence) for the child—an irreducible reality of development in its own right that supersedes any outside or inside influences understood as existing separately from each other and from the child acting in the environment. The point is that it is in principle insufficient to consider influences (in any of their combinations or hierarchy) on development in order to understand how this process comes about and progresses. Infinite number of factors, in an infinite number of combinations, influence development at any particular time, starting from even the most general ones such as the forces of gravity and solar power (including fluctuations in climate changes), and ending (metaphorically speaking) with societal structures, access to cultural resources, influences of proximate others, biological characteristics of the organism, and so forth. However, no research into these factors and influences per se, however meticulous and broad in scope, would ever be sufficient to illuminate development unless attention is paid to the reality of development itself as a process in its own right which, while not shielded from external and internal influences, proceeds on its own grounds and according to its own logic. These influences are not ignored; rather, they are understood to remain indeterminate in their effects until they are absorbed by the evolving activities between the child and the environment and thus transformed into dimensions or aspects of development.

In this rendering of Vygotsky's project, the dichotomies and dualism of culture versus nature (including a 'hybridity' expression of this dualism) is dialectically superseded by positing that development forms a reality sui generis not reducible to a sum of influences (internal or external) extraneous to its own unique realm and ontology. As I discuss in the next section, in struggling to formulate these views of development as a process in its own right, Vygotsky turns out to be in the company of today's scholars (especially those developing relational accounts of development including Developmental Systems Theory) who rarely associate themselves with his works but de facto continue and elaborate on a similar set of ideas.

Conceptual Revolution in Developmental Sciences

A conceptual revolution in the fields of developmental biology and psychology has been taking place in the last decade, although many scholars working in these fields are still often unaware of the sweeping changes in their respective disciplines. This conceptual revolution provides an integrated account of human development and is associated with the ascendancy of relational and developmental systems approaches that move away from the assumptions typical of the mechanistic and essentializing worldview. Although still far from being the mainstay of research, these relational and dynamical approaches have become quite prominent across areas such as developmental psychology (e.g., Lerner, 2004; Thelen & Smith, 1994), ecological studies (e.g., Ingold, 2000), cultural anthropology (e.g., Holland, Lachicotte, Skinner, & Cain, 2001), organizational studies (e.g., Engestrom, 1990), studies of communication and cognition (e.g., Clark, 1997; Cole, 1996; Hutchins, 1995), and education (e.g., Barab & Roth, 2006; Gutierrez, 2002; Hedegaard, 2007; Lantolf & Thorne, 2006; Lave & Wenger, 1991; Rogoff, 2003).

What underpins all of these approaches is a relational worldview that posits mutually influential relations between the organism (in biology) or person (in psychology) and the world as the basic process at the core of development. The central assumption of this worldview has to do with challenging the central essentialist premise about phenomena in the social world being 'thing-like' entities that exist separately from each other and the rest of the world (if not without some extraneous influence from other independently existing entities). In opposition to this view, many of today's approaches are based on the notion that social and psychological phenomena are processes that exist in *the realm of relations and interactions*—that is, as embedded, situated, distributed, and co-constructed within contexts. The most evident common rationale across these approaches (though varying in the degree of its explicitness) is the need to overcome the Cartesian split between the object and the subject, the person and the world, the knower and the known, and to offer instead a radically different *relational ontology* in which processes occur in the realm *between* individuals and their world. In this broad worldview-level approach, for example, development and learning are not seen as products of solitary, self-contained individuals endowed with internal machinery of cognitive skills that only await the right conditions to unfold. Instead, they are seen as existing in the flux of individuals relating to their world, driven by relational processes and their unfolding logic, and therefore as not being constrained by rigidly imposed, pre-programmed scripts or rules.

Thus, the reductionist metaphor of separation (typical of the previous mechanistic worldview) is replaced with the metaphor of 'in-between-uity,' that is, of mutual co-construction, co-evolution, continuous dialogue, belonging, participation and the like, all underscoring relatedness and interconnectedness, blending and meshing—the 'coming together' of individuals and their world that transcends their separation. With its broad message of the meta-level, this perspective has profound implications for practically all steps in conceptualizing and studying phenomena in the social world, including the self, identity, mind, knowledge, and intelligence, as well as human development at large.

Much of this conceptual revolution in psychology and other social sciences can be attributed to (or at least associated with and supported by) the recent breakthrough advances in biology—a discipline that is today at the forefront in establishing and ascertaining a dynamic view on development (for excellent overviews, see Lewontin, 2000; Lickliter & Honeycutt, 2003a, 2003b; Oyama, 1985, 2000). In particular, whereas from the mid-20th century and up to 1990s the core concepts in biology focused on the role of genes as the singular vehicles by which instructions for development are transmitted across generations, the situation has dramatically changed in recent years. The more recent concepts highlight a much more dialectical picture of development and move away from the dichotomy of two types of causal factors operating in development—the genes (nature) on the one hand, and the environment (nurture) that 'interacts' with genes to provide the conditions necessary for the expression of information encoded in these genes (see Lickliter & Honeycutt, 2003b, p. 461), on the other. What recent works in developmental system theory contest is the nondevelopmental "phylogeny fallacy" (Lickliter & Berry, 1990), according to which ontogeny and phylogeny are alternative means by which information is made available to the developing individual. Instead, the emerging consensus today is that the bodily forms as well as physiological, behavioral, and cognitive processes never are, and in principle cannot be, pre-specified in advance of the individual's development (for further discussion see Lickliter & Berry, 1990; Oyama, 1985; cf. Lickliter & Honeycutt, 2003b).

The hallmark of the Dynamic System Theory (DST) is its call for a 'constructive interactionism' that argues against any pre-specification of traits, characteristics, or behaviors including psychological processes in even their 'skeletal forms.' Instead, development is posited to be a *self-organizing*, probabilistic process in which pattern and order emerge and undergo changes in the course of individual development as a result of complex interactions and relations unique to each organism. As Lickliter and Honeycutt (2003b, p. 462) claim

> From this framework, behavioral or cognitive development cannot be represented as the unfolding of a fixed or predetermined substrate, independent of the activity, experience, or setting of the individual. This relational focus on the ontogenetic construction of phenotypes undermines any meaningful opposition between genetic and environmental sources of information for development, a framework still common in several subdisciplines with the behavioral sciences …

Importantly, DST implies that development is not the result of the summation of genetic and environmental factors, as neither operates independently and cannot be seen as alternative causes for the expression of a trait or characteristic. The importance of this claim is not only that genetic and environmental factors (nature and nurture) interact or mesh with each other in individual development, but that the organism itself, together with all of its traits and characters, *must be constructed—rather than expressed or brought to realization—in individual ontogeny.* A focus on the organism coactively constructing itself in the course of its life undermines any claims that cognitive modules pre-exist individual development and lie dormant awaiting activation or realization under certain conditions and extraneous influences.

Thus, this newly emerging perspective amounts to a clear rejection of the concept of development as being an additive, hybrid product of a confluence of factors (either internal or external) extraneous to development itself. Instead, development is understood as a process of self-organizing activity by the organism—activity that unfolds and undergoes constant changes during individual life course. The difference between this position and the hybrid-type, additive approaches (where genetic and environmental influences are thought to interact with each other but are taken to be independent of the self-organizing activities by the organism) is tacit but extremely significant. This difference continues to evade many scholars even among those who attempt to move away from unidirectional understanding of development (e.g., in socio-cultural traditions) but reincarnate the duality of development in new guises, for example, as a duality of gene–culture co-evolution. As Susan Oyama (2000) has commented,

> The concepts of trait transmission and *developmental duality* are linked by a way of thinking about the role of genes and environment in ontogeny that ensures that we will continue to find ways to carve up the living world into innate and acquired portions, no matter how vociferously we declare the distinction to be obsolete. (p. 21; emphasis added)

> Even though the distinction between the innate and acquired has been under attack for decades ..., and even though it is routinely dismissed and ridiculed in the scientific literature ..., it continues to appear in new guises. The very people who pronounce it obsolete, manage, *in the next breath*, to distinguish between a character that is a 'genetic property' and one that is only 'an environmentally produced analogue ... Vocabulary and styles of description shift, but the conviction remains that some developmental courses are more controlled by the genes than others' .(p. 22; emphasis added)

Vygotsky as a Relational Theorist

Vygotsky is not often associated with the premises of relational ontology, with recent interpretations of his works often focusing, as mentioned in the previous section of this chapter, on the importance of the effects of social context on human development, suggesting a model in which outside influences are seen as forces that shape development and learning. However, much of Vygotsky's efforts can be read as an attempt to re-conceptualize human development based on relational premises, that is, in terms of an organism–environment nexus in which the two continuously determine each other so that neither one can be conceived independently. In fact, one of Vygotsky's core achievements was that he substituted for the fixed, preformist views on development the notion that development exists in flux and constant change, with fluid and ever-changing, open-ended dynamical processes linking organisms and their environments. For example, Vygotsky (1997, p. 100) challenged the then accepted view that development could be understood as a set of static, predetermined steps when he wrote:

> Least of all does child development resemble a stereotypic process shielded from external influences; here [in child development], *in a living adaptation to the outside milieu* is the development and change of the child accomplished. In this process, ever newer forms arise, rather than the elements in the already preordained chain being simply stereotypically reproduced. (emphasis added)

In this and similar instances, Vygotsky insisted that development cannot be seen as an unfolding of pre-specified internal potentials enclosed in some potential form present at preceding stages of development; such an understanding, according to Vygotsky, describes not so much a process of development as a process of growth and maturation. In an alternative account, development consists in the new stage arising not out of unfolding of potentials enclosed in the preceding stage, but out of *an actual confrontation between the organism and the environment and an alive adaptation to the environment.*

Vygotsky's affirmation of relational ontology is also evident in his statement that "relations to the environment stand at the beginning and at the end" of development (Vygotsky, 2004, p. 194). And in yet another place, he asserts that his approach eventually resolves the argument between nativism and empiricism by showing that "*everything* in personality is built on a species-generic, innate basis and, at the same time, *everything* in it is supra-organic, contingent, that is, social" (Vygotsky, 2004, p. 190; emphasis in the original). In formulating these views, Vygotsky directly, and even quite literally, intuits the developmental system theory (DST), according to which any psychological process is "fully a product of biology *and* culture" (Lickliter & Honeycutt, 2003a, p. 469; emphasis in the original) and what counts as 'biological' falls entirely within the domain of what counts as 'cultural' and vice versa (cf. Ingold, 2000).

What these examples underscore is that at its most fundamental level, and drawing on groundbreaking advances in natural sciences in the late 19th and early 20th centuries, Vygotsky's project (the Vygotsky–Leontiev–Luria theoretical framework) was based on the premise that living organisms exist and develop in dynamic interchanges with the environment—as part of (or a moment in) a dynamic system of relations connecting organisms with the environment. It is the open-ended, ongoing, dynamical, reciprocal, and bi-directional (give-and-take) relationship with the environment that constitutes, according to CHAT, the foundation of life and ultimately defines all characteristics of organisms such as their structure, functioning, morphology, and development (both in evolution and in ontogenesis). In this view, no organism and no aspect or dimension of its functioning (including psychological processes) exist outside of or prior to a dynamical relationship with the environment. Therefore, development can neither be studied nor understood in abstraction from this relationship; instead it needs to be understood as a dynamically expanding and ever-changing relationship between the organism and the world.

Crucial to Vygotsky and his followers, adopting and further elaborating the relational and dynamical worldview was their acquaintance with and enthusiastic reception of Darwin's ideas of animate nature as a process imbued with *collective, relational, and historicized dynamics.* Importantly, Darwinian insights have been merged into Vygotsky's project with the growing knowledge about the physiology of the nervous system and the brain (e.g., Helmholtz, Sherrington, Sechenov, and—later—Pavlov, Ukhtomskij, Bekhterev, and Bernstein). Following on from these two important strands, the CHAT founders viewed processes in the animate world as being in constant flux, subject to change, variation, chance and development, entailing the position that these processes neither have predestined constraints nor follow preprogrammed paths, algorithms and ordered stages.

This general relational approach set the stage for the CHAT founders to attend to questions about the place and role of mind in the broader context of life (i.e., in regulating activities of organisms in their environment), rather than in the workings of physiological processes or narrowly defined behavior. They saw their task as having to do with conceptualizing mind as being a part of this organism–environment nexus, rather than existing in organisms taken in isolation. Vygotksy's early works can be interpreted as focusing on elaborating the dynamical notion of development consistent with the relational worldview (bearing much resemblance to Deweyan transactionalism). In particular, Vygotsky expanded insights about the open-ended, fluid, and dynamical character of natural processes into the realm of psychology, essentially defining mind as representing part of nature. For Vygotsky and his followers, mind evolves from matter and can be seen as involved and immersed in life activities of organisms-in-environments. This dynamical process of interrelations with the environment calls for and gives rise to regulatory mechanisms that allow for it to be carried out. This idea, formulated in its incipient form by Vygotsky, became central to Leontiev (e.g., Leontiev, 1979) in his works on the phylogenetic origins of the mind. Much of CHAT is devoted to exploring how more and more refined mechanisms of regulation, in the form of increasingly complex psychological processes, have emerged as a result of increasingly complex exchanges between organisms and their environments and evolutionary pressures to adapt to the ever more complex demands of life associated with growing levels of unpredictability and uncertainty.

The truly original contribution of CHAT, however, goes beyond the premises of relational and dynamic systems theoretical approaches. Though not finalized by the CHAT founders and containing many ideas only implicitly, this contribution has to do with conceptualizing the very type of relations that link humans to their world and will be expansively articulated in the following section while adding a number of specifications and extensions.

Transformative Collaborative Activities as the Foundation of Human Development

Whereas most relational and dynamic systems theories described in the preceding section (including those following Dewey and Piaget) treat human beings as no different than other biological organisms—thus keeping up with the notion that 'nature makes no drastic leaps'—Vygotsky and his followers postulated precisely such a leap and turned to exploring its implications. In doing so, these scholars followed the Marxist dialectical materialist view according to which "... [the] base for human thinking is precisely *man changing nature* and not nature alone as such, and the mind developed according to how human beings learned to change nature" (Engels, quoted in Vygotsky, 1997, p. 56; italics in the original).

According to this view, the evolutionary origins of humans have to do with an emergence of a unique relation to the world realized not through adaptation but through the social practice of human labor—the collaborative (and therefore sociocultural), transformative practice unfolding and expanding in history. Through this collaborative process (involving development and passing on, from generation to generation, the collective experiences reified in cultural tools, including language), people not only constantly transform and create their environment, they also create and constantly transform their very life, consequently changing themselves in fundamental ways while, in and through this process, becoming human and gaining self-knowledge and knowledge about the world. Therefore, human activity—material, practical, and always by necessity social, collaborative processes aimed at transforming the world—is taken in CHAT to be the basic form of human life, that is, of human relation to the world.

This new transformative relation to the world, precisely as a new form of life brings about the emergence of human beings, supersedes adaptation and natural selection, as well as the distinction between nature and culture, and establishes the centrality of human practice in its unity of history, society, and culture as a supreme ontological realm for development and learning. This conceptual turn is actually quite radical because the shift from adaptation to transformation is taken to signify the end of biological evolution and a transition to processes now taking place in the realm where forces of history, culture, and society reign. This turn by the CHAT scholars is of a truly dialectical sort because it posits that human development is both continuous with and radically different from the processes in the rest of the animate world. Human history and life entail a radical break with nature, while at the same time continuing it. Thus, with the transition to humans there is a drastic leap away from biological laws and regularities that govern the animal world. In this leap, nature negates itself, turning into a radically new reality—the reality of cultural history of human civilization that proceeds in the form of a continuous flow of collaborative practices of people aimed at transforming their world. Human development, from this perspective, can be conceptualized as a sociohistorical project and a collaborative achievement— that is, a continuously evolving process that represents a 'work-in-progress' by people as agents who together change their world and, in and through this process, come to know themselves, while ultimately becoming human.

Human nature, in this perspective, is not an immutable, pre-given evolutionary residue that rigidly defines development within the constraints of biological endowment and functioning. Neither is it a product of various factors and influences acting on human beings from outside of their own activity. Instead, human nature is a process of overcoming and transcending its own limitations through collaborative, continuous practices aimed at purposefully changing the world. In other words, it is a process of historical becoming by humans not as merely creatures of nature but as agents of their own lives, *agents whose nature is to purposefully transform their world*.

It is the simultaneity, or in even stronger terms, the unity of human transformative practice on the one hand, and the process of becoming (and being human) and of knowing oneself and the world on the other, that is conveyed in this conception. Human beings come to be themselves and come to know their world and themselves *in the process and as the process* of collaboratively changing their world (while changing together with it)—in the midst of this process and as one of its facets—rather than outside of or merely in connection with it. This conceptualization of human development moves beyond the dualistic designation of nature and culture and does so not by simply stating their bi-directional relation or hybridity. Instead, the collaborative human practice is posited as the new unified—and unique— ontological realm that takes over and dialectically supersedes (or supplants) both nature and culture, absorbing and negating them within its own, and radically new, transformative ontology.

In the transformative ontology, culture is *immanent* to people's activities (and hence their development) rather than an outside source of influence or a pool of artifacts. Culture is neither inside nor outside human beings; moreover, it is neither something that people have nor just a milieu that they exist in or relate to – an extraneous world out there to be discovered. Instead, culture is the *quality of human life* that people continuously *do and enact* – a unique quality of them *collaboratively* engaging their world through *collective* efforts.

Positing a continuous flow of collaborative transformative practices as the foundation of human life and the 'substrate' (or 'fabric') of development entails a number of implications (for details, see Stetsenko, 2005, 2008) such as the centrality of contribution to these collaborative practices from an authentic subject position as the grounding for human subjectivity. Given that transformative engagement with the world is taken as ontologically and epistemically supreme, and because transformation can only be achieved from a certain position and with certain goals in view, the ethical/moral dimensions become central to understanding human development. In this sense, the expanded Vygotsky project, as suggested herein, invites a vision for a unified human science that brings together the question of acting, being/ becoming, and knowing on the one hand, and the question of values and commitment to transformation on the other. That is, it brings together the questions of what is, how it came to be, how it ought to be, and how all of this can be known—with each question foregrounding the other questions (i.e., being answerable only in light of the others, and with the question of 'ought' taking the center stage). It is the stance that affirms that society, especially education, could be different, therefore demanding that we discern why things are as they are at a given point in history by looking at how they came to be, while also considering how things could be otherwise and how they ought to be. And because acting, being, and knowing are seen from a transformative activist stance as all rooted in, derivative of, and instrumental within a *collaborative historical becoming*, this stance cuts across and bridges the gaps (a) between individual and social and (b) among ontological, epistemological, and moral-ethical (ideological) dimensions of activity.

Conclusions

In this chapter, I suggest that it is time to move beyond understanding Vygotsky as asserting the centrality of culture as a force extraneous to human development that shapes this process from afar and as an addition to biological factors. The foundation for moving beyond this view is built on the relational ontology now actively pursued in a variety of disciplines in conjunction with important advances in developmental sciences such as those in Developmental Systems Theory. Relational frameworks focus on the transactional nature of development and learning and present these processes as taking place at the interface between the organisms (persons) and their environment. The dialectical expansion of the framework proposed herein—undertaken in the spirit of a Vygotskian project that pioneered but has not completed this task—consists in dialectically supplanting the notion of relationality with the notion of *collaborative purposeful transformation* of the world as the core of human nature and the principled grounding for learning and development. According to this expansive position, people come to know themselves and their world as well as ultimately come to be human *in and through* (not in addition to) the processes of collaboratively transforming their world in view of their goals and purposes.

An activist transformative stance is proposed to capitalize on all human activities (including psychological processes and the self) being instantiations of *contributions to collaborative transformative practices* that are contingent on the vision for the future and therefore as profoundly imbued with ideology, ethics, and values. This conception arguably opens up ways to overcome the narrowness of both (a) the individualist views of positivist and humanist traditions that posit the primacy of an individual as some supreme entity existing prior to social practices and (b) the social reductionism 'upwards' of unidirectional collectivist accounts that tend to exclude individual processes and human subjectivity. This approach invites a vision for a unified human science that brings together the processes of acting, being/becoming, and knowing on the one hand, and the values and commitment to transformation on the other. Importantly, it also invites researchers to become activists in the pursuit of new social arrangements and practices grounded in ideals of social justice and equality that could better serve the needs and expectations of the generations to come.

References

Barab, S. A. & Roth, W.-M. (2006). Curriculum-based ecosystems: Supporting knowing from an ecological perspective. *Educational Researcher*, 35, 3–13.

Clark, A. (1997). *Being there: Putting brain, body and world together again*. Cambridge, MA: MIT Press.

Cole, M. (1988). Cross-cultural research in the sociohistorical tradition. *Human Development*, 31, 137–151.

Cole, M. (1996). *Cultural psychology: A once and future discipline*. Cambridge, MA: Harvard University Press.

Cole, M. (2002). Culture and development. In H. Keller, Y. H. Poortinga, & A. Schoemerich (Eds.), *Between culture and biology. Perspectives on ontogenetic development* (pp. 303–319). New York: Cambridge University Press.

Cole, M. (2003) Vygotsky and context. Where did the connection come from and what difference does it make? Internet, retrieved from http://communication. ucsd.edu/lchc/People/MCole/lsvcontext.htm. Accessed 2 March 2008.

Cole, M., Gay, J., Glick, J. A., & Sharp, D. W. (1971). *The cultural context of learning and thinking*. New York: Basic Books.

Cole, M., & Gajdamaschko, N. (2007). Vygotsky and culture. In H. J. Daniels, M. Cole, & J. Wertsch (Eds.), *Cambridge Companion to Vygotsky* (pp. 193–211). New York: Cambridge University Press.

Engestrom, Y. (1990). *Learning, working and imagining. Twelve studies in activity theory*. Helsinki: Orienta Konsultit.

Gelman, R. (1990). Structural constraints on cognitive development. *Cognitive Science*, 14, 79–106.

Gutierrez, K. D. (2002). Studying cultural practices in urban learning communities. *Human Development*, 45, 312–321.

Hedegaard, M. (2007). The development of children's conceptual relation to the world, with the focus on concept formation in preschool children's activity. In H. Daniels, M. Cole, & J. V. Wertsch (Eds.), *The Cambridge companion to Vygotsky* (pp. 246–275). New York: Cambridge University Press.

Holland, D., Lachicotte, W. Jr., Skinner, D., & Cain, C. (2001). *Identity and agency in cultural worlds*. Cambridge, MA: Harvard University Press.

Homer, B. D. & Tamis-LeMonda, C. S. (2005). *The development of social cognition and communication*. Mahwah, NJ: Lawrence Erlbaum.

Ingold, T. (2000). *Perception of the environment: Essays in livelihood, dwelling and skill*. London: Routledge.

Lantolf, J. & Thorne, S. (2006). *Sociocultural approach to second language learning.* New York: Cambridge University Press.

Lave, J. & Wenger, E. (1991). *Situated learning: Legitimate peripheral participation.* New York: Cambridge University Press.

Leontiev, A. N. (1979). The problem of activity in psychology. In J. V. Wertsch (Ed.), *The concept of activity in Soviet psychology* (pp. 37–71). Armonk, NY: Sharpe.

Lerner, R. (2004). Diversity in individual-context relations as the basis for positive development across the life span: A developmental systems perspective for theory, research, and application. *Research in Human Development*, 1, 327–346.

Lewontin, R. C. (2000). *The triple helix: Gene, organism, and environment.* Cambridge, MA: Harvard University Press.

Lickliter, R. & Berry, T. D. (1990). The phylogeny fallacy: Developmental psychology's misapplication of evolutionary theory. *Developmental Review*, 10, 348–364.

Lickliter, R. & Honeycutt, H. (2003a). Developmental dynamics: Towards a biologically plausible evolutionary psychology. *Psychological Bulletin, 129*, 819–838.

Lickliter, R. & Honeycutt, H. (2003b). Evolutionary approaches to cognitive development: Status and strategy. *Journal of Cognition and Development*, 4, 459–473.

Oyama, S. (1985). *The ontogeny of information.* Cambridge: Cambridge University Press.

Oyama, S. (2000). *Evolution's eye.* Durham, NC: Duke University Press.

Rogoff, B. (2003). *The cultural nature of human development.* New York: Oxford University Press.

Sawchuk, P. & Stetsenko, A. (in press). Sociology for a non-canonical activity theory: Exploring intersections and complementarities. *Mind, Culture and Activity.*

Stetsenko, A. (2005). Activity as object-related: Resolving the dichotomy of individual and collective types of activity. *Mind, Culture, and Activity*, 12, 70–88.

Stetsenko, A. (2008). From relational ontology to transformative activist stance: Expanding Vygotsky's (CHAT) project. *Cultural Studies of Science Education*, 3, 465–485.

Stetsenko, A. & Arievitch, I. M. (2004). Vygotskian collaborative project of social transformation: History, politics, and practice in knowledge construction. *International Journal of Critical Psychology*, 12 (4), 58–80.

Thelen, E. & Smith, L. B. (1994). *A dynamic systems approach to the development of cognition and action.* Cambridge, MA: MIT Press.

Vygotsky, L. S. (1987). Thinking and speech. In R. W. Rieber & A. S. Carton (Eds.), *The collected works of L. S. Vygotsky: Vol. 1. Problems of general psychology* (pp. 39–285). New York: Plenum Press.

Vygotsky, L. S. (1997). The problem of the development of higher mental functions. In R. W. Rieber (Ed.), *The collected works of L. S. Vygotsky: Vol. 4. The history of the development of higher mental functions: Cognition and language* (pp. 1–26). New York: Plenum Press.

Vygotsky, L. S. (1998). The problem of age. In R. W. Rieber (Ed.), *The collected works of L. S. Vygotsky: Vol. 5. Child Psychology* (pp. 187–205). New York: Plenum Press.

Vygotsky, L. S. (2004). Fundamentals of defectology. In R. Rieber & D. Robbinson (Eds.), *Essential Vygotsky* (pp. 153–199). New York: Kluwer Academic/Plenum.

8 A Cultural–Ecological Perspective on Early Childhood Among the Luo of Kisumu, Kenya

Jonathan Tudge and
Dolphine Odero-Wanga

Introduction

One way of thinking about the global–local distinction is the difference between the epistemic child (what all children, or all humans, hold in common) and the more anthropological approach of focusing on what is different between groups, particularly the impact of culture. To understand both the extent to which children are the same the world over and the differences between children, a good deal of research has been conducted on child-rearing practices in many different cultural groups. In order to show just how varied children's experiences are, cross-cultural psychologists have largely been interested in "maximizing the differences" between the groups studied, often comparing White middle-class practices in some part of the industrialized world (typically North America) with practices from rural and/or poor areas of the "majority" world (Kağitçibaşi, 1996; Rogoff, 2003; Whiting & Edwards, 1988).

One problem in this approach is that some particular types of majority-world experiences are brought to the fore, and treated as though they are the norm in the society or cultural group being studied. Typically these experiences are those that most clearly serve to distinguish between experiences in the researcher's home society or cultural group. Cultural differences, in other words, are reduced to being something exotic. An alternative approach is to take seriously the heterogeneity that exists within any cultural group and to identify cultural variations even among groups that are not maximally different.

Kenya provides a good case in point. Child-rearing in Nyansongo featured as one of the Whitings' original *Six Cultures* studies, and data from several Kenyan tribes were included in the follow-up book (Whiting & Edwards, 1988). Nonetheless, only Weisner (1979) studied the impact of city life on young children's experiences, contrasting the lives of Abaluyia children living in Nairobi with those in rural areas. For the most part scholars have left the impression that Kenya is populated with non- or semi-educated parents who raise their children in rural areas. Kenya, clearly, has large and complex cities—Nairobi, Kisumu, etc.—which include families that are very well-off by the standards of the society, many who live in large slums and struggle to find work and bring in enough money, and children who are living on the streets, either having been orphaned by the growing AIDs crisis or because their parents cannot afford to feed them (Swadener, 2000). Are ways of raising children in the city similar or different to rural ways in Kenya? Weisner's data suggest that there might be some important differences. One also has to recognize the impact of the passage of time—ideas about raising children have changed since the days of the *Six Cultures* study, although this may not have been adequately accounted for (see, for example, Weisner, Bradley, & Kilbride, 1997; Whiting, 1996).

Our goal has therefore been to do research in different societies, from both the industrialized and majority worlds, while holding certain factors constant (all families come from cities, medium-sized by the standards of the society, that allow a range of occupational and educational possibilities). In addition, we have deliberately chosen to study families drawn equally from two groups that differ by the parents' educational background and current occupation. Although we are interested in comparing the experiences of children in these different groups, the goal is not to judge on a single measuring stick (a way of assessing which groups do better or worse), or to look at what is standard across all children, but to study the ways in which culture and children's development are intertwined among groups that are not maximally different. What this allows is an examination of both "global" factors (do parents from different societies who are well educated and have professional jobs raise their children in ways that are different from their working-class counterparts?) and those that are more local (when holding constant city living, educational level, and type of occupation, what are the differences among ways of raising children?).

In this chapter we will focus on some of the everyday activities and interactions in which young Kenyan children from Kisumu engage, comparing them with the activities and interactions engaged in by children in cities in the United States, Russia, Estonia, Korea, and Brazil. What we will show is that social class, in a city such as Kisumu, is as important in helping to explain the children's experiences as is the broader society of which they are a part, and that global considerations, as well as those that are local, play an essential role.

How have young children in Kenya been portrayed, or, more specifically, how have previous scholars described the way in which they spend their time? By comparison with the children from the US and Western Europe, a good deal more of their time is spent in work. As Martha Wenger pointed out, the amount of time children in Kenya spend "contributing to the household economy" is "one of the most striking differences" between them and American children (1989, p. 92). Authors writing about Kikuyu, Gusii, and Giriama children from as young as two or three have shown them as often engaging in little chores and helping their mothers in the fields, and girls, by the age of five, looking after their younger siblings (LeVine & LeVine,

1963; LeVine et al., 1994; Wenger, 1989; Whiting, 1996; Whiting & Whiting, 1975).

The amount of work that these children were involved in did not mean that they had no time for play, however. In part because the Giriama boys studied by Wenger (1989) had more unstructured time than did girls and also because their work generally occurred outside the household area, they had more opportunities for social play with their peers; girls, as might be expected, were more often found playing with infants or toddlers. Adults were conspicuous by their absence from the play of these children from different groups in Kenya. As LeVine and LeVine (1963) reported about Gusii families in Nyansongo: "Mothers do not play with their children, fondle them, or display affection for them openly" (p. 165). Although mother–child relationships were described as "relatively informal" mothers did not typically reward their children, even verbally, and were far more likely to use fear to control their children's behavior. Giriama children also learned early not to expect their mothers or other adults to engage with them in play. In fact, children "are reluctant to attract adult attention, since this often incurs an undesirable consequence, such as the assignment of some task" (Wenger, 1989, p. 96).

Siblings, as we know from the work of Weisner and Gallimore (1977), play a key role in the development of young children in all parts of the world, but do so particularly in communities in which play and conversation involving young children and adults are not considered appropriate. This has certainly been the case in many Kenyan communities, as documented by Edwards and Whiting (1993) in Ngeca, the Embu children studied by Marion Sigman and her colleagues (1988), as well as Gusii (LeVine et al., 1994), Kipsigis (Harkness & Super, 1985), and Giriama children (Wenger, 1989).

Heterogeneity

The studies done in different parts of Kenya, featuring children from different tribes, reveal a good deal of similarity in the types of activities and typical social partners. This should not be taken to mean that there is homogeneity of experience. Much of what we have learned about children's activities in the various parts of Kenya comes from studies in rural areas of the country. That is perhaps not surprising, given that at the end of the twentieth century only about 20 percent of the population was living in urban centers (Odero, 2004). The urban population is growing rapidly, however, with greatly increased pressure for housing, employment, and adequate food (Swadener, 2000). Some earlier data from Nairobi, the capital, reveal a pattern that is quite different from what has been reported from Kenyan villages, with children engaged in far less work than their counterparts in rural regions, and different types of interactions with adults, particularly their mothers (Weisner, 1979). Weisner found that few of the typical chores mentioned earlier, so helpful in a rural setting, were needed in the city, and the rural children that he also studied were observed doing twice as many chores as were those who lived in the city. Weisner also found that the children in Nairobi, much like their counterparts in the United States or Western Europe, were more likely to seek interaction from their mother, and were more likely to want attention or praise from her.

The other major source of heterogeneity has to do with the passage of time. Most of what we know about young children's lives in Kenya comes from the observational studies conducted as part of the *Six Cultures* research, started in the 1950s with additional research in different parts of Kenya in the 1970s (Whiting & Edwards, 1988). These data are somewhat misleading, however, because they have mostly failed to address the issue of the huge changes that have occurred in Kenya since independence in 1963. Jomo Kenyatta, in one of his first acts after independence, promised free and universal primary education, believing that education was going to be the means to modernize the society. A decade later all school fees for the first four years of school were abolished, and by the mid-1970s almost 80 percent of the children were enrolled in primary school. This is particularly impressive, when we know that it was not until the 1940s that it was considered appropriate for girls to go to school (Whiting, 1996). The number who move on to secondary school is currently far less, and is partially based on exam results in primary school (although girls are far less likely than boys to move on to secondary school regardless of exam scores). "The result is a highly expanded educational system that rivals those in the most industrialized countries in terms of its complexity and competitiveness" (Buchmann, 2000, p. 1350).

Participation in formal schooling, and preparation for formal schooling (in child-care centers), still coexists with children's work, although it is increasingly clear that children have less time to work as they spend more of their time in school (Buchmann, 2000). By the turn of the century more than 80 percent of children, whether from rural or urban areas, were enrolled in school (Swadener, 2000). Girls are thus no longer as available to look after their younger siblings, although sometimes the latter accompany their older siblings to school (Swadener, 2000). As noted by Edwards and Whiting (1993), when the Ngecha study began in 1968 children (primarily girls) who were aged five to ten were the ones primarily responsible for looking after toddlers. A few years later, as children of this age were primarily attending school, the responsibility for looking after toddlers had fallen to children as young as four. The recognition of the impact of these types of historical changes was highlighted by Edwards and Whiting (2004) in the title of their most recent book, *Ngecha: A Kenyan village in a time of rapid social change.*

The Role of Fathers

We have hardly mentioned fathers so far, and in part this reflects the prevailing belief, as reported in the literature, that in Kenya the raising of children is primarily the work of females, whereas the male role is that of providing food, clothing, and (in more recent times) the money for school fees for the children. Kipsigis fathers' roles with toddlers were restricted to verbally disciplining them and occasionally teaching them chores (Harkness & Super, 1992). Among the Logoli, too, contact with the father occurred far less frequently than it did with the mother (Munroe & Munroe, 1992). The LeVines pointed out that: "The Nyansongo father is viewed by his child as an awesome and frightening person, and with some justification. Fathers do not play, fondle, or praise their children, and, unlike mothers, they do not feed them or comfort them when hurt" (1963, p. 178).

The Cultural Ecology of Young Children Project

The information that we have about young Kenyan children's everyday experiences provides some clear contrasts with what we know about children's lives in much of the industrialized world. However, what we know has been heavily influenced by the types of studies that have been done, and the overwhelming focus on children living in rural parts of the country. Our feeling was that this focus has not done justice to the changes that have taken place in Kenyan society, with increasing numbers of Kenyans living in urban areas and schooling having taken on a good deal of importance. In fact, scholars need to take seriously the profound impact of the growth of schooling and urbanization in many parts of the majority world, and be careful not to confuse the "Kenyan" experience with the lives of Kenyan children growing up in rural areas at a time when schooling was not so important.

We therefore decided to collect our data in Kisumu as part of the Cultural Ecology of Young Children project, a cross-cultural and longitudinal study conducted in seven different societies, the United States, Russia, Estonia, Finland, Korea, Kenya, and Brazil (Tudge, 2008). In each of these societies we selected a single city, medium sized with at least one institution of higher education and a wide range of occupations. The children in the study were drawn from middle- and working-class families, with the parents' educational background and occupation being the criteria for social-class membership. When the children were three years of age, each child was observed for 20 hours, in such a way as to cover the equivalent of one complete day. Our focus was on the activities and interactions going on around the children, those they became involved in, their manner of involvement, their partners in those activities, and so on.

Cultural–Ecological Theory

The theory on which the first author bases his work is named cultural–ecological theory, at least in part because it draws heavily on the theories of both Lev Vygotsky and Urie Bronfenbrenner. Central to the theory is the idea that development occurs in large part through the typically occurring everyday activities and interactions involving developing individuals and their social partners. It is in the course of engaging in these regularly occurring activities and interactions that children come to fit into their cultural world. They learn what is expected of them, the types of activities considered appropriate or inappropriate for them, how they are expected to engage in these activities, the ways other people will deal with them, and the ways in which they are expected to deal with others. Children often initiate activities themselves, and try to draw others into those activities, and it is in the course of these activities that they try out different roles and observe the roles of others, both with regard to themselves and with others.

The culture within which these activities and interactions take place clearly plays a central role in influencing the types of activities and interactions that are available to the young of that culture, and influences which of them the children are encouraged to participate in (or discouraged from). The group's values and beliefs about raising children, the practices they consider normative or appropriate, the resources and settings available to them, and so on, are clearly implicated in the children's typically occurring activities and interactions. As Tom Weisner (1996) wrote, if you want to know how a child will develop, the most important single thing to know about that child is the cultural group of which he or she is a part.

But so too are the children's own characteristics. In any cultural group there are children who are differentially inclined or motivated to learn some skills, ideas, practices than are others. Children themselves change the nature of the activities and interactions in which they engage simply because of their own unique natures. The same is true, of course, of the other people (children and adults) with whom they are interacting.

The young of the cultural group thus do not simply imitate or internalize the practices of those who are more competent in the ways of the culture but recreate those practices in the course of engaging in them. There is thus always the possibility that those practices will change over time. The same is true for values and beliefs about raising children. Although the older generation may try hard to transmit those same values and beliefs to their young it is not always the case that the younger generation accepts their parents' ideas. In cultures in which tradition is considered highly important there is greater pressure on children to accept their parents' ways; in other cultures, however, in which creativity and independence are more valued, one should expect to find faster change. Cultural groups are thus themselves developing under the influence of the new generation while at the same time they are helping that new generation become competent in the ways of the group.

In other words, cultural–ecological theory treats development as a complex interplay among cultural context, individual variability, and change over time, with the key aspect being activities and interactions, where context and individual variability intersect. We want to use this theory to make sense of child rearing among the Luo of Kenya, or at least those who were living in Kisumu during the late 1990s.

To this point we have written about individuals being members of specific cultural groups, but have not so far provided a definition of culture. The definition that we use stipulates that cultures consist of groups that share a general set of values, beliefs, practices, institutions, and access to resources. The group may have a sense of shared identity, or the recognition that people are in some way connected and feel themselves to be part of the group, and the adults of the group should attempt to pass on to the young of the group the same values, beliefs, practices, and so on.

By this definition of culture, members of different countries or societies constitute different cultural groups. Or rather, if we are able to show that members of different countries or societies have sets of values, beliefs, practices, institutions, etc., that they feel themselves to be part of the same group as other people of the same country or society, and share a commitment to pass on those values, etc. to the next generation, we should feel comfortable saying that these different groups constitute different cultures. However, precisely the same point should be made about different groups within any given society or country. Any group for whom the above definition holds may in this case be considered a cultural group. Within a given society's politically defined borders may be found many different cultural groups, and people thus have to be considered members of more than a single cultural group. Different ethnic groups, different socio-economic groups, regional groups, and groups that are more locally constituted may all constitute cultural groups, so long as they conform to the above definition.

It is important to remember, however, that these types of cultural differences do not *determine* the activities and interactions in which individuals engage. Actions and interactions are a complex amalgam of individual characteristics, the particularities of the setting, and the culture as it is currently constituted.

Kisumu and Our Participants

Kisumu obtained the status of a city in 2001, is the third largest urban area in Kenya (with a municipal population of a little over 200,000, with more than twice that number in the broader Kisumu area), and is situated about 300 miles (500 km) from Nairobi on the shores of Lake Victoria. The town was founded in 1901, originally with the name Port Florence, and achieved the status of Municipal Council in 1960. It is the major administrative, commercial, and industrial center for Western Kenya. Agriculture is the primary industry, with textiles, sugar and molasses production, and fishing also found in the region. Tourist attractions in the area include the wild life (hippos, leopards, hyenas, and impalas can all be found), and Lake Victoria is also a draw for tourists (Odero, 1998). The town is also home to Maseno University, one of six State universities in Kenya. Close to Lake Victoria, the city has asphalt roads and six- or eight-story buildings, with a bustle of cars and bicycles, but in other areas the roads are gravel or dirt, and one of the main modes of transport is the bicycle taxi.

A number of different ethnic groups live in Kisumu, but the large majority (85 percent) is Luo, the second largest ethnic group (of a total of almost 50) in Kenya. They are descended from pastoralists who had originally moved from Sudan, several centuries ago, and who settled primarily in the area of Lake Victoria. The Luo, traditionally, worshipped their ancestors, and although many were converted to Christianity their religious beliefs still combine both traditional and Christian practices. There is a similar duality of marriage arrangements, with "statutory" (monogamous) marriage going hand-in-hand with "customary" (polygamous) marriage, with both being recognized by the Kenyan government (Odero, 1998).

Kisumu is divided into "estates," approximately one square kilometer in size. The estates are differentiated by social class, with some estates having larger and better-appointed houses or apartments and being home primarily to families with college education and professional occupations, whereas other estates feature smaller and simpler residences and are occupied by working-class or poor families. In addition, many families now live in large slum areas, with very small structures occupied by many individuals, and increasingly children and families have no fixed home, but live on the streets of Kisumu (Swadener, 2000).

The families in this study were recruited in the mid-1990s primarily through the local office of birth records. We initially tried to contact the parents of all 30 children who had been born two to three years earlier in five different estates (three middle-class estates and two working-class estates). In the middle-class community seven of 16 families had relocated; of the remaining nine families six agreed to participate (67 percent acceptance). In the working-class community nine of the 14 families who had had a child three years earlier had already left the area, but the remaining five families agreed to participate (100 percent acceptance). Eleven other families (four middle class and seven working class) were contacted by "snowball" methods, with information on the presence of these families being provided by families who had already agreed to participate. Two of the working-class families who were approached in this manner declined to participate, but the remainder were happy to do so. A total of 20 families, equally divided by social class, were thus included in the study.

In the middle-class group, all mothers and fathers had had at least some college education, and some had a graduate degree. Fathers' occupations included university lecturer, sales manager, public administrator, and owner of a travel agency. All of the middle-class mothers worked outside the home, with occupations such as high school teacher, registered nurse, and nutritionist. The houses in which they lived were much larger than those of the working-class families, having between three and five bedrooms, two or more bathrooms, in addition to a living room and kitchen. The rooms had a mixture of carpets and tiles on the floors, and paintings on the walls. Each house was on its own lot of between ¼ acre and 1 acre, typically behind a fence. The children thus had a lot of room to play, but it was not easy for them to interact with children from neighboring houses because of the fences between them. Mostly, then, the children played with their siblings or with friends who had been invited over to play. Of the 10 middle-class families, five rented their homes and five had bought the land and built the houses.

The working-class fathers were primarily skilled and semi-skilled manual laborers, and had jobs such as plumber, pipe fitter, store clerk, and messenger. None of the mothers had a fornal occupation, with the exception of one who had a job as clerk, but all of them engaged in some type of subsistence selling (vegetables, fruit, bread, etc.) to supplement the family income. One of the fathers had had some college education, but in the remainder of cases the level of education ranged from primary education to the completion of high school. The working-class families who participated in our study mostly lived in houses that had one or two bedrooms, a living room, and bathroom. Larger families in these estates often have the older children sleeping in the living room (or sometimes in the kitchen), whereas the younger ones sleep with their parents in the bedroom. The floors tended to be of cement, with no covering, and the walls featured family pictures, calendars, and sometimes cuttings from the newspapers (Odero, 1998). Eight of the ten working-class families shared bathrooms that were built outside the houses, and they also had to fetch water from a well in the center of the estate. Three of the families did not have electricity, and relied on lanterns. These families shared compounds with their neighbors, and only in two cases did houses have any type of fence. This meant that the children were free to mingle with the other children in the compound, playing one minute in and around their own home, and the next in another child's home.

All families were ethnic Luo, and all but two were monogamous. The two children who were from polygamous families were both working class, and lived in different sections of town with their mothers. Fathers in polygamous families divided their time between the wives' households, although one of these fathers spent the majority of his time with the family that included the child who was being observed, as this child was the only male child that he had with either wife. The middle-class families tended to be smaller (1–4 children) than those of working-class background (2–7 children). The experiences of the two groups of children were also quite different, in that the middle-class children all attended some type of private preschool, which were well equipped with commercially made learning and play equipment. These children spent their weekends going to the lake, a museum, shopping with parents, or taking swimming lessons (seven of them did that). Many of the working-class children did not attend any preschool, which fits with the fact that, at the start of the 21st century, fewer than 30 percent of Kenyan 3- to 6-year-olds attended preschool (Swadener, 2000). Working-class children who attended went to community schools in which the playthings were made from locally available materials (for example, a doll made from banana leaves, a car made from cans of juice with bottle tops for wheels). These children also went shopping but they, unlike their middle-class peers, went alone or with other children, to buy something for the family.

Methods

In the CEYC project we were interested in the typical everyday experiences of children. Our approach to observations is that we simply followed the children, putting no restrictions on where the child went or on the people who interacted with the child. We followed each of the children in our study (who were all between 28 and 48 months of age when the study began) for 20 hours over the course of a week. We did this in such a way that we covered the equivalent of a complete day in their lives, observing on one day when the child woke up and for the few hours following, another day the hours before he or she went to sleep for the night, and on other days during the hours in between. Using this technique, we hoped to have a good sense of the types of activities in which the child was typically involved, the partners in those activities, the roles taken, and so on.

Although each observer observed for a total of 20 hours, data were only gathered systematically during a 30-second period every six minutes. The remainder of the time was spent coding and writing field notes, while continually tracking what the participants were doing. Time was signalled in such a way that the participants were unaware of when their behaviors were being coded, and the child who was the focus of attention wore a wireless mike so that the observer could hear what was being said while staying at a distance from the activity.

Our approach captures children's activities in an ethnographically appropriate way. For example, children were not separated from their context and we tried to change nothing except the change that necessarily occurred because an observer was present. Our aim was thus to get a sense of what the child's experiences typically were. We observed for enough time, we believe, to give a reasonable sense of the types of activities that typically occur in these children's lives. The approach also allows us to examine the types of activities that are going on in which the children do not participate, or those in which they would like to participate but are discouraged from so doing. The major activities in which we are interested are displayed in Table 8.1, and are divided into five major groups (each of which is subdivided into numerous subgroups), comprising lessons, work, play, conversation, and "other" (sleeping, idleness, eating, bathing, etc.). For more details about the coding scheme, see Tudge (2008).

Results

Engagement in Activities. One of the questions in which we were interested was the extent to which the children in these various cities engaged in similar or different types of activities. At first glance, just focusing on the broadest categories, the Luo children in Kisumu did not look different from children in any of the other cities. They were observed in play, for example, in a little less than 60 percent of our observations, almost exactly as often as were their counterparts in Greensboro (United States), Tartu (Estonia), and Porto Alegre (Brazil). They played less than did children in Suwon (Korea) and Oulu (Finland), but were more likely to be observed in play than were children in Obninsk (Russia).

There was a good deal more variability across cities in the extent to which the children were observed in lessons, but those in Greensboro and Kisumu were observed in this type of activity in about 6 percent of the observations—

Table 8.1   Definitions of major activities

Lessons	Deliberate attempts to impart or elicit information relating to:
Academic	School (spelling, counting, learning shapes, comparing quantities, colors, etc.);
World	How things work, why things happen, safety;
Interpersonal	Appropriate behavior with others, etiquette etc.;
Religious	Religious or spiritual matters.
Work	Household activities (cooking, cleaning, repairing, etc.), shopping, etc.
Play, Entertainment	Activities engaged in for their own enjoyment, including:
Toys	Play with objects designed specifically for play or manipulation by children;
Natural objects	Play with objects from the natural world, such as rocks, mud, leaves, sand, sticks, etc.;
No object	Play that does not feature any type of object, such as rough and tumble play, chase, word games, singing, etc.;
Adult objects	Play with objects that were not designed for children, such as household objects, games designed for adolescents, etc.;
Pretend play	Play involving evidence that a role is being assumed, whether part of the normal adult world (a mother shopping, a teacher) or purely fantasy (being a super-hero, fantasy figure, or baby);
Academic object	Play with an object designed with school in mind, such as looking at a book, playing with shapes or numbers, etc., with no lesson involved;
Entertainment	Listening to radio, going to a ball game, circus, etc.;
TV	Watching television, video, or DVD, whether school-related, child-focused, or not designed with children in mind.
Conversation	Talk with a sustained or focused topic about things not the current focus of engagement.
Other	Activities such as sleeping, eating, bathing, etc. and those that were uncodable.

less than children in Obninsk and Tartu (approximately 10 percent), but more than children in Oulu, Suwon, and Porto Alegre (between 2 percent and 4 percent) of their observations.

Children in Kisumu were involved in conversation in about 7 percent of their observations, but children in Greensboro, Obninsk, Tartu, and Porto Alegre were similarly involved; their counterparts in Suwon were observed conversing a little less, but children in Oulu were the ones who stood out—they were about twice as likely to be involved in conversation.

The one type of activity in which Kisumu children led the way was in terms of the extent to which they were involved in work—about 15 percent of their total observations, which was three times the amount of their counterparts in Porto Alegre. However, the children in the remaining cities were observed being involved in work in between 8 percent and 13 percent of the observations. Even in this case, therefore, it is difficult to argue that children's lives in Kisumu are as different from those in other parts of the world as scholars have traditionally portrayed.

One might be tempted, therefore, to make the argument that local variations are not particularly important, at least when considering children who are around three years of age. They all spend the majority of their time in play, and are involved in the other activities much less, and not to a greatly different extent. However, there are two ways in which these preliminary conclusions may be misleading. First, even if children around the world spend a majority of their time playing, it is worth considering what they are playing with, and with whom. Second, as we argued earlier, even within a single city, with families from a single ethnic group, it may be possible to see differences in activities because of the families' social-class background. It is by looking in more detail at children's activities and interactions that it becomes very easy to see the impact of local forces.

For example, in terms of the objects with which they were playing, the Kisumu children (from both social-class groups) look very different from all other children. They were the only children who played pretty much evenly with toys, objects from the natural world, with no object at all, and, most common of all, objects from the adult world. Children were observed playing with Vaseline containers, bottle tops, an old oil bottle, a tube of toothpaste, old cassette tapes, a spice container, a box of cookies (without eating any of them!), a walking stick, climbing on the fence, and with innumerable other objects from the adult world.

The children in Kisumu were also far more likely to be observed playing either with objects from the natural world (leaves, branches, clay) or with no objects at all than were the children in the other cities. Children in Kisumu were much less likely to have been observed watching television than children in the other cities, although this finding cannot be explained simply by the relative absence of television sets in the working-class Kenyan families we observed, as the middle-class children in Kisumu also watched very little television, despite the fact that their families owned televisions.

The same type of point can be raised about the type of lessons in which the Kisumu children were involved. Middle-class Luo children were actually involved in more than twice as many academic (school-relevant) lessons (over 4 percent of their total observations) as were any other group of children (including their working-class counterparts in Kisumu) in the entire study. White middle-class children in the United States are usually portrayed as being often engaged in rather didactic lessons (see, for example, Rogoff, 1990, 2003; Tudge, 2008). It is therefore noteworthy that they were involved in only half as many academic lessons as were the Luo middle-class children. The working-class children in Kisumu were also involved in twice as many academic lessons as were their White counterparts in Greensboro.

Similarly, although the Kisumu children did not look so different from the children in the other cities in terms of the amount of conversation in which they were involved, child–child conversation occupied a far higher proportion (about one-third) of their total conversations than was true in any other group. As other scholars have found, children in Kisumu were much less likely to be involved in conversation with adults. This was because in Kisumu children spent a lot of their time in the company of other children.

As noted earlier, these Luo children were more involved in work than were children in any other city. However, when looking separately by the social-class background of their families, it was clear that it was only the working-class children who were quite heavily involved in work. We actually have two measures of this involvement. First, we considered the extent to which the children were either doing some work themselves or were watching someone else at work but not involved in a more active way. The working-class children were involved in this looser sense in approximately 20 percent of their total observations, far higher than any other group. By contrast, their middle-class counterparts were only involved in work in less than 10 percent of their observations, a percentage that was less than that of the children in Obninsk (Russia), Tartu (Estonia), or Oulu (Finland), and similar to that of the African American children in Greensboro.

When we looked at *actual* participation in work (doing chores, going to fetch something from a local shop, etc.) we found that the working-class Luo children from Kisumu did indeed participate more in work (8 percent of their observations) than did children from any other group, but not greatly more so than did children from Obninsk and Tartu (around 6 to 7.5 percent of their observations). In other words, these Luo children did work, but not to a much greater extent than children from parts of northeast Europe. More interestingly, their middle-class counterparts in Kisumu participated in work only a quarter as often, in just 2 percent of their observations, a proportion that was lower than that of children everywhere except Porto Alegre!

The impact of child care. To this point we have focused simply on the activities in which the children were observed, but we can understand better why it was that the Kisumu children engaged in the activities in which they did by looking at where they spent their time and with whom. Across the entire set of cities where we gathered data, children spent between 60 percent and 80 percent of their time in and around the home. Children in Kisumu and Tartu (Estonia) were most likely to be observed there, children in Greensboro and Porto Alegre (Brazil) the least likely. One of the reasons was that the Luo children were relatively unlikely to spend much time in some type of formal child-care setting—less than 10 percent of our observations. It is worth noting, however, that the children in Tartu and Suwon (Korea) were less often observed in child care, although children in Porto Alegre were observed almost 30 percent of their time in child care.

However, as we have already pointed out, there were some clear class differences. Six of the ten children from middle-class backgrounds spent more than 20 percent of their time in a formal child-care setting, whereas only one of the working-class children did so. It is clearly worth looking at the types of activities in which the children engaged when they were within child care or outside. Although the children obviously spent far more time away from child care than within, all of the Luo children who went to child care spent a much smaller proportion of their time engaged in play when in child care than when in other settings. In this they were similar to the African American children in Greensboro, but quite different from the children in the White communities of Greensboro and children in Oulu and Porto Alegre, all of whom actually spent a greater proportion of their time playing within child care than elsewhere.

What is even more noteworthy is that virtually all of the children, in each group where some children spent at least 20 percent of their time in a formal child-care setting, spent somewhat more time playing with school-relevant objects (looking at books, playing with mathematically shaped blocks, etc.) inside child care than outside. In the case of the children in Kisumu, however, the differences were dramatic. The middle-class Luo children, for example, were observed engaging in some type of school-relevant play in 15 percent of their observations in child care, compared with just 5 percent when not in child care. One working-class Luo child was actually observed in this type of play in 25 percent of the observations in his child-care center, but virtually never outside of it. To put these findings into perspective, children in the other groups were typically observed playing with school-relevant objects in less than 5 percent of their observations within child care.

The findings were even more striking when looking at school-relevant lessons. In all other groups, the proportion of these types of lessons observed within child care was similar to the proportion observed when the children were in other settings. The range of observations of these lessons was from virtually none, among the working-class children in Porto Alegre, to around 5 percent in Greensboro. By contrast, the Luo children (middle class and working class alike) were engaged in school-relevant lessons in no fewer than 20 percent of their observations within child care, and 1–2 percent elsewhere. A further 10 percent of their observations within child care involved interpersonal lessons, or lessons on how to get along with others, tidying up after oneself, and so on. In terms of the other activities, Kisumu children were much less likely to be involved in conversations and work within child care compared with elsewhere, as was true of virtually all other groups of children.

Clearly, the function of child-care centers in Kisumu is to give children experience with school-relevant objects and concepts—around half of the time that children spent in child care was devoted to explicit or implicit preparation for school. By contrast, in most of the other groups the function of child care seemed to be more related to allowing children to play. This is not to say that the child-care teachers were not interested in preparing children for school, but perhaps had the idea that children learn in the course of their play.

It is worth comparing the experiences of the children who did not attend child care with those who did; regardless of social-class background, those who did not attend were observed very rarely in any type of lesson, but those who attended child care were often involved, but only when they were in child care. In their observations outside of child care, those who attended were equally unlikely as those who did not attend to engage in lessons. In other words, it cannot be the case that only children who were particularly interested in learning were sent to child care.

Partners in activities. To this point we have simply written about the various activities in which the Kisumu children were involved. The literature uniformly states that Kenyan adults do not see play as something that they should get involved in, and Kenyan children are highly likely to play with other children. To some extent this was born out by our data. Adults (mother, father, grandparents or other extended family members, or teachers) were only observed as a partner in their children's play in less than 10 percent of the observations, which was far less than for any other group (the next fewest was about 30 percent in Greensboro and Suwon, Korea). By contrast, about 50 percent of the Kisumu children's observations of play featured one or more other child. This was not so different from the proportion in the other cities, however, where the proportion ranged from a low of about 30 percent in Porto Alegre to 40–45 percent of the observations in each of the remaining cities. Somewhat surprising, certainly in comparison with the literature, is that in almost 40 percent of our observations of these Luo children playing, they were playing by themselves. (This does not mean that others, children or adults, were not around, simply that no one else was participating in their play.) These proportions did not differ greatly by social class in Kisumu, although the middle-class children were more likely to play with adults than were those from working-class families.

This does not mean, however, that adults were uninvolved with their children in other types of activities; they were involved with them in over 50 percent of the work and lessons in which the children were engaged. This was not so different from the situation in Greensboro (about 60 percent in each case), although of course the Luo children (or at least the working-class Luo children) spent a greater proportion of their time involved in work than was the case in Greensboro and the other cities. The Kisumu children, as we mentioned earlier, were less involved in conversation than were the children elsewhere, but when they were involved child–child conversation only occurred in about 40 percent of the observations of conversation, with adults being involved in the remaining 60 percent of cases. This was still less than the proportion elsewhere (from a high of 80 percent in Porto Alegre, Brazil, to 70 percent in Suwon, Korea, and about 75 percent elsewhere), but our data certainly do not support the idea that adults are uninvolved in young children's activities in Kenya.

Although adults could include teachers in child care, extended family members, or completely unrelated adults, we looked with particular interest at the role of the child's own mother and father. Our expectation was that mothers would be more involved in all activities with their children than would fathers. This expectation was based partly on prevailing beliefs in many countries about the respective roles mothers and fathers should take with their children, but also because mothers may simply be around their young children more than are fathers. Because we always noted whether the mother and father were present in the same setting as their child we are able to assess not only the extent to which the parents were involved with their children but also the proportion of the time that they were engaged, given their availability to their children.

In each city, mothers were far more involved with their children in lessons than were fathers. However, when examined proportionally, in only two cities were fathers as involved in lessons as were mothers—in Kisumu and in Porto Alegre, and the Luo fathers were more likely to be involved in their children's lessons, once they were present in the same setting as their children, than were fathers in any other city. The same was true of the work in which their children were involved—Kisumu fathers, given their presence in the same setting, were more likely to be involved with their children in work than were fathers elsewhere (although in this case mothers were still more involved, both actually and when considered relative to their availability to their children). Only in Porto Alegre were fathers as involved in work with their children as were mothers, once availability was taken into account.

As mentioned earlier, neither mothers nor fathers in Kisumu were greatly involved in their children's play. Mothers, in fact were far less involved here than were mothers in any other city. The Luo fathers were not much less involved in their children's play, however, than was the case in Greensboro or Obninsk (Russia), and they were actually more involved in their children's play than were the fathers in Suwon. When expressed as a proportion of availability, however, Kisumu fathers were actually more likely to be involved with their children in play than were the mothers. (The same was true in Suwon, and in Porto Alegre, again, fathers and mothers were equally involved, given their availability to their children.) The situation was similar in terms of conversation; again as noted earlier, Luo mothers and fathers were not much involved in conversation with their children, and fathers in Kisumu were both less involved in fact and proportionally than were mothers, as was true in all cities except Suwon.

Discussion and Conclusion

The everyday activities in which these Kenyan children were involved appeared to be quite different from those reported in the literature (the children engaged in much less work, were far more involved in preparation for school, and there was more evidence of parent–child engagement). The Luo children we studied, in general, do not look so different from those in the other countries, which perhaps speaks to a global phenomenon, given historical trends, of children playing, and engaging to a much lesser extent in work, lessons, or conversations. However, a closer look reveals some striking differences in experiences as a function of social class, and by presence in child care.

One possible reason for the differences in data reported here and elsewhere is that we collected our data only from a single urban setting, and from middle-class and working-class families. If data collected in similar ways in rural regions revealed patterns more in line with the previous literature this would be clear evidence of the heterogeneity that exists across Kenya, and should serve as a challenge to those who refer simply to "Kenyan" child-rearing practices.

Another reason, one that seems at least as likely to explain some of these differences, is that the introduction of formal schooling, as opposed to more informal ways of learning what one needs to attain competence within one's cultural community (see Rogoff, 1990), has had similar effects as have been seen in many parts of the world (Cole, 2005; LeVine, Miller, Richman, & LeVine, 1996; LeVine & White, 1986). This is surely part of a global trend that is reflected equally in the Kenyan government's signing the 1989 United Nations Convention on the Rights of the Child, the 1990 African Charter on the Rights and Welfare of the Child, and the 2000 Millennium Development goals. As others have argued (see Freitas, Shelton, & Sperb; Göncü, Özer, & Ahioğlu; and Elliott, this volume), it is easy to see the impact of globalization at this level.

However, as Freitas and her colleagues noted, global forces meet local possibilities. The pressure for children to spend more time than ever before in settings designed explicitly for them may be a global phenomenon, but how it is reflected varies greatly not only among different countries but also within the same country. Both Kenya and Brazil are considered part of the majority world, but children's child-care experiences in Kisumu and Porto Alegre could not look much more different! (Tudge, 2008). In one case, children are being prepared for formal schooling and in the other they're being given opportunities to play in a safe environment. We make no claims whether one approach is "better" than another—such a judgment surely depends on the society's current values and beliefs.

Moreover, even within these two countries can be seen different approaches to child care. In Kenya when children of the poor spend time in a child-care center they are much more likely to be cared for rather than educated. As Swadener (2000) has documented, the major goal behind providing settings for young children in tea and coffee plantations and other agricultural areas is to make it easier for mothers to work. Children of wealthy families, however, go to a child-care center in order to ensure that they will be able to enter one of the more prestigious schools. A very similar claim can be made for both the United States and Brazil (see Freitas et al., this volume), with two parallel systems of care and education being developed.

It thus seems clear that in order to understand children's development, one cannot only consider the forces of globalization that, at this particular historical period, appear to be treating certain values and practices as "better" than those viewed as traditional. The impact of local forces can be seen in the different ways in which globalization has influenced different societies from the majority world—as we have shown in this chapter, although there is global pressure for schooling and preparation for schooling, children's activities and interactions in child-care settings are quite different in Brazil and Kenya. Moreover, even within Kenya there are clear differences in children's typical activities in rural versus urban areas, and even within a single Kenyan city parents have different ideas about the types of settings into which to place their children and the types of activities and interactions they view as appropriate for them. The majority world is far from homogeneous, and its enormous heterogeneity must be taken seriously when trying to understand the development of its children.

References

Buchmann, C. (2000). Family structure, parental perceptions, and child labor in Kenya: What factors determine who is enrolled in school? *Social Forces*, 78 (4), 1349–1379.

Cole, M. (2005). Cross-cultural and historical perspectives on the developmental consequences of education. *Human Development*, 48 (4), 195–216.

Edwards, C. P. & Whiting, B. B. (1993). "Mother, older sibling, and me": The overlapping roles of caregivers and companions in the social world of two- to three-year-olds in Ngeca, Kenya. In K. MacDonald (Ed.), *Parent–child play: Descriptions and implications* (pp. 305–329). Albany, NY: SUNY Press.

Edwards, C. P. & Whiting, B. B. (2004). *Ngecha: A Kenyan village in a time of rapid social change.* Lincoln, NE: University of Nebraska Press.

Harkness, S. & Super, C. M. (1985). The cultural context of gender segregation in children's peer groups. *Child Development*, 56 (1), 219–224.

Harkness, S., & Super, C. M. (1992). The cultural foundations of fathers' roles: Evidence from Kenya and the United States. In B. S. Hewlett (Ed.), *Father–child relations: Cultural and biosocial contexts* (pp. 191–211). New York: Aldine de Gruyter.

Kağitçibaşi, C. (1996). *Family and human development across cultures: A view from the other side.* Mahwah, NJ: Lawrence Erlbaum.

LeVine, R. A., Dixon, S., LeVine, S., Richman, A., Leiderman, P. H., Keefer, C. H., & Brazelton, T. B. (1994). *Child care and culture: Lessons from Africa.* New York: Cambridge University Press.

LeVine, R. A., & LeVine B. B. (1963). Nyansongo: A Gusii community in Kenya. In B. B. Whiting (Ed.), *Six cultures: Studies of child rearing* (pp. 14–202). New York: John Wiley.

LeVine, R. A., Miller, P. M., Richman, A. L., & LeVine, S. (1996). Education and mother–infant interaction: A Mexican case study. In S. Harkness & C. M. Super (Eds.), *Parents' cultural belief systems: Their origins, expressions, and consequences* (pp. 254–269). New York: Guilford Press.

LeVine, R. A., & White, M. (1986). *Human conditions: The cultural basis of educational development.* London: Routledge and Kegan Paul.

Munroe, R. L., & Munroe, R. H. (1992). Fathers in children's environments: A four-culture study. In B. S. Hewlett (Ed.), *Father–child relations: Cultural and biosocial contexts* (pp. 213–229). New York: Aldine de Gruyter.

Odero, D. A. (1998). *Everyday activities and social partners of Luo children in an urban Kenyan setting: The roles of culture, class, and gender.* Unpublished doctoral dissertation, University of North Carolina at Greensboro.

Odero, D. R. (2004). Families of Kenya. *National Council on Family Relations Report*, 49 (4), F13–14, December.

Rogoff, B. (1990). *Apprenticeship in thinking: Cognitive development in social context.* New York: Oxford University Press.

Rogoff, B. (2003). *The cultural nature of human development.* New York: Oxford University Press.

Sigman, M., Neumann, C., Carter, D. J., D'Souza, S., & Bwibo, N. (1988). Home interactions and the development of Embu toddlers in Kenya. *Child Development,* 59 (5), 1251–1261.

Swadener, B. B. (2000). *Does the village still raise the child? A collaborative study of changing child-rearing and early education in Kenya.* Albany, NY: State University of New York Press.

Tudge, J. R. H. (2008). *The everyday lives of young children: Culture, class, and child rearing in diverse societies.* New York: Cambridge University Press.

Weisner, T. S. (1979). Urban–rural differences in sociable and disruptive behavior of Kenya children. *Ethnology,* 18 (2), 153–172.

Weisner, T. S. (1996). Why ethnography should be the most important method in the study of human development. In R. Jessor, A. Colby, & R. A. Shweder (Eds.), *Ethnography and human development: Context and meaning in social enquiry* (pp. 305–324). Chicago: University of Chicago Press.

Weisner, T. S., Bradley, C., & Kilbride, P. L. (1997). *African families and the crisis of social change.* Westport, CT: Bergin & Garvey.

Weisner, T. S., & Gallimore, R. (1977). My brother's keeper: Child and sibling caretaking. *Current Anthropology,* 18 (2), 169–190.

Wenger, M. (1989). Work, play, and social relationships among children in a Giriama community. In D. Belle (Ed.), *Children's social networks and social supports* (pp. 91–115). New York: Wiley.

Whiting, B. B. (1996). The effect of social change on concepts of the good child and good mothering: A study of families in Kenya. *Ethos,* 24, 3–35.

Whiting, B. B. & Edwards C. P. (1988). *Children of different worlds: The formation of social behavior.* Cambridge, MA: Harvard University Press.

Whiting, B. B., & Whiting, J. W. M. (1975). *Children of six cultures: A psycho-cultural analysis.* Cambridge, MA: Harvard University Press.

9 An Environmental Affordance Perspective on the Study of Development – Artefacts, Social Others, and Self

Jytte Bang

The Activity Setting

The aim of this chapter is to present an interpretive method by which the researcher might study possible developmental novelties emerging out of child–environment reciprocity in activity settings. By *activity settings* we mean temporally and culturally re-occurring events organized in relation to institutional arrangements for children (home, kindergarten, school, after-school activities, sport clubs, cultural activities, etc.). Children participate in many different activity settings, like getting ready for kindergarten in the morning (home), playing with toys in the playground (kindergarten), having a lesson (school), playing baseball or soccer, riding horses, playing an instrument or dancing (club activities), etc. Researching a child's development therefore means researching participation across the variety of activity settings in the everyday life of the child. This wholeness perspective puts into focus when and how a child participates in what activities and how she experiences/feels about her participation. By doing so, it hopefully becomes possible to study the personal trajectories (Dreier, 2008) and development of the child *in situ*, that is, in and across the child–environment reciprocity of the activity settings; this unit of analysis hopefully also helps re-integrate what is often studied in fragments: social development, cognitive development, etc. The chapter seeks to argue for a methodological and theoretical wholeness approach to the study of development (see also Hedegaard et al., in press).

The Concept of Human Environment – Artefacts, Social Others, and Self

In the present paper, the term 'activity setting' is a theoretical construct which hybrids Barker and Wright's term *behaviour setting* with the term *activity* within the cultural-historical perspective on psychology. The hybrid term suggests a synthesis of that which is *immediately present* (the present present) and directly available to a perceiving agent with that which is historically and culturally present (the absent present) to a perceiving agent; hence the term activity setting suggests the concept of environment to be a wide one, in that it embraces the dialectics (the mutually inclusive nature) of immediateness and mediateness.

In their Midwest studies, Roger G. Barker and Herbert F. Wright (1966, 1971) put much effort into the development of a proper ecological unit of analysis with the aim of conceiving real-life activities of children in institutional settings. Barker and Wright use the term 'behaviour setting' as a community unit for their study in psychological ecology; they define it as a standing behaviour pattern together with the context of this behaviour. 'Activity', on the other hand, is a core unit of analysis within the cultural-historical tradition and activity theory. According to this theoretical perspective, developmental changes in individuals are dialectically connected with the transformation of human environment by humans themselves. Anna Stetsenko expresses the central pillars of this approach:

> One of the central pillars (...) is the idea that human development is based on active transformations of existing environments and creation of new ones achieved through collaborative processes of producing and deploying tools. These collaborative processes (involving development and passing on, from generation to generation, the collective experiences of people) ultimately represent a form of exchange with the world that is unique to humans – the social practice of human labor, or human activity. In these social and historically specific processes, people not only constantly transform and create their environments; they also create and constantly transform their very lives, consequently changing themselves in fundamental ways and, in the process, gaining self-knowledge. Therefore, human activity – material, practical, and always, by necessity, social collaborative processes aimed at transforming the world and human beings themselves with the help of collectively created tools – is the basic form of life for people. (Stetsenko, 2005, p. 72)

This view forms the basis for the study of child development as well, in that it puts the focus on how history and processes of reification form part of the child's environment and, further, how a child as a human agent contributes to his or her own developmental changes by contributing to collaborative processes in those particular environments. This summarizes the concept of human environment to include three general dimensions: *artefacts, social others,* and *self.* School, for instance, is a societal institution with a specific history and like in other institutions this history is reified in the form of *artefacts* (things) with specific properties that are intended to sustain certain practices; *social others* like classmates and teachers as well as the child her*self.*

By arguing that potentials for developmental novelty are embedded into the child–environment reciprocity of the activity setting it also is argued that those potentials might be studied *directly* when interpreting the observational data. Studying potentials for development in an activity setting means studying forwards by focusing on potentialities rather than studying in retrospect by filling out gaps between sequences of micro-genetic studies. This implies that what the researcher studies in-progress is greatly unsettled but nevertheless the researcher may throw light on how it is to be a child participating in the process of *becoming*. The particular activities are historically and culturally embedded. They are part of an ongoing flow of life that transcends particular pockets of time and space. Experienced meaningfulness is what connects the immediate activity with the flow of life for the child; it provides the "who am I?" and "who am I becoming?" questions with certain contours and possible pathways. This point suggests that the researcher should make observations of the child in different activity settings over a span of time. By doing that, it may be possible to study the dialectical nature of development, that is, of how the heterogeneity of a child's participation in different activity settings across a span of time and institutions may contribute to her development.

Small and Great Novelty

In an attempt to conceptualize the relations between potentials for development embedded into the activity setting and the developmental movements going on over a longer span of time, I suggest the terms *small* and *great* novelty. We have to do with great novelty when particular developmental pathways seem to occur; and when general capabilities emerge which allow for the child to expand her activities, interact in new ways and/or with new people; and when the child begins to experience herself and her life in new ways. Great novelty, hence, is novelty on an ontogenetic level. Small novelty, on the other hand, refers to the ongoing flow of everyday activities in the activity settings into which the child takes part and to which he or she contributes. The child may find new ways of viewing things or of appropriating new environmental properties and things (artefacts). She may find her way in not so well-known surroundings. She may develop new actions, relate to new people or to well-known people in new ways. She may experience herself as a participant in new ways, etc. The list of small novelty is unlimited and it is assumed that great novelty rests on developing heterogeneous patterns of small novelty which the child unfolds in her activities across different settings in her ongoing life.

An Environmental Affordance Perspective

As suggested above, the notion of *environment* presented here views environment as the dynamic unit of *artefacts*, *social others*, and *self*. Hence, environment (or context) does not just refer to that which surrounds (Cole, 1996) but to the particular reified wholeness of cultural and historical processes available in an activity setting. This view makes environment an antithesis to that which is *immediate* even though that which is immediate is the starting point of the study of individual–environment reciprocity.

The concept of environment should refer not only to the presence of things and people in specific contexts but *also* to the presence of an absence (temporality/historicity) of societal processes. This is what the child interacts with in his or her environment – the intentions of humans. Marx Wartofsky

(1979) stresses the general intentional nature of human environment. He says:

> The objectification of human intention is embodied both in the tools used in production, in the skills acquired and adapted to this use, and in the forms of symbolic communication which develop in language, in art, in dance and poetry, in their origins ... 'environment' is itself not a neutral term, but is what is functionally adapted to, and changed by an organism, or a population of organisms ... the very environment itself, as a space of action, is invested with the characteristics of an artefact. (pp. 205–206)

Following this perspective, human environments do not only have *historical* properties (which might be described on a formal level), they have *functional* properties as well, that is, properties which are regarded relative to some individual (or group of individuals). Environment is loaded with values. In relation to the view presented in the present chapter this implies that potential developmental novelty should be studied where the *historical values* (from the perspective of a given society or community of practice) intersects with the *functional values* (from the perspective of the individual who is the one who enters the activity settings as a heterogeneously interested agent).

To better grasp the intersection of historical values with functional values relative to a child, it seems fruitful to incorporate James J. Gibson's (1966) concept of *affordance* into the perspective being outlined. More precisely, I shall do so by following Heft (1988), who suggests a synthesis of Gibson's concept of affordance with Barker and Wright's (1966) concept of behaviour setting. Heft finds that Gibson's concept of affordance provides an alternative interpretation of the data collected by Barker and Wright in their Midwest studies. Barker and Wright's (1966) study is a record of what a seven-year-old boy, Raymond, did and what his surroundings did to him on a specific day of his life from when he woke up in the morning until he went to bed in the evening. The study of Raymond's day is part of a larger ecological study of the children who grew up in the late 1940s in a particular town (Midwest) in the United States. The study is a rich and detailed description of who Raymond meets during his day, how he relates to people and how they relate to him; the activities are embedded in shared, social and institutional activities. The observation covered activities like 'jumping down off something', 'picking up an object and breaking it', 'hiding behind something', etc. Each of such activities requires a particular environmental property to support it. 'Riding a bike', for instance, requires a relatively smooth, flat surface. Gibson (1966) regards exploratory action to be a basic unit of analysis which makes information about the environment available for an actively exploring organism. "The affordances of the environment are its *functionally significant* properties considered in relation to an individual" (Heft, 1988, p. 29). When integrating Gibson's ideas with those of Barker and Wright, he finds that: "An individual entering a behaviour setting will experience 'pressures' to act in a manner consistent with the perceived character of the setting, which contributes to maintaining a particular behaviour-milieu synomorphy" (Heft, 1988, p. 31); further, the affordance analysis offers "… a descriptive framework for conceptualizing the environment in terms of its functional possibilities" (p. 34).

What is appealing about this integrated ecological perspective on environment is the fact that it offers an opportunity for the researcher to move beyond a 'photo-like' concept of the human environment. In Heft's terms, this is viewed as a 'form-based' description which is problematic. He finds that our everyday terminology makes it difficult to get behind the so-called *form-description* of everyday life and everyday surroundings. A form-based approach to environment would be like describing what is in a photo or a painting: what is at the front, what is behind, etc. The properties of environmental features are considered independently of an individual. In fact, Heft finds that form-based descriptions are quite abstract compared with the immediate experience of the environment. A given environmental feature may have multiple affordances whereas form attributions are mutually exclusive. Alternatively he suggests that psychology should focus on *function* properties when describing the environmental properties relevant to a child. By suggesting a shift from form to functional descriptions, *intentionality* as a general theoretical perspective is being brought into focus and the child's surroundings are being looked upon with the child's eyes. Heft is interested in describing the function of *objects* (natural as well as human artefacts) and he suggests that different objects – such as bench, fence, and tree, for instance, may afford 'climbing on', while, on the other hand, one specific object may have a variety of different functional values. Water, for instance, affords splashing; pouring; floating objects; swimming, diving, boating, fishing; mixing with other materials to modify their consistency. The limitations of form-descriptions, hence, are that they do not reveal much about the *interest* some individual (child) may have in her interacting with specific environmental properties and objects. Rather, Heft finds that the transactions a child and her environment are being organized with regard to the *types of activities* that are expressed. Each type of activities requires a particular environmental feature to support it (like 'jumping down off something', 'picking up an object', 'hiding behind something', etc.). So, what are being put into focus in the first place in this alternative taxonomy of the environment are the 'types of activities' being available in some environments relative to a child.

Summing Up

Studying potentials for small and great novelty within an activity setting means studying what kind of activities are going on in which particular environment, how a child participates in ongoing activities and how she experiences/feels about this. The concept of 'environment' is an important one; a central point is that environment should be studied from an integrated historical/cultural *and* a functional perspective, that is, it should be studied at the intersection of reified intentions (the historical and societal nature of artefacts and institutional practices) and subjective intentions (the individual child participating in ongoing activities). This widens the concept of environment to include the dialectics of what is immediate and what is mediate (the present present and the absent present). Each action of a child relates to those aspects simultaneously. This, further, calls for a functional perspective according to which environment is not a neutral term; rather, beginning with the 'types of activities', as suggested by Heft, the environment of a child becomes that which the child perceives as available to action. Much child development has to do with appropriating and exploring availability. From a cultural-historical perspective, availability and affordances transcend the immediately perceived physical properties of an object (for a discussion of social affordances from a Gibsonian perspective, see for instance Schmidt, 2007); cultural artefacts, social others, and the child herself afford activities, only those affordances are historically, culturally, and personally developed and include the reified intentions of other people (who are not present in a particular activity setting) as well as the personal history of the child herself.

An Example: Having a Lesson

In the next section I shall work through an analysis and interpretation of a specific activity setting on the basis of the theoretical understanding of the child–environment reciprocity outlined above. It is intended to illustrate the general theoretical and methodological considerations rather than to specify or focus on a particular practical research domain. The study is from a school in Copenhagen which has a very high percentage of children coming from homes where Danish is the second language. The children in the study are third graders which means that the children are 9–10 years old. The parents and grandparents of the children come from countries like Turkey, Pakistan and Somalia. This means that the children's grandparents, or maybe even their parents, do not have a background in Denmark; very many of them are in the process of learning about Danish traditions, locations, geography, etc. The teachers cannot take for granted that the children have a broad knowledge about various matters well-known to children with a Danish family background; they need to include the children's perspectives on information and activities when working with them. The following example illustrates how a teacher tries to imagine and to include the children's probable perspectives and their assumed lack of specific knowledge due to their home background and everyday lives in a particular part of Copenhagen.

In the near future, the class is going on a camp close to a city about 60 km from Copenhagen. The children are not familiar with the place they are going to, and so the teacher talks with the class about the trip in an attempt to help them learn and feel good about it. The scheme (Table 9.1) is inspired by Hedegaard et al. (in press). On the left is the transcribed observation and on the right is the initial interpretation which is an attempt to condense the ongoing flow of action.

Table 9.1   Example lesson

1.	In a few weeks the class is going on a camp at another city (Holbæk) for a few days. The teacher wants to prepare the class so that all of the children will know about the trip and what to expect from it. As they sit at the tables, the teacher tells about the ticket that they have to buy and asks if anyone knows where Nørreport is (the station where the trip begins). He pulls down the map of Denmark so that the children can see where Holbæk is in relation to where they live.	The teacher introduces the trip by help of a map.
2.	Abdul goes find the cities they have to pass on their way.	Abdul uses the map.
3.	The teacher explains and points at the small city Vig outside of Holbæk where the camp is.	The teacher point out the destination.
4.	Hamid asks how long the trip will take?	Hamid asks a question.
5.	The teacher pulls up the map, cleans the blackboard and writes "bus".	
6.	Teacher: We will have to wait for the bus for about ten minutes and then it will take about 30 minutes to reach Nørreport Station. He asks the children to take up their folders and they do so immediately. He says that he wants them all to write down what he is now going to write on the blackboard.	The teacher gives a longer answer to Hamid's question by writing the details, shifts and timetable of the travel on the blackboard.
7.	The teacher writes: Travel Camp – time School: 8.00am (says: this is where we get on the bus) Nørreport St.: 8.45am (says: then we go to Holbæk) Holbæk St.: 9.45am (says: and then we have to go to the camp) Vig: 10.28am (says: this is where the camp is)	
8.	Teacher: Well, where are we beginning our trip and where does it end?	The teacher asks a control question.
9.	Absia: We begin at Nørreport Station and then we go to Holbæk, and then we go from Holbæk to Vig.	Absia answers

continued …

Table 9.1   continued

10.	The teacher writes on the blackboard: "1) How long are we going to spend on the train?"	The teacher writes two questions
11.	Child: Are we supposed to write it all down?	A child asks about the procedure.
12.	Teacher: Yes.	
13.	The teacher continues writing: "2) How long does the trip take?"	
14.	Teacher: Absia, will you read aloud the two questions, please?	The teacher asks Absia to read, and she does so..
15.	Absia reads the questions aloud.	
16.	The teacher tells the children to finish writing in their folders and then raise their hand to tell him where they want to be when they continue working with their maths folders. He communicates with the class about this.	The teacher organizes the group work
17.	All of the children find a partner after a little while and each couple fetch a small carpet which is put on the floor. Each couple now sits quietly on their carpet around in the classroom so as not to disturb other couples.	Each couple of children work on a blanket
18.	The teacher says that he wants to be able to see all of them and to make sure that everything goes well. He repeats that they are going to try to answer the questions.	The teacher wants to keep in control.
19.	Several children talk about whether they can have their mom and dad with them on the travel.	Some children would like mom and dad to join them.
20.	The teacher says that we are not going to talk about that now.	The teacher stops it.
21.	The children are now very, very quiet as they continue working. One child can be heard whispering to her partner.	They work quietly.
22.	After a while a boy asks the teacher if he is the only adult joining them.	A boy is interested in who will join them.
23.	The teacher says that there will be two other teachers as well.	The teacher answers.
24	The children continue working.	They work again.

Interpreting the Lesson From an Environmental Affordance Perspective

As can be seen, the teacher introduces the children to the trip very carefully and in detail. He utilizes the organization of the classroom and certain available artefacts in his attempt to help the children focus on the details and in an attempt to make them participate actively by having verbal exchange with him. I shall try to apply the environmental affordance perspective by analysing the three general aspects of an activity setting: artefacts, social others, and self.

Artefacts

The activity setting exemplified is from a school. Therefore, the artefact analysis should focus on what kind of artefacts are available and utilized in the classroom, when they are pulled into activities and with what purpose, how that contributes to the ongoing activities, the children's participation, their experiences, etc. The general list of available artefacts, of course, is long; among other things, it includes the architecture of the school, particular outdoor facilities, indoor facilities, practical arrangements and decorations of the room, furniture, tools, the cafeteria (or lack of one), the location and organization of teachers' rooms, organization of schedules, time planned for different activities, posters, photos, books, exhibits, etc. All of those possible artefacts have a historical as well as a functional value relative to the individuals who inhabit the particular environment and keep up the social practice. A book, for instance, affords looking into or reading (in addition to culturally less reified intentions like standing on, throwing, etc.). Artefacts present in school constitute environmental properties which may help initiate action through exploration and appropriation. After a period of practising, most newcomers learn how to read; hence, reading appears in its generalized form as an ability which often encourages the child to continue reading and so the child will gradually become more skilled and come to know about books in general (to be read) and about herself (as a skilled reader having fun reading). Reading is not a neutral cognitive skill in the child; it is a way to appropriate more of his or her world with the help of the book as an artefact and herself as an interested and exploring reader. To follow Heft, reading can be seen as a type of activity which helps the child experience the affordance of books. In this sense, reading expands the child's world and self-perception. These *generals* are always embedded into *particular* activities and serve as examples of the immediate–mediate dialectics presented earlier. In the example presented above, particular artefacts seem to play an important and prominent role in organizing the flow of the activity setting. The presence of those artefacts and what they afford is to be analysed. Table 9.2 lists the artefacts (on the left) as well as what they seem to afford (on the right).

Table 9.2   Artefacts and what they afford

Artefacts	Afford
Chairs and tables	Sitting on; sitting at; working at; leaving, returning to, remaining quiet; listening to social others; talking with classmates etc.
Map	Way finding; orienting oneself about places, directions, and distances; working with abstract representations; etc.
Blackboard and written information	Writing on; focus shared attention on matter presented; communicating about matter; unfolding/structuring events and processes in representational form; mediating information; imagining things and events; etc.
Folders and pencils	Writing/drawing in; writing/drawing with; 'playing' with artefacts; keeping information; unfolding imaginative processes; etc.
Carpets	Putting on the floor; walking/standing on; sitting on; putting something on; being the base for shared activities; etc.

Interpretation of the Affordances of Artefacts

How are the artefacts being used to organize activities among participants in the lesson? I shall attend to that question by working through the transcription above.

Chairs and tables in general afford *sitting on* and *sitting at*. Following the cultural norm in school; they further afford *working at*. Often, they are a 'base' for the child which means that they afford *leaving* and *returning to*. Further, when the children sit at their table, they afford *remaining quiet*, *listening to social others* and *talking with classmates*, etc. Quite often, sitting at one's table means listen to the teacher and answering questions when asked. It is common that children for shorter or longer periods of time inhabit a certain chair-and-table in the classroom and in this respect the children have something like a small 'home'; it works as a base for each particular child and occupying another child's base may be a reason for conflict. In this lesson there are no such conflicts; each child seems to respect what chairs and tables 'are for' in school (1–16).

The map is an artefact which the teacher includes to help the children know and understand about the upcoming trip. It affords *way finding* and *orienting oneself about places, directions and distances*. Also, the map in general affords *working with abstract representations*. In the lesson the map is used as a means for helping the children understand about the destination as well as how far from home the camp is and which places to pass to get there; it is used to help the children *imagine* details about the trip, that is, make the trip concrete with the help of representational means. Abdul uses the map accordingly as he points out the towns to pass on the train; hence he helps his classmates to have a general imagination of what to expect in the near future (1–3).

The blackboard and the written information similarly are being used to specify details about the trip; in a classroom, a blackboard generally affords *writing on* as well as *focusing attention on shared matter* and *communicating about matter*. Further, it affords *unfolding/structuring events and processes in representational form* as well as *mediating information* and *imagining things and events*. This is also the case in this particular lesson; the teacher wants the children to focus their attention on the timetable of the travel which is being written slowly and in detail on the blackboard (5–9). Afterwards, the teacher writes questions on the blackboard (10; 13) which children are going to answer independently in pairs as they write it all down in their folders.

Folders and pencils which the children also use (11–16; 21–24) afford *writing/drawing in* and *writing/drawing with*. Also, they afford *keeping information* as well as *unfolding imaginative processes*, etc. In this case, the children use their folders to write down information from the blackboard; in this process information given is being transformed into an externalized (reified) form of memory. The processes that basically constitute the human societies (as described by Stetsenko), also seem to occur in children's appropriation of human artefacts. The folder and pencil therefore also afford *extending memory* as well as *'playing' with artefacts* (words, numbers, …), *keeping information* to be used later on, not to speak of *unfolding imaginative processes*. In this case the children are expected to write down information from the blackboard and to use the information shortly after as they do the calculations and try to answer the two questions asked by the teacher.

A carpet is an artefact rarely seen in Danish schools, especially the way it is used in this particular lesson (17–24). Most often, a carpet affords *putting on the floor, walking/standing on* as well as *putting something onto* (like furniture). Further, it affords *sitting on* which, in this school context, is being utilized to make the carpets function as the *base for shared activities* among a few students. In the lesson it is the sitting on affordance which is relevant in that it helps organize the classroom activities and hence facilitates certain aspects of the learning process. The sitting on affordance facilitates *working independently and quietly* and often also *collaborating with classmates*. This expanded affordance character is due to the special needs and organization of the classroom practice as well as to the role that carpets play in the lives of the children. The carpets mediate between different cultural practices and hence symbolize the simultaneous values of ordinary school practice and other practices which are well known to the children in their home life.

Social Others

As a child interacts with other children (like classmates) or adults (like a teacher) about some shared matter (like an upcoming trip or some calculations), she also learns about ways of doing things in the ongoing activity settings as well as about general mutual positions which include distributed responsibilities and power-relations. The child learns about 'who am I' in relation to social others in the particular institutional setting. With being a schoolchild, for instance, follows certain responsibilities to be appropriated if ordinary social exchange with others should continue to go smoothly. Classroom activities are expected to be taken seriously and a child will easily get into trouble if she does not live up to the culturally defined norms for proper actions and behaviour.

Through interactions with teachers the child comes to know about a variety of general expectations, activities, and values; the child comes to know about the teacher as an *agent* and as an individual who inhabits the general cultural/institutional *position* of teaching children in a classroom; hence, in general terms the teacher's presence represents the functional value of experiencing and living up to the valued order set by others in school (accepting power-relations). Also, the child comes to know about herself as an agent *and* as someone inhabiting the position of being a schoolchild among other schoolchildren. By interacting with classmates she comes to know about classmates as individual agents *and* as someone who inhabits the position of being 'like-me' (a schoolchild in this class); because of this position, the child also comes to know what counts as important in the classroom compared with what counts as important in recess, in after-school activities, on the playground, etc.

The analysis offers an opportunity to reveal the possible general positions among participants in different institutional activity settings; the analysis, of course, may reveal tensions, resistance, coping with the inevitable, etc. as well as how different general positions can contribute differently to the development of the child. Children do not just adapt to the general expected norms and patterns of interaction; their development is not homogeneous or uni-directional. This is why a detailed environmental affordance analysis may help focus on the varieties, richness, ambiguities, and contradictions of embedded potentialities in (and across) activity settings.

In short, studying an activity setting offers opportunities to follow how a child manages to be herself as an agent who (in the institution) is *also* a schoolchild among other schoolchildren who all contribute in non-linear ways to the ongoing practice of school. The child may feel conflicted or the child may experience conflicts with others; the child may prefer some activities rather than others; she may be more affectionate to some peers and adults rather than to others; she may participate and collaborate with great joy, participate with degrees of open resistance, resign and withdraw, give up participating and remain quiet and unnoticed.

The affordance perspective of Gibson is occupied very much with physical properties. However, because individuals are intentional agents one has to include into the affordance perspective the intentional nature of interpersonal relations in the activity setting. This calls for a *double-perspective* on what social others afford relative to the child. An agent (in this case a teacher or a classmate) affords certain actions. This is due to the shared history of particular interpersonal relations between the child and that other agent, as well as to the general positions available and possible in an institutional activity setting. A double-perspective on individuals is needed to grasp the simultaneity of the teacher being *a representative of the specific cultural practice* on the one hand and *a socially interacting human being* (agent) on the other hand. The child who interacts with the teacher comes to know about both sides simultaneously and develops a subjective position which mirrors specific experiences throughout the history of interaction. Similarly, classmates are perceived simultaneously as subjects with personal histories and as having the position of being classmates contributing to the activity setting. Because of the nature of human exchange, an affordance analysis *must* grasp the double-perspective of social others as inhabiting pro-active agency *and* institutional positions. Being an intentional agent with a position, the teacher, for instance, affords *being listened to/listen to* – simultaneously expressing the institutional position related to being a teacher *and* the position of being an intentional interacting agent which demands of the child to listen. At the same time the teacher is an intentional agent and someone who inhabits an *artefact-like* cultural position which affords activities specific to the activity setting.

While interacting with social others, the child attends those affordances. The child *must* include her own agent position while paying attention to (for instance) the teacher. The child must, for instance, include her own agency when *receiving instruction* (the agent aspect of what the teacher affords) when the teacher *instructs* (the cultural position aspect of what the teacher affords). In other words, the environmental affordance analysis concerning human interaction must be an interactive one.

Table 9.3 lists (part of) what is afforded by social others in a particular lesson.

Interpretation of the Affordances of Social Others

In this particular activity setting the social others to a child are the teacher and the classmates. Most of the time is spent having a dialogical exchange

Table 9.3 Social others and what they afford

Social others	Afford
Teacher	Being listened to/listen to
	Instructing/receiving instruction
	Performance/performing
	Organizing/receiving organization
	Controlling/being controlled
	Being communicative/communicate with
Classmates	Performance/performing
	Asking questions/ask questions
	Living up to expectations/live up to expectations
	Communicating/communicating with
	Obeying/obey
Partner	Collaborating/collaborating with

between the teacher and the class, but in the end of the observational sequence, each child communicates with another child in group work. This situation is initiated by the teacher who offers a possibility for the children to have a closer interpersonal exchange. Let us first take a look at the teacher. In the eyes of the children, the teacher probably is viewed as carrying the values of the school as a cultural arrangement of educational activities for children (a *quasi-artefact*). By that is meant that much of his agency and individual energy is being spent on how he, on his part, can live up to the interwoven multiplicity of demands which follow from his position as a teacher. The children relate to him in an interactive way and hence learn about their own position as students. This interactive aspect of what the teacher affords can be observed in the particular activities. When the teacher explains to the class about the trip, he affords *being listened to/listen to* (1–20; 22–23) which means that the children's actions mirror the social arrangement of the teacher talking and the children listen to him. In general, the teacher is responsible for organizing the lesson and giving instructions along the way which means that he affords *organizing/receiving organization* as well as *instructing/receiving instruction* (1–24). The teacher asks questions but also he is open to the children asking him questions which means that *being communicative/communicating with* occurs to be an affordance in the children's exchange with the teacher. In the conversation with the class, the teacher twice asks children to help the class, that is, when Abdul is asked to find the place on the map where the camp is located (2), and when Absia is asked to read aloud the questions that the class is going to work with (14); hence, the teacher also affords *performance/performing* in front of the class. In the conversation and later as the group work is being organized on the carpets, the teacher keeps control with the aim and the focus (20), as well as with where the children sit on their carpets – they should sit in places that allow the teacher to watch them all (18). The affordance of *controlling/being controlled* therefore seems to be an important aspect of the flow of the lesson.

When joining the activities in a classroom, a part of the environment for a child are their classmates. By watching what classmates do, like pointing spots out on a map (2), reading aloud (15), writing in folders (11; 16; 24), etc., a child becomes aware of general expectations and arrangements – including power relations – concerning participation and he or she is provided with a basis for evaluating activities relative to her- or himself. In this particular lesson, two classmates are asked to perform in front of the class: Abdul is asked to point out the towns to pass on the map and Absia is asked to read aloud the questions that the class is going to work with. Hence, classmates afford *performance/performing* as well as *living up to expectations/live up to expectations* and *obeying/obey* because they do as they are asked. The nature of the exchange between the teacher and the class seems to be quite relaxed in the sense that the children are allowed to ask questions and they expect the teacher to give some answers to questions, questions are not being ignored. To a child, classmates therefore afford *being asked/asking* (2; 4; 6; 8; 10; 11; 13–14; 19–20; 22–23). A further aspect of interaction among the children is being introduced in the form of group work arranged on the carpets. In this case, a child participating also experiences classmates as partners who afford *collaborating/collaborating with* (17–24) which is a direct interaction between each child and a classmate, rather than an observed one.

Self

Along with experiencing her own participation in the activity setting, the child also experiences herself as an experiencing participant. Hence, the child's personal experiences of self are phenomenological in a double sense in that they are being an experience and a meta-experience of participation. In the present chapter, this double dimension of phenomenological self-experience is theoretically proposed to be a key to understanding how a child actively contributes to her own development. In this sense, the child is not only the centre of agency, she also experiences her agency (first-person perspective) from the side of the possible and available cultural positions (third-person perspective) during the interactions with social others. One might say, therefore, that the child also inhabits an agent position in relation to herself. Being an experiencing agent, her agency includes her institutional position being negotiated and renegotiated in practice – and in this process the child emerges as a social other to herself. Baldwin already points to this dialectics of social exchange and child development (1899/1973) in his analysis of self and other; as he stresses, 'ego' and 'alter' are born together. According to this notion of 'self', the child's thought of herself is filled up with her thoughts of others and her thoughts of others are filled up with herself.

During participation in the activity setting, the child gradually perceives and conceives the phenomenological double-ness of participation. She learns about own social position in relation to others, about own contributions, performances, values, failures, etc. As time passes, it all merges into more or less generalized versions of 'who am I?' and 'who am I becoming?' Being a social other to others, the child affords a variety of actions to others (teacher, classmates); but the child also affords actions to herself. The child is inescapably embedded into the social negotiation of positions which includes the negotiating of herself. In a positive variant of this point, the child may experience self as a source of *self-inspiration*. There may be a self-stimulating aspect of experiencing self while participating in activities which seems similar to what Baldwin (1899/1973) calls the '*try-try-again*' tendency (a tendency which I believe might develop into a complex and ambiguous notion of try-try-not-again, try-try-again-with-resistance, etc. which breaks with conformity of imitation). Baldwin's try-try-again tendency points to the fact that developmental changes are dialectically related to persistent imitation. In different societal institutions for children, different activities give rise to different experiences concerning the self-stimulating aspects of participation. Different activity settings unfold different repeated patterns of activities which add to constituting the values of a particular institution. Each child will need to explore what it means to be a participant in relation to those institutional activities. Hence the child's *motives* and *interests* emerge and develop along with participating in socially shared activities about some matter; the motives for or against this or that activity perhaps become strengthened or undergo changes – the researcher should expect those motives to be of a complex and ambiguous nature. Hence, it is proposed that the affordance perspective on self throws light on emerging and developing interests and motives for actions as well as on feelings and values in a child. The development of interests in a child, Vygotsky (1998) stresses, is the dialectical resolution of the 'inner' and 'outer' tendencies. The emergence of new interests and needs in a child often leads to changes in the character of things relative to the child rather than to certain actions.

According to a wholeness approach to child development, the development of motives in a child should be researched along with her *capabilities* to manage different activities. Being capable of playing baseball and experiencing the capability as something personally important and valued may be a motive for the child to play again – to practise skills and have a joyful time. Capabilities or skills themselves do not say much about development, but what they afford to the child does. This becomes possible if a child experiences the *quasi-otherness* of self as something positively valued; if the first-person perspective merges with the third-person perspective.

A small novelty of such personally experienced capabilities is suggested to emerge as a budding greater developmental possibility. Small novelties often emerge relatively unnoticed in the activity settings and the researcher has to focus on details when studying child development in a larger scale. Over a longer time-span small novelties may give rise to greater novelties which have an influence on the future motives and activities of the child. Greater novelties may see the light if the shifting and complex stream of experiences result in observable configurations of who the child experiences herself to be and who the child experiences herself to become; or it may result in changes of activities, interests, motives, values, etc. In general, different developmental potentialities in ontogeny are assumed to emerge on the basis of the child's exploration and appropriation of culturally available positions and artefacts in her environment. No matter how the child explores the available positions and artefacts of an activity setting and no matter with what the child becomes skilled, she will co-experience what her life is about and who she is (becoming), with what she has to struggle, where joy is to be found, etc.

In Table 9.4 the phenomenological double-ness as the basis for emerging capabilities and motives is described relative to the example. On the left side are listed the first-person experiences of being a participant in the activities. On the right side are listed the quasi-otherness position which allows for a child to experience capabilities as something that may (or may not) afford further activities as a potential resource for the move from small to great novelty in a child's life.

Table 9.4   The basis for emerging capabilities and motives relative to the example

Self-experience	Motives	Self-experience	Motives
(1.p.p. on activities)	(quasi-otherness)	(1.p.p. on activities)	(quasi-otherness)
Listen to the teacher	Listen-to-able	Share the imagined matter with others	Share-imaginations-able
Listen to the classmates	Listen-to-able	Understand a map	Understanding-representations-able
Sit still	Sitting-still-able Accepting	Imagine specific future coordinated actions	Transfer-of-information-able Exploring-imaginations-able
Remain quiet	Remaining-quiet-able Accepting-order-able	Write in folders	Write-able Externalize-memory-able
Do what one is asked to do	Understanding-order-able Obeying-order-able	Do calculations	Do-calculations-able
Answer when being asked	Answering-able Obeying-order-able	Collaborate in groups	Being-collaborative-able
Be able to ask questions and feeling free to do	Asking-questions-able Expressing-oneself-able Being-interested-able	Linking from home to school	Considering-connections-able
Use information on a blackboard	Understanding-representations-able Transfer-of-information-able	Share the limited space of the classroom	Accept-shared-conditions-able

Interpretation of the Affordances of Self

I shall now interpret the relation between the self-experience (which refers to the child's experiencing herself participating in available activities) and the affordance nature of the self-experience (which means that the child experiences herself as someone who experiences participating). The idea is to put into focus the child as someone who acts *interdependently* (Valsiner, 1987) with the environment in *valuating* ways. Of course, the valuation of a child in general refers to who the child is and who she is becoming. Children have different family backgrounds, different available social and academic resources, different views of themselves, their futures, etc. Therefore, the researcher should expect to find subjectively very different ways of joining available activities in a setting – some children may show open resistance, for instance or hide themself away from the teacher's control, if things going on are felt to be too remote from the child's 'world of daily life' (Schutz, 1971). The child's personal valuation, on the other hand, surely is connected with the variety of expectations embedded into the activity setting as they constitute culturally developed arrangements for children. As Schutz (1971) says, only a small part of the world originates within the personal experience of the child's personal world. Constructions made have to be formed in accordance with the system of relevances accepted from the anonymous unified point of view of the group which the child belongs to. It is within this world of daily life that the affordance nature of the experienced self-experience grows to become motives and interests. This implies that a child must be able to experience the quasi-otherness aspect of herself. Affordance, in this case, refers to the potential motivational inspirations of experienced capabilities in relation to participation (or incapability leading to, let us say, de-motivation and disappointments, etc.). The experience of listening to others (teacher, classmates) affords listen-to-able. Because of his position as the organizer of the activity setting etc., the teacher seems to suggest a variety of self-experiences like *sitting still* and *remaining quiet* as the teacher talks with the class (1–16), *answer when being asked* (2; 8; 14), *do what one is asked to do* (2; 9; 11–12; 14–15; 16; 17; 21; 24), and *be able to ask questions and feeling free to do so* (4; 11; 19; 22), which all are associated with the social expectations related to the school structure. While participating in activities that imply such self-experiences, the child may co-experience him- or herself as someone who is *listen-to-able, remaining-quiet-able, understanding-order-able, accepting-order-able, answering-able, obeying-order-able, asking-questions-able, expressing-oneself-able*, and *being-interested-able*. The child, hence, cannot escape valuating what it is like to be 'me' participating in the ongoing co-construction of the teacher–child (power) positions of the classroom practice. In modern times, those experiences go along with working with the subject matter. In this case potential self-experiences related to the subject matter occur to be the *use of information on a blackboard, share the imagined matter with others, imagine future coordinated actions* (4–9), *write in folders, do calculations* (11; 16–24), and *collaborate in groups* (17–24).

Further, some of the children are occupied with making *links between school activities and their homes* (19) and when it comes to working on the carpets, they are willing to *share the limited space of the classroom* (17–24). When participating in those school-related activities a child may co-experience herself as being *share-imaginations-able, understanding-representations-able, transfer-of-information-able, exploring-imaginations-able, write-able, externalize-memory-able, do-calculations-able, being-collaborative-able, considering-connections-able*, and *accept-shared-conditions-able*.

The Activity Setting and Developmental Novelty

It is now time to relate the analysis of the particular example to the theoretical considerations earlier in the chapter. In focus, of course, is the search for potential developmental novelties which might offer the participating children opportunities to experience participation as meaningful on a personal level. In this brief observational example, those potentials can only be sketched. To study a particular child's development more focus is needed on this particular child in different activity settings over time. However, let us begin with the 'types of activities' which Heft suggests to put into focus in an attempt to grasp the functional nature of child–environment interaction. In the lesson, there seems to be a close connection between types of activities organized very much by the teacher and potentials for a child to experience self while participating. Potential developmental novelties in general are assumed to emerge within such action–experience units. In the lesson, the phenomenological experiences are related to types of activities like reading aloud for the class, finding one's way on the map, writing in folders, collaborating on carpets, etc. The particular artefacts present in the classroom are being utilized to support the aim set by the teacher and co-constructed by the children. The presence of chairs and tables, a blackboard, a map, carpets, folders and pencils, etc. help sustain a certain general order of the classroom; this order is being kept up recurrently as a synthesis of 'who does what', 'by help of what' and 'with what purpose'. The map, for instance, is in front and close to the teacher's location in the classroom so that it can be seen by the children who sit in rows and look in the teacher's direction; at the same time the teacher is in control with the performance of the child who points out cities on the map. The carpets, on the other hand, are spread out like small 'islands' with a relative freedom from the teacher's control – but only relative, he wants to be able to see them all, probably to be able to help as well as to keep in control. The carpets are not ordinary artefacts in a Danish classroom. By choosing the carpets as a means for organizing group work the school most likely tries to include dimensions from other parts of the children's lives. This is an example of how the present present includes the absent present, that is, it illustrate the presence of history and cultural practices in the particular reifications. The carpets might be viewed as a reification of the human intention to make the classroom more 'comfortable' to the children; hence, one should expect a motive like respecting the particular children's conditions for participation to lie behind the reification. If so, what the children are hoped to perceive in the immediateness of the carpet is the mediateness of this particular history. Each artefact and organizational order is such an expression of intentions through reifications. In general, the organizational properties of the classroom, the presence of certain artefacts, and the control aspect of the activities are mutually supportive dimensions which set up the conditions for the children to experience participation as schoolchildren.

Because small novelty should be searched for from the perspective of the participating children, it occurs to be insufficient to keep up the analytical separation by which the analysis is worked through. It is, for instance, *not* a point that working with a map or with written representations on the blackboard in itself will add equally to each child's cognitive development, such as in general improve so-called cognitive skills; or that collaborating with classmates will always improve the social development of each child. The types of activities in the lesson are but opportunities offered to those children in this lesson in that Danish school. According to the environmental affordance perspective, 'cognitive' or 'social' should not be studied as if we have to do with separate elements of development; the study of developmental novelties needs to include the experiences of self in the children. The analysis, in fact, should serve as an argument against instrumental approaches to developmental novelties.

Conclusions

Based on a historical and functional approach to the human environment the aim of the chapter has been to outline an interpretive method for the study of potential developmental novelties. The focus has been on general theoretical considerations as well as an analysis of general potentialities available in a particular lesson in a Danish school. By looking at 'types of activities' in relation to potential self-experiences of the participants, the researcher has a chance to study small developmental novelties directly rather than only in retrospect. Even a temporally short setting like the one analysed here shows a broad variety of potential self-experiences which may afford motivational experiences to a child. In general, one of the aims of the chapter is to point out the richness of potentialities embedded even in a brief observational study. The environments of children are rich and they constitute a flow of history and practice which is being kept up, added to, or changed over time; the interpretive method suggested in this environmental affordance analysis suggests that the researcher studies carefully the details and richness of potentialities while at the same time focusing on those who appear to be culturally and personally meaningful and important. The chapter has aimed to provide an interpretive method by which the researcher can make herself aware of the environmental richness and dynamics so that she will not end up being 'blind' to those all too well-known environmental features and properties as well as those all too well-known practices of her own culture which may hinder her from unfolding a rich and dynamic developmental analysis.

References

Baldwin, J. M. (1899/1973). *Social and ethical interpretations in mental development.* New York: Arno Press.

Barker, R. G. & Wright, H. (1951). *One boy's day – a specimen record of behavior.* New York: Harper & Brothers.

Barker, R. & Wright, H. (1971). *Midwest and its children – the psychological ecology of an American town.* Hamden, CT: Archon Books.

Cole, M. (1996). *Cultural psychology – a once and future discipline.* Cambridge, MA: The Belknap Press of Harvard University Press.

Dreier, O. (2008). *Psychotherapy in everyday life.* Cambridge: Cambridge University Press.

Gibson, J. J. (1966). *The senses considered as perceptual systems.* Boston: Houghton Mifflin.

Hedegaard, M., Fleer, M., Bang, J., & Hviid, P. (in press). *Studying children. A cultural-historical approach.* London: Open University Press.

Heft, H. (1988). Affordances of children's environments: a functional approach to environmental description. *Children's Environments Quarterly*, 5 (2), 29–37.

Schmidt, R. C. (2007). Scaffolds for social meaning. *Ecological Psychology*, 19 (2), 137–151.

Schutz, A. (1971). The problem of social reality. In *Collected papers.* The Hague: Martinus Nijhoff.

Stetsenko, A. (2005). Activity as object-related: Resolving the dichotomy of individual and collective planes of activity. *Mind, Culture, and Activity*, 12 (1), 70–88.

Valsiner, J. (1987). *Culture and the development of children's action: A cultural-historical theory of developmental psychology.* Chichester: John Wiley.

Vygotsky, L. (1998). *The collected works of L. S. Vygotsky: Volume 5.* New York: Plenum Press.

Wartofsky, M. W. (1979). Perception, representation, and the forms of action: Towards an historical epistemology. In *Models: Representation and the scientific understanding* (pp. 188–210). Boston: D. Reidel.

10 Radical-Local Teaching and Learning

A Cultural-Historical Perspective on Education and Children's Development

Seth Chaiklin and Mariane Hedegaard

Formal education for schoolchildren in state-regulated systems is usually aimed both at preparing and motivating children to participate in a society's existing economic, political and cultural practices, and to acquire a foundation for a personally meaningful life. Smiles often appear when schoolteachers (and others) look at the specifications in national or ministry documents – in recognition that currently-existing teaching practices and conditions do not usually address or realise these (often sensible) goals.

Do collectively-shared understandings exist about how to realise such educational goals as helping children to 'get confidence in their own possibilities' and 'background to form positions and act' – so that the problem is merely to have adequate resources to implement the appropriate institutional practices? Or do the smiles also indicate that we do not know how to realise these goals given the diversity found among schoolchildren – even if sufficient institutional resources are available and the goals are clear?

The focus of this chapter is to present radical-local teaching and learning – a conceptual perspective for creating educational practice that can address this tension between valued general goals of education and the diversity found in schools today (Hedegaard & Chaiklin, 2005). The key idea is to integrate and relate a general theory of children's development with the acquisition of academic knowledge and skills. In particular, the aim is to develop motives and competencies that are relevant for the child's societal life, through a dynamic between general subject-matter content and concrete practices in specific historical, local conditions. This gives a way to understand how education can contribute to the personal development of children in relation to their historical and cultural conditions, as well as a general conceptual perspective for planning appropriate educational interventions likely to achieve many of the widely-held goals for formal education.

To give a background for this perspective, we start with analyses about the relations between education and children's development, first in general, and then in relation to societal practices, which will require additional relation to explicate the meaning of education more precisely, and how education is mediated in relation to children's development. Radical-local teaching and learning is grounded in a cultural-historical psychological perspective about the nature of knowledge and children's development in relation to societal life.

We present a brief overview of development in a cultural-historical perspective, introduce main ideas of radical-local teaching and learning, and give concrete illustrations of how these ideas can be used to make developmentally-relevant educational practice.

Relation Between Education and Children's Development in General

In its most abstract form, the relation between education and children's development is simple – it is generally believed that education is necessary for children's development. This point is also found as part of a system of ideas within the cultural-historical tradition, articulated initially in Vygotsky's arguments about the relation between instruction and children's development (e.g., Vygotsky, 1987, pp. 194–211), and elaborated and extended subsequently by his colleagues and their co-workers (e.g., El'konin & Davydov, 1975; Davydov, 1988a, 1988b, 1988c) into the developmental teaching–learning approach, which focuses on the role of subject-matter learning in relation to children's development.

We start with the assumption that education and children's development are not completely independent of each other.[1] That is, education has some influence or consequence for children's development, while characteristics of children's development have consequences for educational practices. Education is larger than children's development (i.e., many aspects of educational practices are not relevant to children's development such as learning to operate computer equipment or rules of grammar), while children's development is larger than education (i.e., some aspects of development are not dependent upon education such as social relations with peers), but (a) education and children's development are not completely independent (i.e., education has an important role to play in relation to development), and (b) their specific relation is hard to specify (beyond that they are dependent, but not exclusively or exhaustively). This formulation may give the (wrong) impression that future research should try to identify what percentage of education contributes to children's development. More productive is to explicate and investigate the specific forms of interaction between education and children's development (i.e., in what ways can education contribute to development and what implications does development have for education), which will require that we elaborate the meaning of education and children's development more fully, so that we can better understand the content and possibilities for interactions.

Relations Between Children's Development and Education in a Societal Perspective

The analysis of the general relationship between education and children's development starts with some general definitions of education and children's development. While not intended to be comprehensive and exhaustive, these definitions are meant to move past the everyday use of these terms. This is particularly important in relation to the polysemous concept of education, which requires a longer discussion. The basic ideas to be elaborated are that (a) children's development is a consequence of their participation in societal practices, (b) education is a societal practice, and (c) therefore education has a significant role in children's development.

Children's Development in a Cultural-Historical Perspective

A central tenet of the cultural-historical perspective is that psychological development is a consequence of participation in historically-formed societal practices, arising through engaged actions in relation to the demands and conditions of the practices. Conversely, the perspective rejects the idea of a natural or normal form, telos, or state of development – both from biological and historical points of view. Persons are not determined primarily by their genetic, physiological or cultural characteristics, nor can one merely describe the current state of historical development in a society and expect that it alone will reveal any necessary or fundamental characteristics of children. While existing practices create conditions for children's development, often nothing is required or necessary about the particular forms of these practices. Therefore, it is not simply a matter of examining existing conditions. While one can explore the possibilities for children's development found in existing societal practice, it is also possible to investigate the consequences of new forms of action that could be realised within existing forms of societal practice.

The main implication of this perspective is that significant aspects of children's psychological development arises from their participation in practices, which in turn have significant consequences for their possibilities to participate in societal life. In the present case, the focus is on possible contributions of education as a societal practice in relation to that development. This requires that we elaborate an analysis of education as a societal practice within which children develop.

Education in Three Perspectives

In everyday usage, the term 'education' refers to a variety of phenomena and issues. We want to preserve the simplicity (and seeming clarity) of being able to refer to 'education', but systematic analysis of the relation between 'education' and 'children's development' will require that three perspectives encompassed in the concept of education are differentiated and elaborated. We start with an abstract idea of education (in an 'analytic' perspective) and move with increasing concreteness to the idea of education as 'societal practice', and 'concrete societal practice'.

The analytic perspective notes the main defining criteria for education as product and process, but these criteria do not specify the societal practices by which the process and product of education are realised. There are many 'societal practices' which attempt to realise the analytic goals of education. We analyse the general relations that organise one significant form of 'education as societal practice', namely state-regulated schooling, followed by a discussion of 'education as a concrete societal practice', which concretises the abstract relations of education as a societal practice in relation to the historical moment of a particular society.

Education in an Analytic Perspective

In everyday usage, the term *education* can refer both to the *process* (e.g., upbringing, instruction, disciplining) by which persons become educated, and to the *product* (e.g., knowledge formation, personality development) produced from this process. Whether these two meanings of education, as process and as product, can be differentiated unambiguously in all cases (e.g., to separate a specific product from a specific process) is not important, because in each case they presuppose the other's existence.

From a 'product' perspective, the term 'education' has been used historically to refer differentially to several kinds of formation – most commonly the formation of intellectual knowledge and skill, usually through systematic instruction. Sometimes it is used more broadly to refer to the formation of other cultural characteristics (e.g., 'physical education' or 'moral education') or character formation. These products can be understood in both retrospective and prospective senses (see Figure 10.1).

In a *retrospective* sense, the 'product of education' refers to that which remains for a particular individual as a consequence of experience (often from formal instruction), where the 'process' refers to the collection of activities by which a person becomes educated. In a *prospective* or normative sense, the 'product of education' refers to preferred qualities to be realised (as expressed in a phrase like 'well-educated'), where the 'process' now refers to the activities by which one expects to achieve these particular educational products. Both senses are meaningful, though they are not usually articulated or differentiated in everyday usage.

	Education as ...	
	Process	*Product*
Retrospective	Historical	Achieved
Prospective	Planned	Ideal

Figure 10.1 Analytic forms of education

Education as a Societal Practice

In most societies, there are many societal practices (e.g., families, religious institutions, sports clubs, music schools) that institutionalise processes directed intentionally to educational products. Furthermore a variety of possibilities for individual action (e.g., as self-study, practice, experiences from concerts, films, museums, travels) have educational consequences. A comprehensive analysis of the relation between education and children's development would need to consider this range of practices.

Because this chapter is focused on the possibilities for systematic instruction to lead development, the analysis of education as a societal practice is limited to processes that involve *schooling* (i.e., institutionally-organised traditions for educational provision). Without the (analytic) idea of education, it is unlikely that schooling, at least in its current historical form, would exist in contemporary societies, and schooling is the most common institutional form within which systematic *instruction* is conducted for educational purposes. Schooling is usually organised (or regulated) by the state, and in this way, *societal interests* are expressed through processes and conditions of schooling and instruction.

These three concepts – schooling, instruction, and societal interests – have important 'conditioning' relations with each other. Each is dependent upon, influenced by, and necessary to the others, but without determining the others (either alone or in pairs). These conditional relations are symbolised in Figure 10.2 by the dashed lines. Joined together, these relations mediate a predominant form of 'education as societal practice'. This form realises both the process and product of education, in an analytic sense, mediated through the relations described in Figure 10.2.

In this form of societal practice, while education as process and product cannot be achieved without instruction, it cannot be reduced to or equated with instruction (even if it is necessary), because of the other relations in the model. As already noted, schooling is the predominant institutional form

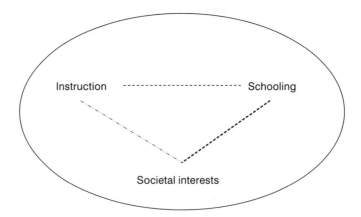

Figure 10.2 Model of predominant form of 'education as societal practice'

where instruction takes place, and therefore necessarily provides conditions within which instruction can be realised. Furthermore, both the conditions for schooling and instruction are conditioned by societal interests. Societal interests usually have more opportunity to influence schooling (including here the demands of the curriculum) than instruction (which is more dependent on individual teacher action, including interpreting or ignoring the curriculum). This differential influence is symbolised in Figure 10.2 by fewer dashed lines between societal interests and instruction.

Societal interests (i.e., norms, visions, and goals for education) are expressed in a variety of ways both through (a) state administration, mediated with such instruments as official documents (e.g., national school law, national curriculum, ministry policies), financial resources, practical resources (e.g., schoolbooks, computers, other instructional materials), inspectors, and organisation of working conditions (e.g., number of hours and days for instruction), and (b) often more weakly, through civil society in such forms as journalism and parent associations.

Presumably these concrete expressions are all directed at influencing the institutional conditions of schooling and instruction within which education is realised. It is not possible however to go directly from a societal interest (e.g., that children should desire to learn) to an educational result (i.e., that children actually acquire this desire), even if there are clear visions of the goals of education. These interests are necessarily expressed through their indirect or mediated forms, which influence how schooling and instruction will realise the educational product. There is no guarantee that these concrete mediating forms (e.g., laws, curriculum) are consistent with the intended goals, nor that they will yield influences to realise ideals – hence the 'smiles' mentioned at the beginning of this chapter.

The relations shown in Figure 10.2 underlie a significant form of 'education as societal practice', which has important consequences for children's development. As mentioned before, there are other societal practices which are educational but not school-based. These practices may involve different central relations (e.g., a different model would be needed in relation to instruction that is part of home study), so all forms of 'education as societal practice', cannot be reduced to the general relations in Figure 10.2.

Education as a Concrete Societal Practice

Education as a 'societal practice' describes the main general relations that organise different societal practices that produce educational products. However, these general relations do not specify the concrete forms found in a particular society. Education as a 'concrete societal practice' is focused on concretising the relations in a 'societal practice' model for a historical moment in a particular society. In the case of the model shown in Figure 10.2, this means specifying societal interests, instructional forms, and schooling conditions for a particular society.

An important implication of the model in Figure 10.2 is that normative goals (expressed as societal interests) are part of the predominant form of education as a societal practice (regardless of whether these are formulated in political documents or found within civil society). State documents in particular give one kind of generally-recognised and widely-accepted proposal for normative expectations for education (to some extent, they can be considered a proxy for norms found in a significant part of civil society). These documents usually express a mixture of interests, and within a societal tradition there are often different views about the needs that must be addressed or the visions to be realised by education. These documents often reflect a tension between viewing education from (a) a national perspective (with a focus on the needs of the nation-state and the national economy and the individual citizen within the national state), (b) a personal perspective (with a focus on helping individuals to develop societally-valued characteristics in the form of knowledge, skills, values and orientations), and (c) a societal-political perspective (e.g., belief that education can serve as a great equalizer, giving all children the opportunity for economically comfortable and societally responsible life).

For example, the first paragraph in the 2007 Danish school law sets out the aim or purpose of schooling (Undervisningsministeriet, 2007). Some of the societal goals expressed in this paragraph include the expectation that the school 'should prepare the pupils for participation, co-responsibility, rights and duties in a society with freedom and democracy' (national perspective), give 'knowledge and skills that prepare them for further education' (national-economic perspective), and 'make them familiar with Danish culture and history, give them understanding for other countries and cultures, [and] contribute to their understanding of man's interaction with nature' (societal-political perspective). There are also goals that pupils should 'develop understanding and imagination, and get confidence in their own possibilities and background to form positions and act' (personal perspective).

Comparable formulations of this partial presentation of goals from the Danish school law can be found in other countries. For example, the aims of the national curriculum in the United Kingdom for 11–16 year olds include such points as enabling all young people to become 'responsible citizens who make a positive contribution to society' (national perspective), 'successful learners who enjoy learning, make progress, and achieve' (societal-political perspective), and 'confident individuals who are able to live safe, healthy, and fulfilling lives' (personal perspective) (Qualifications and Curriculum Authority, 2008).

This quick glance at school law and national curriculum highlights that educational researchers do not need to make their own normative decisions about the goals of education (which express societal interests). They are embodied in part in these formal documents. The challenge is to form concrete instructional forms, within institutional conditions of schooling that respond to these goals.

The remainder of this chapter concentrates on presenting a cultural-historical perspective about education as a societal practice. First a general analysis is presented about the relation between children's development and education in a cultural-historical perspective, which provides a framework for forming specific interventions aimed at supporting children's development through education. Subsequently, the idea of radical-local teaching and learning is introduced as a perspective for constructing instructional approaches for concrete educational practices. This perspective reflects the general theoretical analysis about the relation between education and children's development, which focuses on a developmental approach to education, with a particular interest in educational goals directed to a personally meaningful life (i.e., personal perspective).

Cultural-Historical Theory of Children's Development

A basic assumption within the cultural-historical perspective is that human abilities are formed through interaction in meaningful human practices, as opposed, for example to the unfolding of inborn characteristics (Ilyenkov, 2007). In this perspective, children's development is also a result of participation in practice. From this point of view, one cannot simply describe the current state of historical practices – at least it does not reveal any necessary or fundamental characteristics of children. While existing practices create conditions for children's development, often there is nothing required or necessary about these practices. Therefore, possibilities for children's development cannot only be discovered empirically by simply examining children in relation to existing practices. Some possibilities for children's development may be realistic, even if they do not currently exist. Particularly relevant for the present discussion is the possibilities for children's development that might lie within educational practice. It may be possible to formulate ideals of children's development, which in turn place a demand on forming practices that can realise these ideals (in relation to the historical conditions and demands).

The concept of development in the cultural-historical tradition is organised around the idea of periods (Vygotsky, 1998; El'konin, 1999). Each period is defined by a set of psychological characteristics that are related to the child's social situation of development (i.e., a general relationship between the child's existing capabilities and the demands in relation to societal practice; Vygotsky, 1998, p. 198). These demands give both conditions and possibilities for the development of new capabilities for a given period, which gives the foundation for the next period.

For school-age children in industrialised societies, the demands and main capabilities, as hypothesised by Vygotsky, are learning to think with concepts and the acquisition of concepts within many different spheres of human knowledge and practice. In this perspective, instruction should have a leading role in relation to children's development. That is, rather than equating instruction and learning with development, or waiting for certain intellectual developments to occur before starting instruction, the main assumption is that instructional interventions can serve to support developmental changes for schoolchildren. We continue along those lines, but add the idea of theoretical thinking (as elaborated initially by Davydov, 1990) as an important objective in this period.

Subsequent to Vygotsky's general arguments about children's development, the concept of personality (in terms of development of motives) was formulated within the cultural-historical tradition (see especially El'konin, 1999). The concept of personality – as used within this tradition – provides a way to conceptualise individual development in relation to education, where instruction, in appropriate forms, can have important consequences for leading the personality development of the schoolchild. This is the key theoretical idea for how to address the relation between education and child development. For primary-school children in all modern societies, the main source of personality development results from their acquisition of learning activity, including the development of a perceived need for learning. This conception does not overturn Vygotsky's argument. Rather it better locates his focus on conceptual thinking within the child's practices.

Within the cultural-historical tradition, the concept of 'personality'[2] has a fairly specific technical meaning – even if there are ongoing debates about fine details within this general perspective (Chaiklin, 2001). As the concept is defined in cultural-historical psychology, an individual acquires personality; it is not fixed or determined from some physiological or genetic characteristics at birth (Leontiev, 1978, p. 107). The idea of the cultural-historical concept of personality, expressed in everyday terms, is reflected in the sum of a person's attitudes and orientations in relation to the particular practices of their societal life, where attitudes and orientations are usually dependent on a person's possibilities and capabilities for acting in these practices. In the theoretical terms of cultural-historical psychology, this idea would be described in terms of 'motives' and 'personal sense'. Roughly speaking, we can say that a motive is a concrete, but general, objective in a societal practice towards which a person's actions are organised. 'Personal sense' is an individual's feeling (positive or negative) about their relation to this collective societal motive.

Motives and personal sense only exist psychologically as part of participating in 'activity', which is a specific theoretical concept used in cultural-historical psychology to refer to the complex relation between a person's actions and the general product (i.e., motive) toward which actions are striving to produce. Societal practices are organised in relation to motives. As a simple illustration, consider the phenomenon in which young children (around 3–5 years old) will engage in play activities around reading (even if they are not able to read in the usual sense of extracting semantic meaning from written words). In this case, we can speak about a motive to read, which is realised by the actions in the play activity.

The acquisition of motives (in relation to different activities) together with one's personal sense of motives are major features of personality development as formulated by Leontiev (1978). Motives and personal sense develop through participation in societal practices, and are dependent on the acquisition of specific actions (including substantive thinking) to realise motives. The development of psychological capabilities and actions serve to change a person's relationship to those practices, often connected with a person acquiring new motives and/or developing existing motives, always with a personal sense. In acquiring motives (through instructional activities), a person becomes oriented to acquire knowledge and skill that supports the realisation of motives and is oriented to using this knowledge in relation to these motives. The development of motives changes a person's relationship to those practices, both with new possibilities to act in relation to existing motives and/or the acquisition of new motives. The acquisition of personal sense in relation to these motives is called personality development.

The key idea here is that societal practices are organised around motives. As a result of acquiring one or more of a practice's motives (which depend in part on knowledge and skill), children become oriented to engaging in these practices, which give possibilities for further development. In developing personality (i.e., acquiring motives for societal practice), children are then oriented to developing the action capabilities in relation to these motives, which gives better possibilities to participate in these practices. Schooling is the main institution used to prepare children to participate in their societal traditions. Because motives are acquired through participation in societal practices (e.g., the reading motive mentioned before can arise from seeing [significant] others using newspapers, instruction sheets, billboards, street signs, and other printed forms in everyday life), it is easy to see how and why formal schooling can be important for the development of motives, and hence of personality.

Radical-Local Teaching and Learning and Children's Development

The previous section introduced general theoretical concepts within the cultural-historical tradition used for analysing children's development. These concepts provide a foundation for addressing the relation between schooling and other aspects of societal life, and facilitate conceptualising education as a societal activity and not just an intellectual process. Using these concepts, we think it is possible to realise many national educational goals for schooling in a way that not only teaches children subject-matter knowledge and competence, but also contributes to their general development.

This section presents radical-local teaching and learning – a conceptual perspective grounded theoretically in the cultural-historical tradition, and aimed at constructing instructional approaches that could be used in concrete educational practices. We first explain the idea of radical-local teaching and learning in general terms, discuss a general instructional approach to realise this idea, and then present a concrete educational practice in which a radical-local instructional approach was used. In this presentation, we highlight the use of models in teaching and ways that everyday and academic concepts can be integrated, while engaging with the children's life situation. These examples are meant to illustrate more precisely how one can work with subject-matter teaching in a way that engages with general educational goals, while supporting personal development.

General Ideas of Radical-Local Teaching and Learning

The main focus of radical-local teaching and learning is on how subject-matter teaching can support children's development in relation to the societal conditions within which they live. This focus is grounded in an assumption that schoolchildren's cultural background and the historical conditions within which they live can and should have consequences for the content of teaching. The designation 'radical-local' is meant to emphasise the integration of general intellectual concepts ('radical' in the sense of 'root') with local content and conditions in the children's lifeworlds (which may not always be physically local). An example of general conceptual concepts for social studies is explained in the core conceptual relations between family – living conditions – resources – work.

The main idea is that core conceptual relations within subject-matter areas have to be related specifically to children's life situations so that this academic knowledge can become integrated with local knowledge, thereby qualitatively transforming children's everyday concepts and their possibility to use this knowledge in their local practice. The key approach to realising the main idea is to develop children's capacity to think theoretically in relation to their local and historical life conditions, through which they develop intellectual tools to understand and relate to the living conditions of their community. Facts alone are not sufficient. Children need some way to make sense of these facts. The basic idea of theoretical thinking is to use abstract principles to analyse concrete situations (Davydov, 1990). These principles are often formed in conceptual models that express basic relations in a problem area, and provide an analytic tool for developing and organising substantive content. The use of conceptual models in teaching gives the possibility to help children learn to use them as tools for analysing concrete phenomena and solving problems.

These tools are worthless, however, if children have no interest in formulating questions or, having formulated questions, do not know specific procedures for seeking answers. Children's interests and motivation for the content of teaching come through their active exploration of problems, conflicts and contrasts. Additionally, a focus on content from their lifeworld as a direction for their explorations, often serves to engage their interest, provided they have a way to actively explore this content. This does not mean that the scope of subject-matter teaching should be limited to children's knowledge and experience; rather for everyday concepts to be integrated with academic concepts, both subject-matter concepts and children's everyday concepts have to be taken into consideration in planning educational tasks. As children master intellectual tools (concepts and investigative procedures) for a given content area, they become able to explore a problem area more systematically. Supported by the academic concepts, they often have interests and possibility to explore topics that go beyond their local situation. The development of theoretical thinking (using investigative procedures in relation to core conceptual relations) is an important part of motive development, as these actions make it possible to act in relation to motives. The challenge in planning educational tasks is to engage with the children's life situation, while integrating conceptual models (i.e., academic subject-matter content) in a way that supports the development of motives, knowledge, and skill.

Instructional Approaches to Radical-Local Teaching and Learning

There may be several possible instructional approaches that could realise the main idea of radical-local teaching and learning. In our case, we have worked with the 'double move' approach (Hedegaard, 2002), which was inspired by Vygotsky's analysis of everyday and scientific concepts, and Davydov's account of theoretical thinking (1990), his ideas on learning activity (e.g., 1999), and his developmental teaching–learning approach (e.g., 1988a, 1988b, 1988c). While Davydov was oriented theoretically to the idea of personality development in relation to instruction, his analyses and investigations focused primarily on subject-matter learning, without relating it to the children's lifeworld, and without taking into account that children have an active relation to the material with which they are working.

The double move approach gives a more prominent position to children's personal knowledge and interest, as well as more attention to children's family and community background. It also gives a way to address the goal of working with subject-matter knowledge, structured in models of core conceptual relations. Each teaching session is planned according to theoretical principles that aim to integrate themes from the children's everyday world along with their experiences and imaginations with the subject matter concepts – where class dialogue is important for this purpose (see Hedegaard, 2002, Chap. 6; Hedegaard & Chaiklin, 2005, Chap. 6 for more details). Therefore we have used this approach in constructing instructional activities that aim to realise radical-local teaching and learning.

Integrating Academic and Everyday Concepts Using Models in a Radical-Local Teaching and Learning Project

Because the focus of this chapter is on the role of education in relation to development, we want to highlight the idea of how working with subject-matter content in a radical-local perspective can contribute to children's development. This is done by presenting two aspects from a specific radical-local teaching–learning project that illustrate how we provide conditions for children to develop theoretical thinking and motives.

After providing a general orientation about the radical-local teaching–learning project from which these examples come, we describe a series of activities used across several teaching sessions for developing the under-standing of a single core conceptual relation. Rather than tell children directly about conceptual relations in a core conceptual model, the idea is to use many different examples of a particular relation, embodied in different activities and investigations, so they can develop a concrete understanding of the relation and how it can be investigated. Then, to show processes by which academic concepts can be integrated with everyday experience, we describe the interactions in a single teaching session, and discuss how these interactions contribute to developing both a learning motive as well as more general motives about using these concepts in relation to societal issues (in this particular case in relation to social justice). Remember that personality development is based in motive development.

Processes of motive development and academic concept development (including the ability to use them generally across different situations) occur over a longer period, through many practical experiences. We do not trace the development processes here, but we hope the presentation gives a sufficient impression of the kinds of activities conducted across and within teaching sessions, so that one can imagine how this way of working could realise the general aims of radical-local teaching and learning to integrate academic and everyday concepts in relation to motive development.

General Orientation About the Project

The examples presented here come from a radical-local teaching learning project conducted within an afterschool programme at a local community centre in East Harlem, New York City (Hedegaard & Chaiklin, 2005). Participation in the project was voluntary and open to all 8–12 year old schoolchildren who came to the centre. Most of the children came from Puerto Rican families (a significant cultural minority in New York City). The aim of the project was to make a significant step in addressing the problem of how to provide the children with tools (in this case, social science concepts and investigation procedures) for analysing their societal conditions so that they can explicitly relate their own cultural traditions and history to the more dominant one within which they live. At the same time, we wanted to address widely-held goals for formal education, which focus on personal development of children in relation to their historical and cultural conditions.

The particular focus in this project was to develop a general understanding of the relations in a core conceptual model (see Figure 10.3) by comparing and contrasting living conditions and family life in Puerto Rico and New York City at the start of the 20th century and at the present, together with a specific focus on the community in which the children lived. The model in Figure 10.3 expresses basic relations that can be used to characterise all societies.

To achieve this aim, four main, interrelated teaching objectives must be addressed simultaneously: (a) introducing children to substantive content about Puerto Rican culture and history, while (b) developing their capacities

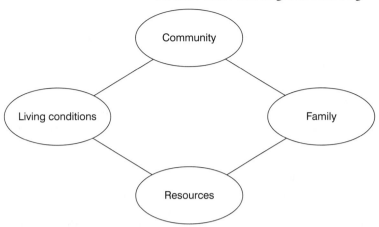

Figure 10.3 Core model of conceptual relations that mediate living conditions

for formulating theoretical models that can be used as tools for analysing this substantive content in relation to their lived world, (c) forming their interest in and motivation for investigating this substantive content, and (d) developing knowledge of specific procedures for evaluating and elaborating conceptual relations in models (i.e., social science methods). Each teaching session was planned with attention to these four objectives. In this way, the children could acquire knowledge of the history of where they are living (i.e., New York City) and the place from which they (or their family) had emigrated (i.e., Puerto Rico), which gives them the possibility to integrate different kinds of social worlds: the world of their parents, their own community, and the larger community of New York City, as well as ways to form a critical understanding of the formation of their current living conditions.

Creating the First Core Relation

This section outlines the main teaching content and the variety of activities conducted with the children in order to formulate and investigate the relation between the general social science concepts of 'living conditions' and 'family'. The aim was to develop the children's understanding of this relation, which is part of the core conceptual model shown in Figure 10.3, by using basic methods of historical research, while introducing them to some aspects of their culture and history that would be unknown but interesting to them. Over the course of the entire project, we worked with three main themes: (a) living conditions in Puerto Rico at the beginning the 20th century, (b) current living conditions in New York City, and (c) current living conditions in their East Harlem community. In the teaching activities described here, the contrasts in these three themes were focused on the relation between family and living conditions.

We started by giving the children photographs that were selected to show the family and living conditions in Puerto Rico around the beginning of the

20th century. In the class dialogue, we focused on the differences between the life then in Puerto Rico and the life now in New York. This historical contrast helped to highlight specific aspects of family life and its relation to living conditions.

The children then learned how to use interview methods, first practising on the teacher and parent aides in the classroom, after which they interviewed their parents or grandparents about how life used to be in Puerto Rico. They continued their investigation by preparing and asking questions about family life and living conditions of a 90-year-old man, who had emigrated from Puerto Rico to the United States in the mid-1920s. Based on their interviews, the children and the teacher created a chart that compared living conditions of the family in Puerto Rico at the beginning of the 20th century and in their community in New York in the present day.

To introduce more contrasts about living conditions in New York City and Puerto Rico, the children saw a film about a Puerto Rican boy's everyday life in New York City in the mid-1980s, followed by another film about the life of a peasant family in Puerto Rico in the 1930s. This film also focused on their relation to the landlord and his family. Through viewing these films, together with their interviews and personal experience of living in New York City, the children had empirical material for comparing a Puerto Rican way of life in the past and a contemporary life in New York City, with a focus on the relation between family and living conditions.

Integrating Academic and Everyday Concepts: Exemplified in a Single Radical-Local Teaching Session

The following presents a single 45-minute teaching session, describing the activities and discussions that occurred during the session, followed by an interpretative explanation of how these interactions contribute to the integration of academic concepts with everyday concepts.

The particular session described here occurred just after the children had seen the second film (about four months into the teaching year). The comparisons between the peasant family and the landlord family in the film led the children to bring up the distinction between being poor or rich today and at the beginning of the 20th century, which was the specific focus of this teaching session.

> The teacher started the session by asking the children to tell some of the things they saw in the movie in the previous session, and to make a list of these things. One child spontaneously asks to use the categories for living conditions and to make a chart, as they had done with their interviews. All the children contribute and are somewhat excited. They follow eagerly as the teacher writes down their answers about the living conditions, lying over the table to see her writing. The children have a lot of comments and are eager to discuss the different aspects of living conditions in the movie.

The children spontaneously introduce the terms 'rich family' and 'poor family' to refer to the two families in the film, and start by characterizing the differences between houses in which they live, the characteristics of tobacco crops, and then the role of money, where the children say that the rich man got money for his work, but the poor man did not. One child introduces the point that all the persons in the poor family worked, including the children, and that they needed shoes and clothes but that the rich family had everything. Another child points out that the radio used batteries.

The teacher recapitulates twice the living conditions that the children described from the film. The second time she uses general categories to classify their descriptions: clothes, electricity, farms, work, transportation and entertainment, and then contrasts that the poor people worked on the farms that were owned by the rich people. This process provides a start to engaging the children's conceptions of characteristic of living conditions with academic concepts.

The children discuss differences between the poor and rich. Several get very indignant about the difference in living conditions between the rich and the poor. Some complain that this is not fair. One jokes about it and says it's fair, but then hurries to add that it is not fair, and that he is joking, and that the poor family cannot buy the same things as the rich one. One says they have different experiences. Another child comments that we all have different experiences and it influences the way we think. A third makes a comparison between the rich people today and the rich people in Puerto Rico, saying that they are alike today, because they all have a lot of stuff. They do not use their hands to wash clothes and they use money to buy things. The teacher stresses this comparison and adds that the rich do not work, but now we work for money. Somebody says that the rich give money to the poor. One says that they should all share.

Discussion of Teaching-Session Example

In this example, we engage in practices, in the sense of helping children to acquire general intellectual practices, which they can then use to analyse societal practices within which they live. Academic concepts – such as examining the relation between living conditions and family relations – do not come initially from the children, but they are able to recognise examples of this relation from their everyday concepts. At the same time, children's interest is created because instructional tasks are directed at relations, which give them an opportunity to use intellectual tools to explore content related to their everyday life in new ways, and to elaborate their everyday understandings through academic concepts.

In this example, one can see the children's engagement with these tasks. The children had pressed the teacher to show the film about the peasant family, after she wanted to postpone it. We would not normally expect children to be excited to see a relatively old film in Spanish about life in Puerto Rico (where the teacher translated a good part of the dialogue), or to be thrilled by the task of formulating characteristics of living conditions that they observe. We interpret this engagement as a sign that they have started to master some analytic tools and substantive issues, and have an interest to work further with these tools and ideas. We also take this as a sign of the development of a general learning motive. Similarly, their engagement with questions about rich and poor is viewed as contributing to personality development, where they start to connect their subject-matter analysis to fundamental relations about social justice and the organisation of society.

This focus on relevant topics does not result in a dilemma or contradiction in which the teacher must choose between academic relevance and personal relevance. It is necessary, however, to help children integrate their experience and information into a theoretical model or perspective for understanding the significance of events and conditions, and not simply draw on children's experience or provide them with specific historical facts that are culturally relevant. Ideally, such a model or perspective functions as a foundation from which children can continue to analyse and interpret their life situation. By bringing the methods of investigation of a subject-matter discipline into the classroom as a working approach, the teacher, in collaboration with the children, can develop specific substantive results which can be related to the children's concrete situation. More generally, through this process, one aims to help children acquire knowledge and skills for understanding and developing better relationships to their life conditions. In developing the capability to work with this content, the children are developing motives and skill to work in relation to these motives – but it is integrated in the ways of working with the content (not as a separate focus on personality development).

Concluding Remarks About the Relation Between Education and Children's Development

This chapter presents a cultural-historical analysis about the relation between education and children's development, elaborating the relations that mediate them, and emphasising the role of education (as a societally-embedded practice) in defining and realising this development. In the cultural-historical perspective, children's development is seen as a consequence of participation in practices, and conceptualised in terms of personality development (which is consistent with a practice perspective). However, this assumption only provides a starting point for analysis. One must continue by analysing the possibilities that particular practices give for the formation of motives and psychological capabilities (which is the basis for development). In this approach education is viewed as a societal practice and not just an intellectual process. A major form of education as societal practice embodies a historically-accumulated complex of cultural values and norms, mediated through instruction and schooling. Thus education (as a concrete societal practice) provides conditions and contributions to personality development by forming motives and action enabling qualitative changes in a person's relation to their life practices.

In relation to this chapter's focus on the predominant form of education as a societal practice grounded in schooling, the choice to conceptualise education in relation to personality development does not resolve any problems. This theoretical frame simply introduces new perspectives and issues to be addressed and elaborated as part of forming interventions. We conclude by highlighting four of them.

First, we believe it is important to preserve the analytic relation between 'education' and 'children's development', even though this relation is mediated by general societal practices, such as schooling and instruction. As the analysis in Figure 10.2 shows, education can be differentiated into mediating relations. While one can distinguish between instruction, schooling and education to some extent (as was done in Figure 10.2), it is not possible to separate them completely into independent, analytic categories, nor describe them additively (e.g., 'schooling' does not equal 'education plus instruction' or 'education' is not 'schooling plus instruction'). These tensions are important to preserve in thinking about education in relation to children's development, even if they introduce ambiguities, complexities, and seeming paradoxes in the analysis, especially if the particular sense of education (as analytic, societal practice, or concrete societal practice) is not specified. For example, by preserving the analytic relation between education and children's development one must address the different general mediating relations involved in how education is developmental. One of these relations, societal interests, allows one to keep a normative focus, which tends to be lost with the more limited and operational concept of instruction. And conflicts between societal interests usually have consequences for the conditions within which schooling and instruction are conducted, which in turn have consequences for children's development. Concrete attempts to address educational practice must consider this complex of relations.

Second, we mentioned previously that there are other societal practices directed toward education, which are not organised around schooling. This was not meant to suggest that all educational practices have equal value or significance in relation to children's development. From a theoretical point of view, we believe that systematic instructional activities have the possibilities for certain kinds of developments that may be difficult or impossible to achieve in other ways.

Third, the model in Figure 10.2 helps to clarify some of the demands for forming developmentally relevant instruction, and ways to conceptualise interventive efforts. While teaching and learning (i.e., instruction) depend on the conditions of schooling and societal interests, they are not entirely determined either. Instruction is one of the main mediators in relation to education, so instructional forms can have important consequences for education, and prospectively for children's development. Given that instruction is only weakly determined by other aspects of education as a societal practice, there is space for investigating the possibilities of instruction directed toward children's development, while still addressing societal interests (e.g., national goals for education), but not limited by currently-existing historical conditions for schooling (e.g., teacher preparation, state-imposed curriculum and accountability), or empirically-observed development under particular historical conditions.

Finally, the radical-local approach to teaching and learning was presented as a conceptual perspective for planning instruction that aims to develop theoretical thinking for analysing and solving problems in ways that change a child's relations to their world in a developmental way. Given that radical-local teaching and learning focuses on instruction, it cannot address all that is relevant to education as a societal practice; but it is more than an instructional technique or principle because it provides a way to think about instruction grounded in a view about the relation between education and children's development.

Notes

1 Other views conceptualise children's development as independent of or equivalent to education. These views are addressed only implicitly by presenting an interactive view in the present chapter.

2 The scientific concept of personality did not appear until the end of the 19th century, when it was used in clinical contexts in relation to persons with psychological disorders (Danziger, 1997, p. 124). Subsequently this concept was given different meanings by different theoretical traditions. The meaning given here – which diverges both from other psychological traditions (which often use the concept to refer to traits) as well as everyday meanings – must be understood within the terms of its own theoretical system, and not as an alternative proposal to address an intended meaning from other theoretical traditions.

References

Chaiklin, S. (2001). The category of 'personality' in cultural-historical psychology. In S. Chaiklin (Ed.), *The theory and practice of cultural-historical psychology* (pp. 238–259). Aarhus: Aarhus University Press.

Danziger, K. (1997). *Naming the mind: How psychology found its language.* London: Sage.

Davydov, V. V. (1988a). Problems of developmental teaching. *Soviet Education, 30*(8), 15–97.

Davydov, V. V. (1988b). Problems of developmental teaching. *Soviet Education, 30*(9). 3–83.

Davydov, V. V. (1988c). Problems of developmental teaching. *Soviet Education, 30*(10), 3–77.

Davydov, V. V. (1990). *Types of generalization in instruction: Logical and psychological problems in the structuring of school curricula* (Soviet studies in mathematics education, Vol. 2; J. Kilpatrick, Ed.; J. Teller, Trans.). Reston, VA: National Council of Teachers of Mathematics (original work published 1972).

Davydov, V. V. (1999). What is learning activity? In M. Hedegaard & J. Lompscher (Eds.), *Learning activity and development* (pp. 123–138). Aarhus: Aarhus University Press.

El'konin, D. B. (1999). Toward the problem of stages in the mental development of children. *Journal of Russian and East European Psychology, 37*(6), 11–30 (original work published 1971).

El'konin, D. B. & Davydov, V. V. (1975). Learning capacity and age level: Introduction. (A. Bigelow, Trans.). In L. Steffe (Ed.), *Soviet studies in the psychology of learning and teaching mathematics: Vol. 5. Children's capacity for learning mathematics* (pp. 1–11). Stanford, CA: School Mathematics Study Group (original work published 1966).

Hedegaard, M. (2002). *Learning and child development: A cultural-historical study.* Aarhus: Aarhus University Press.

Hedegaard, M., & Chaiklin, S. (2005). *Radical-local teaching and learning: A cultural-historical approach.* Aarhus: Aarhus University Press.

Ilyenkov, E. V. (2007). On the nature of ability. *Journal of Russian and East European Psychology, 45* (4), 56–63.

Leontiev, A. N. (1978). *Activity, consciousness, and personality* (M. J. Hall, Trans.). Englewood Cliffs, NJ: Prentice-Hall (original work published 1975).

Qualifications and Curriculum Authority (2008). *The aims of the curriculum.* London: QCA. (Available at: http://curriculum.qca.org.uk/key-stages-3-and-4/aims/index.aspx)

Undervisningsministeriet (2007). *Bekendtgørelse af lov om folkeskolen* (LBK nr 1049 af 28/08/2007). Copenhagen: Undervisningsministeriet. (Available at https://www.retsinformation.dk/forms/R0710.aspx?id=25528&exp=1)

Vygotsky, L. S. (1987). Thinking and speech (N. Minick, Trans.). In R. W. Rieber & A. S. Carton (Eds.), *The collected works of L. S. Vygotsky: Vol. 1. Problems of general psychology* (pp. 39–285). New York: Plenum Press (original work published 1934).

Vygotsky, L. S. (1998). The problem of age (M. Hall, Trans.). In R. W. Rieber (Ed.), *The collected works of L. S. Vygotsky: Vol. 5. Child psychology* (pp. 187–205). New York: Plenum Press (original work written 1930–1934).

11 Cultural–Historical Psychology In The Practice Of Education

G. G. Kravtsov and E. E. Kravtsova

Translated from the Russian by
Sue March, in consultation with
Alex Kostogriz and Marilyn Fleer

Any pedagogical practice has its corresponding theoretical foundation, even if that foundation is not realised by that practice. The theoretical principles of teaching are, to a large extent, based on psychological concepts, and psychological theories, in their turn, carry with them certain philosophical ideas. Popular contemporary educational practice also has its own psychological theories and its own philosophical basis. The philosophy, which for many long years sustained and justified Russia's educational practice, was elevated to the rank of the state ideological philosophy of dogmatised Marxism.

However, it was not so much the direct influence of Marxism on Soviet pedagogy that had more impact, but rather the mediatory influence of the corresponding psychological theories. Russian/Soviet psychology was dominated for many years by the activity-based approach (*deyatel'nostnyi podkhod*), the influence of which, in many respects, remains to this day. This approach posits objective activity as the ultimate explanatory principle. Correspondingly, whatever we consider – personality, thinking, will, communication, any psychological phenomenon – all would be treated as activity, or as its structural components and elements, or as some of its constructs. For example, personality has proved to be from the hierarchy of activities or their motives. The reductionism inherent in this approach particularly perniciously reveals itself in application to the problem of personality. The most essential characteristics of human beings, such as personality, have proved themselves to be beyond the possibilities of this approach. Thus, practically all researchers agree that personality has integrity. But the activity-based approach is not in a position to consider a human being as the subject of the study as integrity This approach has intensified the division of psychology into cognitively-oriented psychology (*intellektualisticheskaya psikhologiya*) and psychology that focuses on the deep exploration of personality (*glubinno-lichnostnaya psikhologiya*), reducing the content of the notion of personality[1] to the motivational-need sphere (*motivatsionno-potrebnostnaya sfera*). In this treatment, personality is a part of the psyche.[2] Correspondingly, another part of the psyche, so to speak, "depersonalizes itself" (*"obezlichivaetsya"*). In this case the integrity of the personality proves to be, in principle, impossible.

In pedagogical practice the division of psychology into cognitively-oriented psychology and psychology that focuses on the deep exploration of personality, about which D. B. El'konin wrote, manifested itself in the separation of upbringing (*vospitanie*) from teaching (*obuchenie*).[3] Moreover, in generally accepted models of education there is not only a separation of teaching from upbringing, but also a one-sided domination of the values of teaching over the values of cultivating the child's personality and emotional well-being.

The idea of continuous and uninterrupted education, which has been expounded by many researchers, educators-practitioners and organisers from this realm of public life, encompasses the intention of an integral approach towards determining the path of education reform. This idea is also orientated towards securing the integrity of the education system itself. The ever-topical problem of continuity in the education system is testimony to the fact that existing educational practice is acutely in need of establishing its own integrity. Schools and kindergartens are actually separated from each other. Primary school and nursery school teachers' criticisms against each other are well-founded and result from the separation of schools and preschool institutions. No less significant are the separation of primary schools from the middle years and the isolation of general education schools from education in tertiary institutions. The idea of continuous and uninterrupted education also implies that today adults "are condemned to" ("*prigovoren k*") continuing learning. Of course, periods of adult study differ from school learning and from the education of students, but even in these cases the problem of continuity remains extremely acute and unresolved.

There is a basis for thinking that the reform of a complex system in its entirety, especially such an unwieldy and conservative one as education, is possible in the case where there are clear theoretical ideas about a new educational model and where effort is applied to the point which is most adaptable to change. The most significant and substantial parts of the theoretical foundations of pedagogy lie in psychology. And in this the central part takes the theory of the child's psychological development – the theory of personality formation in ontogenesis.

The most theorised, researched and promising concept in Russian/Soviet psychology is L. S. Vygotsky's cultural-historical theory which has become world renown. Without expounding the cultural-historical concepts, below we will reproduce and interpret some of L. S. Vygotsky's ideas, those which are the most significant for the present project.

One of the central themes of L. S. Vygotsky's work was the idea of development (*razvitie*). This acted as a focus in bringing together his many interests. His foundational research and scientific thinking were linked to the problem of development. "At the centre of Vygotsky's attention," writes D. B. El'konin, "was the explanation of the main laws (*zakonomernosti*) of the child's psychic development." In a series of his works L. S. Vygotsky directly and immediately deals with the laws of psychic development. However, more often this problem is not emphasized though has supreme significance. The direct output of this idea in pedagogical practice should be a priority orientation towards development which is of value to the child, and not towards any other secondary features, for example, the interests of the state, parental preferences, nor pedagogical regulations and traditions, etc.

- L. S. Vygotsky links the mechanism of psychological development with two fundamental ideas, namely, with the idea of systemic and meaningful structure of consciousness (*sistemnoe I smyslovoe stroenie soznaniya*), and also with the idea of mediation of psychological processes (*oposredstvovanie psikhicheskikh protsessov*). In accordance with L. S. Vygotsky's first idea: "Change in the inter-functional links, i.e. change in the functional structure of consciousness, constitutes the main and central subject-matter of the very process of development as a whole". In the course of ontogenetic development various specific psychic functions and processes change their place, significance and interconnection with all remaining functions. They come across from the peripheral regions onto the central highway of psychic development, and, then depart once more for the periphery, but already in a different quality.

In pedagogy the idea of systematic and sensitive structure of consciousness is, on the one of its aspects, the need to take into account the psychological specifics of a particular period in the child's development, depending on precisely which psychic function of that age-period coincides with the main direction of development and the way the rest of functions relate to it. In particular, in light of this idea, the renowned sensitive periods (*senzitivnye periody*) in the child's development receive scientific explanation. However, no less important is the establishment of well-defined pedagogical ideas about what knowledge is obviously not suitable for children of a particular age-period on the grounds that it is premature and does not correspond with their development.

- The idea of mediation (*oposredstvovanie*) was one of the most important of L. S. Vygotsky's teachings. Closely linked with this is the concept of interiorisation (*interiorizatsiya*) – the transfer of the external into the interior. However, amongst L. S. Vygotsky's students and followers this idea has undergone important changes. To the author of cultural-historical theory, interiorisation signified a transfer into the interior of so-called psychological means (*psikhologicheskii sredstva*), i.e. of the instruments that organise one's own activity and psychic processes. Sign was the most universal means. After L. S. Vygotsky the concept of interiorisation received wide-spread interpretation. The term interiorisation began to be understood as the assimilation of social experience and the mastery of the accumulated knowledge of a culture. Thus, the main content was lost – both the idea of mediation and the understanding of interiorisation.

In the pedagogical practice L. S. Vygotsky's ideas of the mediation of psychic processes and the concept of interiorisation are reflected in the differentiation of the subject material to be acquired during the study and of the meta-object content which is to be not only acquired but also interiorized, i.e. to become a component of the individual's psychic organisation. In other words, the programmed content of school subjects and disciplines should include not only learning per se, but also psychologically-based sign structures, corresponding to the particular age-period in the child's development. This means that the deep psychologising (*glubokaya psikhologizatsiya*) of school programmes and the pedagogical process as a whole is necessary.

- L. S. Vygotsky considered the problem of unity of affect and intellect (*edinstvo affekta I intellekta*) as a corner-stone of his theory of the child's psychic development. However, he believed that this unity appears not as a stable connection between affect and intellect, but as a dynamic connection. L. S. Vygotsky emphasised: "The whole point is, that thinking and affect represent parts of a unified whole – human consciousness." Unity of affect and intellect reveals itself in the qualitatively changing mutual connections and mutual influences of these aspects of the psyche on each other at each stage of psychic development. Each stage in the development of thinking has a corresponding stage in the development of the affect. We think that psychic reality is not exhausted by these two spheres. Above affect and intellect, that is above emotions (*chuvstvy*) and the mind (*um*), there is the volitional sphere (*volevaya sfera*) of the psyche. Will is the higher mediational function due to which free action becomes possible. The principle of unity of affect and intellect allows the integrity of the child's personality development process to be retained. This principle also makes it possible to arrive at an understanding of the determination of this process, not in the light of mechanistic causalities, but as the logic of self-directed movement (*samoobuslovlennoe dvizheniye*) that is directed towards the child's discovery of new possibilities.

In pedagogical practice, the principle of unity of affect and intellect could be the theoretical pivot, which permits the union of teaching and upbringing, the private life of the child and organised activity, family and school. This principle could become the key to the problem of eliminating alienation (*otchuzhdenie*) in education. The ideas put forward by L. S. Vygotsky on the integrity of psychic organisation and that of the child's personality, together with the reasonable approach to the organisation of all the main sphere's of the child's activities should be realised in an educational practice instead of being merely theoretical. However, such practice essentially does not coincide with existing systems today. In the new practice, the child would be not the object of teaching and upbringing, but the subject of self-development: a subject that, from the outset and on an ongoing basis, exists as a sovereign individual in a pedagogically-based system, in newly-fashioned relationships and in cooperation with other children and adults.

In cultural-historical theory the main element in the process of child's psychic development process is the transformation of the lower, elementary or "natural" (*"natural'ny"*) psychic processes into higher, cultural ones. This happens, according to the thoughts of L. S. Vygotsky, by means of specific psychological tools (*orudii-sredstva*). Following the era of Russian/Soviet psychology, the notion of development as self-development, as mastery by means of one's own behavioural and psychic processes was lost. That notion was displaced and replaced with other ideas. L .S. Vygotsky was seriously criticised by his opponents, as well as students and followers over the division of the psyche into higher and elementary functions. However, it was precisely this methodological approach that allowed L. S. Vygotsky to form a starting point towards the integrity of personality and the integrity of the child's psychic organisation

In the field of pedagogy, L. S. Vygotsky's notion of natural and higher functions is linked with the fact that, from the outset, each child has an initial peculiarity and individual uniqueness. The so-called "natural" psyche (*"natural'naya"psikhika*) is that potential and basis, which makes self-movement (*samodvizheniye*) possible in the child's psychic development. Recognising the natural psyche in the sense that it was revealed in cultural-historical theory, we ourselves place the child's individuality at the centre of attention of pedagogy. The very process of every child's development proves to be different, it cannot follow a general standard, but reveals and manifests peculiar features of the individual, that is, it is a process of individualisation (*individualizatsiya*) and self-discovery (*samoobretenie*) in the growing person.

- The decision of the problem of sense and meaning (*smysl i znacheniye*) proposed by L. S. Vygotsky is of utmostimportance: multidimensional personal sense is primary (*mnogomernyi lichnostnyi smysl*) while the meanings are derived from it and form an established zone of sense. According to L. S. Vygotsky, "meaning is only a brick in the edifice of sense." It should be noted that in A. N. Leontyev's activity-based approach exactly the opposite solution was put forward, according to which, subjective, personal sense and objective meanings belong to spheres of reality that differ in principle. These different approaches theoretically legalised the division of psychology into cognitively oriented (*intellektualisticheskaya*) and personality-focused (*lichnostnaya*). Moreover, the process of education was interpreted psychologically as the process of acquisition of social experience and the process of appropriation of objectively existing normative knowledge. According to the approach expounded by cultural-historical theory, there is in fact no direct assimilation of the objective meaning set by society. Behind the external process of knowledge acquisition there always lies a deeper layer of movement from individual sense towards normative meaning.

The pedagogical projection of the problem of sense and meaning is regarded as the principle solution to the problem of the place and the role of the adult, the teacher and the "upbringer" in the education process. The "categorical imperative" (*kategoricheskii imperativ*) for the professional pedagogue can be formulated following the direction shown by the author of cultural-historical theory: "Do not teach and do not 'bring up', but live an interesting life together with children." The conditions for solving specific educational tasks which are of the direct interest not just for the children, but also for the adults, can always be found within this life.

Russian/Soviet psychologists, even those who call themselves Vygotsky School, have not managed to fulfil the ideas and realise the possibilities of cultural-historical theory. Thus, Vygotsky's idea about leading activities (*vedushchie deyatel'nosti*) and their role in the child's psychic development was taken up and well detailed in his disciples' works. In particular, that very idea became the fundamental criterion, determining the psychological age of the child and the periodisation (*periodizatsiya*) of D. B. El'konin. However, other ideas worked out by L. S. Vygotsky, which were no less fundamental for age-period psychology, have not been taken up. Amongst them attention should be paid to the idea of central psychological new formations (*novoobrazovaniya*) of both stable and critical ages. After all, according to L. S. Vygotsky, it is these psychological new formations that determine the most important subject matter of development at a given stage of ontogenesis. But the concept of the social situation of the child's development is not less heuristic. This concept notes, on the one hand, the uniqueness of the interconnection and the unity of extrinsic means and the inner world, i.e. the environment and the motivational-needs sphere of a specific child at a particular stage of development, and on the other hand, the main contradiction, which is the mechanism (*dvizhushchaya sila*) of development at a given psychological age. Actually, this concept could become no less powerful and effective determinant of psychological age than the idea of leading activities. Finally, there remains an absolutely undeveloped idea of L. S. Vygotsky about the central functions: those functions, which at a given moment become main in the process of psychic development. This L. S. Vygotsky idea may be the key to understanding the main laws in the transition from one psychological age to another, that is, the laws of the transition from one leading activity to another.

The further development of the ideas of cultural-historical theory is a topical and promising direction for scientific research. However, if such research is to be undertaken in a purely academic manner, then they will be ineffective, so, another L. S. Vygotsky idea should be implemented. He formulated it in his work *The Historical Meaning of the Crisis in Psychology*. Reflecting on the fate of psychology, L. S. Vygotsky comes to the conclusion that it is vital to include psychology in the "fabric" and "material" of practice. The most important practice, where psychology can be implemented, is the area of education. The mutual self-interest of educational practice and the science of psychology stand in sharp relief when practice starts to be constructed in the light and context of the ideas of cultural-historical theory.

The present state of education is linked to the critical condition of contemporary psychology. One of the most important causes of this state of affairs appears to be the isolated and independent development of pedagogy and psychology. From these positions, the development of a personality-oriented system of education and the departure of psychology from crisis are possible only in the creation and development of a new model of education based on the psychological foundations.

The distinctive feature of constructing a new system of education is that of changing all its links and stages, commencing with preschool and ending with higher pedagogical education. In the West there is experience of constructing such systems: Waldorf education, Montessori centres and the Genetic Epistemology Centre of Jean Piaget that are famous throughout the world. In the present work we describe the experience of constructing a pedagogy built on L. S. Vygotsky's ideas.

The distinctive feature of the new educational practice is that it combines two global values which in the experience of existing educational institutions are considered to be mutually exclusive. They are the value of teaching and the goal-oriented development of children by means of education, and value of the emotional well-being and comfort of each child. Usually either one or other value dominates and so determines the whole educational process, as well as the child's way of life in the educational institution. The main idea of the project described is the following. Education and mental development of children can be effective only if it is closely linked with an effective development of the emotional sphere of the child.

The organisation of preschool and primary school education carried out according to the "Golden Key" (*"zolotoi kluchik"*) programme differs in the following ways.

- School life is organised on the principle of the family, where all adults, without exception, participate in the upbringing of the children, and all children are fully fledged members of this large social family, which is a continuation and extension of the child's own family.
- The children's parents and other family members are involved in the life and problems of the children's life at the institution, taking part in all the events together with the children and teachers.
- The institution is a centre (*kompleks*) uniting the features of both a kindergarten and primary school, where children from three to ten years old live and learn together.
- The children are placed in multi-age groups with fifteen to twenty people in each one, with an equal representation of children of all ages – preschool as well as junior school.
- Two educators specially prepared for the work according to this programme, work with each group for the whole day.
- For the older children, commencing from six years of age, teaching at a special kind of lesson is provided. Every lesson lasts no longer than 20–30

minutes a day for the six-year-olds and no longer than 1–1.5 hours a day for the schoolchildren.

- The foundation of all the school's activity of the institution and the pedagogical process is a special system of events, undertaken by the children together with the adults, which enables the children's initiative to be aroused and introduces the children in a sensitive context of cultural traditions.
- The solving of the majority of educational tasks, and also the mastery of the basic volume of knowledge and practical skills, takes place in multi-age communication of children both with each other and their educators. This is realised in balanced collective, micro-grouped and individual activities, in diverse games and dramatisations, in planned and unexpected events.

The results of working according to the "Golden Key" programme have shown that the basic content of the standard preschool educational programme is acquired by the children without any difficulty, as well as the programmes of primary classes including even greater volume of material provided in the "Golden Key" programme. In the case of the children with behavioural difficulties and difficulties in psychic development, a natural psychocorrection (*psikhokorrektsiya*) takes place. On the whole, the children who study according to this programme differ in greater openness, the ability to find an activity for themselves, skills in collective activity and are more creative. An unexpected, but quite natural occurrence has been the significant reduction in the rate of the children's being sick, although there were not taken any special measures aimed at the achieving of this result.

The "Golden Key" programme in the first four years of the school's operation has some specific features, connected with the fact that the age cohort of the children changes. The older children do not graduate from the groups for three years, before the end of primary school. Accordingly, the very character of the multi-aged children's groups as an integral organism also changes. There is an increase in receptiveness, ability to work as a group with learning material, to consider and comprehend difficulties and problems and find a way to solve them. Accordingly, even the material from year to year becomes more complex and more profound and more diverse. The level is set by the age specifics and abilities of the older children. But, notwithstanding, in general, the jointly-experienced events or business provide the possibility of including children of a younger age in a given level suitable to them. In this way, material which a child of a particular age, for example a four-year-old, is capable of mastering is varied depending on how many years the multi-age group has existed. The "older" the group, the greater the learning possibilities of the children.

The introduction of general educational material and the tracking of its acquisition are carried out according to four main directions. All of these directions exist at each moment of the life of a child of any age and, none the less, in various phases and at various levels of the cycles of mastery of any given educational material these four constituents, which are inseparably-linked to each other, build to a particular hierarchy. These four components, easily observable in the daily life of a person of any age, are as follows.

- The ability to act in the space surrounding the child. The skill to organise one's personal space according to the goals of the activity;
- Orientation in time, the skill to develop, construct a sequence of actions and to plan them;
- The ability to work with various materials, to use their properties and peculiarities in one's own activity;
- The development of the ability to analyse one's own actions, reflect and understand oneself as the subject of these activities.

In each of the "Golden Key" centre's first four years of work, one of the directions described above becomes the most important and comes to the foreground. For the first year's work it is orientation in space – the construction of their own space by a group of children together with adults and each child individually, the familiarisation with the space of the group, the whole centre, the grounds and the adjoining area. This task is solved with the aid of specially worked out methodological means. They include the establishment by the children of varied plans, schemes and models, which make part of the children's life. Towards the end of the first school year the older children are already well oriented in the space of the children's centre, the grounds and the adjoining area; they orient themselves in familiar places by the direction of light (by the sun), they know the signs of a southern slope (sides of the house, edges) in comparison with a northern one; they are able to graphically represent on a plan of the room the path to known places, they can put up stage decorations for a performance; they know the direction of light on a map and are able on a physical map of the world to show the way to the North Pole, Africa, Japan and America.

The centre's second year of work differs in that the "time" constituent comes to the foreground. This time measurement of activities takes place on the same varied levels: from micro-intervals (each time you bob up and down for half a minute you must stand on one leg for a minute, etc.) to longer historical times.

Groups in their second year of work have an axis of time on which children travelling in a time machine record all the points where they "touch down". This is the world of the cave-dwellers as well as the future with space travel and, of course, the present time. Particular work is linked with the basic knowledge of Russian history, for example, children celebrate the anniversary of the battle of Borodino. The study of some historical events coincides with the opening of the first class in the centre. Historical material is one of the bases for the study of mathematics. Apart from historical times, children in the centre learn to deal with the matters that demand planning and the development of actions in time. These are serious games that continue for several days, e.g. "at a film studio" or "script writers", "directors", "actors", "animators", etc.

By the end of the second year in the "Golden Key" children's centre, the older children (including first-years) acquire general understanding of historical times and the milestones in history. All children develop an age-appropriate ability to understand and cope with their own time, to be aware whether they are doing something quickly or slowly, and succeed in carrying out a plan in the necessary time space (clearly determined with the aid of hourglasses). Children have an understanding of what constitutes one minute, five, ten minutes, half an hour, an hour and of what one can manage to do within this amount of time.

In the third year of work at the children's centre the priority becomes activities with various materials, productive activities and specific methods, which the children master. All this takes place against a background of deepening and broadening their knowledge and skills in orientating themselves in space and time. The year results in the older children gaining a sufficiently clear understanding of the different fields of art, including folk art, and also the first experience of working with various materials – with wood, straw, clay, bast,[4] small pieces of smalt.[5]

The fourth year of the centre's work is the final one in the introductory period of its existence. That is the year when children mainly develop their ability to analyse their actions, reflect on them, and correct them if necessary. These aims are achieved with the aid of formative methods directed at teaching the child to detach him or herself and his or her activity from the general flow of daily life, to separate him or herself from others and to fit into various personality positions in relation to others. All these formative impacts are based on the content which includes those forms and methods of activity which the children have acquired over the preceding three years. At the same time the children are immersed in cultures new to them – in the culture of Ancient Egypt and in Russian culture of the time of Peter the Great. The children's geographic knowledge also broadens, due to greater specific knowledge about various countries and climatic zones.

The teaching of school children in preschool and primary school centres according to the "Golden Key" progamme carries a range of peculiarities, differentiating it from general schools. The essence of these differences lies in establishing the necessary conditions for creating valuable educational activities for each child. According to the concept of education on which the "Golden Key" programme is based, educational activities in its development goes through several stages. All the stages are characterised by the advantage of a definite form of work with children. It is practically impossible to realise these forms of work using the standard lesson-based approach to the organisation of education. The most important forms of work with children of primary school age are individual tasks and the cultivation of business-like co-operation (*delovoe cotrudnichestvo*), as well as partnership relationships (*partniorskie vzaimootnosheniya*). These forms of work are the necessary stages in the development of educational activities. Without implementing these stages, the approach to such complex group-assigned activity as the learning one is also not possible.

The practice of educating children according to the "Golden Key" programme has shown that a single path to forming high-quality and content-rich learning activities, which are topical for the children involved, lies through cultivating business-like, team-work relationships in the process of learning. The establishment of business-like relations based on learning material, in its turn, is possible only through partnership with the educating adult, through individual education.

Apart from individual work with children, work with micro-groups of children and conducting lessons (general, not divided according to subject), primary school teachers working with the "Golden Key" programme have one more, very significant and important aspect of work. That is work in groups, where the pupils of their classes live together with young children and educators. The outline script for the life of the group of the children's centre envisages participation of school children in all business and events. This participation is almost always of the nature of continuing education, strengthening the knowledge and skills acquired in school, and sometimes also the creation of problematic situations, for which the means for resolving them can be found in school.

On graduating from the education centre the children master valuable educational activities, which means that they:

- can understand a learning task/problem and work on it;
- independently choose and master general methods of solving a problem;
- have the skills to adequately evaluate and control themselves and their actions;
- use the laws of logical thinking;
- make use of theoretical generalisations;
- have mastered various forms of communication;
- know how to take part in group-assigned forms of activity; and
- have a high level of independent creative activity.

Notes

1 The Russian word *lichnost'* can be translated as both personality and individual. Here we use the most appropriate English term for the given context.
2 The Russian word *psikhika* can be variously translated as psyche, mind, and its derivative *psykhicheskii* as psychic(al), mental and, in certain contexts, as psychological. Here we use the most appropriate English term for the given context.
3 In Vygotsky's time *vospitanie* (the moral-ethical domain of education or "upbringing") and *obuchenie* (the epistemological domain of education or teaching) were inseparable. The idea of unity is captured in the Russian word *obrazovanie*, or education.
4 A type of fibre.
5 Blue powdered glass.

12 Developmental Education

Improving Participation in Cultural Practices

Bert van Oers

Political Ambitions and Practical Concerns

One of the important insights of the educational sciences in recent decades is that education entails more than a purposeful and reflective organisation of the relationship between educator and child (see Daniels, 2001). It has become clear that cultural institutions (like family, school) and cultural tools (like language) embody structures that largely influence human activity explicitly or tacitly. Because of the intrinsic relationship between activity and human development, human development is also prone to be (at least partly) determined by cultural institutions and tools.

Society and its institutions are not stable, unchanging structures. Emerging economic, political and cultural changes modify the ways people act and interact, and these changes also may have significant influences on human cultural development. However, the influence of changing societal structures on human activity and development is not a deterministic process. It depends on how these changes are perceived and how people cope with them. The recent transition of the global society into a knowledge economy is changing people's interactions, including their expectations, and the demands that are made on people. It is important to study the effects of these sociostructural changes on human activity, learning, and development. The present chapter explores some of the consequences the knowledge economy may have on education and children's development, and proposes a way of dealing with these consequences.

The notion of knowledge economy is based on the idea that knowledge and information are fundamental commodities for modern cultural life. Like all commodities, knowledge and information can be economically valued, codified and traded among people, institutions and nations. The concept of the knowledge economy pervades our modern society, and the dominant position of economy in all parts of our society transforms the society into a knowledge society. The knowledge society has rapidly turned into a political concept that is used for the organisation of economies and institutions (including school). The members of the European Union for example made an agreement in March 2000 (the so-called Lisbon strategy) which stated that by 2010 Europe should become '*the most competitive and dynamic knowledge-based economy in the world, capable of sustainable economic growth with more and better jobs and greater social cohesion'* (Report of the EU Education Council, 2001, p. 4). The council also stresses the important role of schools to realise this ambitious political goal.

In the Netherlands, as elsewhere, several attempts have been made to explore the educational consequences of the knowledge society and translate them into educational proposals and regulations. These discussions resulted, for example, in proposals for canonisation of mandatory school contents, standardised goals, prioritising children's adaptation to and performance in school, especially literacy and numeracy. The tendency to focus on essential contents, programme-based schooling and accountability by frequent testing had been growing since the 1980s, but this tendency was still more strengthened by the increased emphasis on the knowledge economy. Gradually, schools were put under pressure to embrace the ideal of teaching for the knowledge society. The idea of the knowledge society was embraced by many politicians, policy makers, and practitioners as a valid basis for the innovation of schools. Given the tenets of the knowledge society (and economy) there is a strong predilection to favour schools as places for transmission of cultural knowledge and skills. The transmission-type schools, which already had a long tradition in our society, were reinforced by the emergence of the knowledge society.

Both international and national discussions, however, have also critically evaluated these developments. Hargreaves (2003) puts the point aptly when he writes:

> Teachers and others, therefore, must think about how to teach not only *for* the knowledge society but also *beyond* it, so we address other compelling human values and educational purposes in addition to those that make a profit—purposes concerned with character, community, democracy, and cosmopolitan identity. (p. 57)

The future society, according to Hargreaves, should go beyond uniform knowledge transmission and skill training, and advocate education at school that helps students to become emancipated, responsible human beings, who can 'think and act above and beyond the seductions and demands of the knowledge economy' (p. 60).

However, on the national level (the Netherlands), since the 1980s there has also been a deep concern among a small group of educators and investigators about the dominating transmission-type of education in schools. The concern was that this type of teaching/learning does not optimally promote the pupils' broad identity development, and results in mechanically learned outcomes that will not function properly in new problem solving contexts. One of the critical groups drew on the educational ideas of Vygotsky and developed the idea of 'Developmental Education'. The basic idea of this approach is that pupils can only meaningfully learn in school when this learning is embedded in practices in which they participate with peers and teachers. The purpose of education should always be to support the broad identity development of pupils as well-informed participants in sociocultural activities.

We named this educational concept '*Developmental Education*' (or in Dutch: 'Ontwikkelingsgericht Onderwijs'). Over the decades, this new educational concept was gradually elaborated and implemented in a number of schools, beginning with the lowest grades of primary school (ages 4–8), but recently spreading to the upper grades as well (8–12). It is still a minority in the Dutch educational field, but we estimate that about 10 per cent of Dutch primary schools have committed themselves (in varying degrees) to this concept. In the following sections, I will describe the fundamental notions of Developmental Education, and show how we deal with the exigencies of the knowledge society. Finally, I will give details of the infrastructure that is necessary for the implementation of the Developmental Education concept in classroom practices.

Developmental Education: Basic Concepts and a Practical Outline

Basic Tenets

Developmental Education in the Netherlands started out in the 1980s from two initiatives. On the one hand there was the practical concern for early childhood education that tried to prevent young children from the age of four from being squeezed into a drill and practice curriculum that was supposed to prepare them for the primary school curriculum (Janssen-Vos, 1990). On the other hand there was the research paradigm, based on the ideas of Vygotsky, Gal'perin and Davydov, which was meant to elaborate a new theory for school learning that could promote the cognitive development of pupils (van Parreren & Carpay, 1972). These two movements merged in the 1980s into a collaborative enterprise to improve both early childhood education practices and educational theory (e.g. Janssen-Vos & van Oers, 1992; Janssen-Vos, 1997). The core idea of this concept was based on Vygotsky's optimistic view on human developmentability. Good education, as Vygotsky (1978) once pointed out, should always be one step ahead of pupils. It is supposed to promote human development through meaningful interactions with children, by offering them the cultural tools for meaningful participation in the cultural life of their social communities.

From the beginning, the Developmental Education movement represented a theory-driven approach to the development of educational practices. However, from the beginning we were also aware of the fact that Developmental Education should not be narrowly focused on finding the one effective method that could promote pupils' development. We also realised that this method itself is also an ever-developing system that depends on the professionalism of teachers, researchers, curriculum developers, and teacher trainers, as well as how they interpret the demands of society. Improved teaching abilities and teaching conditions optimise the conditions for pupils' learning.

The theoretical basis of Developmental Education was elaborated over the years through numerous discussions between researchers and practitioners, and through critical exchanges with (international) Vygotskians. We learned how to articulate the theory in such a way that it optimally served our aims, while still being consistent with the spirit of Vygotsky's cultural-historical theory.

As a way of presenting the Developmental Education approach, I will discuss some of the basic concepts briefly, and eventually employ them for the explanation of how Developmental Education deals with the demands of our modern (knowledge) society.

Emancipation: The main aim of Developmental Education is the *emancipation* of the learning individual, including his educators. Emancipation, however, is a deeply problematic concept that cannot go without further explanation. At first sight, emancipation in the context of a cultural-historical approach seems paradoxical, as it seems to suggest a glorification of the individual, while the cultural-historical conception of the human being is essentially a sociocultural construct. In this context, emancipation refers to a further qualification of identity development. From a cultural-historical point of view, identity consists – in the Bakhtinian sense – in a polyphonous construct that is voiced by a situated person. Identity, like cognition, is a distributed phenomenon that can only exist thanks to the wealth of cultural resources that we can use for our personal enterprises. However, the potentials of the individual can only be optimally developed when he or she has meaningfully appropriated the influences from others. The integration of the different voices and contents into one meaningful whole requires a critical appropriation process, in which a person not only acquires new knowledge, skills or understandings, but also critically evaluates them in the process of creating ownership and assuming personal responsibility for what is appropriated. Emancipation, then, means the development of a critical identity for participation in sociocultural practices.

Practice: The aim of Developmental Education can also be described as the enhancement of persons' abilities to participate independently and critically in the sociocultural practices of their community. A practice can be defined as a culturally evolved constellation of integrated activities that aim collaboratively at the production of specific products. Take for example the practice of a bakery. For the achievement of its product, the baker has to integrate activities of calculating, reading, writing, maintenance of his machinery, selecting and buying ingredients etc. Developmental Education aims at developing proficiency in different activities that are required for participating in sociocultural practices. It is interesting to note, that the teacher him/herself is also participating in a cultural activity when he/she teaches. The aim of improving the teachers' ability of participating in this teaching practice is also one of the objectives of Developmental Education.

Activity: A culturally developed, systematic, and tool-mediated way of dealing with a specific category of objects; each activity can be carried out in different ways. Activities can follow different formats, depending on the goals, the ideology of the actors and stakeholders, or on material conditions. Every format contains one or more (more or less mandatory) *rules*. The rules help defining the activity. Formats can also differ in the extent to which they require personal engagement. This dimension runs from enforced participation (no engagement) to complete *involvement* on the basis of personal motives and values. Finally, formats of activity differ in the extent that they allow the participants in an activity more or less *freedom of action and choice*. From our Developmental Education perspective we believe that meaningful learning that can stimulate critical identity development can only blossom in activities that have adopted a format that is based on clear rules, that stimulates involvement in the actors, and that allows (at least) some degrees of freedom. This format is characteristic for play activities (see van Oers, 2005), but we extrapolated the format to all meaningful activities in the Developmental Education curriculum. That is why we characterise the whole Developmental Education curriculum as a *play-based curriculum*. This includes both playful learning activities in the primary grades, and inquiry-based learning activities in the upper grades of primary school. This format of the activities in school creates the basic conditions for emancipation, identity formation and meaningful learning.

Meaningful Learning: As can be inferred from the previous explanations, Developmental Education aims at meaningful learning processes. For a good understanding of our classroom practices, it is important to keep in mind that meaningful learning always and principally implies two dimensions. Learning must be meaningful in the sense that it promotes the (critical) mastery of cultural meanings that can be applied and recontextualised for personal purposes (see van Oers, 1998). On the other hand, the learning must also be meaningful in that it makes personal sense. To put it differently: personal meaning (sense) is a process of valuation of learning processes and outcomes from the perspective of one's own motives and emotions (see Leont'ev, 1977 for further explanation of the differences between meaning and sense; see also González-Rey, 2008). From the perspective of Developmental Education, learning in school or outside must always be meaningful in this double way.

Zone of Proximal Development: Above, I quoted Vygotsky, saying that good education should always be ahead of pupils. That was his way of expressing that education can and should promote pupils' development. In his view, human development is not fully defined by summarising what humans have already individually achieved, but developmental potentials strongly depend on the quality of the interaction humans are engaged in. When other people take account of those aspects of activities that we have not yet mastered ourselves, we can accomplish that activity even if we wouldn't be able to do it alone. This is one of the descriptions Vygotsky gives of the zone of proximal development (see Vygotsky, 1978, p. 86). However, taking this description as a definition is misleading, as it does not give any indication of the sense of this action or learning. Taken on its own, this 'definition' legitimises any imposed learning that pupils cannot accomplish alone. It can be taken as a reference to what they can achieve when assisted by a strict 'scaffold' or direct stepwise instruction. Such learning can already be taken as meaningful, when it transmits cultural meanings, but lacks the element of personal sense.

For the definition of the zone of proximal development, we start out from Vygotsky's remark that the core of the zone of proximal development is basically in the concept of *imitation* (van Oers, 1987, 2007b). Vygotsky explains that he does not refer to mechanically copying behaviour. His notion of imitation should be understood as *participation in cultural activities*. Insofar as this imitation of cultural activities is a self-chosen activity, it is meaningful in the double sense. The new actions that a child can learn within this context with the help of adults or more capable peers indicate the zone of proximal development within that context at that moment. This conception of the zone of proximal development does not legitimise learning of anything new, but is restricted to the content of activities persons are meaningfully involved in.

Dialogue and Polylogue: When we define learning in terms of appropriation of meanings, dialogue becomes a crucial concept. As a negotiation of meanings, dialogue is the many-sided process in which participants of a communicative activity exchange utterances on a topic and decide which of these utterances can be legitimately accepted as a predicate to that topic (see van Oers, 2000, 2006, 2007a). Important as this process is, it leads at best to local consensus among the participants in this conversation. A culturally and historically relevant consensus, however, must also be permanently tested against other views, particularly experts that may not be present in the context (contemporary or historical authorities). In order to assess the cultural-historical relevance of consensual meaning, the dialogue must be extended with virtual participants, represented by texts. Following Davydov (1983) we call this type of extended conversation 'polylogue'. It is a fundamental step for academic discourse and the development of scientific concepts (see also Carpay & van Oers, 1993; Davydov, 1996). As we shall see below, Developmental Education takes this polylogue seriously in the learning processes of pupils. It is the main course from local dialogues and consensus-finding to the critical appropriation of the culturally relevant understanding our society needs.

Developmental Education in Practice

In Developmental Education, teachers' basic intention is to help pupils with becoming critical and autonomous participants in sociocultural practices. A basic strategy for the teachers is to get children involved in meaningful activities, in ways which relate to the children's cultural life and that make personal sense for the pupils as well. In the lower grades of primary school, children are, for example, involved in thematic activities related to a particular meaningful theme, such as for example a hospital, a barber's shop, a toy factory, etc., but also to such cultural activities as mathematising, or communicating (story-telling, writing, reading, making stories, playing out stories, explaining). In all activities, pupils are assisted to figure out the rules, appropriate relevant tools, knowledge and strategies. They are encouraged to explore these activities freely and with the help of experts in the classroom or outside. To acquaint themselves with the possibilities of (for instance) communication in this broad sense, they visit a museum on communication media, or arrange a conversation with an advertiser or a mailman. But they also learn reading, writing, making presentations, etc. in order to improve their ways of communicating and their participation in communicative activities of their community (for more examples, see Janssen-Vos, 1997; van Oers, 2003a, part II). When pupils progress through the primary school curriculum to the higher grades, they get involved in more complex communicative activities, or cultural activities like producing a newspaper, organising elections, running a store or a catering company, or keeping a garden, growing vegetables or flowers (many examples of such activities in classrooms can be found in Pompert, 2003). Of particular relevance here is also the pupils' involvement in the cultural practice of knowledge production (science, investigations). By participating in this type of practice they learn to formulate research questions, reflect on methods, gather data and literature, argue on data and research outcomes of others, etc. Obviously, primary school pupils need much assistance for meaningful participation in such activities, but it is clear that they can learn to take part in such academic activities: reflect on methods and outcomes, appropriate new knowledge and strategies, and report on the outcomes of investigations (see also Wells, 1998). Particularly in such academic activities the role of polylogue is of outstanding importance. Through the inclusion of texts of other experts, the activity of the pupils is cultural-historically informed, which (with proper guidance) leads to intertextual products. Pupils in Developmental Education schools also learn to write texts (stories and reports) from the beginning of their school career. Reporting is an essential part of their academic activities. Cultural history settles into the activities of young learners in this way. The integration of opposing views from their classroom community or from literature can help pupils to become critical.

Instead of dwelling longer on detailed practical examples from our classrooms, it should be clear from the information given above that Developmental Education aims at improving pupils' abilities for participation in many different practices. These practices become the real zones of proximal development for the pupils, in which they can appropriate new tools (knowledge, skills, strategies) in a meaningful way, with the help of actual or virtual others, as represented by texts and other forms of communication. Although systematic empirical evidence is still lacking with regard to identity development, it seems theoretically plausible to assume that the permanent collaborative reflection on alternative meanings within the context of these cultural activities has the potential of educating critical participants.

From this background, Developmental Education schools define their positions regarding the knowledge society and its demands. The basic question is: what do people (both teachers and pupils) need for critical participation in relevant practices of the knowledge society? On the basis of theoretical analyses and practical experiences, we arrived at the following categories:

(a) *General strategies for dealing with (textual) information:* This relates to both reading and writing strategies (questioning, summarising, predicting, organising, etc). In Developmental Education reading and writing is a core activity. With regard to thinking strategies, emphasis is given to strategies that make the complexity of situations manageable, such as schematising and modelling (van Oers & Poland, 2007; Poland, 2007; van Oers & van Dijk, 2004).

(b) *Reflective attitude:* Much emphasis is given to discourse on topics and problems; this collaborative reflection is supposed to build up a positive value regarding reflective approaches to actions and problem situations. The systematic reflection is stimulated by the teacher (if not by peers), and focuses on both cognitive, moral-ethical and aesthetical aspects of an activity.

(c) *Practice-relevant knowledge and skills:* Proficient participation in cultural practices requires the mastery of subject matter understandings and skills that are necessary for autonomous and critical participation; during the thematic activities children learn vocabulary, concepts, rules, skills that are necessary for participation. Availability of knowledge not only supports the ability for participation but also enhances the ability to expand one's abilities (e.g. better reading and getting to know the practice better through external written resources); reading, writing and knowledge acquisition with regard to the practices pupils are involved in, is an important element of Developmental Education.

(d) *Arts:* At the moment this is the least developed part of Developmental Education practices; within the context of Developmental Education, children's involvement with arts is primarily based on aesthetic thinking that engages children in a process of figuring out what they would define as art. The development of art skills (painting, music, dance, etc.) is secondary and should be a spin-off of an individual's need to acquire new means for expressing his view on art (van Oers, 2003b). The development of aesthetic thinking is conceived as one of the antidotes for the seductions of the knowledge society, and probably one of the basic dimensions of identity formation (van Oers, 2003b).

We cannot suggest that Developmental Education has already solved all the problems of learning and development in a knowledge society. From our theoretical perspective and on the basis of growing research, we build confidence in the value of this approach for human development that is sensitive to the demands of the modern society.

Establishing an Infrastructure

Improving participation in cultural practices is, as we have argued, not simply a matter of teaching relevant knowledge and skills from our present understanding of human cultural development. Society changes and our understandings of learning and development change. Hence there is a permanent need for improving the educational system itself and enhancing the professionalism of its workers. Developmental Education is itself both a *conceptual view* on development under institutional conditions, a type of *classroom practice*, and an evolving educational system that serves as an *infrastructure for innovations.*

As it turns out, the evolution of this infrastructure is partly a theory-driven process, but also conditioned by practical political constraints (like budgets, official policies, dominant economic ideology, etc.). The infrastructure for Developmental Educational practices and research is basically a hybrid system. When we interpret this infrastructure as an activity system by itself (in the sense of Engeström, 1987), we can infer that the optimal workings of the infrastructure can only be managed when we organise the structure in such a way that the internal contradictions within the system can be solved or mitigated.

To create optimal conditions for the improvement of Developmental Education practices, we have built up over the years an infrastructure that can optimise the chances for Developmental Education (both as a practice and as a theory). Special effort was put into optimising the developmental conditions by setting up a *community*, creating necessary *artefacts*, and defining *rules* for collaboration (see Engeström, 1987). In order to characterise the infra-structure, I will elaborate these three pillars below.

The Community

The community involved in our collaborative innovation of Dutch education, consists of people who are somehow committed to this concept of Developmental Education. This includes teachers, principals, teacher educators, counsellors, innovators, researchers, students, inspectors. This view is the central binding force of the community. Formally, this community is organised in an association called the Academy of Developmental Education (Academie voor Ontwikkelingsgericht Onderwijs, see www.ogo-academie. nl). The reasons for membership of this community are various among different types of stakeholders, depending on the nature of their expertise and practices (see van Huizen, van Oers, & Wubbels, 2005).

It is evident that the members of the community have quite different reasons for being involved, and their interests vary accordingly. In order to bring the various interests together, the association created a number of communication platforms where members can exchange ideas, discuss and develop new ideas together.

There is a *journal* (called *Zone*, four issues per year) with an editorial board that recruits its members from the different 'sections'; one of the policies of the editorial board is to invite practitioners and researchers to write articles together, or to reflect on each other's work. Every issue of the journal includes articles about theory and practice informing about new developments. The journal is a main channel of communication for the members of the community.

There is a bi-annual *conference* where teachers present their work, where researchers and young students can present and discuss their research, and where new practical developments are presented; the attendants of the conference come from all sections. In the organisation of the different conference sessions care is taken that academic researchers, innovators and practitioners are able to interact and exchange ideas; for example, researchers that serve as discussants for a practical presentation (or vice versa).

The association encourages members to form *interest-based platforms* where particular practical problems are addressed; for example a platform that develops new projects for the upper levels of primary school, a platform that addresses problems of emergent literacy. Again, the Association takes care that every platform also includes academic researchers and practitioners.

There are specialiscd institutions for teacher training, focusing on developmental education. First there is the *institute for in-service teacher training* ('De Activiteit' see www.de-activiteit.nl). Academically trained workers who assist schools with the innovation of practices according to the ideas of developmental education run this institute. This institute is also a very important communication platform for integrating theory and practice. In addition, some of the initial teacher training institutes in the Netherlands adopted the perspective of developmental education as the main philosophy for their teaching programme.

There are research centres that investigate the theory and its practical implications. Part of the research is currently related to a *university chair* 'Theory of cultural historical education' that is based at the Free University of Amsterdam. Part of the research is also related to a *lectureship* 'Ontwikkelingsgericht Onderwijs' (Developmental Education), that is based at the university of vocational (teacher) training in Alkmaar. Both centres initiate research on the analysis, evaluation, design and application of Developmental Education.

Artefacts

Researchers' Tools: In the development of the activity system of Developmental Education, several instruments (artefacts) involved regulate the activity of the members of the community. Of course every 'section' of the community (teachers, educators, researchers, etc.) has tools that are specific for their respective practices. The researchers have their statistical and methodological models, and they will use them when they think it is necessary. However, in the choice of research designs the researchers from this community often choose informed designs that include teachers' interests and ideas as much as possible (e.g. design experiments); in designs like case-studies or quasi-experimental designs the focus is primarily on educational arrangements that include both teachers and pupils in interaction; these studies more often than not give results that are recognised by teachers as relevant for their practices. Researchers will never just impose ideas or programmes top down (as in an RDD approach), but develop innovations through boundary crossing, i.e. through collaborating with practitioners, teacher educators, and other innovators, up to a point that every participant can agree with the outcome.

Teachers' Tools: From a practical point of view there is another category of artefacts that directly influences the everyday practices of developmental education classrooms. These are the tools of the teacher for the implementation of developmental education in his/her classroom. The tools have been developed on a theory-driven basis very close to the needs of the practitioners. In the realisation of developmental education, a number of theories are involved and each of them finds material expression in practical tools. Take a look at the following theories.

Theory of Learning and Development: The basic theory here is the Vygotskian approach to learning and development, which holds that learning can promote development when it is embedded in activities in which pupils can meaningfully participate and in which they get assistance for optimal participation in this activity. Learning is here defined as a process of qualitative improvement of actions or activities (see van Oers, 1996). For young children, meaningful learning is conceived as a process that is intrinsically related to activities in a play format. That means that pupils can participate as agents with personal interests and needs. Play is seen as a leading activity for young children. Within the playful activities learning should be promoted by the teacher. The learning process of the pupils can be explicitly promoted through five dimensions that are described as the 'five impulses' that the teacher should try to employ in his/her interaction with pupils (from Janssen-Vos, 1997), see Figure 12.1.

Curriculum Theory: As a consequence of the theory of learning and development the curriculum of the younger children (4–8 years) is seen as a play-based curriculum (see above; van Oers, 2003b). As a course for learning, the curriculum is conceived as a learning trajectory of individual pupils that is constructed in the classroom through the interaction between teacher and pupils. It is, however, important that the teacher has an overview of important subject matter that can be introduced into the children's activities at moments when this is relevant. Frea Janssen-Vos (1997) developed a diagram with the relevant areas of learning that can be used by the teacher as a heuristic means for the guidance of pupils (see van Oers, 2003a, p. 100). No strict uniform learning route is imposed on the pupils. A similar diagram was developed for the upper grades of primary school (for ages 8–12), which will not be discussed here.

The core of the curriculum is the well-being of the pupil. The first task of the teacher is to take care that the pupils feel safe, free, and confident to explore and to express. This is the basic resource from which the pupils start exploring the world and building up needs for specific tools, rules and help. From this starting point the teacher can try to get children involved in broadly conceived new activities (like communicating, problem solving, cooperating, planning, etc.) in which children may participate in their own ways and don't need to obey (not yet!) the strict rules that govern these activities in the adult culture. Strict rule following is for later. But when

- *Orientation*: Encourage the pupils to reflect in advance on what they are planning to do;

- *Extension to other activities*: Like connecting pupils' construction activities with drawings of construction diagrams, or maps, or connecting their play in a grocery store with mathematical activity or reading;

- *Deepening and structuring*: Help children to see the point and structure of an activity: a child that is playing doctor by putting a stethoscope on all parts of a puppet's body can learn where the stethoscope should be put, can learn that there is more to being a doctor than just using the stethoscope (prescribing pills, writing prescriptions, interviewing the patient, etc.);

- *Adding new actions*: Within the activity of the child, new actions are introduced that enhance the child's ability to accomplish that activity, such as applying a bandage or a sling when playing doctor, or writing a prescription that can be read in the drugstore, etc;

- *Reflection* after the activity, looking back on what went well or where the problems are, trying to draw lessons from these reflections.

Figure 12.1 The 'five impulses' that the teacher should try to employ in his/her interaction with pupils

engaged in these activities, the teacher constantly spots opportunities where she/he can encourage and support the child to appropriate new specific actions. For example, from the feeling of well-being and freedom, the child may decide to participate in a role-play in a supermarket. In this play, the child initially plays his role in a personally meaningful way, and the teacher tries to support the pupil in whatever he picks up. At some moment the pupil will encounter the need to buy things from the store and pay at the counter. There the teacher or more knowledgeable peers can help the pupil with improving this counting action. This will produce specific learning outcomes in a meaningful way.

The learning trajectory is always constructed in collaboration with the pupils (see for example Janssen-Vos, 2003). For literacy development (Knijpstra et al., 1997) and mathematical development (Fijma & Vink, 1998) in the lower grades of primary school, special hypothetical trajectories have been developed that show main goals and thinking strategies that pupils should be able to achieve during their learning trajectory. More tools are provided to support teachers' planning activities, but these will not be discussed here (see van Oers, 2003b, part II). The course through the curriculum in the higher grades is organised in a similar way.

Observation Theory. A core ability of teachers for the accomplishment of developmental education is the ability to observe pupils, and identify their position and needs in the developmental process. In order to guide pupils through an appropriate learning trajectory, the teachers need to trace the pupils' actual progress very carefully. In order to assist teachers in their observation, evaluation and registrations a manual was developed that materialises the observation theory of the developmental education approach. The core of this theory conceives of observation as an inquisitive process driven by hypotheses. The materialisation of the observation theory is consolidated in a manual (HOREB – a Dutch acronym for Action-Oriented Observation Registration and Evaluation in Basic Development, see among others Janssen-Vos, 2003; Fijma, 2003). The observation manual consists of different sections that deal with different subject matter and with general developmental characteristics. As such, the manual also incorporates (and materialises!) subject matter theories (like Reading as Communicative Act, or Realistic Mathematics Education) as well as developmental theories.

The teacher constantly makes notes about the pupils in a diary, and tries to infer the needs for new steps from these observations. These new steps are always hypothetical and have to be put into practice to find out if and how a pupil reacts to this attempt by the teacher. This action leads to new learning, new observations and new plans for further learning. If an attempt by a teacher to promote new actions and learning does not work out, then the hypothesis must be revised. A new hypothesis is formulated and examined in the interaction with the pupil.

The observation manual is a material expression of the observation theory. Teachers are supported to appropriate this manner of observing children, and accordingly planning their learning trajectories.

These theories and their materialisations are themselves artefacts that teachers can use to organise pupils' learning processes. The teachers are expected to use these heuristic theoretical tools as tools for thinking and not as a fixed set of guidelines. In the development and application of these theories and tools, it is again significant how communications take place. The development of the theories was the work of scientific researchers, but the material embodiments of the theories have been constructed in close connection with practical needs. The construction of these tools is mainly the work of the teacher educators and innovators who developed them through observation in classrooms, through observing and listening to teachers, and through discussion with researchers. In practice, it turns out that teachers have lots of difficulties in applying these tools in their classrooms. This should not surprise us, as the tools were meant as tools for thinking. As a consequence, we also had to develop strategies for assisting teachers to develop their thinking with the help of these tools and with the help of teacher educators. This calls for strategies of communication between the designers of the instruments, the teacher educators and the teachers. I will describe some of them by clarifying the rules for this inter-professional communication.

Rules

It is obvious that every profession involved in the Developmental Education project has its own rules. These rules have been developed in the history of that professional community and have to be taken into account when professionals participate in the development of the activity system of Developmental Education. The way in which professionals negotiate with their own professional communities about the rules of their work is an interesting but complicated matter. I shall not deal with it here.

What is more interesting for us now is how professionals within the community of Developmental Education communicate among the different specialists, especially how they communicate with the teachers who are responsible for bringing the ideas of Developmental Education into practice. In order to clarify this I will focus on the teacher educators' communication with the teachers. The teacher educator is in many cases mediating between researchers, innovators and teachers.

In the work in schools the teacher educators abide by a number of rules:

- The building of a community of practice at school is a fundamental condition for school innovation. So as a rule the teacher educators always *work with whole teams.* Most of the time a school is dissatisfied with its way of working, because of bad results, negative evaluations by the inspectorate, or just as a result of innovatory forces within the team (maybe a new principal!). In cases where the team decides that Developmental Education might answer their needs, they contact the teacher educators and the process starts. The teacher educators always start with a stage of negotiation with the team on a shared plan for innovatory work. They choose for a main issue for their reform process, an issue that is considered relevant for the school (e.g. strengthening of the language policy of the school, improve the language/literacy development of all pupils, enhancing art education). They make suggestions of how to address this problem in one or two years, how the progress will be monitored and assessed.
- When the initial negotiations are finished, the real processes of team discussions and *individual coaching* will begin. For the individual coaching, the educators again have a number of basic communication rules that they will follow:
  - *Address the problems and questions of the individual teachers* that are covered by the main issue (for instance, under the main issue of language policy fall specific questions regarding vocabulary learning, comprehensive reading, how to include ethnic minority pupils, etc.);
  - *Work with the teachers in their own classrooms:* the teacher educator frequently visits the teachers in their own classrooms, and tries to find points for improvement related to the teachers' problems;

- *Reflect with the teacher on his/her classroom activities* with the help of the theory-based tools and demonstrate how the tools work and how they can contribute to their practical problems;
- *Develop new strategies for classroom activities:* better strategies for observing children, using the HOREB system more consistently, make more detailed plans for the hypothetical learning trajectories of pupils; the teacher educator is constructing a zone of proximal development with the teacher;
- *Assist the teachers in the implementation of the innovation plan in their classrooms:* those elements of the plan that the teacher cannot yet do on her/his own will be carried out by the teacher educator, and reflected on later; the teacher educator now applies the concept of zone of proximal development, and helps the teacher where she cannot carry out the required actions on her own;
- *Provide models* that the teacher can emulate in her own classroom, and which they can critically reflect on afterwards, taking into account their personal beliefs, standards and limits;
- *Share the outcomes of individual progress with the whole team* and reflect on each other's developmental processes to build up a body of common experiences and knowledge; in this process the teacher educator explicitly relates the outcomes, experiences and plans with the conceptual framework of Developmental Education;
- *Encourage the team to become self-supporting* and to interiorise the assistance given by the teacher educator. We believe that most of the time bringing an innovation with incidental help to schools is not enough. A period of interiorisation is needed to empower the team for a self-sufficient approach of new steps in their permanent development; this increases the innovatory potential of the school.

In these communicative rules we see how the teacher educator mediates between theory and practice. She or he does not impose new ways of working on the school but constructs with the team a new teaching strategy until the point that all participants feel that the solutions fit in with their conceptual framework and answer their individual and collective needs. This is characteristic for multi-perspective collaborative innovation: the final product is appropriated as a product of one's own efforts, although it is not an exclusive possession of one or other of the involved parties.

Conclusion: Developmental Teaching in the Knowledge Society

Children need assistance to improve their abilities for participation in cultural practices. Developmental Education intends to offer children this assistance in a way that gives each of them access to the basic tools for participation. However, the mission of Developmental Education is not merely to adjust children to the demands of the knowledge society, but to make them critical members of a democratic society, that is committed to excellence and fairness, using and improving cultural heritage(s) for the benefit of all.

From Vygotsky's view on human (cultural) development, we argued that the main aim of such education should be the transformation of human beings into identities that can participate autonomously (in an intellectual and moral way) and critically in cultural activities with others. As we have shown, in recent decades, we have made important steps in developing both the tools for teaching, and the infrastructure for the innovation and implementation of these tools in classroom practices. This is essentially an unending process that requires further empirical and theoretical research. We will continue on this road, with the help of critical teachers and teacher trainers who share an honest commitment to the potentials of humanity in social communities.

References

Carpay, J. A. M. & van Oers, B. (1993). Didaktičeskie modeli i problema obučajužčej diskussii. [Didactical models and the problem of classroom discourse]. *Voprosy Psichologii*, 4, pp. 20–26.

Daniels, H. (2001). *Vygotsky and pedagogy*. London: Routledge.

Davydov, V. V. (1983). Istoričeskie predposylki učebnoj dejate'nosti [Historical conditions or learning activity]. In V.V. Davydov (Ed.), *Razvitie psichiki škol'nikov v processe učebnoj dejate'nosti* . Moscow: PN.

Davydov, V. V. (1996). *Teorija razvivajuščego obuçenija* [Theory of developmental education]. Moscow: INTOR.

Engeström, Y. (1987). *Learning by expanding: An activity-theoretical approach to developmental research*. Helsinki: Orienta-Konsultit Oy.

EU Education Council (2001). *The concrete future objectives of education and training systems*. Retrieved from: http://ec.europa.eu/education/policies/2010/doc/ (May 2008).

Fijma, N. (2003). Mathematics learning in a play-based curriculum. How to deal with heterogeneity? In B. van Oers (Ed.), *Narratives of childhood* (pp. 146–162). Amsterdam: VU Press.

Fijma, N. & Vink, H. (1998). *Op jou kan ik rekenen* [I can count on you]. Assen: van Gorcum.

González-Rey, F. L. (2008). Subject, subjectivity, and development in cultural historical psychology. In B. van Oers, W. Wardekker, E. Elbers, & R. van der Veer (Eds.), *The transformation of learning. Advances in activity theory* (pp. 137–154). Cambridge: Cambridge University Press.

Hargreaves, A. (2003). *Teaching in the knowledge society. Education in the age of insecurity*. New York: Teachers College Press.

Huizen, P. van, van Oers, B., & Wubbels, T. (2005). A Vygotskian perspective on teacher education, *Journal of Curriculum Studies*, 37, 3, 267–290.

Janssen-Vos, F. (1990). *Basisontwikkeling*. [Basic Development]. Assen: van Gorcum.

Janssen-Vos, F. (1997). *Basisontwikkeling in de onderbouw* [Basic development in the early grades of primary school]. Assen: van Gorcum.

Janssen-Vos, F. (2003). Basic development: Developmental education for young children. In B. van Oers (Ed.), *Narratives of childhood* (pp. 93–109). Amsterdam: VU Press.

Janssen-Vos, F. & van Oers, B. (Eds.) (1992). *Visies op onderwijs aan jonge kinderen.* [Visions on early childhood education]. Assen: van Gorcum.

Knijpstra, H., Pompert, B., & Schiferli, T. (1997). *Met jou kan ik lezen en schrijven* [With you I can read and write]. Assen: van Gorcum.

Leont'ev, A. N. (1977). *Tätigkeit, Bewusstsein, Persönlichkeit* [Activity, consciousness, personality]. Berlin: Volk und Wissen.

Oers, B. van (1987). *Activiteit en begrip* [Activity and concept]. Dissertation. Amsterdam: VU Press.

Oers, B. van (1998). From context to contextualizing. *Learning and Instruction,* 8 (6), 473–488.

Oers, B. van (2000). The appropriation of mathematical symbols. A psychosemiotic approach to mathematics learning. In P. Cobb, E. Yackel, & K. McClain (Eds.), *Symbolizing and communicating in mathematics classrooms. Perspectives on discourse, tools, and instructional design* (pp. 133–176). Mahwah, NJ: Erlbaum.

Oers, B. van (2003a). *Narratives of childhood. Theoretical and practical explorations of early childhood education.* Amsterdam: Free University Press.

Oers, B. van (2003b). *Dwarsdenken. Essays over Ontwikkelingsgericht onderwijs* [Cross thinking. Essays on developmental education]. Assen: van Gorcum.

Oers, B. van (2005). *Carnaval in de kennisfabriek.* [Carnival in the knowledge factory]. Inaugural address. Amsterdam: VU Press.

Oers, B. van (2006). An activity theory approach to the formation of mathematical cognition: Developing topics through predication in a mathematical community. In J. Maass & W. Schlöglmann (Eds.), *New mathematics education research and practice.* Rotterdam: Sense Publisher.

Oers, B. van (2007a). Helping young children to become literate: The relevance of narrative competence for developmental education. *European Early Childhood Education Research Journal,* 15 (3), 299–312.

Oers, B. van (2007b). In the zone. *Children in Europe* (August), special Vygotsky issue, 14–15.

Oers, B. van & van Dijk, I. (2004). Curriculum and the development of model-based thinking. In J. Terwel & D. Walker (Eds.), *Curriculum as a shaping force. Toward a principled approach in curriculum theory and practice* (pp. 51–72). New York: Nova.

Oers, B. van & Poland, M. (2007). Schematising activities as a means for young children to think abstractly. *Mathematics Education Research Journal,* 19 (2), 10–22.

Parreren, C. van & Carpay, J. A. M. (1972). *Sovjetpsychologen aan het woord* [Soviet psychologists speaking]. Groningen: Wolters-Noordhoff.

Poland, M. (2007). *The treasures of schematising. The effects of schematising in early childhood on the learning processes and outcomes in later mathematical understanding* (Dissertation). Amsterdam: VU Press.

Pompert, B. (2003). *Thema's en taal* [Themes and language-education]. Assen: van Gorcum.

Vygotsky, L. S. (1978). *Mind in society.* Cambridge, MA: Harvard University Press.

Wells, G. (1998). *Dialogic Inquiry.* Cambridge: Cambridge University Press.

Part III

Global Politics Shaping Local Childhoods

13 Motivation and Behaviour in Russian Schools

The Impact of Globalisation upon the Soviet Educational Legacy

Julian Elliott

Recent reforms to education systems across the world have, unsurprisingly, tended to place great emphasis upon school practices as the means to raise standards and cope with what is widely perceived to be declining behaviour on the part of young people across many of the world's countries. While it is a truism that teachers, and schools, are of vital significance in inculcating positive student attitudes and behaviour, it is nevertheless important to recognise the impact of broader socioeconomic and sociocultural influences that play a major role in everyday interactions and practices (Bronfenbrenner & Morris, 2006). As influences at all levels of any given ecosystem are typically reciprocal (Elliott & Tudge, 2007) it is often difficult to separate out the ways by which each plays a part in fostering children's development. However, the experience of Russia since 1991 offers a unique and invaluable perspective on the interplay of key factors that may help when considering motivational and behavioural challenges confronted by all societies

The Soviet legacy

Education in the former Soviet Union was long considered to be one of its success stories (Canning, Moock, & Heleniak, 1999) with high standards of behaviour and achievement being notable features (Muckle, 1990). In this section I outline some of the ways in which this was achieved. A key component appears to have been a remarkable sense of continuity between the 1930s and the early 1990s (Hufton & Elliott, 2000) in which relatively minor changes arose incrementally through researched and planned development. Classroom practices, expectations of students and the classroom assessment system were remarkably consistent over this period. As one Western researcher visiting Soviet classrooms (Schweisfurth, 1998) noted:

> Teachers were bemused and amused when queried about the reasoning behind such classroom routines as putting books in a certain place on the desk, or raising hands in a certain way. Things had always been so and they hadn't really thought about it. (p. 3)

Given this scenario, it is hardly surprising that the upheavals of the late 1990s proved to be so traumatic for teachers and parents. It was also a troubling time for a whole generation of children for whom so much of their cultural legacy seemed to be ill-equipped to help them to cope with future challenges.

The main outline of the schooling system was put into place in the early and mid-1930s. Schools (and classes) were comprehensive in their intake, and served a particular geographical area. Although there were attempts to develop distinctively communist curricula shortly after the Revolution, Lenin had been concerned to maintain an element of European high culture which he considered had a meaning beyond class (Fitzpatrick, 1999). Lenin's wife encouraged the importation of progressive American educational approaches (Dewey being particularly influential at this time) but Stalin's subsequent rise to power saw the end of experimental approaches and, with it, Russia's "brief flirtation with Western progressivism" (Alexander, 2000). Stalin, concerned that experimental curricula might be incompatible with the specialised division of labour for the new Soviet State to achieve its modernising aims, oversaw the deployment of an academic and encyclopaedic curriculum, a formulation that could be traced back to Tsarist times. (For a detailed discussion of schooling under Stalin, see Holmes, 2005.)

Under the Soviet system, academic education was conceived as part of the highly important process of "upbringing" (*vospitanie*) – guiding the child towards becoming "a new Communist man" (*sic*). Undoubtedly the Soviet education system contained highly indoctrinatory elements, but *vospitanie* also incorporated many elements of the socialisation and acculturation of the young (cf. Bereday, Brickman, & Read, 1960) that are, arguably, also found in non-Communist societies. Other earlier roots can be found in Russian Orthodoxy, which perceived a relationship between the state, family authority and values and the development of spiritual merit.

As noted above, Western observers have often remarked favourably upon the high levels of motivation and discipline of Russian children (Muckle, 1990; Alexander, 2000). In his many observations in Russian schools, four decades ago, Bronfenbrenner was similarly struck by the positive behaviour of most Soviet youngsters:

> In their external actions, they are well-mannered, attentive, and industrious. In informal conversations, they reveal a strong motivation to learn, a readiness to serve their society, and—in general—ironically enough for a culture committed to a materialistic philosophy, what can only be described as an idealistic attitude towards life. In keeping with this general orientation, relationships with parents, teachers and upbringers are those of respectful but affectionate friendship. The discipline of the collective is accepted and regarded as justified, even when severe as judged by Western standards ... it is apparent that instances of aggressiveness, violation of rules, or other antisocial behaviour are genuinely rare. (Extract from Research Report at the 1963

International Congress of Psychology, reproduced in Bronfenbrenner, 1970, p. 76)

Behaviour was strongly conditioned by the influence of peers. The work of Makarenko in the 1920s and 1930s, with abandoned and delinquent children, demonstrated how skilful adult intervention in a cohesive children's grouping could be a powerful means for bringing about growth in moral and social learning (although see Holmes, 2005, pp. 76–78 for discussion of the Makarenko "mythology"). Children's natural desire for affiliation and friendship could be channelled through their shared participation in valued, common tasks which, in turn, gained reflexive importance as a means of affiliation and friendship. It was part of the "upbringer's" (parent's or teacher's) competence, especially in the early stages of education, to develop the child's social skills for, and an attachment to, collective ways of working. In his classic study of childhood socialisation in the US and the Soviet Union, Bronfenbrenner (1970) described in detail the ways by which these early socialisation experiences impacted upon later behaviour. Between the ages of three and six years, most young children left their home for supervised group activities. As part of these, children learned how to cooperate, to subjugate their own desires to those of the group, and to defer to the authority of adults (Tudge, 1991). Formal schooling in Russia commenced at the age of seven. Having absorbed and internalised the importance of deferring to the needs of the group, Soviet children learned patriotic songs and stories that would underpin both their education and moral upbringing (Markowitz, 2000). This was often a far from negative experience as many children benefited greatly from the warm, nurturing and caring environment that these settings usually provided (Markowitz, 2000). For any who found it difficult to accept the behavioural standards expected, the threat of exclusion from the Pioneers (ages 9–14) or when older, the Komsomol, was both real and potent. In general, however, most children were accepted into these organisations, albeit after several recruiting rounds, yet clearly, the threat was still meaningful and influential.

As well as in its impact in the area of moral education and character formation, the collective offered teachers a powerful means of managing class and individual motivation for academic learning. In effect, the class could be brought to share in standard-setting and to exert a peer discipline on student misbehaviour or lack of effort in study at home or in class. Thus the use of the collective resulted in the harnessing of powerful peer group influences that supported and maintained existing adult values and objectives.

> Not only does the peer group in the U.S.S.R. act to support behaviour consistent with the values of the adult society, but it also succeeds in introducing its members to take personal initiative and responsibility for developing and retaining such behaviour in others. (Bronfenbrenner, 1970, p. 80)

Bronfenbrenner (1967) noted that the role of the peer group in the Soviet Union was not, as in the US, left mainly to chance but rather, was the "result of explicit policy and practice" (p. 206) whereby the peer group was used as an agent of socialisation geared to encouraging identification with societal values.

In his writings, Bronfenbrenner (1970) highlighted the Soviet state's systematic attention to detail that prevailed at this time. To illustrate, he drew upon a manual written for teachers and Pioneer leaders that provided direct guidance on appropriate procedures. Here there exist elements of both competition and collaboration. Addressing the children's very first day in school, for example, the manual notes that instructing them to "All sit straight" does not "reach the sensibilities of the pupils and does not activate them". Rather, the teacher should say, "Let's see which row can sit the straightest" as it has a number of psychological advantages:

> The children not only try to do everything as well as possible themselves, but also take an evaluative attitude towards those who are undermining the achievement of the row. If similar measures arousing the spirit of competition in the children are systematically applied by experienced teachers in the primary classes, then gradually the children themselves begin to monitor the behavior of their comrades and remind those of them who forget about the rules set by the teacher, not to forget what needs to be done and what should not be done. The teacher soon has helpers. (Novikova, 1959, cited in Bronfenbrenner, 1970, p. 55)

While the phrasing that the teacher is recommended to use here would not be dissimilar to that observable in many Western contexts, it is the deliberate and systemic emphasis upon developing positive peer influences that renders its meaning very different. Although the Russian teacher was initially key in setting and maintaining standards, gradually the children were encouraged to take on monitorial roles. In the first grade of primary school, monitors had responsibility for recording teacher evaluations; during the second grade, they were taught to make the evaluations themselves. In the third grade, they were taught to make criticisms publicly. But, more importantly, the children were asked to see if they could enter into competition with the monitors to highlight their own areas for improvement. For some Westerners, this may seem like an Orwellian exercise in mind control; for others it may be construed as a powerful means of inducing self-regulation and self-discipline.

Bronfenbrenner argued that, in contrast, American peers were more likely to encourage deviance from adult norms. In one comparative study, Bronfenbrenner (1967), found Russian twelve-year-olds to be more resistant than Americans to promptings to engage in anti-social behaviour and more responsive to adult standards of behaviour. While this was particularly true for Russian girls (see also Muckle, 1998), Bronfenbrenner found that Russian boys were also more adult oriented than their counterparts in the other countries that he and his research team studied. In another study, he and his colleagues (Devereux, Bronfenbrenner, & Rodgers, 1965) found that the negative influence of peers was even stronger in England, with children readily following the promptings of peers to engage in socially disapproved activities.

For all the faults of the Soviet educational system in producing a sometimes crushing uniformity, in offering an overloaded and overtaxing curriculum, in limiting students' freedom of expression and opportunities to challenge received knowledge (Muckle, 1990), the Russian school at the end of the Soviet period was largely characterised by high educational standards and disciplined and engaged students (Alexander, 2000; Elliott, Hufton, Willis, & Illushin, 2005). While moves towards greater democratisation of learning and adult–child relationships were evident at this time, these were, in the main, successfully accommodated, no doubt in part because of the longstanding Russian tradition of respect for teachers and schooling. Such pressures, however, were to increase considerably in the decade following the end of the Soviet Union.

Educational Continuity at a Time of Social Discontinuity

The end of the Soviet regime resulted in significant social and economic upheavals in Russian society with what appeared to be obvious consequences for schooling. However, my research, undertaken during the 1990s (Elliott, Hufton, Hildreth, & Illushin, 1999; Elliott, Hufton, Illushin, & Lauchlan, 2001a; Elliott, Hufton, Illushin, & Willis, 2001b; Elliott, Hufton, Willis, & Illushin, 2005; Hufton & Elliott, 2000; Hufton, Elliott, & Illushin, 2002, 2003) suggested that Russia's tradition of impressive educational standards, underpinned by high levels of motivation and engagement (Bucur & Eklof, 1999; Bronfenbrenner, 1970; Canning et al., 1999), was continuing (see also Alexander, 2000). To the surprise of our research group, during the second half of the1990s, we found that despite intense social, economic and ideological change, and reduced and insecure funding for education, there seemed to have been little impact on either students' attitudes and behaviours, or teachers' practices, in the many schools that we visited. Like Alexander, who was conducting a detailed cross-cultural study of primary education at this time, we found that schools appeared to be marked by:

> ... a continuity and stability in pedagogic values and practices from Soviet days which contrasted markedly with post-Soviet policies and rhetoric and with the economic and social dislocation of the world outside the school. (Alexander, 1998, p. 19)

During this period, schools appeared to be remarkably similar to those that had been described during the Soviet period, and shortly afterwards by Bereday et al. (1960), Grant (1972), Dunstan (1978, 1992), Shturman (1988), Muckle (1990), Holmes, Read, and Voskresenskaya (1995) and Schweisfurth

(1998). Far from being disrupted by the wider social turbulence of the time, it seemed as though schools were acting as enclaves for the preservation of at least a measure of familiar normality, both for their students and for their communities (O'Brien, 2000; Alexander, 2000).

Our studies in St. Petersburg, conducted in the second half of the 1990s, reported student behaviour and orientations that strongly echoed findings from Bronfenbrenner's studies of a very different world operating some three decades earlier. In our observations, behaviour in class and around the school was overwhelmingly positive and the students we interviewed, both formally (Hufton et al., 2002; Elliott et al., 2005) and informally, presented accounts in which they were actively pro-learning and in which they shared precepts of propriety and due behaviour with their teachers. Where we observed a small proportion of children in the classrooms who were seemingly less motivated and engaged than their peers, the typical response was more likely to be cognitive withdrawal rather than disruption, a phenomenon similarly noted by Glowka (1995) in a comparative study of German and Russian students

In addition to the high standards of behaviour and motivation that we observed at this time, we were particularly struck by two highly influential factors that had persisted from the Soviet period: a) continuing belief in education as, primarily, a means to personal development, and b) continuing and powerful pro-adult peer influence.

The Purpose and Value of Education

The importance of education in any society will largely depend upon the traditional value that scholarship and erudition have held and the current economic and vocational opportunities that pertain (Broadfoot, Osborn, Planel, & Sharpe, 2000). In the Russia of the mid-1990s these two influences appeared to be pulling in opposing directions. However, in comparing the attitudes of students in St. Petersburg (Russia), Kentucky (US) and Sunderland (England) (Elliott et al., 1999, 2001a; Hufton et al., 2002) we found that our Russian informants (aged 14–15 years) were still strongly resistant to the highly instrumental views of education that were held by the English and American students. Russian children in our studies prioritised the role of education as, first and foremost, a means of self-improvement: scholarship was widely seen as a means to become erudite and cultured. For these students, interviewed during the economic turmoil that followed the end of the Soviet Union, education should not be seen in wholly instrumental terms. As one sixteen-year-old informed us,

> (Being educated) … is more … important [than merely making money]. It may be the aim of life.

More than half of those whom we canvassed in a large survey (Elliott et al., 1999) highlighted "Being an educated person" as the main reason for working hard in school, a factor significantly under-emphasised by their English and US peers who, unsurprisingly, highlighted instrumental reasons: access to college and a well-paid career.

Even more telling were the responses of our Russian adolescent informants in in-depth interviews where the importance of being cultured/educated again emerged as a common feature:

> It is good to become an educated person to deal with people from a certain circle.

> An educated person will always feel well in the society.

> It is good to talk with an educated person.

> It is nice to feel yourself educated, to be able to talk with other educated people, feeling that you have got the same level of knowledge they do.

At this time ostentatiously wealthy "new Russians" were beginning to emerge, many of whom were benefiting from new commercial opportunities that did not appear to require high levels of education (Nikandrov, 1995). Our questioning explored whether pursuing high levels of education was desirable given the economic possibilities available out of school. The great majority of informants rejected such a suggestion, one stating:

> I think that we are to become persons, not machines for making money ... A man doesn't live for money only ... something else is also important.

When asked what this was, she replied:

> Well, spiritual values, a soul ... not only material things.

Another informant agreed that the suggestion that leaving school to pursue greater wealth was understandable given that many educated people such as teachers, scientists and doctors did not lead wealthy lives. She found the situation personally upsetting:

> Some people observing this may think, "What do I need education for? – I'll live better without it." Well, for me now, education is obligatory. I wouldn't be able to live without it. I need a sort of spiritual thing to live on. The sort of life when you are rich and not educated – I think that this can't satisfy me.

Reflecting the view of education as a means of personal development, one informant stated:

I personally think that money is not something to value. In this world it is more important to build your personality. I would think that you haven't reached your potential.

Similar findings were discovered in a comparative Russian–Finnish study (Laihiala-Kankainen & Rasčetina, 2003) in which upper-secondary school students were asked to write essays on the purpose of education. While students in both countries attested to its importance, the Russians tended to see education as having an absolute value in itself, while the Finns placed greater emphasis upon its instrumental function in the acquisition of useful skills. In line with the traditional emphasis upon being cultured, the Russians were more likely to say that education helped one to be "interesting", to be capable of entering into conversation, and to be respected by others.

In undertaking this series of interviews we had sought a sample that would reflect varying degrees of commitment to academic achievement. However, despite the anonymity and confidentiality of our research process, we found it hard to find students who were prepared to decry the importance of education. However, the response to our questioning by one student, identified by his teachers as unmotivated, was particularly telling:

Many teachers say I'm clever ... but I became lazy recently, so I don't do homework properly. I think that if I start doing everything at home, I may become much better. To be honest, I feel like putting all my lessons aside and doing nothing. The thing I love to do most of all at the moment is just to lie on the sofa and dream about something.

When asked what he was dreaming about, he replied

About everything ... how to change the world ... like in the story *Oblomov* that you may know.

Here we have a highly revealing anecdote about the importance attached to erudition in Russian culture. Despite his seeming detachment from school and his difficulty in motivating himself to study, our informant was still eager to present himself as in some way analogous to a famously slothful character from nineteenth-century Russian literature. Such a remark could hardly be imagined coming from the mouths of any of our English or American informants. Indeed, the great majority of Kentucky students tended to see education primarily as helping them to avoid a life of "flipping burgers" or "pumping gas". Given the importance placed upon monetary success in American society (Merton, 1938), the Kentucky State Department's motto "Education Pays" would appear to be a highly percipient means of motivation.

Peer Influences

As noted above, the positive pro-adult influence of peers was a key factor identified by Bronfenbrenner in his study of Soviet socialisation practices in the 1960s. When we conducted our interviews in St. Petersburg some three decades later, children's socialising experiences were no longer heavily underpinned by Soviet ideology or by organised groupings such as the Pioneers or Komsomol. Nevertheless, an adolescent counter-culture in school was still not evident. In line with traditional expectations, we found Russian students reporting that their classmates exerted pressures in a prosocial fashion (Elliott et al., 1999, 2001a; Hufton et al., 2002). In our surveys, Russian children were significantly more likely to state that their classmates spurred them to engage in their classwork and conduct themselves as their teachers would wish. In a comparative study of 9- to 10-year-olds (Elliott et al., 2001a), for example, the ratio of those reporting positive to negative influences was 7:1. In contrast, our sample of English children was more likely to report negative, rather than positive, peer influences (by a ratio of 2:1).

Unlike classrooms in England and the United States, where students are often eager not to appear too enthused, lest they be dismissed as nerds or swots (see Elliott et al., 2005, pp. 118–132), high-achieving students in Russia were still generally admired and respected as long as they exhibited desirable personal qualities such as modesty and generosity towards their peers:

> I think that how a person is studying is less important than what sort of person he is. How he treats others, what sort of relationships he has … The most important thing is that he doesn't become snobbish.

> I think that the pupils who have a sort of "brain", who think well are the popular and attractive ones. … They are respected for their cleverness.

> I respect those who work hard and do well. In our class, there is no envy, we feel positively about (hard-working) students.

For these, and other, reasons, student behaviour in Russian schools during the 1990s continued to be quite different to that of many Western countries (Akiba, LeTendre, Baker & Goesling, 2002; Alexander, 2000; Elliott et al., 1999, 2001a). However, despite the positive impressions gleaned by Western observers, a growing disquiet about the orientations of young people in Russia was beginning to emerge within Russian society.

The Impact of Globalisation at a Time of Social Upheaval

> In times of dramatic social changes, it is particularly true that adolescents are the last children of the old system and the first adults of the new. (Van Hoorn et al., 2000, p. 4)

As the millennium drew to a close, Russian academics and social commentators began to report diminishing levels of motivation and engagement in school, and expressed concern about a weakening of educational standards (Dolzhenko. 1998). It appeared that the remarkable continuity of the experience of schooling across several generations could no longer hold in the face of such major social, political and economic upheaval. Factors that were seen as particularly influential in undermining schooling processes included changes in employment practices, widespread shifts in broader societal values, an apparent weakening of the prestige of education and the professions, and a diminishing role for education as a means to achieve social mobility.

Reflecting global influences, strong trends towards competitiveness and individualism were being reflected in the education system by a plethora of structural and pedagogic reforms resulting in potentially divisive and alienating educational hierarchies and inequalities (Andriushina, 2000; Konstantinovskii & Khokhlushkina, 2000). A massive proliferation of specialist schools catering for more able, or more wealthy, students, resulted in the demoralisation of young people and teachers in other, often impoverished, under-resourced schools. This contributed to the rise of an alienated student underclass, many of whom dropped out of schooling altogether (Cherednichenko, 2000; Grigorenko, 1998; Karpov & Lisovskaya, 2005). The opportunities for the new wealthy to gain educational advantage contrasted with an underlying belief that schools in Soviet times were more or less equal. This was not wholly true, as various specialist schools did exist, but these were primarily for a very small proportion of the political elite, or for the exceptionally talented.

The new educational environment was also seen to be affecting the nature of teacher–student relationships. Schmidt (2001), for example, noted that the growth of a selective and competitive educational "market", together with the decline in the perceived importance of *vospitanie*, combined to threaten the traditional way that Russian teachers had catered for the emotional needs of their students. In surveys in a number of Russian cities, reported by Schmidt (2001), many students stated that they miss the warmth and affection shown by their teachers in the past. Similarly, Rimashevskaia (2007) comments that the divisions between rich and poor students have led schools to lose the character of tolerance that was inherent to them.

Broader social and economic changes were seen by many Russian commentators at the turn of the century as leading to an increased emphasis upon materialism, high levels of impoverishment resulting in serious deterioration in the quality of nutrition and young people's health (Baranov, 1998), and a general breakdown of traditional moral codes and values (Rutkevich, 1997). While the country is now becoming stronger economically, during the immediate post-Soviet years the adverse material position of most young people in Russia appeared not to be greatly influenced by how hard they worked or by their educational level (Zubok, 1999). Rather, what affected income levels was the nature of their employment, something that often appeared to be independent of performance at school or university. Indeed, in the mid-1990s, it was noted that, "… the more education one has nowadays, the less money one earns" (Nikandrov, 1995, p. 54).

A further complication was the radical shift in the social order: many of those at the socioeconomic top of society had been at the margins only a few years ago, whereas those who were recently at the social pinnacle now found themselves at the margins, with practical skills appearing to be more valuable than the advanced analytical abilities of the more educated (Sternberg & Grigorenko, 2000). Observing the growing disparity between the new, rather poorly educated, wealthy and the impoverished majority (often seen as including university professors and schoolteachers, although, for this group, the situation is now improving), the importance of education began to be questioned by students who increasingly sought to position themselves more favourably in their rapidly changing world. Although some highly educated individuals have succeeded in the new Russia, primarily those in professions such as business and law, a large proportion of the intelligentsia has become part of the newly poor (Ryvkina, 2007). In a telling anecdote, White (2001) describes an encounter with a woman who tearfully recounted a conversation in which her son scornfully rebuked his father's poverty:

> You have two degrees, yet you come to me begging for cigarettes. (p. 11)

As a result of these multiple influences, the value of education as a means for individual growth (an element so strongly portrayed in our earlier interviews) gradually declined. The only kinds of knowledge and skills that were deemed to be of worth were those that could bring the possessor immediate material benefits (Andreev, 2003).

In addition to economic instability, the weakening of the traditional mechanisms of social regulation that largely operated through state and societal institutions during the Soviet period resulted in a social and moral vacuum. Shorn of the old ideals of country and collective and perceiving the views of their elders as outdated and irrelevant, growing anxiety and alienation on the part of young people was attributed by social commentators to the loss of longstanding cultural and historical values. Instead, key sources for how to live one's life were seen as being largely gleaned from mass culture and mass media (Karpukhin, 2000). The effect of this is captured beautifully in the lament of one Russian intellectual:

> ... the desanctification of attitudes toward the world and society, the decline of the ideal, exalted, romantic aspect of life, have been accompanied by its banalification, rendering it more bourgeois and susceptible to the laws of the market, converting it into a commodity. The old symbols and imagery, which expressed lofty and oftentimes unattainable ideals are being turned into products of mass spiritual assimilation—but an assimilation that is illusory, limited to audio-visual familiarity. Ideals are

being turned into products of mass spiritual consumption rather than assimilation. (Erasov, 1994, p. 217)

Given these rapid changes, young people at the end of the last century began to question the authority of the adult world as the experience of their forefathers appeared to have lost its value. It proved difficult for many Russian parents to have confidence in the messages they would wish to pass on to their children, or for children to learn from their parents' example (Shurygina, 2000). As parental influence began to wane so did those of other adult authorities (Bocharova & Lerner, 2000; Sergeev, 1999). Students became increasingly alienated in school, not because these institutions had changed for the worse but because they proved so slow to change to better prepare young people for the economic realities of adulthood (Iartscv, 2000). Illustrating this point, Schmidt (2001) cites an interview with a 16-year-old girl who stated:

> School doesn't teach what's important any longer ... How to live, how to go on living in this almost unimaginably difficult world. (p. 131)

Such confusion was heightened by teacher uncertainty about the messages they should give their students. Teachers in Russia (Elliott & Tudge, 2007) and, indeed, in other former Soviet societies (Harkness et al., 2007), have struggled to reconcile traditional teacher–student hierarchies with calls for youth to have greater independence and autonomy. Globalising (i.e. predominantly Western) influences that emphasise individualism, personal choice and agency and detachment from traditional ties and settings (Inglehart & Welzel, 2005) appear to have reduced adults' ability to harness peer influences in ways perceived as desirable. Socialising with peers appeared to gain prominence over more intellectual activities such as reading (Zvonovskii & Lutseva, 2004). In his examination of child socialisation in the US and the Soviet Union, Bronfenbrenner (1970) warned of the dangers to US society of highly autonomous peer groups, separated from the adult world. Ironically, as Russian peer groups become more autonomous, increasingly akin to those in Western societies, the traditionally powerful pro-adult, pro-school peer influences characteristic of Russian contexts (Bronfenbrenner, 1967; Elliott et al., 2001a; Hufton et al., 2002) appear to be declining – a factor which, if sustained, is likely to have major implications for classroom practice and behaviour (Elliott, 2007).

While lauding the high academic and behavioural standards of the Soviet period, many commentators, both Western and Russian, (e.g. Eklof, 2005; Markowitz, 2000; Muckle, 1990; Westbrook, 1994), were critical of the strong ideological component that minimised debate and controversy and often undermined students' individuality. Soviet teaching methods were seen as overly authoritarian and inflexible (Polyzoi & Dneprov, 2003) and schools were perceived as unresponsive to those students who failed to accept the emphasis upon control and conformity (Froumin, 2005). Markowitz (2000) is critical of the student passivity that resulted, whereby less-motivated students tended to withdraw rather than disrupt:

> Children learned to be passive recipients of what their elders doled out, and parents in all but the most exceptional cases were in complicity with teachers and the school administration ... Parents knew from experience that if their children were to rebel against the order of things they would risk the worst punishment of all – exclusion from the only game in town. In the main, however, it did not often occur to anyone to rebel. (p. 50)

In an age when independence of thought and the need to adapt to high challenging times are emphasised in modernised societies (Giddens, 1991), such criticisms were widely recognised as meaningful by Russian progressives and by the end of the Soviet period many Russian educators had come to believe that the time for change had arrived. Responding to calls for more democratic and individualistic emphases, new legislation, the 1992 Law of Education in the Russian Federation, was introduced that sought to increase opportunities for personal self-determination, democratic relations and the need to foster each individual's unique potential.

However, as one might expect from the simple importation of values without any corresponding means of changing what Bronfenbrenner (1995) terms "proximal processes" (these constitute the interactions between the human organism and the persons, objects, and symbols in their immediate environment), teachers were largely unaware as to how to put these ideas into practice, particularly as their professional skills and knowledge were closely bound to long-established methods (Elliott & Tudge, 2007). Some paid lip service (Eklof & Seregny, 2005) while others actively resisted calls to change, believing that traditional methods were necessary for addressing Russia's difficulties (Belkanov, 2000; Mitter, 2003; Polyzoi & Dneprov, 2003). Given these uncertainties, it was not surprising that tensions continued to build.

As other societies that have long experienced high levels of traditional adult authority move towards more democratic schooling practices, it is highly likely that problems such as those seen in Russia will be reproduced. It is sometimes poorly understood that in placing a strong emphasis upon children's autonomy and capacity for self-determination, extremely skilful classroom management is essential (Elliott & Stemler, in press), particularly in schools characterised by socioeconomic disadvantage – it is no accident that the shift to democratic student–teacher relationships played out more successfully in the elite Russian schools (Froumin, 2005). In cultures that place a premium upon individualism, individual autonomy and self-determination, teachers (and other adult authorities) will need to ensure a school climate underpinned by student self-discipline in order to avoid the anarchy that might otherwise result. However, this is particularly difficult to achieve where teachers lack confidence in their own authority and are uncertain about their professional practice. The experience of highly individualistic societies, such as those of the UK and the US, provide a salutary lesson for those nervously observing the increasing demands of young people for greater control over their lives (Elliott & Nguyen, in press). Alexander (2000), for example, describes the tensions he observed in elementary schools in the US. While high value was placed upon student autonomy and empowerment in these settings, he noted that realisation of these ideals became problematic as teachers sought to maintain order and discipline. Alexander found a strong contrast between the US and Russia where:

> In the one context the substantive messages about the nature of knowledge, teaching and learning and about behavioural norms and expectations were unambiguous yet also—bar the occasional brief reminder—tacit; in the other context they were the subject of frequent reminders by the teacher and often intense encounters ranging from negotiation to confrontation. (2000, p. 318)

Such difficulties result from pedagogic practices that reflect very different underlying value systems:

> In an authoritarian teaching culture routines will not be negotiated or contested because teachers simply will not permit this to happen, while in a teaching culture that espouses democratic values routines not only will be negotiated and contested but by definition must be. The combination of complex classroom organisation, unpredictable lesson structure and avowedly democratic pedagogy, such as we found in Michigan, is a sure-fire recipe if not for conflict then certainly for the constant testing of regulatory boundaries. (2000, pp. 385–386)

Alexander (2004) writes of the tensions he found in American schools where teachers often promoted values that seemed to be in opposition: self-fulfilment and altruism, consumerism and environmentalism, cooperation and competition, while, in the wider US, a strong sense of communal commitment was at odds with "rampant" individualism. These tensions were manifested not only in formal education goals but also in the everyday discourse and actions of both students and teachers.

After a flirtation with the West in the 1990s, disillusionment gradually set in (Elliott & Tudge, 2007; Schmidt, 2001). Many teachers, initially beguiled by Western pedagogical theory and practice actively advocated in Russia by various international bodies such as the World Bank (1996) have retreated to their former practices (Froumin, 2005). However, in keeping with the new age, they have found reduced willingness on the part of Russian students to accept their authority unquestioningly (Bocharova & Lerner, 2000).

However, more promisingly, it appears that academic success is being perceived by young Russians as increasingly important. This is in direct contrast to the 1990s where social connections, good luck and risk-taking behaviour were widely seen as more important than educational qualifications for achieving success, status and material well-being (Lisauskene, 2007;

Vishnevskii & Shapko, 2007). Drop-out rates have begun to fall and more students are spending longer in education (Arapov, 2005; Cherednichenko, 2005).

Despite ongoing concerns about deterioration in the behaviour and morals of Russian youth (Krug, Dahlberg, Mercy, Zwi, & Lozano, 2002; Ol'shanskii, Klimova, & Volzhkaia, 2000; Pickett et al., 2005), it would appear that classroom behaviour continues to be superior to that of many other industrialised nations (OECD, 2003). However, the traditional regard for education as something intrinsically valuable has been replaced by more instrumental drivers. As social turbulence lessened and Russian society gradually shifted from one largely based upon knowledge to one based upon consumption (Maksakovskii, 2006), the economic benefits of education have become more salient. As in the West, education is now widely seen as the key to entry to prestigious universities and high-paying careers. As a result, the importance of intellectual life has declined (Vishnevskii & Shapko, 2007) and "[t]he paramount function of education associated with the acquisition of knowledge, has basically disappeared" (Lisauskene, 2006, p. 8).

The Russian experience has provided a fascinating "natural experiment" in which globalising influences have been variously welcomed, accommodated and resisted by students, their parents and teachers (Elliott & Tudge, 2007). A breaking away from traditional attachments and identities, a greater emphasis upon individualisation, and the seeming inability of existing institutions to guide young people is not solely a Russian experience but, rather, a phenomenon of all late-modern or postmodern societies (Giddens, 1991; Inglehart & Welzel, 2005). To observe the influence of growing instrumentality and individualism, the increasing tendency for adolescents to be critical of their teachers, the growth of powerful peer cultures with the concomitant decline of adult influence, and the physical or intellectual withdrawal of a significant minority of students from schooling, is to witness some of the problems of the Western world being superimposed upon a very different culture with very different traditions.

Bronfenbrenner (2001) has remarked upon the "growing chaos" in the lives of American children, marked by growing cynicism, disillusionment, mistrust, self-centredness and a loss of faith in their society's basic institutions. Is this a vision of the future that will prove difficult for all modernising societies to avoid?

The Future for Russian Education

> The individual's own developmental life course is seen as embedded in and powerfully shaped by the conditions and events occurring during the historical period through which the person lives. (Bronfenbrenner, 1995, p. 641)

While a cursory glance at this statement might suggest a deterministic conception in which we are all wholly conditioned by powerful external forces, this is far from the position espoused in Bronfenbrenner's dialectical theory. Context, while important, does not act in a unidirectional fashion upon individuals (see Elliott & Tudge, 2007; Tudge, 2008). Rather, both broader context and characteristics of individuals affect the nature of those proximal processes that are key to development.

For this reason, we should not see the trends in Russian education that have been outlined in this chapter as slavishly following an oversimplified "western" trajectory. The initial attraction, to many Russian educationalists, of "modernising" educational ideas and practices enthusiastically promulgated by Western educational advisers, consultants and funding agencies, declined as many teachers who were initially persuaded of their value subsequently struggled to put the ideas and principles into practice. Elliott and Tudge (2007) note that it is hardly surprising that large macro-level changes have not translated speedily into modifications of those educational practices that have evolved over many years, particularly where new approaches and ideas have originated in cultures with very different basic values. Teachers who have participated in a particular set of educational practices for generations are likely to be more resistant to change than their students who may well be better equipped to profit from whatever the new system has to offer.

Rather than perceiving students and teachers as passively shaped by global forces, we need to ascribe to them a greater degree of agency; significant and long-lasting shifts in human behaviour do not simply occur solely because of changes at the level of culture or society. As today's Russian students grow up, they will necessarily influence their culture's values and beliefs. As new generations of teachers, schooled during the post-Soviet years, emerge, the long-lasting continuity of Russian school practices may slowly dissipate. What will be particularly interesting to observe over the next few generations are the ways by which traditional Russian educational values and practices are reconciled with the seemingly inexorable drive towards "modernisation".

References

Akiba, M., LeTendre, G. K., Baker, D. P., & Goesling, B. (2002). Student victimization: National and school system effects on school violence in 37 nations. *American Educational Research Journal*, 39, 829–853.

Alexander, R. (1998). *Culture in pedagogy, pedagogy in culture.* Coventry: University of Warwick, Centre for Research in Elementary and Primary Education.

Alexander, R. (2000). *Culture and pedagogy: International comparisons in primary education.* Oxford: Blackwell.

Alexander, R. (2004). *L'apprentisage, la civilité et la culture: Perspectives internationals.* [Learning, behaviour and culture: International perspectives.]. Paper presented at the third DESCO Conference (2003), Paris. Reprinted in A. Christophe (Ed.), *L'apprentissage de la civilité à l'École: Regards croisés* (pp. 7–14). Paris: DESCO.

Andreev, A. L. (2003). Society and education. *Russian Education and Society*, 45 (11), 89–103.

Andriushina, E. V. (2000). The family and the adolescent's health. *Russian Education and Society*, 42 (4), 61–87.

Arapov, M. V. (2005). The higher education boom in Russia: Scale, causes and consequences. *Russian Education and Society*, 47 (1), 7–27.

Baranov, A. (1998). A real threat to the nation's future. *Russian Education and Society*, 40 (1), 6–16.

Belkanov, N. A. (2000). Pedagogicheskaya sovetologiya kak nauchny fenomen [Pedagogical Sovietology as a scientific phenomenon]. *Pedagogika*, 6 (5), 81–87.

Bereday, G. Z. F., Brickman, W. W., & Read, G. E. (Eds.) (1960). *The changing Soviet school*. London: Constable.

Bocharova, O. & Lerner, A. (2000). Characteristics of the way of life of adolescents. *Russian Education and Society*, 42 (6), 37–48.

Broadfoot, P., Osborn, M., Planel, C., & Sharpe, K. (2000). *Promoting quality in learning: Does England have the answer?* London: Cassell.

Bronfenbrenner, U. (1967). Response to pressure from peers versus adults among Soviet and American school children. *International Journal of Psychology*, 2, 199–207.

Bronfenbrenner, U. (1970). *The two worlds of childhood*. New York: Russell Sage Foundation.

Bronfenbrenner, U. (1995). Development ecology through space and time: A future perspective. In P. Moen, G. Elder, & K. Luscher (Eds.), *Examining lives in context: Perspectives on the ecology of human development* (pp. 619–647). Washington, DC: American Psychological Association.

Bronfenbrenner, U. (2001). Growing chaos in the lives of children, youth, and families: How can we turn it around? In J. C. Westman (Ed.), *Parenthood in America* (pp. 197–210). Madison: University of Wisconsin Press.

Bronfenbrenner, U. & Morris, P. (2006). The ecology of developmental processes. In W. Damon & R. Lerner (Eds.), *Handbook of child psychology*, 6th edn (pp. 793–829). New York: John Wiley.

Bucur, M., & Eklof, B. (1999). Russia and Eastern Europe. In R. F. Arnove & C. A. Torres (Eds.), *Comparative education: The dialectic of the global and the local* (pp. 371–392). Lanham, MD: Rowman & Littlefield.

Canning, M., Moock, P., & Heleniak, T. (1999). *Reforming education in the regions of Russia*. World Bank Technical Paper No. 457. Washington, DC: The World Bank.

Cherednichenko, G. A. (2000). School reform in the 1990s. *Russian Education and Society*, 42 (4), 61–87.

Cherednichenko, G. A. (2005). The life trajectories of young people at different stages of education. *Russian Education and Society*, 47 (5), 7–29.

Chuprov, V. & Zubok, I. (1997). Social conflict in the sphere of the education of youth. *Education in Russia, the Independent States and Eastern Europe*, 15 (2), 47–58.

Devereux, E. C., Bronfenbrenner, U., & Rodgers, R. R. (1965). *Child-rearing in England and the United States: A cross-national comparison*. Unpublished manuscript.

Dolzhenko, L. (1998). The college student today: A social portrait and attitudes toward schooling. *Russian Education and Society*, 40 (11), 6–15.

Dunstan, J. (1978). *Paths to excellence and the Soviet school*. Windsor: NFER.

Dunstan J. (Ed.) (1992). *Soviet education under Perestroika*. London: Routledge.

Eklof, B. (2005). Introduction – Russian education: The past in the present. In B. Eklof, L. Holmes, & V. Kaplan (Eds.), *Educational reform in post-Soviet Russia* (pp. 1–20). London: Cass.

Eklof, B. & Seregny, S. (2005). Teachers in Russia: State, community and profession. In B. Eklof, L. Holmes and V. Kaplan (Eds.), *Educational reform in post-Soviet Russia* (pp. 197–220). London: Cass.

Elliott, J. G. (2007). Ecosystemic perspectives on student behaviour: Why teachers in training need to see the bigger picture. In T. E. Scruggs & M. A. Mastropieri (Eds.), *Advances in learning and behavioural disabilities: Vol. 20. International perspectives* (pp. 57–77). Oxford: Elsevier.

Elliott, J. G., & Nguyen, M. (in press). Western influences on the East: Lessons for the East and West. In T. Oon Seng & D. M. McInerney (Eds.), *Research on multicultural education and international perspectives. Vol. 7. What the West can learn from the East: Asian perspectives on the psychology of learning and motivation*. Greenwich, CT: Information Age Publishing.

Elliott, J. G., & Stemler, S. E. (in press). Teacher authority, tacit knowledge and the training of teachers. In T. E. Scruggs & M. A. Mastropieri (Eds.), *Advances in learning and behavioral disabilities: Vol. 21. Personnel preparation*. Oxford: Elsevier.

Elliott, J. G., & Tudge, J. R. H. (2007). The impact of the West on post-Soviet Russian education: Change and resistance to change. *Comparative Education*, 43 (1), 93–112.

Elliott, J. G., Hufton, N., Hildreth, A., & Illushin, L. (1999). Factors influencing educational motivation: A study of attitudes, expectations and behaviour of children in Sunderland, Kentucky and St. Petersburg. *British Educational Research Journal*, 25, 75–94.

Elliott, J. G., Hufton, N., Illushin, L., & Lauchlan, F. (2001a). Motivation in the junior years: International perspectives on children's attitudes, expectations and behaviour and their relationship to educational achievement. *Oxford Review of Education*, 27, 37–68.

Elliott, J. G., Hufton, N., Illushin, L., & Willis, W. (2001b). "The kids are doing all right": Differences in parental satisfaction, expectation and attribution in St. Petersburg, Sunderland and Kentucky, *Cambridge Journal of Education*, 31, 179–204.

Elliott, J. G., Hufton, N., Willis, W., & Illushin, L. (2005). *Motivation, engagement and educational performance: International perspectives on contexts for learning*. London: Palgrave.

Erasov, B. (1994). *Social Culturology*, Part 2. Moscow: n. p.

Fitzpatrick, S. (1999). *Everyday Stalinism – ordinary life in extraordinary times: Soviet Russia in the 1930s*. New York: Oxford University Press.

Froumin, I. D. (2005). Democratizing the Russian school: Achievements and setbacks. In B. Eklof, L. Holmes, & V. Kaplan (Eds.), *Educational reform in post-Soviet Russia* (pp. 129–152). London: Cass.

Giddens, A. (1991). *Modernity and self-identity*. London: Polity Press.

Glowka, D. (1995). *Schulen und Unterricht im Vergleich: Rusland/Deutschland* [Schools and teaching in comparison: Russia and Germany]. New York: Waxmann Verlag.

Grant, N. (1972). *Soviet education*, 3rd edn. Harmondsworth: Penguin.

Grigorenko, E. L. (1998). Russian "defectology": Anticipating perestroika in the field, *Journal of Learning Disabilities*, 31 (2), 193–207.

Harkness, S., Blom, M., Oliva, A., Moscardino, U., Zylicz, P. O., Bermudez, M. R., Feng, X., Carrasco-Zylicz, A., Axia, G., & Super, C. M. (2007). Teachers' ethnotheories of the "ideal student" in five Western cultures. *Comparative Education*, 43, 113–135.

Holmes, B., Read, G. H., & Voskresenskaya, N. (1995). *Russian education: Tradition and transition*. New York: Garland Publishing.

Holmes, L. E. (2005). Schools and schooling under Stalin, 1931–1953. In B. Eklof, L. Holmes, & V. Kaplan (Eds.), *Educational reform in post-Soviet Russia* (pp. 56–101). London: Cass.

Hufton, N., & Elliott, J. G. (2000). Motivation to learn: The pedagogical nexus in the Russian school: Some implications for transnational research and policy borrowing. *Educational Studies*, 26, 115–136.

Hufton, N., Elliott, J., & Illushin, L. (2002). Motivation to learn: The elusive role of culture: Qualitative accounts from three countries. *British Educational Research Journal*, 28, 267–291.

Hufton, N. R., Elliott, J. G., & Illushin, L. (2003). Teachers' beliefs about student motivation: Similarities and differences across cultures. *Comparative Education*, 39, 367–389.

Iartsev, D. V. (2000). Characteristics of the socialisation of today's adolescent. *Russian Education and Society*, 42, 67–75.

Inglehart, R., & Welzel, C. (2005). *Modernization, cultural change and democracy: The human development sequence*. Cambridge: Cambridge University Press.

Karpov, V. & Lisovskaya, E. (2005). Educational change in time of social revolution: The case of post-Communist Russia in comparative perspective. In B. Eklof, L. Holmes, & V. Kaplan (Eds.), *Educational reform in post-Soviet Russia* (pp. 23–55). London: Cass.

Karpukhin, O. I. (2000). The young people of Russia: Characteristics of their socialisation and self-determination. *Russian Education and Society*, 42 (11), 47–57.

Konstantinovskii, D. L. & Khokhlushkina, F. A. (2000). The formation of the social behaviour of young people in the sphere of education. *Russian Education & Society*, 42 (2), 26–58.

Krug, E. G., Dahlberg, L. L., Mercy, J. A., Zwi, A. B., & Lozano, R. (Eds.) (2002). *World report on violence and health*. Geneva: World Health Organisation.

Laihiala-Kankainen, S. & Rasčetina, S. (2003). What does education mean? Educational beliefs of Russian and Finnish students. In J. Lasonen & L. Lestinen (Eds.), *Conference Proceedings. Teaching and Learning for Intercultural Understanding. Human Rights and a Culture of Peace*. UNESCO Conference on Intercultural Education, 15–18 June 2003.

Lisauskene, M. V. (2006). A new generation of Russian college students. *Russian Education and Society*, 48 (9), 6–17.

Lisauskene, M. V. (2007). The *next* generation. *Russian Education and Society*, 49 (4), 76–86.

Maksakovskii, V. P. (2006). What is hampering the development of our education? *Russian Education and Society*, 48 (3), 18–30.

Markowitz, F. (2000). *Coming of age in post-Soviet Russia*. Chicago: University of Illinois Press.

Merton, R. (1938). Social structure and anomie. *American Sociological Review*, 3, 672–682.

Mitter, W. (2003). A decade of transformation: Educational policies in Central and Eastern Europe. *International Review of Education*, 49 (1–2), 75–96.

Muckle, J. (1990). *Portrait of a Soviet school under glasnost*. London: Macmillan.

Muckle, J. (1998). Review article. [Schulen und Unterricht im Vergleich. By D. Glowka. (1995). New York: Waxmann Verlag] in *Education in Russia, The Independent States and Eastern Europe*, 16 (1), 35–41.

Nikandrov, N. D. (1995). Russian education after perestroika: The search for new values, *International Review of Education*, 41 (1–2), 47–57.

O'Brien, D. (2000). *From Moscow: Living and teaching among Russians in the 1990s*. Nottingham: Bramcote Press.

OECD (2003). *Literacy skills for the world of tomorrow: Further results from PISA 2000*. Paris: Organization for Economic Co-operation and Development.

Ol'shanskii, V. B., Klimova, S. G., & Volzhkaia, N. (2000). School students in a changing society (1982–1997), *Russian Education and Society*, 42, 44–40.

Pickett, W., Craig, W., Harel, Y., Cunningham, J., Simpson, K., Molcho, M., Mazur, J., Dostaler, S., Overpeck, M., & Currie, C. (2005). Cross-national study of fighting and weapon carrying as determinants of adolescent injury. *Pediatrics*, 116 (6), e855–e863.

Polyzoi, E. & Dneprov, E. (2003). Harnessing the forces of change: Educational transformation in Russia. In E. Polyzoi, M. Fullan, & J. P. Anchan (Eds.), *Change forces in post-Communist Eastern Europe* (pp. 13–33). London: RoutledgeFalmer.

Rimashevskaia, N. M. (2007). Children and young people are the future of Russia. *Russian Education & Society*, 49 (2), 70–86.

Rutkevich, M. (1997). Changes in the social role of the general education school in Russia. *Russian Education & Society*, 39, 6–60.

Ryvkina, R. V. (2007). The expiration of the intelligentsia's social role in post-Soviet Russia. *Russian Education and Society*, 49 (7), 5–20.

Schmidt, G. (2001). Upper secondary graduates' perceptions of school in Russia and Germany – A comparative view. In L. Limage (Ed.), *Democratizing education and educating democratic citizens* (pp. 121–139). London: Routledge.

Schweisfurth, M. (1998). *Report on visit to Perm: 2–24 April 1998*. Unpublished paper, University of Warwick, Institute of Education.

Schweisfurth, M. (2000). Teachers and democratic change in Russia and South Africa, *Education in Russia, the Independent States and Eastern Europe*, 18 (1), 2–8.

Sergeev, S. A. (1999). Youth subcultures in the Republic. *Russian Education and Society*, 41 (10), 74–91.

Shen, C. & Pedulla, J. J. (2000). The relationship between students' achievement and their self-perception of competence and rigour of mathematics and science: A cross-national analysis. *Assessment in Education*, 7, 237–253.

Shturman, D. (1988). *The Soviet Secondary School*. London: Routledge.

Shurygina, I. I. (2000). The life strategies of adolescents. *Russian Education and Society*, 42 (9), 5–24.

Siu, S. F. (1992). *Toward an understanding of Chinese American educational achievement (Report No. 2)*. Washington, DC: U.S. Department of Health and Human Services, Center on Families, Communities, Schools and Children's Learning.

Sternberg, R. J. & Grigorenko, E. L. (2000). Theme park psychology: A case study regarding human intelligence and its implications for education. *Educational Psychology Review*, 12, 247–268.

Tudge, J. R. H. (1991). Education of young children in the Soviet Union: Current practice in historical perspective. *Elementary School Journal*, 92, 121–133.

Tudge, J. R. H. (2008). *The everyday lives of young children: Culture, class, and child rearing in diverse societies*. New York: Cambridge University Press.

Van Hoorn, J. L., Komlosi, A., Suchar, E., & Samelson, D. A. (2000). *Adolescent development and rapid social change: Perspectives from Eastern Europe*. Albany, NY: SUNY Press.

Vishnevskii, I. T. & Shapko, V. T. (2007). The paradoxical young person. *Russian Education and Society*, 49 (5), 65–85.

Westbrook, M. (1994). St. Petersburg's independent schools. In A. Jones (Ed.), *Education and society in the New Russia* (pp. 103–117). Armonk, NY: M. E. Sharpe.

White, A. (2001). Teachers in contemporary provincial Russia. *Education in Russia, the Independent States and Eastern Europe*, 19 (1), 2–13.

World Bank (1996). *Russia: Education in the transition*. Washington, DC: World Bank.

Zubok, I. A. (1999). Exclusion in the study of problems of young people. *Russian Education and Society*, 41 (9), 39–53.

Zvonovskii, V. & Lutseva, S. (2004). Young people's favourite leisure activities. *Russian Education and Society*, 46 (1), 76–96.

14 Family Practices and How Children are Positioned as Active Agents

Mariane Hedegaard and Marilyn Fleer

Children develop through everyday activities participating in different practices in societal institutions, but neither society nor its institutions (i.e. families, kindergarten, school, youth clubs, etc.) are static but change over time in a dynamic interaction between persons' activities, institutional traditions for practice, societal discourse, and material conditions. Several different types of institutional practices influence children's life and development. At the same time children's development can be seen as socio-cultural tracks through different institutions.

Theoretically, we position ourselves in the cultural historical activity traditions (Vygotsky, 1998; Leontiev, 1978; Hedegaard, Chaiklin & Jensen, 1999). In this theoretical tradition, activity is a central concept (Leontiev, 1978). This conception of activity is extended in Hedegaard's use of the cultural-historical tradition so that a societal perspective is introduced, and this perspective is formulated as an institutional practice (see also Hedegaard, 1999). "Practice" is a conceptualisation of Leontiev's concept of "activity" when viewed from a societal perspective. By this it is possible to conceptualise the influences of traditions and value positions in institutionalised practices. Persons' activities can be related to institutionalised practices by the perspective of the person that participates or enters the practices. An institutional practice will have multiple activities; in each of these activities one or several persons' motives and projects can be distinguished.

The focus in this chapter is on children's upbringing and education in home practice. We will argue that home can be seen as an institution as well as school and kindergarten. Therefore home practices have to be seen as part of a more elaborated account of a wholeness approach, where different institutional practices create conditions for each other (Hedegaard, in press). From a cultural-historical activity perspective, children are seen as active participants in the activities of upbringing and education in home and school practices, thereby contributing to their own conditions for learning and development. The aim of this chapter is to differentiate the concept of practice in relation to a formal societal, a general institutional and an individual perspective, and to demonstrate how difference in family practices gives different conditions for children's participation in what can be characterised as family practice in late modern society (Giddens, 1984; Andenæs, 1998). Further the aim is to illustrate how imitation occurs during interactions and modelling of other persons' activity with whom they share motives and cognitive competences.

In the first part of this chapter the concept of practice will be related to the different way the three perspectives can be interpreted in relation to home and school. We will analyse how the *formal societal*, the *general institution* and the *individual* perspective relate to difference in conditions within the respective traditions of family and school in order to illustrate that the conception of practice has to differ in relation to the specific institutions. The second part of the chapter will illustrate variation in family practices between two families that have different economic conditions and who are located in different societies, namely Denmark and Australia.

Institutional Practice

The institutional perspective focuses on the everyday practices in institutions. This everyday practice in institutions has to be seen as knotting cultural traditions and values with personal motives and competences. A concrete institutional practice is an integral whole, realised by the activities and interactions among multiple participants. At the same time, in an institutional practice the three different perspectives can always be found and related to conditions for the practices. The *formal societal* is reflected in historically evolved traditions and value positions in a society that are formalised into laws and regulations; the *general institutional* can be found in informal community traditions and discourses related to school and home; and the *individual* traditions can be seen in shared activities of persons in a specific institution (i.e., a specific home or a specific school). Figure 14.1 presents a graphic representation of a model of institutional practice. All three perspectives are necessary to understand an institutional practice and the variations within an institutional practice. If one of these three aspects is missing, then the idea of an institutionalised practice does not exist. Each aspect – formal, general, individual – is a conditions for the others. Within

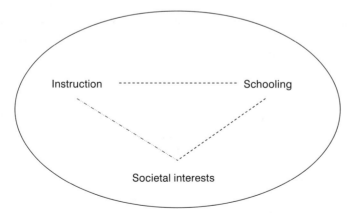

Figure 14.1 A model of institutional practice

or across institutions one can find more or less permanent groups that can be seen as *arenas for activities* (i.e., friendship groups, and neighbourhood groups). From a life course perspective a child's participation in the different institutional practices changes as s/he finishes some and enters new ones, thereby dominating activities in a persons' life change over time. The first institution that a child enters is the family (if we do not count the maternity ward), and this is the one most persons participate in for their whole life, even though its members can change. From an educational research point of view there has been more focus on children's life in school. In this chapter we will focus on children's everyday activity in family practices. We will contrast the theoretical construct of family practice with school practice. However, in our empirical work we will restrict ourselves to children's activities in family practice.[1]

The Family Institution

The first important institution for a child is usually the family. Practice within a specific family is usually unwritten, and often unspoken, including aspects that are *unique for a particular family*. In terms of the model, this is the *individual aspect*. Aspects of individual family practice that are *shared with other families in a community* can be characterised as *general family practice*. The general aspect of family practice is often found in traditions that are common for several generations of family life in a specific society, which through a historical process have become traditions for how to live and act in families. Individual families are often aware, in some sense, of these general traditions (through knowledge of practices in other families, as acquired from personal acquaintance, fictional representations in movies, novels, and theatre, documentary and news reports, and so forth). In our model these traditions would be called the general perspective of family practice. Some of these traditions have become formalised into laws and bureaucratic regulations about family life (e.g., inheritance, divorce, birthright, educational requirements for children). In other cases, societal requirements are imposed or inspired by specific interests – political beliefs, professional consultants, attempts to respond to societal problems. These *formal requirements* are *the societal aspect of family practice*.

The School Institution

Schooling, as an institutional practice, can also be analysed or characterised within this model. In each nation-state, an individual school always has its own characteristics, reflecting the historical actions and decisions of the persons – administrators, teachers, consultants, and children – who have acted in that school in relation to the material resources and conditions that were available. *The individual* aspect of practice for each school within a given nation typically has some characteristics found in all schools, reflecting their interpretation of general practices that have developed within the school system. *The general* aspect is developed and reinforced through teacher-education institutions, further education, professional magazines, and so forth. Individual and general traditions of school practice are developed in relation to *the societal* aspect of school practice, which reflects national or societal interests, such as formulated in formal laws and regulations, curriculum plans, policy papers, instructional guides, specific testing goals, and other official demands on school practice. All three aspects are present in any concrete practice, though the contribution and interaction between aspects will vary for specific, individual practices.

Difference in Practices Between Home and School

This perspective on institutional practice gives a way to understand differences in the forms of practices that dominate at home and school.[2] At home the individual aspects of practices are usually dominant with mild influence from general family traditions. In most homes there is no explicit focus on societal practice (i.e., on laws and regulations) for how families should care for children except in conflict situations such as divorce, mistreatment, or death in the family. In school the societal practice dominates the activities both in content (subject-matter areas, curriculum plans, and examinations) and form (time and space characteristics such as school hours, pupil and teacher locations in the school and in the classroom).

If the societal and general practices dominate more in family practices than the actual needs of the participants in the individual practices, then the human interactions in the home become formal and lacking positive emotional content. In contrast, if the societal and general aspects are not the basis for the school practice, then the societal value of schooling and the importance of theorising activity are neglected. In effect, the school practice becomes "headless" or egocentric.

This difference between home and school in terms of the dominance of individual specific versus formal societal traditions is important to take into consideration when looking at pedagogical perspective and children's learning because children's knowledge, grounded in individual practice traditions from home and community, is informal and often not formulated explicitly. In contrast, the knowledge presented in school is dominated by the societal aspects of practice and is formulated through demands for activity in school and in relation to examinations.

Explanation of Development: Demands and Imitation in Interactions and Modelling and Conflicts in Activities

Children's development has been described as directed forward by their participation in different types of trajectories (Vygotsky, 1998; Riegel, 1975; Elder, 1998; Hundeide, 2004; Dreier, 2008). The main point in using the concept of trajectories in relation to conceptualisation of development is that society with its material and institutional conditions gives different possibilities for a persons' psychological development and for how the biological trajectory for human living can be realised as cultural development. But this conception in itself does not solve the problem of what development is and what works for creating a child's development. Here we will argue for four other concepts as central for understanding children's learning and development. These concepts become relevant when we transcend the analyses of institutional trajectories given by the societal possibilities for practices and look at the diverse activities that can be found in these practices. That is, the demands children meet when entering activities in home and school practice, but also the demands that children put on parents, children's imitation and modelling of parents, teachers, siblings and friends in the activities they share, and the conflicts that arise during interaction with other persons in these activities.

Demands and Imitation

Vygotsky's concept of the zone of proximal development has been central for understanding the importance of social relations for children's development. The concept has been used as a pedagogical concept, where a more competent person demands something from the child. Vygotsky used the concept in relation to development of the children's intellectual capacities. The concept of the zone of proximal development points to the phenomenon that intellectually a child can always do more with the help of a more competent person than s/he can do alone (Vygotsky, 1998). The more competent person can urge the child to imitate. A child's ability to imitate is not limitless and is not the same for all children, but will change corresponding to the child's development so that at each age period a child will have a specific zone of intellectual imitation connected with the actual level of development. Here it is important to note Vygotsky's remark:

> Speaking of imitation, we do not have in mind a mechanical, automatic thoughtless imitation but sensible imitation based on understanding the imitative carrying out of some intellectual operation. ... Everything that the child cannot do independently, but which he can be taught or which he can do with direction or cooperation or with the help of leading questions, we will include in the sphere of imitation. (Vygotsky, 1998, p. 202)

In this quotation Vygotsky points out that the child imitates with a meaningful understanding. However, Vygotsky's concept of the zone of proximal development as a learning concept does not include ideas about the qualitative change that the imitation can accomplish. This conceptualisation of what can be accomplished has to be related both to the practices the child is participating in and the demands that rise from these practices. At the same time, it must relate to the child's motives and interests for imitation and interaction with other persons in the child's social situation.

Children's imitation and learning within the concept of the zone of proximal development has to be seen in relation to how they relate to other persons in their social situation of interaction in specific activities. Here we will turn to Bronfenbrenner's ecological approach which can complement the cultural historical approach put forward by Vygotsky.

Modelling

Bronfenbrenner (1970) points to the significance of the involvement of parents, teachers and other adults that are of importance for a child in his/ her concrete activities, including activities across institutions. In his book *Two Worlds of Childhood* he discusses the importance of the emotional relation for a child to imitate other persons, and especially the importance of adults to take an ethical responsibility in relation to children's possibility to relate to their community and society. Adults' involvement as models for children will lead to children's growing involvement and responsibility on behalf of their own family, community and society as well as to individual autonomy (1970, pp. 165–166).

Bronfenbrenner's contribution that we will take up here is the concept of children's modelling of other persons' activities as central in their development. Modelling is a more encompassing concept than imitation, because the person the child imitates has to be conceptualised as a person. This idea is put forward in Bronfenbrenner's description of the "conditions" affecting a child's modelling processes. Modelling as a part of learning has to be related to the moral concern of the adult and how they relate to the child. Bronfenbrenner used modelling as a process that goes further than imitation of actions and involve relationships with other persons. In Bronfenbrenner's conceptualisation, the child just imitates as outlined by Vygotsky, but by including the characteristic of the model of who is imitated (as a caring or interesting person such as a child's parents, siblings, playmates and other persons who play a prominent role in the child's everyday life), the child's engagement in his/her imitation of the model is included in the analyses. Social reinforcement is a central concept for Bronfenbrenner. But social reinforcement is used in the meaning of interaction with a person that cares for the child; therefore he sees it as a problem if children are "neglected" or in "deprived" conditions.

Under the pressure of a deprived and threatening environment, there is neither time nor temper for playing games with children, answering their questions, or praising their constructive efforts. To the extent that the child gets any attention at all in response to his own activity, it is likely to be when he misbehaves to the point of interfering with the adults. Thus in contrast to the middle-class youngster, who is reinforced for his curiosity and achievement, Brontenbrenner argues that the disadvantaged child grows up in a world of few contingent responses that would let him see the probability of reward arising out of his efforts. Instead, what little he learns about the connection between his own behaviour and its social consequences is counterproductive for the development of the motives and skills required for satisfactory progress in the worlds of school and work (1970, p. 137).

Conflicts Between Demands and Children's Intentions and Motives

To participate in shared activities within family or school practices is a basic condition for children's development. They meet demands in these practices and challenges in their activities. The demands can be found both in the physical conditions and objects and in the activities. Conflicts can arise from not been able to handle objects, also as conflicts between different intentions of persons in the activities, and between different motives related to different activities in the practice.

The conceptual ideas in this chapter focus on children's appropriation of motives and competencies through entering activity settings and sharing activities with other people within cultural practice traditions. What we then want to focus on in the study of children's everyday activities across different institutions, is the demands that children meet in the specific family practices and the demands they put on their parents and how children and parents relate to these demands in their interactions, either to accomplish them or opposing the demands.

Exemplifying our Theoretical Approach with the Project: Children's Everyday Life Across Different Institutions

In a research project Children's Everyday Life Across Different Institutions together with Jytte Bang and Pernille Hviid at the Centre of Person Practice Development and Culture at Copenhagen University, Denmark in cooperation with a parallel project led by Marilyn Fleer at the Centre of Early Childhood, Monash University, Melbourne, Australia, the aim is to look at children's everyday life in a broader perspective and how they throughout different settings are active agents in the activity they participate in through imitating, modelling and solving conflicts. The study seeks through participant observation to capture everyday family activities in home and community with a focus on children's relations to parents, siblings and other persons, and how children's everyday activities both are structured by societal as well as parents' demands and also by themselves as active agents making demands, imitation, modelling, solving conflicts and exploring the different possibilities in their everyday settings. The focus of our research attention is on the children's perspective in their family and how the family's everyday life influences the children. What we will draw on here is how institutional practices in homes influence children's activity when cooperating with parents and siblings with a focus on children as active agents in their learning.

Other studies that have used participant observation to study children's everyday activities in all its diversity are Roger Barker and Herbert Wright in their book *One Boy's Day* (1966) and Susan Grieshaber in her book *Rethinking Parent and Child Conflict* (2004). Barker and Wright focus on how different behavioural settings throughout a day in family and school in a local community together create "the everyday life of one boy". Grieshaber follows four children in four families over several months. She focuses on conflicts in child–parent relations and on the power aspects in this relation. She uses the concepts *regimes of truth about family life* and *regimes of practice in relation to a particular family's life* to describe family practice (2004, p. 64ff). Regimes of truth are found in analysing discourses and refer to what we here have called general practice traditions – the discourse of everyday activities in the community or society. Regimes of practice are how the particular family handles the everyday activities.

In both Denmark and Australia we also followed children in their everyday activities, respectively in four families in Denmark (using participant observation with two observers writing down in the situation) and two families in Australia (using two observers each with a video camera). We followed the children in the six families over nearly a year in three respective two periods of ten visits each, but for several hours each time. It is the children's activities and their social relations that are the focus in our research. We focused on what Vygotsky has named the social situation of development (1998, p. 198), now specified and researched through its activities. Demands and conflicts were seen as part of this. An activity can be compared to a scene in a play, with a beginning and an end. Barker and Wright use the idea of scenes in their description in *One Boy's Day*. Vygotsky uses the concept of the social situation. We want to keep the concept of activity because an activity is always motivated, and this motivation can be seen from the point of tradition, so that a person enters a social situation and takes over the motive, but the person will also have his or her own understanding of the motive of a situation and have different ways of engaging in the social situation. It is the dynamic of the social situation and the scene that is introduced with the concept of activity.

What are the Dominating Activities in the Children's Everyday Life During the Week in the Two Families?

If we view the four main markers of each family's day – morning activities, school time, coming home and the evening meal – as the defining events in their weekdays, then all the other activities the children engage in can be seen as occurring around these. In each family several activities are going on at the same time. The main activities in the two families are listed in Table 14.1.

In this chapter we will focus on the activities at home in the afternoon and dinner and bed activities. The interpretation will look at:

- adults and children's demands
- children's imitation and modelling
- interactions and conflicts in the
  - relation to mother and father
  - relation to siblings and visitors at home.

Table 14.1 Everyday activities in the families

The Australian Family	The Danish Family
Morning activities	*Morning activities*
Rising out of bed	Rising out of bed/getting dressed
Getting dressed	Having breakfast
Looking for food	Playing
Walking to school	Walking to school
School activities	*School activities*
Having breakfast at school	
Class activities in school	Class activities in school
Recess	Recess
	After-school club
Walking home	Walking home
At home – afternoon activities	*At home – afternoon activities*
Playing (riding bikes; playing outside on the swings; playing with balls outside; watching TV (for Nick mostly); climbing furniture; running inside and outside of the house)/homework	Afternoon tea and homework/play (for Sara and Esben)
Dinner and bedtime activities	*Dinner and bedtime activities*
Dinner (guarding food from the dog)	Dinner
	Household chores
Preparing for bed	Playing in the apartment, either the two small children in their shared bedroom or upstairs with the acrobat rings and Lego and a lot of toys; using the computer (in the beginning mostly Louise, but Line and Esben start over the year to join in)
Going to bed	Going to bed

Everyday Practice in a Danish Family and the Conditions this Gives Children for Learning and Development

This is a middle-class family living in a middle-class neighbourhood in Copenhagen, with six members; both father and mother work. The children are Sara the youngest (4), Esben the only boy (6), Line (8), and Louise the eldest child (10).

The Setting

The Danish family is living in an apartment on the fifth floor in a block with several other families with children. The apartment design is oriented toward having four children. There are two floors. One enters directly into a hall–living room; the family's bedrooms and kitchen are also located here. Upstairs there is a big spacious room, and another bathroom. The upstairs room does not have so much furniture, but there is a computer, a dinner table, coffee table arrangement with TV, toys, and two acrobat rings hanging from the roof. Both the computer and the rings are in use most of the times when we visit, when the children do not have to participate in the obligatory activities of homework and help with the housework (setting the table, weekly cleaning).

Children's Move Between Practice at Home, Kindergarten, School, After-School Club and Other After-School Arrangements

There is a fairly consistent daily routine. The family rises in the morning quite early; the parents rise at quarter past six, and the children are called at half past six. They start to eat breakfast at a quarter to seven, and then the mother leaves at a quarter past seven to be early at work, so she can leave and fetch the children from day-care and after-school institution. The father clears the table after breakfast while the children play. He then gets them ready for school and day-care, and they leave at half past seven. There is a short walk to the institutions, five minutes to day-care where all children and father go first to leave Sara. She is always one of the first children in day-care. She goes to the window and waves goodbye and then runs to play. The father takes the three other children to school, again five minutes walk, where he leaves Esben in the kindergarten class, class 0, and walks Line to second grade, Louise just goes by herself to fourth grade. The father comes back and stays in Esben's class until after it has just started with a song. It is a practice that parents stay with their children in this grade for their first activity, and then leave. The teacher organises the first activity so that the parents do not stay the whole period, the father tells us with a smile. The father says that he finds that it is important that the children are not rushed in the morning, so they therefore rise rather early, and take time to walk to school.

In the afternoon the mother leaves work at two thirty in order to be able to fetch the children at three o'clock – first going to the school, to get Line and Esben, and then walking with them through a garden to fetch Sara from the kindergarten. It can take 15 minutes to collect Line, since she likes her mother being around in the after-school club. Usually they end up arriving home at 4 pm. It takes an hour to go home, because the mother does not rush the children, she lets them finish the activities they have started at the different places. Louise walks home herself from the after-school club she is attending.

On coming home the mother makes tea and afternoon snacks (fruit and bread), and the children start doing homework for around an hour. Esben and Sara play, but sometimes Esben starts doing "homework" with help from his mother who invents some activities; at other times he has a friend Tais at home to play with. Sara plays either by herself or with Esben around the "homework" activities. Around half past five the mother starts cooking the dinner and the children play. Then the father comes home, says hello to the children, and then helps the mother if she has not finished cooking the dinner. Often on Wednesdays (not in the summer) the family go together to the swimming bath before dinner from 5 to 6.30 pm. When they do not attend the swimming bath they eat their meal at 6 pm. On Thursdays, Line and Louise go to gymnastics after dinner. The father drives them and fetches them later when they are finished. On other days different activities occur from dinner to around 7 pm and until bedtime, 8 o'clock, i.e., the children participate in cleaning the house, or the children play together or one or two of the children's friends from the other apartments in the house come along. The mother may also arrange a shared play activity. All the children go to bed at eight. Louise supposedly reads a little in bed. The rest of the evening is for the parents.

Saturday and Sunday are different. The children walk around in night clothes up to ten o'clock, play and watch TV. Then different activities take place depending upon the time of year. The family make arrangements, going to the cinema, having events for all the apartments in the block, going to the beach, having birthday parties, having skiing holidays, going to their summer cottage, and visiting family in other parts of the country. The single child will also participate during the week in birthday parties, or events in kindergarten and school sometimes together with the whole family.

Pedagogy in the Family

It is obvious that the parents focus very much on the children's routines, that they do not rush the children, they put great emphasis on children's arrangements with routines, such as dressing, doing homework, eating, going to bed. The children often play together. Both parents stress that they feel happy about the children playing together and having playmates visiting. At home the mother is around both when they play and when they do homework. Homework time starts just after arriving home on weekdays at 4 pm. The arrangement is laid out so that all sit together in the hall–living room when it is homework time, with the eldest actually doing homework, Esben imitating homework and Sara floating around in the periphery preparing for when she should sit at the table to do homework. The mother is together with the children being like an octopus serving them tea and bread, helping the two oldest with homework, talking with Esben and Sara when they need her.

The father does practical things: setting and clearing the table, helping with dinner, participating in cleaning the house. At the dinner table he introduces themes and talks with the children. Occasionally he helps Louise with homework when directly asked, but otherwise this is the mother's task as well as being around when the children play. The father busies himself with tasks when he is around, except at the dinner table where he sits with the family and talks also after they have finished eating.

Extract from Interpretation of the Second Visit to the Family's Home

Wednesday from 4 pm to 8 pm, observers Kasper and Mariane.

Tais (6), Esben's classmate, visits for the whole afternoon and eats dinner with the family.

Activities:

- Play in Esben's room
- Drinking tea around the main table in the living room downstairs
- Visit to the swimming bath (not commented on here)
- Dinner upstairs.

Playroom Activity

Robber play: relation to playmates, sister and friend – Sara and Esben (focus) Tais:

Esben orients himself to both sister and friend. The two boys are together and Sara is the victim. Tais suggests they "kill" her. Esben does not like to pretend Sara has to die, and suggests that she should only faint.

The money activity: relation to playmates, sister and friend: Tais finds Esben's purse and empties it out on the floor, Tais wants to take some money, Esben tries to stop him. Tais turns it into their robber play. Esben does not really want to accept this, but then accepts that they can hide the money.

Conflicts:

The consequences are too big in the play, that Sara has to die, so Esben goes into the "planning sphere" in the play and say that she should only faint.

Tais loses interest in the play and gets absorbed by Esben's money. Esben tries to stop him, by asking him to place his money where it belongs in his purse, when Tais has emptied this. Tais does not want to do this but enters back into the play and says let him hide the money from the enemy in the playhouse, which Esben accepts.

Tais takes 10 kr. of Esben's and wants to buy potato chips with it. Esben accepts and goes to his mother in the other room with this idea. She rejects this but says she will give them some food, since they must be hungry if they are thinking about buying chips.

Drinking tea, doing homework around the main table in the living room downstairs

The three children from the play room gather around the table after 15 minutes together with the older sisters and mother. Esben sits on his mother's lap until she leaves the table to make sandwiches. The two older girls are doing their homework before the trip to the swimming bath. The mother supports their work by being at the table and giving them attention when needed.

Homework: relations to parents and mutual demands: Line is doing her maths, she is not so enthusiastic. She asks her mother for attention when the mother is helping Louise with her English essay. Line asks if 5×4 is the same as 5×7, perhaps Line knows so it is a way to get the mother's attention. The mother advises her how to find out the answer by using the calculation table. Line starts an exercise of writing number four several times on a piece of paper without raising the pencil from the paper. Mother praises her for her way of writing number 4. Line obviously does exercises instead of undertaking her maths calculations. Practising number writing is a task that is too easy in relation to the maths Line is supposed to do (second grade maths). Mother perhaps praises Line to support her to continue with her maths homework. Later, Line wants to leave her homework, but she continues because her mother tells her to.

   Louise seems to enjoy her work with writing a text in English, preparing a play (a fashion show) for the class. Indirectly Louise also seeks her mother's attention by starting to write numbers like Line, when Line is praised, and later when she says she has a lot of homework. Later when the father comes home and enters the room Louise takes out her maths book and shows it to her father. She only has one task left, but she wants to get his attention and asks him for help. Her father helps her to understand the mathematical problem.

Conflicts within the activity: Line has problems with understanding the mathematic problems she is supposed to solve by calculation. The mother and observer help her. Later she wants to skip her homework, but her mother solves this by giving her a specific time limit, connected to a positive event: "You can do it while I am making sandwiches."

Relation to siblings: modelling and conflicts: Louise perhaps competes for the mother's attention, because she starts to do the same as Line, writing the number four. Later she points out that she only has one maths problem left to do (though she earlier said she had a lot of homework). Perhaps she says this because she wants to show that she is more competent than her sister.

Esben's Provocations Trying to Create Conflicts:
Conflicts with Line. Esben provokes Line because he suggests to Tais that they should erase her homework. Line talks to mother and mother solves this conflict by preventing this very quietly.

Play with his mother's purse. When mother goes into the kitchen, Esben tries to provoke the observer Kasper by peeking into his mother's purse and taking money out – the same thing that Tais did to him minutes ago in relation to Esben's purse. The mother comes back and says he must not take her money. Later he is allowed to sit on her lap and take things out of her purse.

Talks very loud. Nobody reacts, so he comments to himself.

Put his legs on the table but takes them down when asked by his mother.

Around the Dinner Table

Demands, modelling and conflicts: The children get some of their favourite food, pizza; they all wait to start to eat until everybody is at the table, except the guest child Tais. Esben looks at him a little amazed and then says he has to wait when he tries to take a piece of pizza. Mother then says that of course he can start.

Modelling and Imitation:

Language associations. The parents make conversation about the activities in the school and kindergarten.

Esben takes jalapeños and mother says they are gruff. Esben then starts to talk about his mother sending each child to bed being gruff, imitating mother's voice. *Sara* also imitates her mother by saying "Now you have to go to bed 'bebser'" in a high pitched voice.

Tais wants Esben to hit the observer Kasper in his forehead (perhaps to get Esben's attention, and make him stop him being attentive to Kasper and the computer). Father uses this as an introduction to a figure of speech "bash on the head". The word association can be seen as a way to take a conflict and to turn it into a language game thereby turning the attention away from an unwanted activity. Later Esben imitates the word game when he constructs his own saying when Tais leaves and does not want to go away with his father; Esben then says that he will give him a "pizza hug".

Computer Use:

Louise gives a great deal of attention to observer Mariane's writing on her laptop and says that she wants a driving licence for the computer. (She does not yet use a computer for her writing, but this will change over the next month. Mother helps her to get started.)

Esben is also very attentive to observer Kasper's writing and wants to try to write on his computer, which he is allowed to do for a short while. (He cannot write words yet, so he just tries out the keyboard.)

Everyday Practice in an Australian Family and the Conditions this Gives Children for Learning and Development

The Australian family discussed in this section lives in a low socioeconomic community in a rural town south of Melbourne. There are six family members: mother, father and four children – Andrew (6), Nick (5), JJ (3), and Louise (2). Neither the mother nor the father has any employment. The family does not have a car, and must walk ten kilometres to go to school, preschool, childcare and return home. The shopping area is approximately three kilometres away from the family home. Limited public transport is available. Because Australia is a large country, homes and facilities within communities are geographically distant and dispersed, meaning that mobility between services assumes ownership of a car.

The setting

The family receives funds from the government, and they live in a free-standing three-bedroom government house. The house has a large backyard which is fully fenced, and a small front yard that is open to a quiet cul-de-sac. The outdoor area has swings, a vegetable garden that was designed and is looked after by the father, and two small sheds which are used for storing toys and tools.

The house has a small lounge room, a kitchen area for cooking and eating, a central hallway, two children's bedrooms, the parents' bedroom, and the bathroom, toilet and laundry area. In the kitchen, there are four chairs and a high chair. That is, there are fewer chairs than there are people living in the house. In the lounge area there are places for five people to sit. The lounge room has a 2.5 metre fish tank filled with tropical fish, a medium-sized TV, DVD player, and one cupboard.

Children's Move Between Practice at Home, Childcare, Preschool, School and Breakfast Programme

Attendance at school punctuates how the family is organised. Because the family does not have a car, they must wake up early in the morning at 6.30 in order to allow enough time to walk to the school – which takes one full hour. In the mornings two of the children are usually awake at 6.30 am (Andrew and JJ). The mother rises and makes herself a coffee, has a smoke (if available), and prepares the children's lunches and Louise's bottles of milk for childcare. As she does this, Andrew walks around the house looking for food, usually staring into an empty fridge. Andrew is usually dressed when we arrive to film. JJ is in his pyjamas. His mother dresses him in the hallway next to his bedroom or in the lounge room. As this occurs, Nick wakes and begins looking for food. He is usually very hungry and becomes upset when there is no food to be found in the fridge. The mother reminds them that they will have breakfast at school. Louise is woken by the mother once all the other children are dressed and standing next to the door ready to walk to school. Louise is dressed and put in the stroller. She is given a bottle. The father usually rises at this time and comes out of the bedroom. The children say goodbye to him, and then walk first to childcare, where Louise and JJ are left, then to school where Andrew and Nick participate in the breakfast programme. When Nick is not at preschool, he remains with his mother, and when JJ and Louise are not at childcare (they attend childcare for 3 days) they also return home with their mother. The walk to school is usually rushed, and Andrew is often late to class because he is still eating his breakfast.

In the afternoon, the mother collects the children from preschool, school and then childcare. If it rains, other families often drive the family home. On Thursdays the father collects Nick from preschool it is impossible for the mother to collect both children because the finishing times do not allow for the long walk between settings.

When the children arrive home they wander around the house moving between rooms, between inside and outside, and between different activities that are concurrently occurring. The children do not watch TV seated for long periods of time, but rather, Nick will sit and watch a favourite programme, whilst Andrew goes outside to play, followed by JJ and Louise, and later Nick, who tends to play with the balls lying in the backyard. Andrew will then return inside to play jumping on the bed, climbing the bookshelf in his room and running between rooms in the house. Riding bikes also occurs in this way – between other activities.

Meal times occur around 6.00 pm. Meal times involve the children being called to the table, with the mother serving up food and standing and watching the children eat for the first 5 minutes. The father is usually in the bedroom or outside, and does not participate in meal times. The mother "comes and goes" into the kitchen whilst the food is being eaten. When Louise needed help with feeding the mother would spoon-feed her and then leave. After a period of unsupervised time, the children tend to gradually take their meals from the table, and continue eating in other parts of the house. After the meal has been consumed, the children continue to move between rooms and between inside and outside. The preferred activities include playing on the swing, going down the slides, running around the rooms in the house, climbing furniture, running outside, riding their bikes, playing with balls, and investigating the vegetable patch. The latter is actively discouraged by the father, because the explorations usually involve pulling out plants.

During the children's play activities after school, the mother will from time to time hear Andrew read his school reading book. The mother either sits down or she stands holding the book at child height, whilst Andrew stands and reads the text in the reading book. The mother puts the book away immediately after reading has finished. This activity usually lasts for 1 minute.

On weekends, the play routine described above continues all day. The breakfast programme is not accessible on the weekends, and the children usually eat leftovers, saved from the night before. The family has many visitors to the house, and the children usually engage the visitors in ball games. The family dog runs with the children and follows them around the house, particularly when the children are carrying food.

Pedagogy in the family

The children will continually be watching out to see what each other is doing. They will run around each other in a kind of dance as they move across time and space within the house and backyard. The mother participates in this continual movement, and can be observed orchestrating interactions, whilst at the same time disappearing from the children's field of vision. However, the mother keenly notes all activities and appears as required, demonstrating that although at times she is absent, she nevertheless knows what is happening. A kind of distant surveillance occurs. The children will observe what is going on, but will also participate in simultaneous conversations with each other. A rapid machine gun firing approach characterises conversations between parents and children. Because there is so much activity, the members of the family have adopted an effective approach to communication.

Extract from Interpretation of the Second Visit in the Family's Home

Wednesday from 4.40 pm to 8 pm, observers Marilyn and Gloria.

They have a male and female visitor. The female visitor stays inside with the mother the whole time. The male visitor stays outside with the father.

Activities:

- Garden presentation
- Meal time
- Inside play
- Outside play
- Bedtime preparation.

Garden Presentation

On arrival, the father and then shortly after the mother, show the researchers the corn they have grown in their garden. They take corn out from the fridge and give some to the researchers. The whole family goes out to look at the vegetable garden, and the produce is discussed with the researchers.

Imitation and adults' demands: The children do the same as the parents, showing the researchers all the produce under the foliage. After presentation to the researchers the father asks the children to leave the garden.

Meal Time

The children go into the house and the mother feeds the children the fish and chips that the researchers have provided. The children begin their meal at the table (except JJ, he is still outside), and then over the course of the meal, they take their food to different parts of the house to eat. Louise stays in her high chair asking for milk. The mother fills the drink container with coke which she does not like. The mother talks to the researchers about school, testing, and food additives whilst the children are eating.

Demands and imitation: The children go to the table and eat, when called upon (except JJ), but when mother leaves the table to talk to the observer, the children do the same. Louise demands milk but gets coke.

Inside Play

Louise is taken from the high chair; the mother mentions that Louise is now 2 years old and that she has had her ears pierced. Observer Marilyn and the children go into Louise's room and look over her new birthday toys. Louise runs up and down the hallway with great pride, showing her "running" achievement to observer Gloria. Louise then goes outside.

JJ and Andrew play with Louise's birthday toys. The mother goes back and talks to the visitor in the kitchen.

Nick sits in the lounge watching TV and eating his food. When he has had enough he wraps his food, goes into the kitchen and asks his mother to put the food away. Nick then goes outside. JJ and Andrew continue to play in Louise's room.

Modelling: Nick models the mother collecting and saving food. Andrew models to JJ when playing on his bike and moving rapidly around the house and backyard.

Outside Play

a) At the Slide

Nick and Louise play outside. The father talks to observer Gloria, whilst the visitor supervises Louise on the slide. He notices her struggling and then spends a long time supporting her with climbing and sliding. Eventually Louise manages to climb and slide without support. He cheers and claps, and at this time the father notices too, and also cheers. Louise continues to slide. During this time Nick plays with the totem tennis, and when Louise is cheered, he goes over to the slide and joins in. The visitor who has been scaffolding Louise has moved physically further and further back from her, so that Louise feels more confident with her own achievements. Because Nick has moved to the slide, the visitor returns to the slide to supervise the interactions between Nick and Louise. Nick climbs up the face of the slide, whilst Louise climbs up the ladder. This means both can slide uninterrupted. Nick solves this problem.

Demands and imitation: The visitor, by helping Louise, places demand on her to continue getting skill at sliding. Nick becomes interested and imitates the sliding. He solves the conflict of the two entering the slide by crawling up the slide.

b) Totem Tennis Batten and Biking

JJ comes out into the yard and picks up the totem tennis batten and hits observer Gloria with it. The father hits JJ. Andrew comes out of the house too, and he takes JJ's bike and rides it. JJ does not like this and objects.

Andrew takes another bike. Louise runs over and joins in with the bike riding. She cannot ride, but she picks up the bikes and toddles around near the riders. JJ goes back to the swing and climbs the frame, eventually sitting into the seat and swinging.

Conflicts:
JJ hits Gloria with the tennis bat, father then hits JJ.

Andrew takes JJ's bike and JJ objects and Andrew finds another bike.

Imitation: Louise imitates Andrew with the bike, though she cannot ride.

Bedtime Preparation

When it becomes dark, the children are encouraged to go inside by the mother. The father reinforces this. The father changes Louise and JJ's nappies in the lounge room in front of the heater. The mother gathers their pyjamas and helps each child to put them on, with the father supporting this process. The mother takes the children's clothes from the room, and the children are sent to their room. Louise is given a warm bottle of milk and is put into her cot with a little swinging game, which Louise clearly enjoys. The room is dark. The mother looks for her soft toys and puts them into the cot with her, and talks to her about how nice they are. The door is closed. When the mother appears from Louise's room, she notes that both JJ and Andrew are still in the lounge room. The mother calls to both to get back into bed. They both return to the room, and then over a period of five minutes the children go into bed, and then go back out again. Nick stays in bed and appears to be happy to go to sleep. Eventually, the mother becomes angry and raises her voice to Andrew, who immediately becomes compliant and stays in bed. JJ continues to leave the room and then the mother tells him about the scary monsters who will get him if he is not in bed. JJ immediately goes into his bed and begins sobbing, and asking about "where they are" showing great fear. For 5 minutes JJ cries and talks about the monsters, with the mother saying to be quiet and to go to sleep. The mother signals that it is now time for the researchers to leave because their routine is now to sit in bed and watch TV. The researchers leave.

Demands and conflicts: The children are called to go to bed when it becomes dark outside. They are expected to go to bed and sleep, but Andrew and JJ create a conflict by getting out of bed.

JJ imitates Andrew. When mother asks Andrew to stop and lay down to sleep he does so but JJ continues to play.

Conflicts: Mother then tells JJ the monster will come and this creates a conflict where he starts to cry, until the mother tells him to stop.

General Discussion of Everyday Practice in Families and How This Contributes to Development

Even though we name the families the Danish and Australian family the idea is not to discuss national differences. Having families from two distinct places that are economically different and who have different physical conditions gives the possibility of seeing how varied family practice can be in families in late modern societies (Giddens, 1984). The idea also is to see how demands from school and kindergarten together with the family practice create possibilities for children's activity and how diverse their activity can be. Through the case analyses we want to see if we can get a deeper insight into how children's activities are framed by family practices and how within these they contribute to shared activities and thereby conditions for their development. To do this we will first frame the shared activities by characterising the formal and general aspects of family practices in the two families.

How School as a Societal Condition Influences Home Practice

It is obvious that the formal practice of school attendance shaped the everyday morning activity and the afternoon activity for both the Danish as well as the Australian family. This also shaped bedtime in the family so the children were sent to bed around the same time to be able to get up early. Thereby they also leave parents with some time for themselves in the evening. Variations between the two families in the formal structuring of the day are not obvious because of this shared way of structuring the day. Variations start to be more obvious when we look at the tradition of handling these demands, even though there are differences across nations and economic circumstances. However, there are also several similarities.

General Expectations and Discourses Upon Family Practice Reflected in the Two Families

An expectation in Western late modern society about family practice is that parents should share responsibility for children. But even in the Scandinavian countries where a very high percentage of women have joined the labour market the expectation is still that the mother is the leading figure in household chores and the father contributes to join in (Andenæs, 1998; Christensen & Ottesen, 2002; Lausten & Sjørup, 2003).

In both the Danish and the Australian families in our case study, the children are walked to school; this is an activity both mother and father contribute to. In the Australian family the mother is the one that takes most of the responsibility to deliver and fetch the children and to supervise them. But the father contributes by fetching Nick once a week from kindergarten, because time demands make it impossible for the mother to do this. The father also changes the children's nappies at night and helps the mother to get the children ready for bed. In the Danish family the mother also takes most of the responsibility for children's care but the parents share collecting and bringing the children to school/kindergarten and often share preparing food. Another general practice at home is children's homework that has to be accomplished each day. Here in both families it is the mother that helps and supervises children's homework. The children are younger in the Australian family and homework does not feature as much in their daily life, but the little that Andrew needed to do was taken care of by the mother.

The real difference between the families can be seen in the concrete material conditions that these two families have. The long walk to school for the Australian family, and the isolation of the family in relation to stores and other facilities, are even more marked in this family than for other Australian families who own a car. The economic situation that makes food for everyday meals a conscious topic for both children and mother is also a dominating difference between this family and the Danish family. Also traditions for shared activities make differences. Eating together and talking together go on very differently. One factor that is important and must be remembered in this connection, is that the children are much younger in the Australian family, from 2 to 6 years, where they are from 4 to 12 years in the Danish family. The two oldest children in the Danish family have much more capacity to enter a conversation and this becomes a model for their younger siblings. So instead of comparing the families to find differences, we will see how demands take place, how conflicts are solved, and how children imitate and model each other and the adults. This means we will try to take the children's perspective and see how they contribute to the social situations, and instead of looking at differences, try to schedule how diverse children can be at different ages in different families.

The Children's Perspective: How they Contribute to Social Situations

The Danish Family: Parents' and Children's Mutual Demands

In the Danish family it is obvious that the routine of shared homework is a demand that children just accept; even though Line actually expresses that she "hates" doing homework, she actually sits at the table with her mother and Louise, and seems in some way to enjoy her mother's attention. Esben starts to join in mostly by sitting on his mother's lap when homework takes place. Sara roams around playing on the floor or sits by herself at the table with some toys. The two youngest children thereby prepare themselves to enter the homework activity. Through the homework activity the three oldest children each create their own space with demands on the mother. Each of them seeks and competes for their mother's attention at the joint homework activity. Louise, who enjoys homework and who actually does not need any help, frequently just poses questions in order to get attention, or as in the example when the mother turns her attention to Line, she starts to demonstrate that she is as competent as Line writing the number 4. The mother focuses especially on Line who needs help. Esben has difficulty keeping his mother's attention on the homework activity since he does not yet have any real homework. In the example here he makes several provocations, by taking the money out of his mother's purse, by talking loudly and by putting his legs on the table. The mother takes these provocations in a rather relaxed way and gives him some attention by letting him sit in her lap and with the money activity she just makes a warning comment and otherwise ignores his provocations.

Demands on the child can turn gradually into the child modelling the mother's demand where the child puts the same kind of demands on others (when he takes the role of the adult). Esben takes the role of the adult when Tais empties his purse and together they turn the money activity into a play that is acceptable for Esben. He also takes the adult role at the dinner table when he demands that his friend keeps table manners and waits for everybody to be seated before he can take a piece of pizza.

In conflict situations parents often use language and play with language to orient the children to other aspects than the activity they do not want. We can see the children modelling this aspect when both Esben and Sara associate the mother's use of the word gruff for the jalapeños to the mother's keeping time when sending them to bed. Also Esben uses language association in the same way as parents to help Tais when he does not want to leave and says that he will give him a pizza hug.

The Australian Family: Demands and Modelling

The demands put on the children in the Australian families are also in relation to getting ready for school and going to bed. The mother manages to get the three oldest children ready in the morning, with Andrew managing his own dressing routine, and Louise being woken and dressed before they walk to school, kindergarten and childcare. The other routine is the demands made on the children in relation to their preparation for bed. The conflict that rises between the mother, Andrew and JJ is connected to this demand. In this scene one can expect that the play was started by Andrew who enjoys his smaller brother (3 years) imitating him, but the younger brother cannot react as fast to mother's demands so he continues to play and then gets into trouble.

The demands in relation to dinner are rather loose. The children are called to the dinner table where the mother distributes the food. There is no expectation that they will stay at the table. The children's demand on the mother is to get food. In this example Louise wants milk, but cannot get this. In the morning the mother cannot give them food when they demand it, as they have to wait for the breakfast programme at the school. Because the food is sparse we see Nick modelling his mother; in this example, he wraps the rest of his leftover food and puts it into the refrigerator.

Since there is not much demand on the children except for the morning walk and the bedtime activities there is an ongoing movement from activity to activity, without a real starting point or ending point. Inside and outside activities flow across boundaries and time. Children will actively be viewing TV or a child will be doing something whilst also spending time going outside to slide down the slide, running back into the house to view TV or to play with one of the siblings again. There is very little conflict between the children and seemingly no competition for parents' attention. But there is neither a shared activity spent together with parents or each other over a longer period, though they are all around at the time. Therefore it is also more difficult to model activity, where they take the role of the father or mother. But the smaller children imitate the older children on several occasions in the example. JJ imitates Andrew, and Louise imitates Nick. The family practices come close to aspects of what Bronfenbrenner has described as deprived in relation to playing with children, and this can also be considered in relation to the limited school-oriented interactions that were occurring in the family. But it seems that visitors to the house, instead of the parents, contributed to playing with the children and supporting their efforts. In this example, the slide generated huge physical demands for Louise through participating in the practice of using a slide designed for older children. Her struggles in managing the equipment were met by the adult visitor scaffolding her action. The interactions she had with the adult visitor in the social situation were significant for realising and accomplishing this competence.

Conflicts Between Demands and Children's Intentions and Motives in the Australian Family

When JJ (3 years) hits the observer, the father at once hits the child, there is no explanation. Later JJ enters into another conflict imitating his elder brother. JJ and Andrew enjoyed the "getting up" and "going back to bed" play that took place when the family announced "it was bedtime". The intention of the mother was to get the children into bed quickly and easily. The intention of the children was to play their game of "getting up" and "going back to bed". When this game went on too long, the mother changed the activity and re-introduced a night fear for JJ – of monsters – in order to ensure he stayed in bed. JJ's motive for play changed as he actively demanded reassurance and safety from his mother against the monster, and he did not seem to get this, but instead the mother demanded that he stop crying and go to sleep.

Conclusion

Barbara Rogoff's (2003) and Jonathan Tudge's (2008) extensive studies of family practices show diversity according to how much children are integrated in the daily chores and work activities of the family or community. Rogoff shows that in different societies the role of fathers and siblings are different, and these roles are connected with other traditions in society. In our study it is the mother who takes responsibility for daily chores. In the Danish family the "regime of truths" is to include the children, but there is not any responsibility distributed to them. Contrary to Rogoff's (2003) research, where she shows that in several Mexican and Mexican heritage families children become involved in household production, children in both the Danish and the Australian family participate in activities that are characteristic for families in late modern society where work, school and home practice is divided between different institutions and furthermore where children mostly are wanted for emotional reasons and thereby become a project in itself for the family.

Both the formal societal conditions as well as material conditions influenced the practice in the two families. What were most obvious were the school demands and the material restrictions in the Australian family, but there were also other institutional demands. For the Danish family it was parents' work that generated the condition. For the Australian family it was the social agents that supervised their lives. The room that these conditions and general practices give the child in relation to putting demands on parents, are also factors that have to be considered in understanding what possibilities children have when they enter into interaction with other people. Possibilities are also generated through the demands they meet, and the demands that they themselves formulate. Finally it must be noted that through the imitation and modelling of family members, these in turn develop motives and competences for other family members. Learning and development viewed in this way provides a deeper understanding of how institutions (as influenced by society) create conditions for furthering children's abilities and knowledge within the everyday practices.

Acknowledgments

The projects reported in this chapter were supported by The Danish Union of Pedagogue's Foundation for Research and Development and the Margaret Trembath Research Scholarship, Australia. For the latter project, special acknowledgment of Gloria Quiñones and Carol Linney is given for their valuable research assistance.

Notes

1 The case examples presented later are drawn on a study of *Children's everyday life across different institutions* but there is only enough room in this chapter to present the analyses of children's participation in everyday practices in families.
2 Day care institutions can be compared to schools, though their individual practices in most cases are not as constrained by formal practice as school practices are.

References

Andenæs, A. (1996). *Foreldre og barn i forandring* [Parents and children in change]. Oslo: Pedagogisk Forum.
Barker, R. G. & Wright, H. F. (1966). *One boy's day. A specimen record of behaviour.* Hamden, CT: Archon Books.

Bronfenbrenner, U. (1970). *Two worlds of childhood: U.S. and U.S.S.R.* New York: Russell Sage Foundation.

Christensen, E. & Ottesen, H. M. (2002). *Børn og familier* [Children and families]. Copenhagen: Socialforskningsinstitutet.

Dreier, O. (2008). *Psychotherapy in everyday life.* Cambridge: Cambridge University Press.

Elder, G. H. (1998). The life course of developmental theory. *Child Development,* 69, 1–12.

Giddens, A. (1984). *The construction of society.* Cambridge: Polity Press.

Grieshaber, S. (2004). *Rethinking parent and child conflict.* New York: Routledge Falmer.

Hedegaard, M. (1999). Institutional practice, cultural positions, and personal motives: Immigrant Turkish parents' conception about their children's school life. In S. Chaiklin, M. Hedegaard, & U. Juul Jensen (Eds.), *Activity theory and social practice.* Aarhus: Aarhus University Press.

Hedegaard, M. (in press). Child development from a cultural-historical approach: Children's activity in everyday local settings as foundation for their development. *Mind Culture and Activity* 16 (1).

Hedegaard, M., Chaiklin, S., & Jensen, U. J. (1999). Activity theory and social practice. An introduction. In S. Chaiklin, M. Hedegaard, & U. Juul Jensen (Eds.), *Activity theory and social practice.* Aarhus: Aarhus University Press.

Hundeide, K. (2004). *Børns livsverden og sociokulturelle rammer* [Children's life world and socio-cultural frames]. Copenhagen: Akademisk Forlag.

Lausten, M. & Sjørup, K. (2003). Hvad kvinder og mædn burger tiden til – om tidsmæssig ligestilling i danske familier [What women and men use their time for – equality of time use in Danish families]. Copenhagen: Socialforskningsinstitutets report, no 03-08.

Leontiev, A. N. (1978). *Activity, consciousness, and personality.* Englewood Cliffs, NJ: Prentice-Hall.

Riegel, K. F. (1975). Toward a dialectical theory of development. *Human Development,* 18, 50–64.

Rogoff, B. (2003). *The cultural nature of human development.* Oxford: Oxford University Press.

Tudge, J. (2008). *The everyday lives of young children. Culture, class, and child rearing in diverse societies.* Cambridge: Cambridge University Press.

Vygotsky, L. S. (1998). *The collected works of L. S. Vygotsky. Volume 5. Child psychology.* New York: Plenum Press.

15 Conceptions of Early Childhood Care and Education in Brazil

Lia B. L. Freitas, * *Terri L. Shelton and Tania M. Sperb*

Over the course of the twentieth century one can see, in many parts of the world, a growing interest in children and childhood. Researchers in many countries have conducted studies about children's growing cognitive capabilities and their socio-emotional and moral development. In part because of these studies, there is a widespread view that children's first years of life are fundamental for healthy development, across the life course, of humans' biological, psychological, emotional, and social potential. When early problems are found, appropriate care and education can help to overcome or minimize problems of development (OECD, Organization for Economic Co-operation and Development, 2001; Shonkoff & Phillips, 2000; Simpson, Jivanjee, Koroloff, Doerfler, & García, 2001). Intervention studies also indicate that this period constitutes a powerful opportunity to ameliorate children's development, lessen cognitive and socio-emotional problems, and stop early problems from becoming more serious (Campbell & Ramey, 1994; Guralnick, 1997; Kellam & Rebok, 1992; Lopez, Tarullo, Forness, & Boyce, 2000; Ramey & Ramey, 1998; Raver, 2002; Williford & Shelton, 2008).

At the same time that society's views were changing about the importance of early care and education it was also possible to observe the local, state, and federal governments taking a greater interest in providing support for the care and education of young children. Prior to the start of the twentieth century, the care and education of young children was seen as the family's basic duty. Thus when both parents had to work in order to provide enough for themselves and their children, the parents were considered either incapable of raising their children or in some way pathological (Howard, Williams, Port, & Lepper, 2001). Nowadays, services for all young children are increasingly considered as a complement to the socialization provided by the family.

The new-found preoccupation with the care and education of young children was probably not simply a function of new understandings that developed over the course of the twentieth century. It also relates to the growing belief that investing in early childhood programs is a good economic development strategy, because of its wide and long-lasting benefits. In the United States, for example, "the Federal Reserve Bank found that early childhood investments make more sense than spending on venture capital funds, subsidizing new industries such as biotechnology, building new stadiums or providing tax incentives for business" (National Institute for Early Education Research, 2003, p. 13). Longitudinal studies on the Perry Preschool program for low-income children in the United States estimate that every dollar spent on such a program yields a saving of up to $17 by the time that the individuals served had reached 40 years of age, based on reducing crime (the major cost benefit), increased earnings, and the lack of need for special education and welfare payments (Schweinhart, Montie, Xiang, Barnett, Belfield, & Nores, 2005). In other parts of the world, other concerns also played a role; for example, following communist revolutions the State wanted to reduce, wherever possible, families' influence on their children (see, for example, Tudge, 1991).

As one of the results of the growing interest of the State in these issues, the last century witnessed the rapid growth of policies designed to support young children's care and education around the world. Some general principles that have permeated these policies have been accepted in a very large number of societies. One example of this is the fact that only two countries (Somalia and the United States) have not ratified the United Nations Convention on the Rights of the Child (UNCRC), first adopted in 1989. Another example is that researchers from various countries have argued that an integrated system of care and education (that is, a system that focuses on a range of children's needs, from health and safety to children's social, emotional, and cognitive development) is essential for young children (Brauner, Gordic, & Zigler, 2004; Campbell, 2002; Cerisara, 1999; Corsino, Nunes, & Kramer, 2003; Knitzer, 1993; OECD, 2001; Oliveira, 1996; Rosseti-Ferreira, 1998; Shonkoff & Phillips, 2000; Raver, 2002; Shelton et al., 2000; Simpson et al., 2001; Vasconcellos, Aquino, & Lobo, 2003).

Because these changes are fairly widespread there may be a tendency to view them as universal. However, the form in which these general principles have been implemented varies greatly not only across different societies but even within the same society, in part because of the society's values, beliefs, and goals, its access to resources, and political decisions about how best to use those resources (OECD, 2001; Tobin, Wu, & Davidson, 1989; Tudge et al., 2006). In this chapter our goal is thus to illustrate how general principles about the care and education of young children take on local nuances. We will accomplish this goal by focusing on a single society, Brazil, showing the ways in which these general principles have been put into practice there over the course of the last century or so.

Rather than attempt to describe the general principles across many societies, however, we will simply draw comparisons between Brazil and the United States. There are some similarities between these two societies. For example, the two countries are similar in size (over 8.5 million square kilometers), and are populated primarily by descendents of immigrants, more recent immigrants, or descendents of Africans brought as slaves, with only a small percentage of people whose roots could be traced back to the original native populations. Both countries also have a federal system of government incorporating states that are of widely differing sizes and have access to very different resources. These states are similar in terms of following federal guidelines but also have the freedom to institute their own policies which also leads to variability.

However, despite these similarities the two nations have quite distinct cultures, histories, and economies. One factor that is clearly relevant to policies regarding care and education is that of resources. Whereas the United States is classified by the World Bank as one of the 24 "high-income OECD countries," Brazil is classified as a "developing" country with a "higher-middle-income" economy. This difference is reflected in the fact that although almost one-fifth of American children aged five years and under are living below the official poverty line (U.S. Census Bureau, 2003), almost half of Brazilian children of the same age live below Brazil's official poverty line (Instituto Brasileiro de Geografia e Estatística, 2000). Moreover, Brazil has a higher percentage of preschool-aged children than does the United States (Instituto Brasileiro de Geografia e Estatística, 2000; U.S. Census Bureau, 2003).

It seems reasonable to suppose, therefore, that similarities in approaches to early childhood care and education reflect trends that are globally influenced. By contrast, differences in the ways in which these approaches have been adopted seem to relate to local cultural, historical, and economic factors. As Vygotsky (1978) argued, citing Blonsky (1921), to understand something one needs to understand its history. We therefore turn to a discussion of the history of early care and education policies in the Brazilian context.

Early Childhood Care and Education: Historical Developments in Brazil

The separation of care and education was forged, in Brazil, by the development of a dual system of education for young children: one for poor children, whose primary goal was "care" (that is, feeding, protecting, keeping off the streets) and the other for children of the wealthy, with the main objective being that of creating "the whole child." As we have written elsewhere (Freitas, Shelton, & Tudge, 2008; see also, Nourot, 2005; Scarr & Weinberg, 1986; Tobin et al., 1989) the parallel development of two systems was also found in the United States.

The first Brazilian institutions for young children, established for those who had been abandoned by or removed from their parents, existed in various cities as early as the eighteenth century (Oliveira, 2002). They provided minimal care at best and had an infant mortality rate of about 50 percent at the end of the nineteenth century (Montenegro, 2001). In 1899 the Institute for the Protection and Assistance of Young Children of Rio de Janeiro became Brazil's first day nursery[1] for the children of Rio's parents living in poverty. This Institute, which also helped poor pregnant women and their newborn children, served as a model for other institutions established in different parts of the country. By 1929 a total of 22 such institutions had been created, half of which included a day nursery. Also in 1899, the first Brazilian day nursery for the children of working-class (but not poverty-stricken) parents was founded by the Corcovado Cloth-Making Company in Rio de Janeiro (Kuhlmann, 2004).

The provision of care for young children primarily for economic (not educational) ends was paralleled, during the same historical period, by a different type of concern. Toward the end of the nineteenth century, Brazil saw the first kindergartens. Freidrich Fröbel had created the first kindergarten in Germany in 1837. He believed that play constituted an innate necessity for children. For this reason, Fröbel held that they should be encouraged to play in school and also that play toys are helpful for learning. Fröbel's ideas were also adopted in other societies, including the United States, where the first kindergarten was opened in 1856 by Margaretha Schurz, a German immigrant who had studied with Fröbel (Nourot, 2005). In Brazil, as elsewhere, these kindergartens aimed primarily at developing children's moral and social sensibilities from three years of age, and were designed to augment the education and socialization of young middle- and upper-class children (Freitas et al., 2008).

As in the United States, in Brazil kindergartens were private institutions for the children of the wealthy, the first to have access to this type of service. Given that their mothers did not work outside the home, the sessions were most commonly for half a day only, rather than the full-day care provided by the day nurseries. Although some people held the view that kindergartens should also be created to serve the children of the poor, no concrete steps were ever taken to put this view into effect. Even when public schools included kindergarten classes, the schools that created them exclusively served the children of the wealthy. An example of this was the kindergarten, founded in 1896 in São Paulo, of the Caetano de Campos school (a school whose main goal was the training of future teachers). In order to differentiate kindergartens from the day nurseries, intended for the children of the poor, it became customary to refer to the kindergartens as pedagogical institutions, rather than those designed simply to take care of children (Kuhlmann, 2004). In other words, the main objective of kindergartens was to educate the children of the wealthy whereas the day nurseries were principally designed to "take care of" poor children.

The process of industrialization during the first half of the twentieth century brought about structural changes in Brazilian society, particularly in the south and south east of the country (Skidmore, 1999). Industrialization meant that increasing numbers of workers (both male and female) were required to work in factories, which meant that children were more likely to be left unsupervised. However, for many years the government did not concern itself with the regulation of services for the care of young children. Even though the work-related legislation of the government of President Getulio Vargas (1930–1945) obligated workplaces to provide nurseries so that breast-feeding mothers could care for their infants while at work, this legal advance failed to be implemented, mostly because workplaces were not closely monitored and penalties for non-compliance were extremely low (Rosemberg, 1993). However, during the second half of the twentieth century a transformation occurred in this situation, not only in terms of an increase in the number of services that were offered, but also in terms of changes in the conception of care and education in early childhood and government's role in it (Xavier, 1992).

Another phenomenon that occurred at approximately the same time in Brazil as in many western European countries and North America was the women's liberation movement of the 1960s and 1970s. This phenomenon clearly led to an increase in the number of middle- and upper-middle-class women who worked outside the home. In Brazil, as elsewhere, there was a concomitant rise in demand for higher quality services for young children. These parents were much less likely than their poor and working-class counterparts to be satisfied with their children simply being cared for; they looked for facilities that encouraged activities that would enhance their children's development. According to Kuhlmann (2004), this demand for better services "also had an impact among working-class parents, who sought educational possibilities for their young children, appropriate to the needs of their working world and life in urban centers" (p. 200). In part to satisfy this new demand, the government, during the years of the military dictatorship (1964–1985) provided more services for young children, including more day nurseries for the children of the poor. This was seen as a way to provide a type of compensatory education. According to the Public Law on the Rights and Bases of Education (LDB, 5.692) of 1971, the goal of preschool education was to ready the children of the poor for learning to read and write, as a way of lowering the high incidence of school failure (Kramer, 1984).

Those who are familiar with developments in the United States and the United Kingdom will again recognize the similarities; children from poor backgrounds were viewed as "deprived" (Bernstein, 1962; Reissman, 1962). A good deal of research showed the impact of social class on individuals' performance, both in IQ and in school tests. Children from the lower socioeconomic groups arrived in school with cognitive skills far less developed than those whose parents were privileged, and those differences became ever greater the longer they were in school (Alexander, Entwisle, & Dauber, 1994; Kerckhoff, 1993). As we have written elsewhere (Freitas et al., 2008), almost simultaneously in both Brazil and the United States the idea that poor children should simply receive care was replaced by the idea that the children, and society, would benefit more by providing education. However, in both countries education took on the character of a "compensatory" process.

Over the course of the following decades, Brazilian scholars became dissatisfied with the notion of compensation, a view that is increasingly controversial (as of course is also true in other societies that have tried the same process for children from poor or lower socioeconomic backgrounds). A good deal of work has been, and continues to be, done to suggest a model with a different conception of care and education, one that builds on strengths rather than apparent deficits (Kramer, 1984; Oliveira, 1996, 2002; Rosseti-Ferreira, 1998). However, change has been slow.

The same idea was apparent in other programs of care for young children, designed to compensate for various deficiencies (nutritional, sanitary, and socio-emotional). In 1977, a federal department responsible for social security (Legião Brasileira de Assistência, or LBA) started a program called the "Cocoon Project" whose job it was to create and maintain community day nurseries for children of the poor. According to Vasconcellos et al. (2003) this program, to the present day, continues to be the major force in the provision of care in the day nurseries. The program "used to believe in rigid and inflexible stages of development and prioritized aspects connected to the health of children (feeding, nutrition, and medication)" (Vasconcellos et al., 2003, p. 244).

According to the same authors, in 1981 the Ministry of Welfare and Social Assistance (in which the LBA was situated) published a paper entitled "Let's Create a Day Nursery!" in which both day nurseries and preschools were to assume, in addition to their function of care, the function of education. In other words, for the first time Brazil witnessed the attempt to bridge the gulf between care and education that had been a feature of the policies involving young children.

The impact of this attempt was not great. Until 1996, day nurseries continued to be under the responsibility of welfare agencies, and usually operated full time. Preschools, by contrast, were more likely to be the responsibility of the education system and to operate part time. But day nurseries and preschools could be either public or private. The following description nicely captures the wide variety of services that existed:

> The public programs are usually free, with the family contributing for school supplies and to the Parents and Teachers Association. Among private programs the preschool generally differs from the day care center [day nursery] in that the former is paid for and serves a richer segment of the population, while the latter may be managed by private charitable, philanthropic, or community agencies and is non-profit. When the day care program is free and depends totally or partially on public money, it serves low resource families. However, there are also private day care centers, which are paid for with parent fees and so serve the children of richer families. [...] Family day care is rare in Brazil. [...] Family-based day care does not seem to have found a place in Brazilian tradition, perhaps because poorer families, who do not use day care centers or preschools, prefer to raise children at home. (Rosemberg, 1993, p. 38)

However, following the country's re-democratization after the military dictatorship and the promulgation of a new constitution (Brasil, 1988), services for children from birth were recognized, for the first time in Brazil's history, as a right of the children themselves and of their families. Two years later, the Statute of the Child and Adolescent (commonly termed the Children's Constitution) (Brasil, 1991) reiterated the rights of children as citizens of the country and defined their rights of protection and education.

By the end of the twentieth century, Brazil had witnessed increasing calls to treat early care and education as inseparable (Cerisara, 1999; Corsino et al., 2003; Rosseti-Ferreira, 1998; Vasconcellos et al., 2003). Finally, with the new Public Law on the Rights and Basis of Education (LDB, 9.394) of 1996, the care and education of children from birth to six was incorporated, by federal law, into the Brazilian education system (Brasil, 1996). This stems from the belief that, from birth, all children have the right to be educated (even if, in practice, the right exists only on paper at this time). An acceptance of that belief led Brazil to ratify the United Nations Convention on the Rights of the Child (UNCRC) in 1990.

Public Law LDB of 1996 (Brasil, 1996) defined early childhood education (i.e., from birth to 6 years of age) as the first stage of "basic education" and affirmed that this "has as its goal the integrated development of children in the first six years of life, in their physical, psychological, intellectual, and social aspects" (Article 29). The same article established the fact that services to young children had to complement the socialization provided by the family and the community. Article 30 decreed that early childhood education would be offered to children up to three years of age in creches (day nurseries), and children from 4 to 6 would be in preschools.[2] Article 62 specified, for the first time, that all teachers of young children had to have some minimum requirements—namely a course of early childhood education during high school, although college was preferred.

One important consequence of the process of attempting to integrate all the various services for the care and education of young children into the educational system was that in 2000 early childhood education was included for the first time in the school census. This census aims at showing, among other things, the number of children enrolled, the success and drop-out rate, and variations across states and in urban and rural regions.

Another important result is the provision of more places for children in preschool institutions. In 1979, approximately 1.2 million children were served; a decade later the numbers had tripled to 3.5 million, of whom 15 percent were in the zero- to three-year-old group. In 1989, public programs were responsible for serving 66 percent of the children between zero and six, an increase from approximately 50 percent in the late 1970s (Munerato, 2001). By 2006, more than 1.4 million children were in day nurseries and another 5.5 million in preschools (Instituto Nacional de Estudos e Pesquisas Educacionais Anísio Teixeira, 2006). Most of the children (72.2 percent) were in public programs. But although one can see a clear growth in the number of children served, the services offered are still far from sufficient.

In 2000, Brazil had more than 23 million children of preschool age, approximately 13 million of whom were children from zero to three and 10 million between four and six years (Instituto Brasileiro de Geografia e Estatística, 2000). Comparing the number of preschool-aged children with the number who are enrolled in day nurseries or preschools provides clear evidence that the right to education from birth, established by federal law in 1996, is still far from being applied in practice for Brazilian children.

Moreover, the distribution of preschools is still far from uniform; the vast majority of services are available in urban areas (92.9 percent of creches and 85 percent of preschools). This means that the right to an education from birth is far from being achieved for all Brazilian children. This is another good example of how even within a single country one can find clear local variations in the implementation of early childhood care and education policies that are supposed to be applied across the entire society.

It is not simply in terms of the number of available places that reality does not mesh with what has been established by law. According to the last school census (Instituto Nacional de Estudos e Pesquisas Educacionais Anísio Teixeira, 2006), only about 70 percent of the children who were currently in a creche were actually between zero and three (many children were retained there, sometimes because of physical or mental difficulties). The same phenomenon is apparent within the preschool, although to a lesser extent; 90 percent of those present are between 4 and 6 years, with some entering preschool before reaching the age of 4, and other children retained there after reaching age 7.

One can see clearly, then, that Brazil has a long way to go before achieving its goal of providing an integrated system of care and education to all children from birth to six. However, a comparison with the situation in the United States is again enlightening. Despite the fact that the United States is a far richer country and has made as many calls for an integrated system of early childhood care and education for all children, far fewer children are served in public programs. The U.S. federally funded Head Start program serves over 900,000 children (U.S. Department of Health and Human Services, 2005), although the program as a whole is still reaching only about one-third of eligible families (Illinois Head Start Association, 2006). The more recent Early Head Start program, started in 1995, for infants and toddlers, only serves an additional 60,000 families (Love et al., 2005). State agencies, to be sure, have also provided prekindergarten programs for young children; currently there are 55 such programs serving approximately one million children (Gilliam & Zigler, 2004).

On the other hand, data about the number of children served is only one part of the story. A lot of effort in the United States has gone into trying to assess both the quality of preschool institutions and the consequences of being in poorer or better quality programs (Freitas et al., 2008). In Brazil, by contrast, Brazilian agencies have not evaluated the educational services that the children are receiving. Although Brazilian policy makers are aware that differences in quality still abound despite the passage of the 1996 law (for example, preschool teachers' levels of education range from none to college degrees in early childhood education), there is currently no systematic attempt to assess the quality of the children's educational experiences (Ministério da Educação, 2005).

Final Considerations

Our goal in this chapter was to describe the development of policies regarding the care and education of young children in Brazil to illustrate the ways in which such policies are influenced both by factors that may be global as well as by local (Brazilian) circumstances. Although the United States hardly represents "global" phenomena, the fact that in both the United States and Brazil similar historical tendencies can be seen suggests that these tendencies are far from unique to a single society. For example, in both countries a dual system of care and education developed over the course of the nineteenth and twentieth centuries. Children of the poor were cared for while their parents worked; children from rich families received socialization aimed at creating the "whole child." When policies were established that aimed at helping children of the poor do better once they entered school, in both societies these policies had the flavor of a compensatory approach to help children who were viewed as deprived. Even when they received education, therefore, the children of the poor were given an education aimed narrowly at preparation for formal schooling, rather than the type of socializing and educational experiences that were expected for children from wealthy homes.

Despite these similarities of historical trends that may be reflective of a broader set of views about how to raise young children, we also noted factors that were clearly different, and that may reflect local ideas. Not all of the differences between U.S. and Brazilian approaches are due to local factors, of course. The fact that Brazil, but not the United States, has ratified the UNCRC is testament to the fact that the former society has been influenced far more (at least in this case) by global movements and not by local considerations.

Nonetheless, the fact that the care and education of children from birth to six was incorporated, by federal law, into the Brazilian education system seems to be due to the belief that only the federal government can ensure that all children have equal access to a good education, regardless of where they live. By contrast in the United States the prevailing (though not universal) belief is that central government should not "interfere" in the ways in which families raise their young children except in extraordinary circumstances (Bronfenbrenner, 1992; Cohen, 1996; Sawhill, 1999). Individual states, however, have started to take a far greater role in the provision of early childcare settings (Gilliam & Zigler, 2004).

In Brazil, however, the belief about the role of the central government is more apparent in ideology than reality. For example, it is one thing to sign a federal law stating that all children have the right to education from birth, but quite another thing to ensure that children have access to education, and yet another to see to it that the education is of high quality. As we have seen, care and education services for preschool-aged children are concentrated in the urban areas, leaving children in rural parts of the country largely lacking. Local, rather than global, considerations are also relevant within any society. It is beyond the scope of this chapter, but it is necessary to consider seriously issues such as historically based inequalities among regions, ethnic groups, and races in Brazil.

As our analysis has shown, Brazilian views and policies about early childhood care and education have changed over the course of the past two centuries. In this chapter, we have tried to show that these changes not only reflect tendencies seen in various western societies but also have local nuances. We believe that in order to understand the global–local tension involved in implementing early childhood care and education policies in any society it is essential to know the history of that society, given that the changes that take place are always a transformation of what had been and not a simple substitution of the old by the new.

Notes

* I gratefully acknowledge the financial support provided by CAPES (Coordenação de Aperfeiçoamento de Pessoal de Nível Superior) that allowed me to spend a year as Visiting Scholar at the Center for Youth, Family, and Community Partnerships, University of North Carolina at Greensboro.

1 Portuguese uses the word *creche*, derived from French (old French: *creche*; modern French: *crèche*). According to the Shorter Oxford English Dictionary, crèche means "a day nursery for infants and young children" (2003, p. 551). Although one usually uses "nursery school" to translate "creche" from Portuguese into English, we decided to follow the Dictionary, especially because, in this article, it is important to distinguish day nurseries from nursery schools.

2 Education in Brazil is currently going through a period of reorganization, with the period of basic education ("ensino fundamental") increasing to nine years, starting at 6 years of age and no longer at seven (Law 11,274, of February 6, 2006). The changes are in transitional stage. Schools have until 2010 to implement what the law requires.

References

Alexander, K. L., Entwisle, D. R., & Dauber, S. L. (1994). *On the success of failure: A reassessment of the effects of retention in the primary grades.* New York: Cambridge University Press.

Bernstein, B. (1962). Language and social class. *British Journal of Sociology*, 11, 271–276.

Blonsky, P. P. (1921). *Essays on scientific psychology.* Moscow: State Publishing.

Brasil (1988). Constituição da República Federativa do Brasil [Constitution of the Federal Republic of Brazil]. *Diário Oficial da União.* Brasilia, DF: Imprensa Nacional.

Brasil (1991). *Lei 8.069: Dispõe sobre o Estatuto da Criança e do Adolescente e da outras providências* [*Public Law 8.069: The Statute of the Child and the Adolescent*]. São Paulo: Satraemfa/CBIA.

Brasil (1996). Lei 9.394, de 20 de dezembro de 1996. Estabelece as Diretrizes e Bases da Educação Nacional [Public Law on the Rights and Basis of Education]. *Diário Oficial da União.* Brasília, DF: Imprensa Nacional.

Brauner, J., Gordic, B., & Zigler, E. (2004). Putting the child back into child care: Combining care and education for children ages 3–5. *Social Policy Report: Giving child and youth development knowledge away, 18*(3), 3–15. Available at http://www.srcd.org/Documents/Publications/SPR/SPR18_3.pdf.

Bronfenbrenner, U. (1992). Child care in the Anglo-Saxon mode. In M. E. Lamb, K. J. Sternberg, C.-P. Hwang, & A. G. Broberg (Eds.), *Child care in context* (pp. 281–291). Hillsdale, NJ: Lawrence Erlbaum Associates.

Campbell, F. A. & Ramey, C. T. (1994). Effects of early intervention on intellectual and academic achievement: A follow-up study of children from low-income families. *Child Development,* 65(2), 684–698.

Campbell, S. (2002). *Behavior problems in preschool children: Clinical and developmental issues,* 2nd edition. New York: The Guilford Press.

Cerisara, A. B. (1999). Educar e cuidar: por onde anda a educação infantil? [Education and care: Where is early childhood education going?]. *Perspectiva, N. especial* [Perspectives, special issue], 11–22.

Cohen, A. J. (1996). A brief history of federal financing for child care in the United States. *The Future of Children,* 6 (2), 26–40.

Corsino, P., Nunes, M. F., & Kramer, S. (2003). Formação de profissionais da Educação Infantil: Um desafio para as políticas municipais de educação face às exigencies da LDB [The training of early education professionals: A challenge for local education policies following the Law on the Rights and Basis of Education]. In D. B. de Souza & L. C. M. de Faria (Eds.), *Desafios da educação municipal* [Challenges of local education] (pp. 278–328). Rio de Janeiro: DP&A.

Freitas, L. B. L., Shelton, T. L., & Tudge, J. R. H. (2008). Conceptions of U.S. and Brazilian early childhood care and education: A historical and comparative analysis. *International Journal of Behavioral Development,* 32 (2), 161–170.

Gilliam, W. S., & Zigler, E. F. (2004). State efforts to evaluate the effects of pre-kindergarten: 1977 to 2003. Retrieved January 2, 2006, from http://nieer.org/resources/research/StateEfforts.pdf.

Guralnick, M. J. (1997). Second-generation research in the field of early intervention. In M. J. Guralnick (Ed.), *The effectiveness of early intervention* (pp. 3–20). Baltimore: Paul H. Brookes.

Howard, V. F., Williams, B. F., Port, P. D., & Lepper, C. (2001). *Very young children with special needs: A formative approach for the twenty-first century,* 2nd edition. Upper Saddle River, NJ: Merril/Prentice Hall.

Illinois Head Start Association (2006). Head Start Program Framework: Eligibility – New. Retrieved January 30, 2006 from http://www.iheadstart.org/eligibility.html.

Instituto Brasileiro de Geografia e Estatística (2000). *Censo 2000* [Census 2000]. Retrieved February 26, 2004 from http://www.ibge.gov.br.

Instituto Nacional de Estudos e Pesquisas Educacionais Anísio Teixeira (2006). Sinopse estatística da educação básica: Censo escolar 2006 [Statistical synopsis of basics education: School census 2006]. Retrieved January 16, 2008 from http://www.inep;gov.br/basica/censo/Escolar/Sinopse/sinopse.asp.

Kellam, S. G. & Rebok, G. W. (1992) Building developmental and etiological theory through epidemiologically based preventive intervention trials. In J. McCord & R. E. Tremblay (Eds.), *Preventing antisocial behavior: Interventions from birth through adolescence* (pp. 162–195). New York: Guilford Press.

Kerckhoff, A. (1993). *Diverging pathways: Social structure and career deflections.* New York: Cambridge University Press.

Knitzer, J. (1993). Children's mental health policy: Challenging the future. *Journal of Emotional and Behavioral Disorders,* 1 (1), 8–16.

Kramer, S. (1984). *A política do pré-escolar no Brasil: A arte do disfarce* [Preschool policy in Brazil: The art of pretense], 2nd edition. Rio de Janeiro: Achiamé.

Kuhlmann Jr., M. (2004). *Infância e educação infantil: Uma abordabem histórica* [Childhood and early education: A historical approach], 3rd edition. Porto Alegre: Mediação.

Lopez, M. L., Tarullo, L. B., Forness, S. R., & Boyce, C. A. (2000). Early identification and intervention: Head Start's response to mental health challenges. *Early Education & Development*, 11 (3), 265–282.

Love, J. M., Kisker, E. E., Ross, C., Constantine, J., Boller, K., Chazan-Cohen, R., Brady-Smith, C., Fuligni, A. S., Raikes, H., Brooks-Gunn, J., Tarullo, L. B., Schochet, P., Paulsell, D., & Vogel, C. (2005). The effectiveness of early Head Start for 3-year-old children and their parents: Lessons for policy and programs. *Developmental Psychology*, 41 (6), 885–901.

Ministério da Educação (2005). Política nacional de educação infantil: Pelo direito das crianças de zero a seis anos à educação [Early childhood education national policy: The right to education for children from zero to six]. Retrieved January 14, 2006 from http://portal.mec.gov.br/seb/arquivos/pdf/pol_inf_eduinf.pdf.

Montenegro. T. (2001). *O cuidado e a formação moral na educação infantil* [Care and moral education in early childhood education]. São Paulo: Educ.

Munerato, R. V. S. (2001). *Educação infantil: Políticas públicas na década de 80* [Early childhood education: Policies in the 1980s]. Bauru: EDUSC.

National Institute for Early Education Research (2003). *The state of preschool – 2003: State preschool yearbook*. Retrieved April 9, 2004 from http://www.nieer.org/yearbook.

Nourot, P. M. (2005). Historical perspectives on early childhood education. In J. L. Roopnarine & J. E. Johnson (Eds.), *Approaches to early childhood education*, 4th edition (pp. 3–43). Upper Saddle River, NJ: Pearson.

Oliveira, Z. M. R. (Ed.) (1996). *Educação infantil: Muitos olhares* [Early childhood education: Different points of view]. São Paulo: Cortez.

Oliveira, Z. M. R. (2002). *Educação infantil: Fundamentos e métodos* [Early childhood education: Foundations and methods]. São Paulo: Cortez.

Organization for Economic Co-operation and Development (2001). *Starting strong: Early childhood education and care*. Paris: OECD Publications.

Ramey, C. T. & Ramey, S. L. (1998). Early intervention and early experience [Electronic version]. *American Psychologist*, 53 (2), 109–120.

Raver, C. C. (2002). Emotions matter: Making the case for the role of young children's emotional development for early school readiness. *Social policy report: Giving Child and youth development knowledge away*, 16 (3), 3–18.

Reissman, D. (1962). *The culturally deprived child*. New York: Harper and Row.

Rosemberg, F. (1993). Brazil. In M. Cochran (Ed.), *International handbook of child care policies and programs* (pp. 33–56). Westport, CT: Greenwood Press.

Rosseti-Ferreira, M. C. (Ed.) (1998). *Os fazeres na educação infantil* [Practices in early childhood education]. São Paulo: Cortez.

Sawhill, I. V. (1999). Investing in children. Policy Brief #1, The Brookings Institution. Retrieved, January 14, 2006, from http://www.brookings.edu/printem. wbs?page=/comm/childrensroundtable/issue1.htm.

Scarr, S., & Weinberg, R. A. (1986). The early childhood enterprise: Care and education of the young. *American Psychologist*, 41 (10), 1140–1146.

Schweinhart, L. J., Montie, J., Xiang, Z., Barnett, W. S., Belfield, C. R., & Nores, M. (2005). *Lifetime effects: The High/Scope Perry Preschool study through age 40*.

(Monographs of the High/Scope Educational Research Foundation, 11). Ypsilanti, MI: High/Scope Press.

Shelton, T. L., Barkley, R. A., Crosswait, C., Moorehouse, M., Fletcher, K., Barrett, S., Jenkins, L., & Metevia, L. (2000). Multimethod psychoeducational intervention for preschool children with disruptive behavior: Two-year post-treatment follow-up [Electronic version]. *Journal of Abnormal Child Psychology, 28* (3), 253–266.

Shonkoff, J. P. & Phillips, D. A. (Eds.) (2000). *From neurons to neighborhoods: The science of early childhood development.* Washington, DC: National Academy Press.

Simpson, J. S., Jivanjee, P., Koroloff, N., Doerfler, A., & García, M. (2001). *Promising practices in early childhood mental health.* Retrieved January 15, 2004 from http://www.mentalhealth.sanha.gov/cmhs/childrenscampaing/practices.asp.

Skidmore, T. E. (1999). *Brazil: Five centuries of change.* New York: Oxford University Press.

Tobin, J. J., Wu, D. Y. H., & Davidson, D. H. (1989). *Preschool in three cultures: Japan, China and the United States.* New Haven and London: Yale University Press.

Tudge, J. R. H. (1991). Education of young children in the Soviet Union: Current practice in historical perspective. *Elementary School Journal, 92* (1), 122–133.

Tudge, J. R. H., Doucet, F., Odero, D., Sperb, T., Piccinini, C., & Lopes, R. S. (2006). A window into different cultural worlds: Young children's everyday activities in the United States, Kenya, and Brazil. *Child Development, 77* (5), 1446–1469.

U.S. Census Bureau (2003). Poverty in the United States: 2002. Retrieved November 16, 2006 from www.census.gov/prod/2003pubs/p60-222.pdf.

U.S. Department of Health and Human Services (2005). *Head Start Program Fact Sheet.* Washington, DC: U.S. Department of Health and Human Services, Administration for Children and Families. Retrieved December 27, 2005 from http://www.acf.hhs.gov/programs/hsb/research/2005.htm.

Vasconcellos, V. M. R., Aquino, L. M. L., & Lobo, A. P. S. L. L. (2003). A integração da educação infantil ao sistema de ensino: exigências e possibilidades pós-LDB [The integration of early childhood education in the education system: Requirements and possibilities following the Law on the Rights and Basis of Education]. In D. B. de Souza & L. C. M. de Faria (Eds.), *Desafios da Educação Municipal* [Challenges of local education] (pp. 235–258). Rio de Janeiro: DP&A.

Vygotsky, L. S. (1978). *Mind in society: The development of higher psychological processes.* Cambridge, MA: Harvard University Press (originally published between 1930 and 1935).

Williford, A. P. & Shelton, T. L. (2008). Using mental health consultation to decrease disruptive behaviors in preschoolers: Adapting an empirically supported intervention. *Journal of Child Psychology and Psychiatry, 49* (2), 191–200.

Xavier, M. L. (1992). Trajetória político-pedagógica das instituições de educação infantil [Politico-pedagogical pathways of institutions for young children]. In M. B. Luce & M. I. E. Bujes (Eds.), *Educação infantil no município: O desafio político-pedagógico* [Early childhood education at the local level: The politico-pedagogical challenge] (pp. 19–25). Porto Alegre: Ufrgs/Protext/Faced.

16 A Cultural-Historical Analysis of Play as an Activity Setting in Early Childhood Education

Views From Research and From Teachers

Marilyn Fleer, Holli A. Tonyan,
Ana Cristina Mantilla and
C. M. Patricia Rivalland

Play is valued in many countries around the world (Wood, 2004). However, how the term 'play' is defined is variable (Ailwood, 2003). There is much debate around what constitutes play (Fleer, 1999; Göncü, Mistry, & Mosier, 2000). Many theoretical perspectives on play have become global forces within early childhood education. This chapter examines how early childhood professionals talked about their everyday, local practices with an eye toward understanding how they use (resist) the global theories of play.

Play is a very powerful discourse in the global early childhood education community, both within theory and practice. Much of the foundational research which has informed current practice in Western heritage communities (and more recently Eastern countries) (Fleer, 1996; Haight, Wang & Fung, Williams & Mintz, 1999), was undertaken quite some time ago (Dockett & Fleer, 1999) and represents a narrow range of cultural and historical contexts (Howes & Tonyan, 1999). Moreover, a brief overview of the literature on play indicates that empirical research has focused on understanding the play of young children within the age range of *three to five years*, looking mainly at specific play interactions, categories, behaviours, activities and/or settings, and their relationship to learning and development of children within this age bracket (e.g. Farver, 1992; Levy, Wolfgang & Koorland, 1992; Göncü, 1993; Howe, Moller, Chambers & Petrakos, 1993; Petrakos & Howe, 1996; Trawick-Smith, 1998; Hestenes & Carrol, 2000; Leseman, Rollenberg & Rispens, 2001; Farran & Son-Yarbrough, 2001; Harrist & Bradley, 2003; Lloyd & Howe, 2003; Robinson, Anderson, Porter, Hart, & Wouden-Miller, 2003; Tonyan & Howes, 2003). As such, more recent and relevant studies of children (particularly those three years and younger) are urgently needed for informing the work of early childhood professionals. In the present study, we sought to better understand the tensions between the global and local as early childhood professionals talk about the play activity of

Australian children through, first, recording the everyday play activities of a sample of eight children in a local child care setting, and second, by studying how their teachers used their own professional (practical and theoretical) knowledge to make sense of the children's play.

Global Discourse: Theories of Play

Ailwood (2003) wrote that in early childhood education '[a] whole language has been created for describing the play of young children ... Such a language enables the rationalizing of play – rendering play workable, knowable, and practical' (p. 295). There are many theoretical traditions that have influenced that language. Some of these theories are still taught explicitly in educational settings but others are now part of global discourses without necessarily having particular scientific weight behind them. Here we provide a brief overview of some of the global discourses we expected to find among local teachers' responses.

Dockett and Fleer (1999) provided an overview of classical theories of play, which included many biologically-driven ideas about play as a way to release excess energy (biological drives) or instinct-driven ideas to provide practice for adult roles and strengthen the instincts that will be needed in later life as well as a focus on the domains in which play may be useful in helping children develop the skills developmental psychologists have come to study (e.g., metacommunication, language, cognition, etc.). These classical theories of play provide a useful backdrop to the more contemporary theories of play that are valued in the early childhood community within Australia. Certainly, the biological drive theories are no longer explicitly taught in early childhood teacher education programmes, but the developmental theories are required reading for many early childhood professionals and, indeed, form part of many assessments, credentialing processes, and accreditation processes, including those tied to funding from the Australian government at the time this research was conducted.

Two theories in particular have been reified in early childhood educational discourse and training in many parts of the world, including in Victoria, Australia where we conducted our research. In considering play as an activity, where Piaget (1962) focused on action, children demonstrate changes in their reasoning abilities. According to this view, play shows what children can do and in play, children practise and repeat actions in order to either fit new experiences with existing understandings or modify existing understandings to incorporate new experiences. By contrast, Parten (1932) focused on changes in the social structure of play. She suggested that children progress from relatively isolated play to cooperative play with infants observed mostly in the vicinity of play without seeking to enter play (*unoccupied* or *solitary*) and as children get older, they move from being an onlooker to *parallel* play (playing near others with little or no interaction), to *associative* play using similar equipment or doing similar things, to *cooperative* play when children work toward a shared goal or implement a shared plan of action.

In many educational institutions, students are expected to first learn these theories and then be able to 'apply' their knowledge to their observations of children by identifying and recording examples of the different forms of play and even being able to plan activities for children based on the kinds of play observed. However, these theories are often presented not as theories to be critiqued and discussed, but as 'facts' about children's play. A survey of the texts available for use in training early childhood professionals reveals very little critique of these theories or mention of the growing numbers of critiques among researchers across diverse fields mentioned above.

We will explain a third theory of play that is part of the global discourse of play in early childhood education at a bit more length for two reasons. First, whereas the above two widely-used theories provide conceptual tools for primarily describing and classifying children's play, Vygotsky's theory makes play central to young children's development and thus affords teachers new possibilities for their own local practice, an idea we explain in more detail below. Second, although some concepts from Vygotsky's writing about play have become part of the global discourse (e.g., zone of proximal development), there is much less consensus in the field regarding how Vygotsky's ideas about play can be incorporated into early childhood practice as we explain below.

One of the central defining features of Vygotsky's (1966) writing on play was his view that play provides a space for the conscious realisation of concepts. For instance, he gave the example of two children who in real life are sisters, and who play out being sisters. He argued that the sisters have an everyday understanding of 'being sisters', but may not have an abstract understanding of sibling relationships. Because playing sisters requires some shared meaning and negotiation, the children consciously focus on the concept of 'sisters', thus paving the way for concept formation. Vygotsky (1966) stated: 'What passes unnoticed by the child in real life becomes a rule of behaviour in play' (p. 9). It is these rules of behaviour in everyday life that are acted out through play. Vygotsky (1966) argued that, in this way, a zone of proximal development is generated through play.

Vygotsky's (1987) description of concept formation differentiates everyday concepts, those embedded in everyday life, from scientific concepts, those introduced through formal schooling. In this view, a dialectical relationship exists between everyday concept formation and scientific concept formation. He argued that through the interlacing of everyday and scientific concepts, children became conscious of their everyday practice (scientific concepts in practice), thus transforming their everyday practice. If play provides a conceptual space for the dialectical relations between everyday concept formation and scientific concept formation, then we have at our disposal a whole new way of thinking about play and learning.

> I think that in finding the criteria for distinguishing a child's play activity from his other general forms of activity it must be accepted that in play a child creates an imaginary situation. (Vygotsky, 1966, p. 8)

Taking a cultural-historical perspective on play means that we look to define play when we notice that preschool children place themselves into an imaginary situation, with rules, and act out the behaviours that are associated with those rules (e.g., being a mum or a sister in play). Vygotsky (1966) stressed that preschool children do not actually put themselves in an imaginary world (that would be a delusion), nor do they simply copy the real world that they observe. Instead, in play, children are actively reflecting on the ideas that they otherwise take for granted. He suggests that play is a *leading* activity, one in which children are learning and developing, and not the *predominant* activity of young children, or where they demonstrate their competencies (as many have interpreted Piaget's work to suggest).

Vygotsky's (1966) theory raises many questions about the nature of play and the development of thinking in play that are prevalent in the global discourse of play. Few contemporary studies of play have drawn upon Vygotsky's work, and as such, the study reported in this chapter makes a unique contribution to the literature. As such, we do not anticipate that the teachers we are studying will make links with Vygotsky's theoretical work on play. However, we believe that a brief overview of his work is important, as Vygotsky's (1966) theoretical position is very different to that of Parten's (1932) or Piaget's (1962) positions. In addition, the study design has been framed from a cultural-historical perspective, and therefore it is important to include a cultural-historical theory of play in the introduction to this study.

A Cultural-Historical Perspective on Teachers' Professional and Practical Knowledge

Although Vygotsky's theoretical work on concept formation was directed towards children, we believe his ideas are useful for informing our study of teacher knowledge in relation to the theory and the practice of play. We have conceptualised teacher's talk about play to involve both everyday concepts of play – those developed through teachers' everyday experiences with play and embedded within local contexts – and scientific concepts of play – concepts they have learned in training and in professional development activities. We believe that by examining everyday and scientific concept formation reflected in the teachers' descriptions of children's play (Vygotsky, 1987) we will offer new insights into how teachers have made sense of past global theories of play within the context of contemporary practice. This approach to researching teacher beliefs and practices about play is unique in the literature. With the exception of Hedegaard (2007) and van Oers (1999), we were unable to locate any other research studies which had used everyday concept formation and scientific concept formation as a conceptual tool for studying teachers' views and practices in relation to play.

In particular, we examined how teachers used their scientific knowledge of play to inform their observations of children and their practice. We believe that different scientific concepts teachers have available to them from global discourses afford different possibilities for their local practice. For example,

Piaget's theory of development downplays the role of teachers and education in children's development and learning and has been interpreted to suggest that teachers foster self-learning, whereas Vygotsky's theory of development emphasises the role of teachers and education in learning and development. For instance, a teacher working from a Piaget (1962) informed scientific concept of play could refrain from interacting or helping a child see the scientific concepts in their play if their theory of play assumes that play must be free of adult direction. It is through discussing with staff the everyday play captured on video that we gained insights into their professional scientific knowledge, the levels of consciousness about their knowledge and the dialectical nature of everyday and scientific knowledge of play in early childhood settings. The dimensions we believe are important here are the relations between teachers' theoretical knowledge of play (see Figure 16.1) and the everyday play practices of children, and how these understandings provide for a richer context for transforming thinking about the theory and practice of play. Through observing children at play, teachers are likely to be drawing on their concepts of play (everyday and scientific) to organise children's learning.

More recent research into academic and everyday concept formation has elaborated Vygotsky's ideas further. Hedegaard (2002) has suggested that, in order to transcend the learning experiences organised in classrooms and to connect with children's real-world life, teachers need 'to acknowledge the student's personal everyday cognition' as a valuable fund of knowledge for building upon and developing. Hedegaard (2002) suggested that the

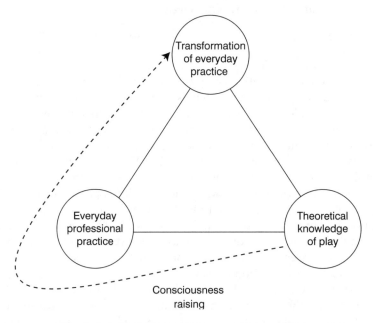

Figure 16.1 Model of play. Modified from Fleer and Raban (2007, p. 17)

challenge for the teacher is 'to create learning activities that connect subject-matter knowledge with students' everyday cognition rooted in their activities both within and outside school' (Hedegaard, 2002, p. 23). In the context of this research, we are examining the teachers' everyday cognition, including both the scientific concepts from the global discourse and the other common themes among the teachers' descriptions of the play activities captured in the videos we recorded, in order to better understand how teachers navigate the global discourses and how we might be able to better help them use alternative scientific concepts that afford them more agency in their everyday practice in local contexts.

Hedegaard (2002) has introduced the pedagogical idea of a double move in teaching. The teacher thinks about both the school subject knowledge (scientific concept formation) and the importance of everyday cognition (everyday concept formation) in order to engage children in 'situated' and meaningful problems. Knowing more about how teachers think and use a double move in teaching in relation to particular theories of play, is important for understanding how professionals work in early childhood centres and how useful particular theories of play may be for informing their work.

Informed by these ideas, one goal of this research was to examine teachers' concepts (both everyday and scientific, and local and global) of play in relation to learning and development. The theoretical understandings of early childhood teachers in relation to play and pedagogy, and the everyday play contexts that are planned or arise through children interacting with things, people and ideas, provide a rich data set for examining how play is organised for learning and development in childcare centres. The importance of teachers' framing play as a double move in early childhood teaching is yet to be determined.

Study Design

Overall International Study

The study reported in this chapter is part of an international study of the play activities of infants and toddlers across nine countries (coordinated by Pramling and Fleer). Participating countries include Australia, Norway, Sweden, Bursa Turkey, Hong Kong China, Wisconsin US, Chile, New Zealand, and Japan. All participating countries have used the same approach to data gathering and the development of the study design. Only results from Australia are reported here.

Participants

Research took place in a university-based childcare centre located in Victoria, Australia. Three of the children were from the 1–2 year-old group (mean age 17 months), two were from the 2–3 year-old group (mean age 30 months) and three were from the 3–4 year-old group (mean age 35 months). Six early childhood professionals took part in the study. The three room leaders had a Technical and Further Education (TAFE) qualification and two of the three assistants had no formal qualifications but had many years of experience working with children. One assistant was currently undergoing her TAFE qualifications.

Methods of Data Collection

In order to capture the daily reality of the different participants within the early childhood context, the target children and teachers were filmed for one full day following a method used in an earlier study by Tobin, Wu and Davidson (1989).

During the formal video recording, the camera-operator situated herself in an inconspicuous area of the room or the garden and used the zoom function and a wireless microphone attached to the target child's clothing to film from a distance; further she did not intervene in any of the activities. One target child from the three rooms was followed for one full day, two pairs of children were filmed on the same day and one child was filmed for approximately 4 hours. A total 25 hours of video data were gathered.

After completion of all video recording, the room leaders were interviewed on the early childhood centre premises and asked to view the videos and record episodes that were representative or showed a different dimension of children's play. To facilitate getting similar information from each of the teachers, teachers were given forms to fill out with spaces to record a name for their chosen episode, the start and end time, and a few notes that would help them remember the video clips during the interview. While teachers were reviewing the video, the assistant researcher was present but did not intervene. After selecting each segment, the teacher was asked to share the thinking underpinning her selection.

Some of the questions and prompts that guided the interview were:

1   What is your philosophy about play and education in relation to play?
2   You have identified these different kinds of play, where did you acquire this knowledge?
3   Do you recall where you learnt that?

Room leaders were also invited to view a selection of play episode that had been chosen by the main researcher. During this viewing time teachers were asked questions inspired by Rogoff's (2003) writing on the three lenses:

1   What can you see that is happening here? (personal lens; Rogoff, 2003)
2   If you were to show this episode at an information night to new/ prospective parents, without explanation, what would they see? (interpersonal lens; Rogoff, 2003)

3   There are many everyday practices that you might not necessarily see anymore. What are the things you hardly even notice anymore? What are the things that didn't surprise you? (institutional lens; Rogoff, 2003)

The same questions and methods were used with the unqualified staff. However, due to staff and time constraints linked to the complexity of the early childhood context, we had only one hour to interview the unqualified staff. In order to maximise this time, these teachers were invited to view the main researcher's pre-selected segments and take part in an audio-recorded interview.

All interviews were transcribed by an experienced transcriber. These transcribed interviews, the play episodes selected by the teachers, and those selected by the main researcher, and the video observation of the eight target children formed the bulk of the data.

Analysis

Each segment of play identified by the teachers or by the researchers was examined in the context of their interview. Vygotsky's (1987) writing on everyday concept formation and scientific concept formation was used to guide the analysis. The unit of analysis was the activity. We analysed the activity on two levels. First, we examined how staff viewed these everyday situations in relation to their theoretical knowledge of play (Vygotsky, 1987). We also used Hedegaard's (2002) writings on the double move in teaching to examine how teachers were moving between everyday practice and their theoretical knowledge. We were particularly interested in those activity contexts where this movement was smooth and segments where teachers were having difficulties drawing upon theoretical knowledge.

Summary of Findings

Using Global Discourse in Local Context: Teachers' Everyday and Scientific Concepts of Play

Our first goal in this research was to examine teachers' everyday and scientific concepts about play. For that purpose, we examined teachers' views about the episodes they selected themselves. These results reflect only the views of the staff with formal qualifications, as described above. Our initial analyses suggested that the teachers identified a wide range of activities as 'play' rather than having clear-cut definitions of play. This is reflected in the wide variety of terms they used to label the play episodes and their responses to our questions about the kinds of play captured in the episodes:

- small group play/cooperative play
- role play
- associative play
- imaginative play

- social play
- dramatic play
- creative play
- sensory play
- relationship play
- gross motor play
- scientific play
- construction play
- dough play
- pretend play
- family play.

When viewing the video recordings of the focus child in their centre, the teachers often categorised the children's activities according to kinds of play. In the following excerpts, the terms that we could link directly back to theories we described in the introduction are underlined. Reflecting the global discourses of play and the dominance of historical theories of play, many of the categories of play used by the teachers can be directly linked to the theories of Parten (1932) and Piaget (1962) even though they were not explicitly identified as such. All the teachers indicated that they had gained these insights in relation to analysing play from their previous education undertaken at TAFE institutes. For example,

> I went to TAFE, during my studies … we were taught there was *solitary* play, um which it tended to be younger, the younger children … because they play on their own, they do interact with other children but they tend not to, you know, build together or they're quite young so that seems to be the younger, and then they, as they get older they advance to *parallel* play which is, say two children, both playing in the home corner, but just next to each other. They're both stirring in a pot or they're both um sitting building with blocks but they're not actually, playing together they're not building together they're not talking together, they're just next to each other but, they've got to that stage where, that's okay, they don't need, cause when they're younger they just want to run away from them and they want their own space. So *parallel* play is where, they've advanced to being next to each other being able to play side by side, and then the *cooperative* play, as they get older again, they're able to, sit down and do a box together or cook in the home corner and hand someone a plate and you know and pretend they're in bed or and things like that things that take cooperation or, sometimes sharing things like that tends to be, um a few children interacting together, in what whatever they're doing. So, yeah got I got that one from TAFE that was what we were taught. (Michelle 12: 547–563)

The teachers had great capacity in easily and quickly identifying how children were playing in their centres, using these global categories to discuss play from their local context. However, teachers also suggested that the categories were limiting at times, and developed their own categories for labelling the activities of the children. For example, Michelle found that many of her children liked to repeat the things they were saying or doing.

> Um, 'experiment' it was a, I made that up. That was a thought that came into my head at the time. Um, and the repit [repetition] repetition that was just, the word I chose to describe, … both of them I just chose and the *dramatic* play is something that we learnt at TAFE as well, a way to categorise, different sorts of play. (Michelle 12: 563–567)

Similarly, teachers also found they blurred categories together at times, as a child moved from one type of play into the next and back. One example shows alternating forms of social play over a long period of time: one child was separated from her play partner, when she moved to another room (due to her age). When she was in the outdoor area, she would move around the boundary of the fence, seemingly playing by herself. However, she would periodically look over the fence and make contact with her play partner. This would occur through gestures, eye contact, passing objects through the fence, or simply calling out sounds that were known to her and her play partner. These expansive play sessions were difficult to categorise by the teachers using traditional labels. A further example of blurring of categories that was common, occurred when play events changed quickly:

> And then the last little segment I called it Tara balancing. She was playing on the short obstacle course with Justin. Not long after she had climbed the ladder and got stuck and could not work out how to get out and from there she started playing on the obstacle course sort of parallel a bit of cooperative play with Justin there is some exchange of language. (Aimee 5: 195–199)

Some of the activities of the infants and toddlers were much harder to discuss in relation to play. For instance, many of the toddlers climbed onto the construction table (which had a lip on it to hold in the pieces and toddlers), and systematically dropped the Lego pieces behind the table.

> I don't know that's kind of difficult to say because, (pause) I don't know it's, (pause) I really couldn't label it I wouldn't know how to label it because it's just, (pause) I don't know it's strange, just throwing blocks I, yeah wouldn't quite know how to label it. (Michelle 5: 222–225)

Contrary to Parten's (1932) suggestion that children under the age of three are capable of only solitary or parallel play, the teachers spoke at length about fantasy play among the children younger than three. For example,

> J: Each child will go through different stages but, from my experience um, they say that certain play will start happening at certain ages or stages of

development but I've actually seen, babies, who are playing cooperatively they're interacting, will be doing the same thing they're mirroring each others, actions and they're laughing together. So that to me is more and that's a stage so that's more a associative or cooperative play but they say babies don't do that, but that happens later on when they get to you know the three to five age group.

I: Yes but through experience you've seen it happening before?

J: It can happen earlier and I also see kinder age children who are mostly engaged, still just in solitary play too. That's just their preference and that's um, their characters that they acquire to children who become very engrossed in what they're doing and perhaps they want others, to share in their play. So it's, the categories are there, because it makes it easier for us to say this is the stage of play but it's varying for each child. It's the categories are very general but, every child is very individual. (Joanna 21–22: 994–1021)

Although the teachers clearly understood that Parten's (1932) theory of play was age based, and on the whole they supported this perspective, they did cite many examples of fantasy play and cooperative play. This is consistent with earlier research undertaken by Fleer (cited in Dockett & Fleer, 1999) who also found many instances in her sample set of children aged 2 to 3 years, engaging in elaborate group fantasy play (with and without objects to support them).

The teachers spoke about the importance of not interfering in children's play, suggesting that they valued their role as facilitators and extenders of children's play. They supported the concept of 'self learning', as this example illustrates:

I'd still say it's very much, um using, the environment, to facilitate self education, by setting the environment up in such a way that the children are, engaged, with the environment and engaged with each other according to their interests and according to their interpretations of how they want to use the materials they've got. So I'm just really the facilitator, I'm, having to do a good job of, of observing what, their interests are, and then facilitating the play based on that and that's something that changes, all the time but some things remain constant like the interest in family play, the interest in role play um, there's a constant interest in animals. Every now and again they mention the animals, the dogs, so it's very much making the environment, a learning experience and the children coming in and utilizing what's there but making sure that everything's appropriate to them, and appropriate to their interests. So that's, sort of how I see my role. I'm not, actively perhaps engaged, in teaching, but I'm, sort of, setting things up so that they're learning. It's self learning but there's some core learning too. There's a core curriculum where I think children need to learn about, um, for instance nature. (Joanna 26–27: 1241–1245)

In this example, it is also possible to see the importance of organising the environment to match the children's developmental level. This orientation to learning is a characteristic of Piaget's (1962) theory, and is consistent with the education that these teachers would have received in the process of obtaining their formal qualifications. The focus on providing a range of appropriate materials, which match developmental levels, is consistent with ideas dominant in many early childhood centres in Australia, although alternative perspectives are becoming evident and being supported in locations around Australia (e.g. see Anning, Cullen & Fleer, 2004; Fleer, 2005, 2006; Fleer & Richardson, 2004; Fleer & Robbins, 2004).

In sum, participants drew from a wide range of ideas from global discourse in describing local activities. They fluently used ideas from the most dominant theories of Piaget (1962) and Parten (1932), but they also created new terms when the terms they knew were not sufficient. Their comments highlight some limitations with the existing discourse in that they found the categories were not useful in describing rapidly changing activity or activity that alternated between solitary and social play or the play of children younger than age three. They also articulated problems with the theory behind Parten's (1932) theory of social play as developing from solitary play to increasingly cooperative play

The teachers' recognition of the limitations of the categories and labels they knew is congruent with the view that theoretical knowledge including understanding of *systems* of concepts and the *relations between them* as opposed to empirical knowledge (e.g., used to categorise) may be an important aspect in professionals' interlacing of everyday and scientific concepts (e.g., see Hedegaard, 2002; Hedegaard & Chaiklin, 2005). Taken together, the data supports the view that the theories of play available to the participants with formal qualifications had limited value for their work in early childhood contexts.

Qualified and Non-Qualified Teachers' Views of the Episodes We Selected

Examining teachers' responses to the video segments we selected provides two important additions to the teachers' descriptions of their own segments above. First, because both qualified and unqualified staff responded to the video segments we selected, we can compare their responses to examine the role of the formal education the qualified staff have participated in. Second, because we selected the segments to represent a range of activities, we can see some more of the limitations of the categories and concepts for teachers when becoming aware of the aim and content of children's play. As we saw in our analysis of episodes selected by room leaders, teachers with and without formal qualifications used a wide variety of labels for the play episodes we identified. For example, many teachers used labels that we saw as linked with Parten's (1932) and Piaget's (1962) theories (i.e., cooperative play, role play, social play, sensory play, construction play and pretend play) to describe episodes we identified. There were, however, some labels used for episodes we identified that were not used for teacher-identified episodes. Room leaders added categories like repetition play, mimicking play and games. Teachers with no formal qualifications used additional labels including independent play, building play, copy play, exploration play and one-on-one play.

Whereas we found that the room leaders used labels and categories for play relatively easily in describing episodes they selected and those we selected, the unqualified staff themselves described difficulties in labelling and categorizing the children's activities without having scientific knowledge to draw upon. When the interviewers asked questions about types/categories of play, or asked them to label what they were observing, unqualified staff would state that they did not know how to do this because they had not received formal training. One of the unqualified staff's answers – when trying to label an episode of a toddler manipulating objects – exemplifies this:

> … I wouldn't label it (pause) I can't I can't think of a word to label it no. There's probably is one but I don't know. […] (pause), it is banging the, (pause) it's not sensory if I'd done that qualification I'd have a word for it but I can't think of what it is. (Carla 3: 103–109)

However, when the questions were related directly to circumstances of the episode (e.g., please tell me what is happening in this episode) and they were not prompted about categories or types of play, unqualified staff would start talking freely and end up categorizing the episodes they were observing – apparently making up their own categories and to a certain extent, struggling with their own ideas. For example:

> Yes I'd say, (pause) yeah bit of copy play role play, because he saw somebody else doing it it's I call that age group the monkey age group they, copy, […] they copy, so you know if one sits on the couch and does his thing well next thing you'll notice you'll have four squashing on the couch doing the same thing you know whereas when you get to the kinder age well, they'll only do it if they really want to do it they don't do it just because she's doing it, you know so that's the difference they, or somebody gets a plate and starts banging it, well you soon have the whole room in this room doing it, you know they all just follow 'oh he's doing that' that's just the way their brain functions, to copy whatever somebody else is doing if I started jumping they'll all start jumping it's just a, monkey see monkey do (laugh). (Louise 5: 217–225)

On many occasions, unqualified staff made use of categories similar to the ones used by room leaders. Categories like sensory, constructive, role and group play were commonly used by all teachers. When referring to children playing by themselves, the unqualified staff were more likely to describe episodes with widely used words like 'independent' whereas teachers with formal qualifications used possibly specialised terms like 'solitary'. These teachers were able to describe episodes in ways that could be directly linked to the focus on social structure characteristic of Parten's (1932) theory. They explained with their own words their understandings of children's interaction and involvement in play. For example:

> ... I think it's still one on one play she's not she's not a child that plays in a group um, (pause) and she's connecting there, you can sense that, she has a connection either [UI](22.23) in something or, (pause) ideas or, and they both are partaking, sort of evenly in the, there's no there's not a controlling, overpowering on one side. (Danielle 6: 290–293)

Both teachers with and without formal qualifications noticed and highlighted some similar aspects of the researcher-selected play episodes. One of the commonly noticed aspects of play episodes related to adults roles. As described relative to the teacher-selected episodes, descriptions of researcher-selected episodes also highlighted the importance of teachers not interfering in children's play. The teachers with and without formal qualifications described this somewhat differently; not surprisingly, teachers with formal qualifications could be characterised as describing their role in more succinct or practised ways:

> I don't want to um in any way interfere with, their thought process or, what they're making or what they're they're doing it more just um supporting them, and encouraging them. (Joanna 14: 623–625)

Whereas teachers without formal qualifications seemed to explain it in a more colloquial way:

> Like you don't want to turn them into, ten children who are in crèche and they've all got to turn out to be the same whereas I think it's important like, you've got to get to know the children's personalities and, you know allow for all their differences, you know [...] (pause) I think we're just there to guide them. Not force your, what you think they should be you're just you're just there to guide them and help them along. (Carla 15: 711–717)

As we had hoped, the analysis of researcher-selected episodes highlighted ideas that had not been noted in the analysis of the teachers' chosen play segments. In general, all teachers struggled to define play but the concepts that they used while undertaking this activity can be classified in the following groups: 'play as everything', 'play as a means of learning', 'play as different to learning' and 'play as fun'. A quote exemplifying each group is given below.

> *Play as everything:* ... children they're sort of stacking bricks or something they're playing, but on the other hand they're also playing if they're just even walking around, doing things because, playing is sort of, [UI]

(4.14) really, [UI](14.05)like exploring but that's still playing, because playing is, is how they learn, to do everything they play at it. [...] For, children playing, because they're all playing, even sitting down they're all, doing their own little thing. (Carla 6: 279–284)

Play as a means of learning: ... play is learning, and how much they learn is what you offer them and how you extend them on, from where they are at to, where they could be but I mean not forcing it also, so there's a, there'd have to be bit of a balance, yeah. (Danielle 25: 1248–1250)

Play as different to learning: ... that's probably more a learning, learning thing that it's time to sit and listen, and of course she made the story interesting. (Louise 7: 326–327)

Play as fun: ... how will I define play I guess having a good time um, finding something interesting um enjoying what they're doing, as soon as they're not enjoying it I guess that's not really play anymore because play is enjoyable we all like to play, don't we? I mean [UI] (23.54) teenage boy [UI] (23.55) play (laugh) it's just something that, and as we get to grow up into adults we just wish we were kids don't we? because play is, supposed to be fun. (Louise 12: 590–594)

Conclusion

Whose Categories of Play – Institutional Universalism

The research reported in this chapter showed that the teacher participants drew fluidly and effectively from global discourse, including scientific concepts, in categorising and describing their everyday, local practices, but also that they were only drawing from a small set of possible global discourse. The discourse these teachers used reflects a dated, Eurocentric norm for how children play rather than seeing play as culturally specific (Fleer, 1996; Gaskins & Göncü, 1988; Göncü, 1993; Göncü, Mistry & Mosier, 2000; Göncü, Tuermer, Jain, & Johnson, 1999; Haight, Wang & Fung, Williams & Mintz, 1999; Rettig, 2002).

Although Ailwood (2003) described the language of play from an institutional perspective as a method of controlling teachers and children, we read our findings to highlight the agency of teachers within the institutions. These teachers, particularly those with formal qualifications, were quite fluent at speaking the language of play prevalent in early childhood, but they also struggled with the limitations and sometimes resisted that language as well. Our research shows an 'institutional' rather than an 'individual teacher' problem. The difficulties noted by the teachers when they used the categories available to them to discuss the play activity of the toddlers point to an urgent need in Australia to go beyond the theories of Piaget (1962) and Parten (1932). As was shown in this study, these theories dominate how staff who work in long-day care learn about play. Although the staff gave critiques of Parten's (1932) categories, and their comments mirror the critiques published since these teachers completed their qualifications (Howes, 1987; Howes & Matheson, 1992; Howes, Phillipsen, & Matheson, 1993; Howes & Tonyan, 1999), the staff were not likely to have had easy access to this work. The current professional climate includes few supports, particularly institutionalised supports, for ongoing professional conversations over time or for developing and refining the language of play. Professionals working in long-day care have long days, and no guarantee of release time for long-term planning or professional development. In our study, the centres were privileged to be able to provide release time for the room leaders, but could not afford to provide as much release time for the unqualified staff.

James, Jenks, and Prout (1998) provide a useful metaphor in their interpretation of Judith Justice's work. In describing the connections between the planners of WHO in Geneva and villagers in Nepal, they suggest that the communication is organized to 'pump' information from the WHO to local villages and rarely in the other direction. Certainly, educators involved in early childhood professional credentialing programmes could benefit from conversations with practising teachers as much as practising teachers could benefit from such conversations, but the flow of knowledge as currently constructed typically moves from training institution to trainees only, from 'global' to local only, rather than facilitating dialogue between the local and global. Not only are many potentially 'educational' programmes where education refers to dialogue and co-construction of knowledge more like 'training' programmes where knowledge from 'expert' teachers is 'delivered' to 'trainees', also many opportunities for ongoing professional development, when available, involve keynote addresses by speakers who present current research findings more often than dialogue. Through personal communication, many professionals have suggested that once in the field they often feel as though they must continue to use and document their use of the reified theories they learned in training for licensing visits. In addition, the language of play may be further politicised when eligibility for government subsidies are tied to accreditation. One of the 'principles' included in the Australian National Childcare Accreditation Council 'Quality Areas' states: 'Staff encourage each child to make choices and participate in play' (NCAC, 2006, p. 6).

At a system level, this study draws attention to the colonisation of Australian early childhood education within the long-day care sector by Western theories of play. Göncü et al. (1999) have argued that 'play characterized in Western theories is only one of many possible cultural models of children's play' (p. 152). Göncü et al. (1999) note the assumptions which prevail when children do not engage in play in the ways that Western theories would suggest. They state 'that the deficits noted justified instituting intervention programs for children whose play did not fit the commonly accepted characterizations of Western theories' (p. 152). As was evident in Smilansky's (1968) original writings, when children did not engage in pretend play in the way her categories would suggest, concern was expressed. Importantly, Göncü et al. (1999) argue 'that interventions prohibited the emergence of efforts to understand the play of children in low-income or non-Western communities, which may not be deficient but may simply be different from the play described in the dominant literature' (p. 152). This critique has also been noted in Australia in a chapter entitled *Universal fantasy: the domination of Western theories of play* [in Australia] (see Fleer, 1999), where a special editor's note at the front of the chapter stated 'The content of this chapter is, I believe thought-provoking and worthy of inclusion in this book. It does, however, challenge some of the assumptions made in other chapters, where the importance of Western-style socio-dramatic play in childhood is usually taken for granted [in Australia]' (Dau, 1999, p. 67). Interestingly, these critiques have not been advanced further in the Australian research literature, despite the enormously diverse cultural community.

Staff Positioning in Play

The teachers who participated in this study described their role in play as actively watching the children's activity and providing 'hands-off' structuring, by providing materials but not interfering. Certainly the position taken by the staff in their role as 'facilitator' and the value placed on not 'interfering' in children's play, does not seem to reflect the emerging cultural-historical view of learning with the accompanying value placed on interaction with experienced members of children's cultural communities (e.g., Farver, 1999; Rogoff, 2003). Interactions within cultural communities have been shown to be culturally specific, and very important for understanding the nature of play between children and their play partners. Göncü et al. (1999) and Haight (1999) have both shown that different readings of play become evident when researchers note the full play context, and keep local context in mind in thinking about how play partners are being conceptualised. Further, Farver (1999) specifically sought to investigate in her study of toddler and preschooler play Western theoretical assumptions in non-Western groups in order to determine how the social settings shape children's interactions and play. She noted in her analysis of both European-American and Korean-American preschool centres different interactional patterns between play partners and values which mirrored child-rearing practices in both communities:

> The activity setting and quantitative analyses of our preschool studies suggest that there were distinct culturally defined social environments that determined children's opportunities for social interaction and play. Adult beliefs about play, the emphasis they placed on the development of particular skills, and the kinds of early experiences they provided for young children produced differences in children's play behavior and in their educational outcomes. (p. 121)

Conceptual Tools for Capturing and Valuing the Diversity of Play

In our study, the teachers were speaking a language of play, but the vocabulary at their easy disposal did not necessarily reflect the changing language of play that has been emerging from more recent theories of play than Piaget (1962) and Parten (1932). We see these results as highlighting the degree to which language and concepts for classifying and labelling play can be useful (or not) in the complex, changing world of contemporary early childhood. Hedegaard and Chaiklin (2005) discuss the differences between empirical knowledge, used for classifying and categorising, and theoretical knowledge, including systems of concepts and the relations between them, in their discussion of the ways in which teachers can frame education around the double-move described in the introduction. We see these teachers as having mastered the empirical knowledge to which they have been exposed, but struggling with the *relations between concepts* that Hedegaard and Chaiklin argue allow individuals to transcend beyond the concrete and transform their practices. How can teacher education and qualification programmes facilitate teachers' mastery of relevant, useful theoretical knowledge? Drawing upon cultural-historical theory, particularly Vygotsky's (1987) writings on everyday and scientific concept formation, has enabled us to examine the scientific knowledge held by the teachers gained through their studies, and the everyday knowledge of play gained through practice. Through the analysis presented in this chapter, we believe it has been possible to see the limitations of teachers' existing scientific knowledge of play, thus pointing to the urgent need for the development of a new theory of play, to help teachers be able to analyse and describe the content and aim of children's play across cultural communities in Australia.

Our research, and the growing number of cultural studies which have questioned Western theories of play, draw our attention to the colonisation that is occurring in Australian long-day care centres. Staff who utilise theories of play derived from Western framed studies, and who have limited opportunities for professional learning, struggle to categorise the diversity of ways they observe children play. The theories of play the teachers drew upon were limiting their practice, and it can be argued that those theories did not give them the conceptual tools needed for working in culturally diverse communities such as Australia. With a broader range of children in a setting, the urgency of having better and more culturally framed theories of play is clearly needed. Australia is a culturally diverse community, and early childhood professionals need other theoretical tools for informing their practices. They need new scientific knowledge of play which foreground the diversity of cultures and contexts in Australia in order to adequately support staff in their educative role in long-day care settings.

References

Ailwood, J. (2003). Governing early childhood education through play. *Contemporary Issues in Early Childhood*, 4, 286–299.

Anning, A., Cullen, J., & Fleer, M. (Eds.) (2004). *Early childhood education: Society and culture*. London: Sage Publications.

Dau, E. (1999). Main editor's note. In E. Dau (Ed.), *Child's play. Revisiting play in early childhood settings* (p. 67). Sydney: MacLennan and Petty.

Dockett, S. & Fleer, M. (1999). *Pedagogy and play in early childhood education: Bending the rules*. Sydney: Harcourt Brace.

Farran, D. C. & Son-Yarbrough, W. (2001). Title I funded preschools as a developmental context for children's play and verbal behaviors. *Early Childhood Research Quarterly*, 16, 245–262.

Farver, J. A. M. (1992). Communicating shared meaning in social pretend play. *Early Childhood Research Quarterly*, 7 (4), 501–516.

Farver, J. A. M. (1999). Activity setting analysis: A model for examining the role of culture in development. In A. Göncü (Ed.), *Children's engagement in the world. Sociocultural perspectives* (pp. 99–127). New York: Cambridge University Press.

Fleer, M. (1996). Theories of 'play': Are they ethnocentric or inclusive? *Australian Journal of Early Childhood*, 21 (4), 12–18.

Fleer, M. (1999). Universal fantasy: The domination of Western theories of play. In E. Dau. (Ed.), *Child's play* (pp. 67–80). Sydney: MacLennan and Petty.

Fleer, M. (2005). Essay review: Studying teachers in early childhood settings. In O. N. Sarach and B. Spodek (Eds.), Information Age Publishing, CT. *International Journal of Teaching and Teacher Education*, 21, 333–341.

Fleer, M. (2006). A sociocultural perspective on early childhood education: Rethinking, reconceptualizing and reinventing. In M. Fleer, S. Edwards, M. Hammer, A. Kennedy, A. Ridgway, J. Robbins, & L. Surman (Eds.), *Early childhood learning communities. Sociocultural research in practice* (pp. 3–14). Frenchs Forest: Pearson Education.

Fleer, M. & Raban, B. (2007). *Early childhood literacy and numeracy: Building good practice*. Canberra: Early Childhood Australia.

Fleer, M. & Richardson, C. (2004). *Observing and planning in early childhood settings: Using a sociocultural approach*. Canberra: Early Childhood.

Fleer, M. & Robbins, J. (2004). Beyond ticking the boxes: From individual developmental domains to a sociocultural framework for observing young children. *New Zealand Research in Early Childhood Education*, 7, 23–39.

Gaskins, S. & Göncü, A. (1988). Children's play as representation and imagination: The case of Piaget and Vygotsky. *Quarterly Newsletter of the Laboratory of Comparative Human Cognition*, 10 (4), 104–107.

Göncü, A. (1993). Development of intersubjectivity in the dyadic play of preschoolers. *Early Childhood Research Quarterly*, 8 (1), 99–116.

Göncü, A., Mistry, J., & Mosier, C. (2000). Cultural variations in the play of toddlers. *International Journal of Behavioral Development*, 24 (3), 321–329.

Göncü, A., Tuermer, U., Jain, J., & Johnson, D. (1999). Children's play as cultural activity. In A. Göncü (Ed.), *Children's engagement in the world. Sociocultural perspectives* (pp. 148–170). New York: Cambridge University Press.

Haight, W. L. (1999). The pragmatics of caregiver–child pretending at home: Understanding culturally specific socializaiton pratices. In A. Göncü (Ed.),

Children's engagement in the world. Sociocultural perspectives (pp. 128–147). New York: Cambridge University Press.

Haight, W. L., Wang, X.-L., Fung, H. H.-T., Williams, K., & Mintz, J. (1999). Universal, developmental, and variable aspects of young children's play: A cross-cultural comparison of pretending at home. *Child Development*, 70 (6), 1477–1488.

Harrist, A. W. & Bradley, K. D. (2003). "You can't say you can't play": Intervening in the process of social exclusion in the kindergarten classroom. *Early Childhood Research Quarterly*, 18 (2), 185–205.

Hedegaard, M. (2002). *Learning and child development: A cultural-historical study.* Aarhus: Aarhus University Press.

Hedegaard, M. (2007). The development of children's conceptual relations to the world, with focus on concept formation in preschool children's activity. In H. Daniels, M. Cole, & J. V. Wertsch (Eds.), *The Cambridge companion to Vygotsky.* New York: Cambridge University Press.

Hedegaard, M., & Chaiklin, S. (2005). *Radical-local teaching and learning: A cultural-historical approach.* Aarhus: Aarhus University Press.

Hestenes, L. L., & Carroll, D. E. (2000). The play interactions of young children with and without disabilities: Individual and environmental influences. *Early Childhood Research Quarterly*, 15 (2), 229–246.

Howe, N., Moller, L., Chambers, B., & Petrakos, H. (1993). The ecology of dramatic play centers and children's social and cognitive play. *Early Childhood Research Quarterly*, 8 (2), 235–251.

Howes, C. (1987). *Peer interaction of young children*, Monographs of the Society for Research in Child Development (Vol. 53).

Howes, C. & Matheson, C. C. (1992). Sequences in the development of competent play with peers: Social and social pretend play. *Developmental Psychology*, 28, 961–974.

Howes, C. & Tonyan, H. A. (1999). Peer relations. In L. Balter & C. S. Tamis-LeMonda (Eds.), *Child psychology: A handbook of contemporary issues* (pp. 143–157). Philadelphia: Psychology Press.

Howes, C., Phillipsen, L., & Matheson, C. C. (1993). Constructing social communication with peers: Domains and sequences. In J. Nadel & L. Camaioni (Eds.), *New perspectives in early communicative development* (pp. 215–232). New York: Routledge.

James, A., Jenks, C., & Prout, A. (1998). *Theorizing childhood.* New York: Teacher's College Press.

Leseman, P. P., Rollenberg, L., & Rispens, J. (2001). Playing and working in kindergarten: Cognitive co-construction in two educational situations. *Early Childhood Research Quarterly*, 16, 363–384.

Levy, A. K., Wolfgang, C. H., & Koorland, M. A. (1992). Sociodramatic play as a method for enhancing the language performance of kindergarten age students. *Early Childhood Research Quarterly*, 7 (2), 245–262.

Lloyd, B. & Howe, N. (2003). Solitary play and convergent and divergent thinking skills in preschool children. *Early Childhood Research Quarterly*, 18 (1), 22–41.

National Childcare Accreditation Council (NCAC). (2006). *Quality improvement and accreditation system handbook*, 4th edn. [Electronic version]. Canberra: Australian Government.

Parten, M. (1932). Social participation among preschool children. *Journal of Abnormal and Social Psychology*, 27, 243–269.

Petrakos, H. & Howe, N. (1996). The influence of the physical design of the dramatic play center on children's play. *Early Childhood Research Quarterly*, 11 (1), 63–77.

Piaget, J. (1962). *Play, dreams and imitation in childhood.* New York: Norton.

Rettig, M. A. (2002). Cultural diversity and play from an ecological perspective. *Children & Schools*, 24 (3), 189–199.

Robinson, C. C., Anderson, G. T., Porter, C. L., Hart, C. H., & Wouden-Miller, M. (2003). Sequential transition patterns of preschoolers' social interactions during child-initiated play: Is parallel-aware play a bidirectional bridge to other play states? *Early Childhood Research Quarterly*, 18 (1), 3–21.

Rogoff, B. (2003). *The cultural nature of human development.* New York: Oxford University Press.

Smilansky, S. (1968). *The effects of sociodramatic play on disadvantaged preschool children.* New York: John Wiley.

Tobin, J. J., Wu, D. Y. H., & Davidson, D. H. (1989). *Preschool in three cultures: Japan, China, and the United States.* New Haven: Yale University Press.

Tonyan, H. & Howes, C. (2003). Exploring patterns in time children spend in a variety of child care activities: Associations with environmental quality, ethnicity and gender. *Early Childhood Research Quarterly*, 18, 121–142.

Trawick-Smith, J. (1998). A qualitative analysis of metaplay in the preschool years. *Early Childhood Research Quarterly*, 13 (3), 433–452.

Van Oers, B. (1999). Teaching opportunities in play. In M. Hedegaard and J. Lompscher (Eds.), *Learning activity and development.* Aarhus: Aarhus University Press.

Vygotsky, L. S. (1966). Play and its role in the mental development of the child. *Voprosy psikhologii*, 12 (6), 62–76.

Vygotsky, L. S. (1987). Thinking and speech. In R. W. Rieber & A. S. Carton (Eds), N. Minick (Trans.), *The collected works of L. S. Vygotsky, Vol. 1, Problems of general psychology* (pp. 39–285). New York: Plenum Press.

Vygotsky, L. S. (1997). *The collected works of L. S. Vygotsky, Volume 4, The history of the development of higher mental functions.* Trans. M. J. Hall (Ed. of English Translation: Robert W. Rieber). New York: Kluwer Academic/Plenum Publishers.

Vygotsky, L. S. (1998). *The collected works of L. S. Vygotsky, Volume 5, Child psychology.* Trans. M. J. Hall (Ed. of English Translation: Robert W. Rieber). New York: Kluwer Academic/Plenum Publishers.

Wood, E. (2004). Developing a pedagogy of play. In A. Anning, J. Cullen, & M. Fleer (Eds.), *Early childhood education: Society and culture* (pp. 19–30). London: Sage Publications.

Woodhead, M. (Ed.) (1998). *Cultural worlds of early childhood.* London: Routledge.

Index